THE END OF
JAPANESE CINEMA

STUDIES OF THE WEATHERHEAD EAST ASIAN INSTITUTE, COLUMBIA UNIVERSITY. The Studies of the Weatherhead East Asian Institute of Columbia University were inaugurated in 1962 to bring to a wider public the results of significant new research on modern and contemporary East Asia.

ALEXANDER ZAHLTEN

THE END OF
JAPANESE CINEMA

Industrial Genres, National Times, and Media Ecologies

Duke University Press · Durham and London · 2017

© 2017 DUKE UNIVERSITY PRESS All rights reserved

Text designed by Courtney Leigh Baker
Typeset in Arno Pro and Din by Westchester Publishing Services

Library of Congress Cataloging-in-Publication Data
Names: Zahlten, Alexander, [date] author.
Title: The end of Japanese cinema : industrial genres, national times, and media ecologies / Alexander Zahlten.
Description: Durham : Duke University Press, 2017. | Series: Studies of the Weatherhead East Asian Institute, Columbia University | Includes bibliographical references and index. | Description based on print version record and CIP data provided by publisher; resource not viewed.
Identifiers:
LCCN 2017012588 (print)
LCCN 2017015688 (ebook)
ISBN 9780822372462 (ebook)
ISBN 9780822369295 (hardcover : alk. paper)
ISBN 9780822369448 (pbk. : alk. paper)
Subjects: LCSH: Motion pictures—Japan—History—20th century. | Mass media—Japan—History—20th century.
Classification: LCC PN1993.5.J3 (ebook) | LCC PN1993.5.J3 Z34 2017 (print) | DDC 791.430952—dc23
LC record available at https://lccn.loc.gov/2017012588

COVER ART: Design and illustration by Matthew Tauch.

CONTENTS

Acknowledgments · vii

INTRODUCTION · 1

ONE ESTABLISHING PINK FILM · 25
TWO PINK TIMES AND PINK SPACES · 63
THREE KADOKAWA FILM · 96
FOUR THE RADICALIZATION OF KADOKAWA FILM · 122
FIVE V-CINEMA · 152
SIX SUBGENRES: *Violence, Finances, Sex, and True Accounts* · 176

CONCLUSION: *Present Histories* · 204

Notes · 225   Bibliography · 273   Index · 285

ACKNOWLEDGMENTS

Without the help and support of a great many people, too many to name here, this book would have remained an unrealized whim, what in Old English was once referred to as a maggot. From mapping a somewhat sprawling dissertation project in Germany to generously long stretches of research in Japan to struggling for a more focused book form in the United States, an immense number of people interacted with and contributed to this project. The following is only a small selection.

At the University of Mainz, my adviser, Thomas Koebner, provided me with complete freedom to follow my interests in topic and approach. I am exceptionally grateful to Tajima Ryūichi, my host at Nihon University, who showed immediate enthusiasm and support for my research from its earliest stage. My research in Japan was made possible by the support of the Ministry for Education, Culture, Sports, Science and Technology and the Johannes Gutenberg University of Mainz. Without question I owe an immense debt to the German public university system.

My sincere thanks go to my inspiring friends and colleagues who provided intellectual companionship, advice, and stimulation. Aaron Gerow and Markus Nornes were immediate and immensely generous mentors, and both the Kinema Club conference series and the Kinejapan mailing list they cofounded were lifelines for me to continue with what was, in Germany at the time, a very lonely pursuit. Jonathan Abel, Stephanie Deboer, Sharon Hayashi, Anne McKnight, Michael Raine, and Steve Clark Ridgeley were encouraging and lucid with their comments when I needed them most. Roland Domenig and Marc Steinberg offered a wonderful mix of friendship and intellectual companionship at, respectively, early and late stages of this project.

Without a doubt I owe an immense amount to my extraordinary mentors and colleagues at Harvard University, who offered invaluable advice when this project needed to be restarted and reframed. Shigehisa Kuriyama, Jie Li, Eric Rentschler, and last but most definitely not least Tomiko Yoda all helped carve this project into book form. Ryan Cook, Yuriko Furuhata, Aaron Gerow, Keith Vincent, and Tomiko Yoda all provided instrumental advice in an authors' workshop they so generously took part in, made possible by support from the Reischauer Institute of Japanese Studies. All of the above helped hammer this maggot into shape.

My editors at Duke University Press, Ken Wissoker and Elizabeth Ault, have my deep gratitude for their continuous advice and support for what must at first have looked like a very unwieldy manuscript. And the anonymous readers of my manuscript went above and beyond with extraordinarily helpful and constructive feedback; their efforts truly deserve a special thanks.

It is even more difficult to name everyone in Japan who contributed to this project, directly and indirectly. Not only was Satō Keiko's support invaluable, she is simply one of the coolest people on the planet. Arai Haruhiko, Hirasawa Go, Fukatsu Junko, Kasuga Taiichi, Kimata Kimihiko, Matsushima Toshiyuki, Mitome Mayumi, Morimoto Junichiro, Sakamoto Rei, Sato Shinsuke, Jasper Sharp, Shibutani Tetsuya, Shiota Tokitoshi, Tanioka Masaki, Tomioka Kunihiko, Tomiyama Katsue of Image Forum, and Yasui Yoshio of the Planet Film Archive represent only a sliver of the many friends and teachers whose generosity often left me humbled. I also thank the dozens of interviewees from all stretches of the film industry in Japan that spared time and energy for my questions; their openness and cooperation was often astonishing and always indispensable.

Finally, the Nippon Connection Film Festival provided a haven for fascinating experiments, valuable insights and contacts, boundless enthusiasm, and generative exhaustion. It was and is a vast team, but I especially thank Jenny Flügge, Marion Klomfaß, Tobias Steiner, and Holger Ziegler for granting me the honor of being part of an extraordinary organization.

INTRODUCTION

Just a month before his film won the Palme d'Or at the 1980 Cannes International Film Festival, Kurosawa Akira performed a historic snub at the glamorous Tokyo premiere of *Kagemusha*.[1] As film producer and media mogul Kadokawa Haruki approached the legendary director to congratulate him, Kurosawa coldly turned away and refused to speak with him, with the room looking on in embarrassment and shock.[2] Yet presumably most of the onlookers understood the reason for Kurosawa's chill-inducing rebuff. Against the odds and seemingly out of nowhere, Kadokawa Haruki had transformed how the film and media business in Japan operated, and he did so to tremendous financial success. For the media industry, Kadokawa was the man who introduced what he called media-mix strategies and who crafted an entirely new system of media production and consumption. For Kurosawa, the larger part of established film criticism, and the old-school film industry, Kadokawa had begun the process of spectacularly demolishing the high art of cinema. Even more than that, what he produced was not even "cinema" anymore; in fact, it was difficult to determine exactly what it was, and what it was becoming.

Kurosawa's deep resentment of Kadokawa Haruki was likely based on the sense that something, some grotesque transformation, was encroaching upon his beloved medium. And while we can assume that Kurosawa was most concerned with the context of Japan, in most media-permeated societies today there is a sense that profound changes have taken place that fundamentally affect how we produce, use, engage with, and understand film and media more generally. To take the case of Japan, imagine that in 1958 one entered a theater to encounter a double or triple bill that might include a comedy from the Company President (*shachō*) series or a special-effects film such as *The H Man* (*Bijo to ekitai ningen*, Honda Ishirō), then returned home or continued on to food and drink. This was cinema proper, defined by a specific mode of production and, importantly, a specific space and practice of spectatorship. By the 2010s, audiences might watch the ninja character Naruto in the anime series on TV while drinking Naruto soda and browsing the Naruto website or playing the online game on their phones. In the morning they could read the manga on the train and receive tweets generated by a Naruto *kyara*-bot while chatting with other fans online. Later they might be preparing to present a self-produced Naruto manga at a fan convention on the weekend, possibly in Naruto cosplay. What was once cinema now entered into a less localizable space of media woven into the fabric of everyday life.

To be sure, this is a transformation that affects all highly mediatized societies. On top of a bounded media text for consumption we find constellations of characters and worlds that are accessible via multiple, multidirectional engagements. We are embedded in these arrangements as much as they are entangled with and coshape our quotidian rhythms. Such a relation is not entirely new—just as film has always entailed connections to other media—but increasingly obvious and consequential. Accordingly, models that assumed the transmission of a media text from an authorial or corporate center to the mass audience that reads the text are increasingly complemented by models that see not a media environment distinct from us but an ecology of media production, circulation, distribution, and redistribution that we are always already part of. Such models frame the relationship between us and media less as one of interactions between cleanly separable individuals and objects or systems than one of what Karen Barad terms intra-actions, actions within interlocked and interpenetrating, barely distinguishable entities or systems.[3] A different economy, media epistemology, and ultimately a different mode of politics follow from such a perspective.

This book delineates the history of film in Japan since the 1960s in order to map transformations in the systemics and experiences of the film and media ecology. To achieve this, it uses genre to track the changing ways that audiences understood and engaged with film. This approach also entails a reconceptualization of what film genre is and a form of reading film that is not fully close nor distant but that we might instead call proximate. Not simply a category based on narratives and film styles, here film genre also includes the structures that produce, distribute, and frame these films, themselves always enmeshed in processes of narrativization and world building.

This book introduces the concept of industrial genres to help describe those historically specific cases in which film-industrial structures and the supposedly bounded feature film textuality that belongs to them overlap on the level of meaning: in terms of narratives, tropes, and politics. Put differently, industrial genres are cases in which, on the level of meaning, film-industrial systems align with their audiovisual texts to propose or critique models of social organization. If, according to Rancière, politics is a question of distribution, systems and texts here are coextensive with each other in terms of working toward common distributive goals, constituting a more cohesive, larger, and legible formation. The Pink Film industry in its structures and practices formulates itself as coextensive of the Pink Film texts' agenda. Even more simply put, the Pink Film industry was itself legible and experienced as a textuality with a specific politics that extended into the screening spaces, posters, and films, and vice versa. It is the common politics of filmic textuality and larger industrial system that makes Pink Film an industrial genre.

This is, to be sure, an unusual use of the term "genre"—one that shifts slightly from category to relation—but one that I hope to show will be useful. That industrial genres multiply at certain points, especially from the 1960s onward, and then begin to fade away as a match between the textuality of the film and the textuality of the industrial structure becomes less probable is in itself significant. Industrial genres, then, will lead us through the trajectory from cinema to new media ecology.[4]

The following chapters describe the formational periods of three industrial genres that were central to film in Japan to trace the larger developments of film and media since the 1960s. This book then takes the beginning of the end of Japan's studio system as its starting point. The breakdown of a Fordist model of film production designed to supply a massive general audience—"supply an audience" in both senses of the term, as both servicing and creating it—is part of the deep transformation of industry, aesthetics, and spectators.

This history begins with Pink Film, a sexually themed type of film that revolutionized the industry from the early 1960s to the mid-1970s. Pink Film positioned itself against a model of postwar Japan that claimed a completely new beginning. It was a system that pushed for an efficient and highly regulated sociality integrated into the Cold War system. In contrast, Pink Film insisted on the messy, confusing, and contradictory experience of Japan two decades after the war. Its highly disturbing focus on sexual violence, predominantly against women, and its production of intensely gendered theater spaces were equally confused and contradictory responses to this experience, formulations of both imagined resistance and vigorous collaboration in the construction of this new Japan. It is here that we first find the formulation of specific forms of confusion to be central, as it will be to each of the industrial genres in this book.

We then continue to Kadokawa Film, a genre that from the mid-1970s to the early 1990s epitomized the immensely influential media-mix strategies that have shaped the media industry in Japan. Kadokawa Film constructed a space in which audiences could imagine Japan as situated in a glamorous global media present, immediated in the sense of films without a time lag or borders to other nations or media.

And third, this history then moves to V-Cinema, a straight-to-video genre that represented an attempt to reimagine film and its role vis-à-vis a new media ecology. From the early 1990s to late in the first decade of the 2000s, V-Cinema retreated from the promiscuous open media space of Kadokawa Film into the living room and destabilized a model of historical sequence via the time-shift technology of video. V-Cinema was expressedly a nostalgic vision, although complexly mediated through a new media technology.

Finally, we turn to developments in the early 2000s, which saw the state develop a tumultuous and intensified interest in the uses of popular media culture, often on the basis of a misunderstanding of new media ecology principles. It is perhaps no surprise that all of the above discourses are deeply permeated with concerns about nation. If print capitalism has been claimed to be one of the foundational factors for the development of the construct of nation, the new media ecology and its platform politics still relate to it, if in more volatile, erratically nostalgic, and utopian ways.

Much of the rapidly expanding body of writing on media in the last two decades that has attempted to understand the shifts in media culture—mostly in the U.S. context—explicitly or implicitly assumes that digital technology is more or less deterministically at the root of a revolution of how we do and make sense of things. Yet practically all aspects attributed to contemporary media culture have been part of mass-media culture from its early stages. A mythic tale of digital rupture inevitably loses sight of long-standing and multifaceted transformations. In its various material forms, film was the paradigmatic medium in the twentieth century and suffered the entire span of these transformations. Film can be, therefore, essential to understanding the deep changes media have gone through and how we have changed along with them. The trajectory of industrial genre is symptomatic to these changes.

The Aesthetics of Industrial Genres

The straight-to-video film *The Tusk of Evil* (*Kyōaku no kiba*, Narita Yūsuke, 1991) is the story of a renegade cop on a rampage, attempting to stop an international arms deal. The rental tape cover features a man in a leather coat and bandana sporting a machine gun. The back cover shows him variably firing the gun, having sex, and fighting one-on-one in an exploding warehouse. The text on the cover declares the main actor, Matano Seiji, to be the "new hardboiled hero," after the late Matsuda Yūsaku, and advertises the film to be full of "hard violence" and set in "streets full of nonnationality."

The Tusk of Evil, while one of the best-selling videotapes of the year, does not appear in any major history of film from Japan. In fact, it does not appear in minor histories of film from Japan, or even in those that focus on the 1990s. Yet one look at the tape's cover suffices for many in Japan to assign the film to the genre of V-Cinema (short for Video Cinema). Indeed, the film, the cover and the images and text on it, the section of the video store where it is located, and the technology it utilizes all converge to form an identity and articulate an argument. In concert with the production system of V-Cinema they reference film history in the form of a deceased star and the films he was associated with in the late 1970s, the 1960s action films from major studio Nikkatsu, and U.S. crime films from the 1970s. This reference extends to the section of the film industry that produced this film, the discourses it produces about itself, and a temporal model it espouses.

Thus V-Cinema qualifies as an industrial genre. The previous example of the media ecology that contemporary media articulations such as Naruto participate in already demonstrates, even leaving questions of reception aside, the difficulty of assuming a single, bounded work. On the level of film, industrial genre points toward a similar but slightly different boundary problem. Here the concept of industrial genres includes the film industry itself, most simply divided into production, distribution, and exhibition, as part of a larger textuality that audiences engage with. For Pink Film, Kadokawa Film, and V-Cinema, industry itself is part of an aesthetic formation to be engaged and decoded, in some way experienced and understood. At least in the formational periods that are the focus of this book, these genres provided specific and meaningful constellations of industrial structures and practices, media texts, and spectatorships.

The concept of industrial genres departs from the conventional usage of the term "genre" in film theory in order to make it attentive to questions of history and location. In film theory, genre has generally relied on concepts and categories developed in literary theory and modeled on U.S. cinema. These two legacies have created immense problems for what is potentially an important tool for mapping landscapes of audiovisual media and for tracking larger change across them.

The main consequence of the transposition of the genre concept from literature to film is that even different conceptions of genre in film define a genre category solely or primarily on the levels of narrative and visual style. Even theorists such as Steve Neale, who argues for taking industry discourse, posters, and advertisements into account in establishing genre categories, ultimately relate all of these aspects back to the filmic work that is being categorized.[5] A main reason for reformulating the concept of genre is to craft a tool that maps change, not static taxonomies, that has a wider scope than simply the filmic text to incorporate the many additional levels on which film makes meaning, and that accounts for specificity of (filmic and social) contexts yet allows us to approximate larger historical trajectories. It thus must be a tool that on the one hand is appropriate to film—which most genre theory arguably still is not—yet does not simply universalize Hollywood categories or even posit Hollywood as the privileged or default reference point.

The primacy of the filmic text has been tentatively softened in film scholarship in recent years. Gerard Genette's idea of the paratext, "a heterogeneous group of practices and discourses of all kinds" that surround the (literary) text, framing and presenting it in ways that decisively codetermine our reception, provided an important early impulse.[6] For film such paratexts would be posters, pamphlets, trailers, or news articles. Yet even Genette's structuralist approach squarely centers on bounded, written, literary texts, for which the paratext is "only an assistant." While aware of the problems the now-destabilized "idol of the closed text" presents, Genette nonetheless retains it for its utility and warns against the "hollow fetish" of the paratext.[7] When Jonathan Gray revives the discussion of the paratext for the media situation of the early 2000s, he cautions, with Roland Barthes, against the equation of work and text, pointing out the "increasingly hazy boundaries between primary and secondary textualities."[8] Ultimately, Gray retreats from the more extensive idea of textuality and retains the division and hierarchy between text and paratext with the more qualified maxim, "To understand what texts mean to popular culture as a whole, we must examine paratexts too."[9]

This book circumvents the need for Genette's distinctions and shifts the emphasis away from static, bounded, and hierarchized texts. Instead it maps shifting textual constellations of industrial structures and practices, media texts, spaces of circulation, and spectatorships. In the case of industrial genres these constellations as a whole are aesthetic formations that actively produce meaning and present a perspective on the world and, usually, the nation.

Not every film necessarily belongs to an industrial genre; in fact the increase and now fading of industrial genres since the 1960s is one of the trajectories this book outlines. The narrative an industrial structure itself spins, as, for example, independent film, does not always match the narratives or tropes of the films it brings into circulation. Finite and historically specific, industrial genres appear and disappear as a discrete and recognizable constellation of discourses, industry formations, practices, and material media objects that together formulate specific and strategic arguments. Anime with its cottage industry and specific parameters of production and distribution, or *jishu* film (amateur or autonomous film) with its local and national distribution networks in the 1970s, may arguably have qualified as industrial genres at certain moments in their existence. The studio system, again at specific times, with its form of production and distribution geared toward producing a specific type of film, may well be said to constitute a very general type of industrial genre. In fact, such an assumption is implicit in many analyses of classical Hollywood cinema, be they formalist or ideological.

Why focus on V-Cinema, Kadokawa Film, and Pink Film to map the broader development of film and media if other industrial genres are available? The films they encompass are not usually recognized as radical masterworks or respectable films. They are not regarded as emancipatory, or even as acceptable in terms of their ethics or their aesthetics. The staff who make them are overwhelmingly not acknowledged by critics or academics as creative geniuses or "great men" (though they are, tellingly, overwhelmingly male), and the films, for the large part, are not seen as paradigm-changing commercial successes. While in all three of these genres we can find impressive examples of the art of film, they are often closer to being the most basically formulaic assembly-line products and are emphatically popular.

Yet the combined roughly eight thousand films that Pink Film, Kadokawa Film, and V-Cinema produced—and are partially still producing—were tremendously important in the transformation of the functions of film and media in Japan. As both mirrors and motors, as symptoms and interventions, these genres catalyzed profound and complex changes that influence any and every kind of media engagement in Japan today. Even if these genres did not cause these immense shifts, they did decisively characterize and coshape them despite their dubious cultural capital.

Each of these genres defined themselves as oppositional to a status quo that they, respectively, defined differently. At the same time it is not difficult to understand their trajectory and that of film in Japan in general from the 1960s to the early 2000s as an avant-garde of practices and attitudes that are often called neoliberal. Pink Film was a forerunner in the casualization of labor in the studio-system-dominated film industry and possibly an enabler of outsourcing strategies that are now well established. Kadokawa Film continued the push toward an atomized, post-Fordist industry and ever more sophisticated systems of consumption. It marketed this shift via the attraction of a Japan reintegrated and resynchronized to world time, aestheticized as a glamorous cosmopolitanism. V-Cinema further intensified the exploitation of labor while delivering deliberately anachronistic visions via video, the technology that makes time itself mobile and commodifiable.

Yet while deeply entwined with the vicissitudes of capitalism in Japan, the arguments these genres made were more complex and layered than a simple drive for more profit. They constructed serialized visions of national moments, respectively bound to the prisms of transforming media technology, practice, and system. Tracking industrial genres provides insights into the emergence of a system of media that functions at ever-higher levels of complexity and the imagination of nation or other communities that shadows this trajectory.

However, industrial genres seem to function as a robust formation only for limited periods of time. That finiteness itself is important in its historical implications. The three industrial genres treated in this book produced and performed cohesive discourses through industry practices as much as in the connected body of films, but they did so most densely in their formational phases, which will accordingly be the focus of this book. It was during these approximately ten-year stretches that they defined themselves against films or industry formations that themselves may not be consistent enough to qualify as parts of an industrial genre. There exists a tipping point, then, when the films and the industrial structures and processes match up and an industrial genre emerges—when Pink films become part of Pink Film. We still however need to allow for categories—even if only discursive ones—of film that rely more centrally on narrative or style within the filmic text, what Rick Altman calls the semantic and syntactic elements of a genre.[10] Here "genre" designates the extended category of industrial genres, while "subgenre" points to categories that are established purely through differentiation on the level of the filmic text, through narrative and audiovisual style, such as the Western or science fiction film.

The history of industrial genres is as much the history of a set of film aesthetics as of an aesthetics of industry. Kadokawa Film's worldview was understood and aesthetically experienced through its business structure and strategies as much as through the films that belonged to it. There is, therefore, a difference between the concept of industrial genre and work commonly being done in film industry studies. While John Caldwell explicitly states that "industry is textualized," the overwhelming majority of work that takes industry into account still relies on some form of base-superstructure model.[11] Caldwell himself lucidly analyzes the discourse the industry produces about itself, yet such industry discourse remains a separate sphere from the spaces, practices, and media texts these industries coproduce. In contrast, I claim that industrial genres put forth an aesthetic argument that is formulated on the level both of a narrative work and of industrial organization and practice itself. If this sounds as if industrial genres possess a degree of agency, it is because that insinuation is intentional: Pink Film, Kadokawa Film, and V-Cinema here are emergent systems that develop their own set of sometimes unexpected internal rules and external consequences, and not only relate to but redefine their environment.[12] These systems include aspects such as labor relations and distribution methods as much as a set of narratives and camera movements or uses of sound, all outfitted with decodable and experiential aspects. This aesthetic strategy lets an industrial genre define its perceived environment and the salient concepts through which it structures it. Such definitions inevitably lead to clashes. Groups such as the PTA (Parent-Teacher Association) or the Tokyo Metropolitan Police perceived Pink Film as oppositional to the status quo not only because of its overtly antiauthoritarian, antigovernment narratives and abrasive stylisms but also because of the specific model of production and distribution it developed and performed against the major studios and the spectatorial spaces it opened up.

To provide a simple example of the limitations a conventional genre concept poses, it is very difficult to distinguish between Pink films and the sexploitation films produced by the major studio Nikkatsu and marketed under the name Nikkatsu Roman Porno purely on the level of narrative and style. Both feature subgenres such as the *danchi-tzuma* (apartment wife) films or the *chikan* (train groper) films, and both have a similar rhythm of sexually themed scenes (approximately once every ten minutes). Yet the audiences, the film industry, and, with considerable consequences, the Tokyo Metropolitan Police Department perceived them as very distinct categories. The different theater spaces, advertising, and type of company producing the films all suggested specific positions, politically and experientially.

This brings us to two basic problems in the way genre has been applied as one of the main tools for ordering films and the history of cinema. First, virtually no one has analyzed the way genre as a system of categorization itself may mean different things within different contexts. Second, to date no genre system has been proposed that might be appropriate to mapping the multiple ways film is understood in different contexts and, especially, at different times. Industrial genres are meant as tools to address both of these issues through emphatic historicization.

The first of the above points is one that has not been addressed significantly despite Alan Williams's 1984 call for genre theory to find a way to "get out of the United States."[13] Beginning with André Bazin's foundational essays on the Western, genre categories have been largely developed on Hollywood models. Indeed, the idea of film genres itself partially relies on Hollywood cinema, and in practice (sub)genre categories have simply been applied to other contexts. Thus films made in the 1950s in Japan about old women transforming into cats to haunt the living are now generally categorized as horror films in both Japan and the United States. Yet that category possessed no relevance for film production or reception in Japan at the time these films were made and seen; they were regarded as *bakeneko* (transforming cat) films. Today, even in Japan a DVD of a bakeneko film may well be found in the J-horror section, erasing categorizations and discourses that provide important insights into the lived media spaces of the time.

Only a handful of projects have even attempted a less U.S.-centric approach to categorizing film.[14] One of the most direct attempts to conceptually address the complex problem of genre in cinemas outside of the United States is Mitsuhiro Yoshimoto's essay "Melodrama, Postmodernism and the Japanese Cinema." Yoshimoto reviews the role of melodrama against the backdrop of postwar Japan to examine the specific function it might have had in that context: "If there is any meaning in carrying on genre criticism, it lies only in the dismantling and deconstruction of generic identity through a radical process of historicizing the institution of genre."[15] Following Fredric Jameson, Yoshimoto defines melodrama as the articulation of societal conflict, in Japan's case the disparity between modernity and modernization. By reading melodrama and its demise in the 1970s as inseparable from the particular sociopolitical air its viewers (and producers and disseminators) breathed, Yoshimoto succeeds in leaving aside questions of otherness and tradition in exchange for a highly productive interweaving of filmic text and context. In one other respect, however, his analysis is problematic. While showing how a genre can be charged with different meanings across varying contexts and emphasizing the constructed nature of generic categories, Yoshimoto restricts himself to observing a genre in isolation, as if it did not relate to other existing ones, and accepts a genre definition that derives all meaning from filmic narrative.

In contrast, including industrial structures, practices, and spaces allows for both a more holistic view on how film makes sense and a more fine-tuned negotiation of the global, regional, national, and very local aspects of film as they manifest in film as practice (of making, of disseminating, of engaging). Using industrial genre takes shifts in the relations of textuality, contextuality, and practice into account—how we intra-act with and understand media.[16]

Second, then, genre, to be useful, needs to account for a complex model for change. The question—not a new one—remains of how to retain traces of history and contingency while accounting for a trajectory.

An astonishing example of the complex relation of continuity and change is that Pink film budgets have remained at around 3 million yen since the mid-1960s. The value of this amount of money has of course changed considerably. This example encapsulates some of the issues concerning the relation of change and continuity that categories such as genres pose. A basic problem of the conventional film genre definition is how it relates to changes over time, more often than not proposing a set of stable narrative or stylistic elements, or a stable set of rules that determine genre change. The approaches to the Western are instructive here. Genre theory in film studies began with André Bazin's writings on the Western, which he saw as a reformulation of myth: "The Civil War is part of nineteenth century history, the western has turned it into the Trojan War of the most modern of epics."[17] As this statement confirms, there is a stubborn connection between Euro-American-centrism and an ahistorical perspective. But even if much of genre theory initially tended toward immutable categories modeled on Hollywood films (and implicitly still often do), there have also been numerous attempts to accommodate genre change. In the 1970s Will Wright detected changes in the Western that he saw rooted in historical change that in turn forced the myth to adjust its narrative structure.[18] This was an important step in the direction of incorporating history, yet it relied on an idealized conception of film as a pure reflection of the social, independent of industrial, legal, media-technological, or other developments within the industry. Increasingly since the 1980s, the question of genre change across time has become central, just as scholars have begun to warn against the "taxonomic trap" (Christine Gledhill). Rick Altman has proposed genre cross-pollination as one of the mechanisms of change. In his well-known model, genres are defined on a semantic level (cowboy hats, horses) and on a syntactic level (garden versus wilderness). Genre change can take place through a recombination of new semantic elements, or those stemming from an existing genre, with syntactic elements from another (or new ones). As this model focuses almost completely on the filmic text, Altman has at other times also attempted to accommodate the question of discourse by including journalism and film marketing to examine the influence on generic labeling. The latter signifies another general shift, the tendency to approach genre categories primarily as a discourse, not as historical or reified categories.[19] Following this direction, Hideyuki Nakamura developed an intriguing approach to film noir. Mindful of his position of a theorist situated in Japan, gazing on a dynamic that initially developed between the United States and France, Nakamura states that "what this book ultimately attempts is not to recognize the general characteristics of the film/text called 'film noir,' nor to provide a clear definition of the concept of 'film noir.' Rather, it is to describe the particularity of 'film noir' as a unique complex of discourse and images, as a long-standing diverse and scattered symbolic practice." For Nakamura, film noir, a genre designation created retrospectively by French critics with regard to an assortment of American films, poses an opportunity to think about the question of categorization and film or, more generally speaking, the relationship of history, media, discourse, and experience.[20]

If we take history or experience into account, how can we track larger, even global developments yet still account for specificity and contingency, both historical and in terms of locality? How to account for change that is not simply an immediate, almost telepathic reflection of audience sentiment, a marketing construction, or free-floating discourse?

Pink Film provides an unruly example of how difficult the relationship of stability and change is to conceptualize even when the focus is not only mainly on the filmic text. Not only the budget, the Pink Film system of production, distribution, and exhibition as well ostensibly remained largely as it had been from the late 1960s to the early 2000s, as did the format of the films, shot at around one-hour length with regularly spaced erotic scenes.[21] Thus Shindō Takae's *Blue Assault: Document of Abnormal Experience* (*Aoi Bōkō: Ijō taiken hakusho*, 1967), about the exploitation of a young woman from the countryside when she moves to the big city, Nakamura Genji's *Beautiful Mystery* (*Kyokon densetsu: Utsukushiki nazo*, 1983), a gay Pink film that parodies Mishima Yukio's personal militia, or the Pink Film version of Meike Mitsuru's *The Glamorous Life of Sachiko Hanai* (*Hanai Sachiko no karei na shōgai*, 2004), the story of a sex worker who gets caught up in a North Korean plot to steal a replica of George W. Bush's finger and becomes Noam Chomsky's biggest fan along the way, all nominally follow this same formal pattern and initial production and release form.

Yet the inflection of meaning that Pink Film's industry, screening spaces, and films charged the genre with has changed significantly. Pink Film at one point quite often used current events and spectacular crimes as source material for the content of stories in order to capitalize on the publicity that the events had generated (director Wakamatsu Kōji's films are the most well known of these outside of Japan).[22] This was only possible because the low-budget production methods demanded, and the customary double role of director-producer allowed for, extremely fast scripting and shooting schedules. On average, a Pink film made it from the first idea to the first public screening in three months, often faster. The location shooting that went along with the low-budget productions supplied a degree of stylistic realism that added to the true crime effect, and the original event was often still fresh in the audience's memory.[23] Moreover, this mode of realism was connected to what some called "erotic realism," which Pink films were associated with, a mode that was in turn connected to pre- and postwar discourses of resistance against political authority. This connotation has changed significantly, partially due to the role of realism in hard-core video pornography. The link between technology and aesthetics alone has helped change the perception and audience practices of Pink Film entirely. Industrial genres then are cohesive in the relations they enact, and the meanings and actions they produce and perform. However, they are also historical, mutable, and finite and allow us to see that level of historicity. Such a model necessarily contests some of the more basic and common narratives of the history of Japanese cinema.

Models of Japanese Cinema History

In 1982 Luise Crom wrote an article titled "Porno and Apocalypse: Japanese Film Today" for the magazine *Merian*.[24] It was a herald of the long relative disappearance of film from Japan from Euro-American film festivals throughout the 1980s. In Japan itself, articles and special issues on the crisis of Japanese cinema have been a mainstay of film journalism from the 1960s onward. By the late 1970s film in Japan, critics and film festival programmers seemed to agree, was primarily interesting as a crash-and-burn spectacle. This is one of several dominant narratives of Japanese cinema that erase a multitude of complex and fine-grained negotiations within it as much as the fundamental change it was subjected to.

Though it has taken increasingly sophisticated approaches, academic research has often implicitly agreed with a variation of the apocalyptic view. It has also tended to focus on respectable formations of the kind that are more difficult to find from the early 2000s onward: the 1930s golden age of cinema, supposedly radical film (auteurs) of the 1960s, or the intriguing (so-called) independent films by young directors in the 1990s. To be sure, there has been work on what is often termed genre cinema, such as films assigned to the J-horror category, or on animated film, which is often cordoned off as separate from live-action film. Despite their constituting more than half of live-action film production in Japan from the 1960s to the early 2000s, academic work on film in Japan hardly discusses or even mentions Pink Film, Kadokawa Film, or V-Cinema.[25]

The focus on male directors—almost never screenwriters, actors, or cinematographers—and (ideally radical) masterpieces represents another of the more permanent aspects of the study of film from Japan. For all the problems associated with such an approach, at one point it did enable films to be examined on common (a)historical ground. Culturalist approaches, such as those taken by Noel Burch or at times Donald Richie, attempted to isolate an enduring and essential Japanese quality in film from Japan, often posited as an alternative to Hollywood. They and their appeal to fundamental continuity across historical upheaval have been largely abandoned. Likewise, formalist approaches most prominently represented by Burch and David Bordwell that prioritize locating distinct styles and defining them in relation to the historical rupture of modernity or to capitalist modes of representation have dissipated.[26] From the first decade of the 2000s onward, many of the major works on Japanese film were part of film studies' general turn to history and its reevaluation of early phases of cinema, aided by the emergence of a generation of scholars fluent in Japanese and with access to historical documents. Focusing on well-delineated groups such as the collective around documentary filmmaker Ogawa Shinsuke, or discourses such as the pure film movement, such work often deliberately problematized the trappings of larger-trajectory narratives and the label of national cinema.[27] This work has been followed by research with a focus on precisely delineated discursive histories that also attempts to widen the scope and contact points of film from Japan. From the late 2000s onward, much research began to set its sights on anime, discourses on moving images (*eizō*) and their relation to architecture or surveillance, or the media mix. Concomitantly the focus began to shift in the direction of media theory and away from the supposedly autonomous medium of cinema.[28]

Despite such transitions in framework and theoretical concerns, the narrative of decline still lives on in the background, in both academic and journalistic accounts. As mentioned, film journals in Japan especially have sported regular features on the crisis of Japanese film from the 1960s onward. Until very recently, almost every account of contemporary film from Japan, be it in Japanese or English, began by juxtaposing the year cinema attendance peaked

(1958), or the year film releases and the number of screens peaked (1960), with the considerably lower contemporary figures. This narrative typically recounts how the annual filmgoing audience shrank by nearly 90 percent from 1,127,452,000 (1958) to 119,575,000 (1996) and how the number of films produced in a given year was reduced by more than half in the same period.

The direction that popular cinema in Japan took did not help its case with many critics. When Satō Tadao, the most prominent living film critic, wrote a history of the oldest major studio, Nikkatsu, for its seventieth anniversary in 1982, he merely subsumed the period following 1972 in a few lines under the section "the period from action films onward."[29] With this he virtually erases everything Nikkatsu produced after it switched almost wholesale to making the sexually themed Nikkatsu Roman Porno films. Satō wrote this at a time when Nikkatsu was the only former major studio still producing and releasing almost seventy films per year, more than one-fifth of the total number of films of around 330. Yet Satō seems unwilling even to touch upon the subject of sex films. Indeed, if one includes Pink films, 1982 saw close to 75 percent of films from Japan positioning themselves in the sexually themed bracket.

The story of decline has an epilogue. "Japanese Film World Rises Again" was a typical headline in 2004.[30] Smaller production outfits replaced the vertically stratified majors as the main site of production. Broadcasters became major players in film production, leading to an influx of capital and a strong increase in the number of movies being made. The industry, supported by the government's burgeoning interest in popular culture for the purpose of national branding, was able to establish new financing methods. Film funds and production committees involving several media companies spread the financial risk, and banks developed an interest in investing in this more transparently regulated system. And while market share would not show steady growth again until around 2004, the international profile of live-action film from Japan rose (again) in the 1990s. In 1997, three films from Japan—*Fireworks* (*Hana-bi*, Kitano Takeshi), *The Eel* (*Unagi*, Imamura Shohei), and *Suzaku* (*Moe no Suzaku*, Kawase Naomi)—won major prizes at the Venice and Cannes film festivals. International interest surged, accompanied by the increasing visibility of anime and manga, which in turn helped inspire the government's "Cool Japan" campaign. Inside Japan the industry seemed to be gaining more secure footing as well, although due to very different films. In 2006, 417 films from Japan were released, up from 230 in 1991, the lowest figure since the mid-1950s. The number of screens climbed to 3,062, up from the 1993 low of 1,734 (the lowest since 1947), and the total box-office gross for domestic films climbed to the third-highest level of all time. Film from Japan, it seemed, was back.[31]

The industrial genres treated here may have been sidelined by academic and journalistic work precisely because they are transitional, because they signal a veering away from the cinema model that the narratives of apocalypse and resurrection rely on. Thus far, academic research has not fully engaged with the live-action films of this "resurgence," unimpressed by the kinds of films that brought about the economic upswing. Overall the films do not fit the focus primarily on "quality" films that can be endorsed due to perceived political or artistic merits. In contrast, accounts of reemergence tack a tale of resurrection onto the narrative of "decline and bankruptcy," as Donald Richie called film from the 1980s onward, that had been in place for the past decades, using box-office numbers and film festival prizes as their meter.[32] Beyond commercial success or very specific forms of appreciation, however, the question persists: what qualitative transformations have taken place over the decades since the 1960s? How has the engagement with film and other media changed, and how does that decisively shape our understanding of the world? What films did audiences in Japan actually watch, and how did they make specific sense of them at respective points in time? Industrial genre will provide a tool to locate cohesive discourses that film shaped and participated in. Each of the industrial genres mapped in the following chapters presents and performs its own version of history, in terms of both film and nation.

We Live in Historical Times

In July 1983, Kadokawa released a double bill of films that would become immensely popular and etch themselves into the collective memory of moviegoers in Japan for decades to come: *Detective Story* (*Tantei monogatari*, Negishi Kichitarō) and *The Little Girl Who Conquered Time* (*Toki o Kakeru Shojō*, Ōbayashi Nobuhiko). Especially the latter fascinated an entire generation with its tale of the involuntary leaps of young idol Harada Tomoyo across time gone awry. Linear time and the sequence it implied were being fiddled with on another level as well: Kadokawa released the films in theaters and on VHS and Betamax II tapes at the same time. Even in this early stage of the video industry, this was a highly unusual move. The hierarchy of different media channels was already in place, dictating a fixed linear sequence in which films moved through them.

As we will see later, Kadokawa Film ripped into the idea of linear sequence with a vengeance, arguing instead for simultaneity on a massive and overwhelming scale. This match of film narrative and business strategy formulates the specific arguments the industrial genre of Kadokawa Film was making, at the time, *about time*. These arguments about time and temporality that Kadokawa Film put forth were deeply tied to the very specific history of Japan shaping itself into a nation that was emphatically intended to be modern. Stefan Tanaka has described how momentous the switch from an assortment of lunar calendars to unified modern time following the solar calendar and modeled on European nations' calendars was in Japan in 1873: "A new reckoning of time was one of a series of events . . . which brought about a truly remarkable and revolutionary transformation of the archipelago. The myriad communities that existed at the start of the era were completely reconfigured both spatially and temporally into one society, Japan. A new temporality is fundamental to this new society."[33] The abrupt and deliberate design of a certain time helped create Japan as nation, and it is no surprise that a complex relationship to time marks many popular culture discourses.

Media then complete the triangle, now composed of media, nation, and time. Conceptions of how time works and how it relates to an explicitly national self—in other words, a specific temporality—are expressed in distinct ways in each of the respective industrial genres mapped here. Benedict Anderson explored how print capitalism enabled and shaped the modern imagined community of the nation, enabling new ways "of linking fraternity, power and time meaningfully together."[34] Similarly, we must ask what new ways of linking the new media ecology facilitate. The different takes on temporality the industrial genres put forth connect them to specific ideas about the nation that are instructive for understanding their respective moments. But they also help to further understand the relation of time-based media such as film and video to questions of nation.

Japan has an anguished history of being sandwiched between time zones. Immensely complex negotiations of temporality ensued after U.S. military power forced Japan into trade in the mid-nineteenth century. Harry Harootunian has written lucidly about the problematic association of spaces such as western Europe and especially the United States with the present or the future, leaving "the rest" to be perennially behind and obliged to catch up.[35] In Japan, a frenzied struggle arose to break that relation in the latter half of the nineteenth century, though it often enough resulted in an in-between state, with Japan in front of its Asian neighbors and eventual colonies, yet still behind Euro-America. The effects of this ongoing negotiation cannot be underestimated, and discourses of historical rupture and continuity are inevitably caught up in this dynamic. These discourses become a major structuring force for industrial genres as well.

The analysis of the respective temporality industrial genres construct thus plays a major role in the following chapters, so what temporality means here needs some elaboration. There is a very general usage of the term that usually refers to a specified relationship to time. More specifically, it is connected to the idea that modernity instituted a different relationship to time, one that really only made time in the modern sense—a linear progression from the past to the future via the present, though one that is contingent and can change direction at any time—possible. This modern temporality also was, as Philip Rosen recounts, the "enabling condition for the 'discovery' of the specific object History."[36]

Recent theory has treated this modern directional time critically, associated as it is with the problematic aspects of modernity: colonialism and its hierarchization into those ahead and behind, capitalist temporal regimes that press social life and labor into life cycles more easily integrated into cycles of consumerism and exploitation, structured by heterosexist and otherwise normative straight time. Many interventions make it their specific goal to upset the oppressive aspect of modern time by locating spaces of resistance to, or at least cracks in, such a temporal regime. Elizabeth Freeman formulates her own project as one that shores up deviations from oppressive time while staying attuned to the swift attempts to reintegrate them: "The point is to identify 'queerness' as the site of all the chance element that capital inadvertently produces, as well as the site of capital's potential recapture and incorporation of chance."[37]

Such approaches agree that modern time is fundamentally massive and homogenously oppressive, and usually assumes that it is centered in the United States. However, even if that were true, the complicated temporal negotiation that different global contexts have gone through already injects a disorderliness into the way the power of modern, homogenous, linear, and sequential time is enacted. Even this hegemonic temporality relies on much less tidy negotiations between competing submodels and experiences of temporality. We must understand how a variety of temporalities grapple with each other to provide a more differentiated view on such a massive formation and how it unfolds locally—industrial genres are one attempt to do so.

One important approach that is useful both within and beyond the Euro-American context comes from the historian Reinhart Koselleck and his idea of multiple historical times (*historische Zeiten*), or, as Fredric Jameson has translated the term, historical temporalities.[38] Koselleck was an early proponent of the idea that the time of modernity had implemented a "temporalization of history," or as Philip Rosen paraphrases Koselleck, the modern idea of "linear or directional time" time was tied to the idea of "principles of change internal to distinctive historical sequences."[39]

Due in part to mistranslation of Koselleck's terms into English, his ideas were initially received in Anglo-American scholarship as a theory of periodization, and were only reassessed in the early 2000s. Indeed, Koselleck proposes historical times as a multiplicity of specifically located temporalities, ones that are at work simultaneously even if separated by time. However, his emphasis lies on the question of experience as the main point where the differing qualities of "progress, decline, acceleration or delay, the not-yet and the not-anymore, the before and the after, the too-early and the too-late, the situation and the duration" manifest.[40] Koselleck splits the question of experience into two different aspects: "As we know it is difficult to illustrate or understand historical time; it is sustained by spatial background meanings and can only be described metaphorically. However there is a possibility of analyzing source material in terms of historical times. Two anthropological categories are suitable for gleaning the time notions implied in language sources. These are the categories of the space of experience [*Erfahrungsraum*] and horizon of expectation [*Erwartungshorizont*]."[41] Koselleck sees the two of these acting together to create a sense of time, not just of things that happened or things that will happen but an *experience* of how time itself structures what happened and what might happen: gradually, catastrophically, or inevitably. Fredric Jameson finds fault with Koselleck's model for being "philosophically neutral," by which he means it does not present an ideological analysis of models of time.[42] However, it does allow us to examine the ideological terrain the respective historical times were navigating. In Japan, maybe more obviously than in some other contexts, that navigation has always been explicit, contentious, ideologically inflected, and political in both broad and very specific senses.

Industrial genres can, considering Koselleck's framework, help to map the temporal experience they both reflected and actively shaped. Far from the "principles of change internal to distinctive historical sequences" that determinist-evolutionary genre models such as those once proposed by Ferdinand Brunetière mirrored, we can focus on a multiplicity of temporalities that are, each for themselves, specific negotiations of a certain experience of time and sometimes appeals for a different one. Industrial genres are enactments of the expectations, experiences of acceleration and stasis, ideas of rupture, and sudden transitions or unwelcome continuities that make up historical time. While Pink Film is a discourse centered on a specific use of corporeality that tries to contain ideas of both continuity and rupture within the postwar system, Kadokawa Film aims for a synchronized world, and *The Little Girl Who Conquered Time* is a utopian appeal for a different historical time less structured by the geopolitical power relations of Japan during the Cold War. V-Cinema plays off of the technology of video to propose impossible rewinds of media history, always in interaction with a historical present it tends to deny, and *Tusk of Evil*, with its multiple references to media history embedded in the new time-manipulation technology of VHS, is part of the historical time that V-Cinema weaves into. It should be mentioned that for all of these industrial genres, the spatial models they navigate, among others in terms of reception spaces, play an important role and resonate strongly with Koselleck's idea of a space of experience. This aspect features throughout this volume and is discussed more centrally in chapter 6.

One of the claims of this book is that all of these genres represented, respectively, a strategic confusion of existing models of historical times. Usually this functioned as a means of formulating opposition to existing models. Pink Film, to which I turn first, specifically con-fused aspects of temporality in the postwar system with the continuity of discourses carried over from the 1930s. Following the war, the Japanese (and the U.S.) government promoted the idea of a complete rupture after 1945 in order to espouse the idea of a new, democratic Japan. However, to do so it retained the linear, directional time directed toward a prosperous future that had helped fuel the colonial effort, now integrating it into the Cold War system. The immediate postwar period saw attempts at breaking through this now differently oppressive, structuring time with a focus on immediacy and corporeal sensation. In this context the so-called literature of flesh argued for an instantaneous time with little trust or belief in the future or the past. Accommodating or rather con-fusing both temporalities, Pink Film's body politics formulated an underlying sense of confusion in the postwar system and made it palatable and commodifiable, enabling both unease and reintegration. While not easily categorizable as resistance, it was a confusion that was as inviting as it was uncomfortable, and it is no surprise that dominant structures faced with the formation of these genres have repeatedly attempted to minimize it.

The End of Japanese Cinema

Kurosawa Akira feared that Japanese cinema was in danger, and he feared correctly. What this book outlines is a trajectory of transformation, yet its title purports to describe the end of Japanese cinema. What, however, would that mean exactly?

"Cinema," "film," and "media" are terms that are used in a variety of ways. Francesco Casetti has explicitly decried the all too common announcement that cinema has expired. "Yet," he explains, "the cinema has certainly not died. Movie theaters, for example, not only continue to exist, but are also increasing in number." (In Japan, as we will see in chapter 6, this is not strictly true; theater screens have increased, at least in comparison to the 1990s, but theaters have decreased.) Casetti's first reflex, then, is to anchor cinema in designated spaces, even if he then, for the purpose of preserving the term in a changing media environment, goes on to define cinema primarily as a "particular way of relating with the world through moving images, as well as relating with these images."[43]

For the purpose of this book, however, "cinema" refers to a more specific discourse of moving image production, circulation, and reception practices. It is a moving image form based on the technology of capturing light and eventually sound on rolls of film material made of nitrate, celluloid, or polyester, to be distributed to cinema spaces for assembled audiences to engage with in the dark. Despite multiple connections to other media, it is often discussed as a stand-alone medium, associated with the studio system and specific models of (Fordist) production and standardization. While producing a specific and highly gendered system of appreciation (auteurism), it established specific avenues of accumulating cultural capital that rely on film critics and an exclusive international (European) film festival system, with the latter tied as much to the Cold War as it was rooted in the idea of nation. It is in this milieu that the idea of a "Japanese cinema" ordered according to "great men" such as Ozu or Oshima could develop and easily be accepted, and Mitsuhiro Yoshimoto has argued that such a model of Japanese cinema was central to establishing and stabilizing the discipline of film studies.[44] It is this milieu itself that has transformed so significantly that the basis for unproblematically thinking the two levels of boundedness that Japanese cinema implies—nation and medium—has crumbled away.

Moving-image forms such as the feature film are still with us, if joined by user-generated clips on Nico Nico Douga, advertising culture, Original Net Animation (ONA), augmented reality objects, and other formations. However, they now by default stand in relation to multiple material bases, media channels, and modes of mediation; this "standing in relation to" is now understood as constitutive of moving image media forms in a way it wasn't before.

If we conceive of the term "film" as closer to the Japanese term "eizō" than to the material of the film strip, then we can think of it in terms of mediated, usually moving, images easily tied to various media-mix models. Yuriko Furuhata has lucidly described how the designation eizō became discussed and popularized in 1960s Japan. Referring to the explicitly mediated image, both moving and still, eizō points to the search for new ways to engage with an

INTRODUCTION · 21

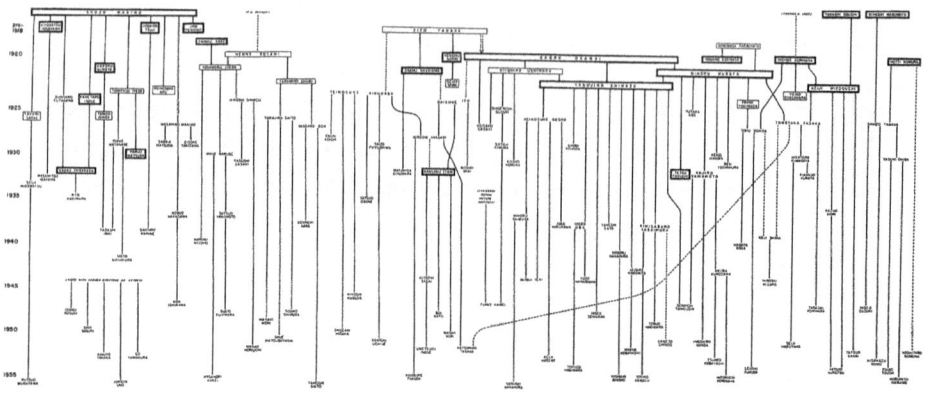

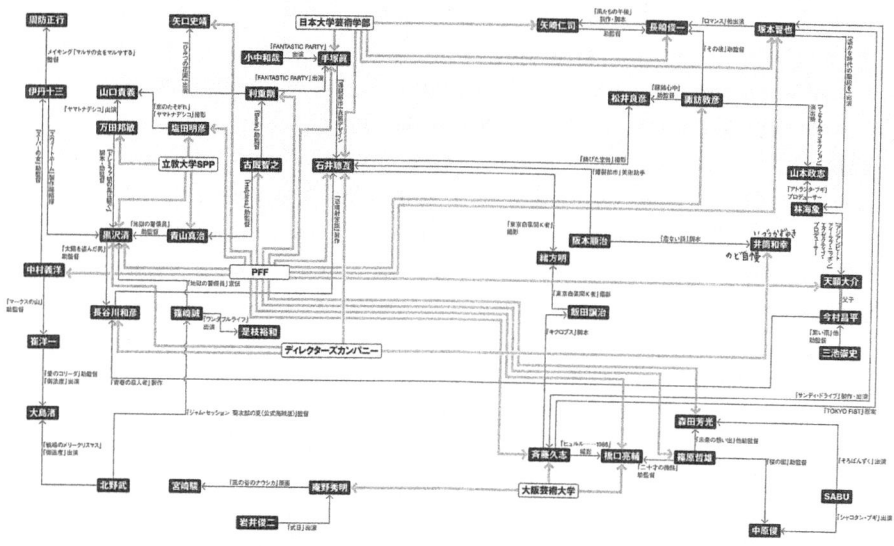

FIGURES 1.1–1.2. Frameworks for understanding film from Japan changed with the structure of the industry. Figure 1.1 shows the chart at the end of Joseph Anderson and Donald Richie's *The Japanese Film*, ordering directors by apprenticeship lineage and studios. Figure 1.2 is an attempt in 2000 to show relations between directors, film schools, film festivals, and production companies, struggling to contain the complexity. From Anderson and Richie, *The Japanese Film*, 432–33, and *Far Away from the Real: Nihon Eiga Nyū Wevu—"Riaru" no Kanate e*, 24–25.

image and media culture caught in profound change.[45] To go a step further, eizō enters an even higher order of relationality when it always already stands in relation to a larger emergent media system, in some way (self-)coordinated and only occasionally centrally controlled (especially in Japan). Throughout this volume we will catch a glimpse of the effects of this transmogrification, a shift from "Japanese cinema" to "film in Japan," with the latter always a priori participating in and understood in relation to larger media or media-mix systems. It is film in Japan that we now need to frame less as a towering stand-alone than as part of an expansive media ecology.

Why then focus on the parts of this media ecology that still very much emerge from the lineage of cinema? Following the industrial genres of Pink Film, Kadokawa Film, and V-Cinema allows us to detect the larger trajectory and the shifts that have deeply affected that genealogy. These shifts manifest in a changing conception of film and media vis-à-vis life, in how they make meaning, in how they help constitute and formulate ideas about forms of collectivity that include but are not limited to the scale of nation and world.

To understand the significant shifts in the epistemology of media that film in Japan allows us to track, it will not help us to view time periods or genres as reified, temporally hermetic units, delineated by eruptive change. Substantial transformations are processes that are composed of layers of influence from different historical moments. Koselleck has termed these time layers (*Zeitschichten*). Such layers each represent disparate experiences of time, operating with a variety of speeds and durations. They are recognizable as something that has ended, but all together form what is perceived as the towering and unstable present moment. This book embarks on mapping such time layers through genres that have been largely ignored despite having constituted the bulk of narrative live-action film in Japan since the 1960s. It begins that journey with Pink Film.

ONE

ESTABLISHING PINK FILM

Market of Flesh (*Nikutai no Ichiba*, Kobayashi Satoru), the film that was later to be called the first Pink film, opened in four theaters in Tokyo on February 27, 1962. It was based on an incident that supposedly occurred in October 1961 and was novelized in the magazine *Bessatsu Naigai Jitsuwa*. Set in the Roppongi section of Tokyo—a central hangout for American GIs and seen as a hothouse of hedonistic, Westernized culture—the narrative depicts Harue and her fiancé, Kinoshita, visiting a nightclub. After Harue is sexually assaulted in the bathroom, a horrified Kinoshita breaks off the engagement. When Harue commits suicide by jumping from the roof of a building, her younger sister, Tamaki, enters the Roppongi club scene to investigate, looking for revenge.[1]

On March 15, 1962, the Japanese police halted the screening of *Market of Flesh* on suspicion of obscenity. It was the first time that the police had taken action against a film with an Eirin mark on those grounds.[2] Eirin, the Administration Commission for the Motion Picture Code of Ethics (Eiga Rinri Iinkai), had passed the film and classified it as *seijin shitei* (adult) on February 17. Eirin sent an open letter complaining to the police department, and after several cuts the police agreed not to raise formal charges. The incident generated a fair amount of publicity and elevated the film to a minor hit. This was the first time that Pink Film, though it would not be called that until later, entered the public eye, and the controversial way that it did set a pattern that would be repeated many times over.[3]

Although there was sensationalizing coverage of the film in weekly magazines, there is virtually no serious critical commentary on *Market of Flesh* from the time.[4] Had there been, we can assume that the film probably would have been considered evidence that the film industry was in disarray. After continuous growth since 1945, audience attendance peaked at over 1.1 billion in 1958, while the number of movie theaters reached their high point in 1960 at 7,457.[5] But within just two years, major film production, distribution, and exhibition entered a period of extraordinary distress, and audience attendance plunged by almost half. Similarly, feature-film production dropped by almost 50 percent to a total of 275 films in 1962, down from 548 in 1960.[6] At the same time, Pink Film proliferated wildly: three films appeared in 1962, twenty-four in 1963, sixty-five in 1964, and in 1965 some counts record an astonishing 213 Pink films, supplying 44 percent of the total feature film output of Japan.[7]

The following two chapters map the formative first ten years of Pink Film, when it performed the painful and turbulent double negotiations of what film and media, and what Japan, were supposed to become. Pink Film's abrupt and extraordinary expansion occurred at the onset of an intense crisis for the film industry and at the tail end of Japan's first period of rapid economic growth after the war. It was a time when the struggle for different visions of Japan's past and its future erupted into the open, attempting to define the shape and quality of community, economy, and the public (media) sphere. Pink Film, as we will see, drew on many of these visions at once, presenting an impossible option that encompassed both resistance against the status quo and stood at the forefront of its most radical visions. Pink Film was the experience of confusion of the first two decades after 1945 made commodity, and a central and violent glue that held this commodity together was gender. How it commodified a conflicted experience for the first approximately ten years of its becoming Pink Film and then shifted away from confusion and into formalism is the trajectory of these two chapters.

There is no record that anyone saw *Market of Flesh* as a beginning, as revolutionary, or as a herald of deep changes to come in the very near future. Nonetheless, *Market of Flesh* is significant in that it combines a number of elements that would later be identified as typical of Pink Film. It contains themes of gendered nationhood framed by postwar trauma that sees the end of the war as a historical rupture. It uses violence and sexuality as central motifs, with the drama troublingly playing out on the abused female body. It was shot in a comparatively short period of time and with a very low budget—

6 million yen (about $16,600 in 1962)—by an (ostensibly) independent production company, and, more importantly, it was independently distributed.[8] The film referenced an actual incident, giving it connotations of actuality and realism, and was written and directed by the same man, Kobayashi Satoru. Finally, it was a point of contention between Eirin, the independent ethics regulatory body, and a metropolitan police that preferred quick and demonstrative action to long negotiations. All of these attributes would become part of the discourse of the Pink Film industrial genre in the decades to come.

Pink Film quickly developed and performed an identity based on opposition: to the major studios; to the status quo of postwar politics, or even the idea of a postwar; and to a set of connotations of national identity. These themes of antiestablishment resistance, oppositional realism, class politics, and independence permeate Pink Film as an industrial genre. They are found in the films' narrative and style but also extend beyond it to industry organization, labor relations, the identity politics of those involved in the industry, and reporting on Pink films. Yet despite being opposed to the majors in terms of product, function, and ideology, Pink Film paradoxically supported, and was indeed integral to, the system that ostensibly shunned it. All of the five major studios that were still operating throughout the 1960s—Shōchiku, Tōhō, Tōei, Nikkatsu, and Daiei—profited from Pink Film's existence, and almost all of them surreptitiously participated in Pink Film production. This tension between resistance and participation in many ways expresses the turmoil of concepts and allegiances that Japanese society itself had been dealing with since the end of the war.

Confusion will serve as a central concept for understanding Pink Film's expansion. The state, with its high-growth strategy and model of postwar democracy, put forth fairly clear ideas about the identity it wanted to fashion for the new Japan: a modern, peaceful, and affluent capitalist nation completely removed from its recent past of militarism and colonialism. Pink Film on the other hand deliberately did not present a cleanly defined and newly born identity, but mirrored an experience. It insisted on the con-fusion of life after the war with its deep changes, ambivalent options, and difficult combination of change and continuity. Georges Bataille has stated that "obscenity is our name for the uneasiness which upsets the physical state associated with self-possession, with the possession of a recognized and stable individuality."[9] In this sense, Pink Film was no doubt obscene, and a danger to the sanitized state order the government was striving for. This obscenity was deeply tied to the confusing of a certain temporal model that was intended to secure the new Japan's identity.

The temporality that high-growth Japan aimed for began with the claim of an *année zéro* and a clean and total rupture with Japan before 1945. It was a flight into futurity that prevented any real assessment of the catastrophe of war and the system and choices that had led up to it. Pink Film injected disorder and distrust into this official narrative, which was tied as much to a specific temporality as to corporeality and control. It instituted what Elizabeth Freeman has called chrononormativity, or "the use of time to organize human bodies into maximum productivity."[10] Pink Film performed opposition to that temporal regulation and provided a kind of volatile epistemology on the levels of production, distribution, exhibition, and reception. Before Linda Williams or Judith Butler considerably complicated the workings of sex films, Catharine MacKinnon—in a statement often criticized by feminist scholars as reductive—claimed that pornography "eroticizes hierarchy."[11] Pink Film, we might say, eroticized confusion, if for very specific audiences.

Pink Film's method should, however, not be stylized into heroic resistance. This confusion was escapist and epistemological, one that mirrored the psychological complexities experienced in personal and societal dimensions. Pink Film organized a constellation of social and political impulses in a way similar to what David Berry calls, in relation to postdigital aesthetics, an asterism: "Following a line of reasoning that capitalism's ability to sublimate and defuse social conflict remains undiminished, there emerges a modulated intensity in terms of what we are here calling a new asterism. Constellations are patterns of concepts that form at a particular historical epoch. The concepts are usually not identical and not necessarily cognate; rather, they lie in the same historical epoch. This explains why the concepts can be contradictory or paradoxical and yet remain in a constellation as such. An asterism is a prominent pattern of concepts that lies within a wider constellation."[12] Commodifying the contradictions of postwar Japan and making them palatable, it addressed them and kept that address in circulation. The genre expressed itself wedged between rarefied capitalism and fiery resistance, and the polyvalent role of representations of sexual violence that suffused it. That Berry applies the concept of the asterism primarily to a "postdigital" regime points to the fact that the increased appearance of industrial genres can be seen as a herald of a media-transitional phase, though one that is not necessarily attached to the principle of the digital.

Any attempt to understand the specific confusion Pink Film was selling and that both denounced and conceded to normative social, political, and economic power relations must take the pervasive and unsettling role of sexual violence in the films into account. The site and enabler of Pink Film's attractive confusion was male power and the insecurities and fantasies that connected gender to a discourse on nation. Pink Film was both soothing and unsettling for its male audiences, and much less ambivalently disturbing for groups that would come into conflict with it, such as the *Haha no Kai* (Mother's Association) or the police. Both destabilizing and laying the groundwork for re-formation of the nation, it functioned as an essential aspect of crisis capitalism in Japan's post-postwar era.

Therefore, a simple oppositional reading of Pink Film as resistance is difficult, as part of its agenda was to present both opposition to and a radical version of the status quo. Decrying the social convulsions of the high-growth economy, it also participated in a larger movement toward efficiency, economic stratification, casualized labor, and commodification. A gap also exists between its status as realism and its highly generic standardization, between ideas of rural authenticity and stylized modernism. There exists a disparity between the ideas of human liberation and the intensely misogynistic imagery Pink Film depicts, in its double play of identification with both victim and assailant. It both claims to take part in the public sphere and drives for gender-oriented compartmentalization and the dividing up of audiences. It was exactly the ability to con-fuse all these contradictions that formed part of the genre's appeal for participants and the audience.

Pink Film wore this confusion on its sleeve until the early 1970s, as it was an important component of its identity and success. It was then that Pink Film, which had previously acknowledged the inextricability of supposed opposites and the continuity of history, slowly became subsumed by an ideology of clean-cut compartmentalization. This and the following chapter focus on the phase of formation of the industrial genre and its aggressive confusion, followed by its fixing into specific forms and spaces.

Pink Stability

Pink Film is often described like a prehistoric mosquito preserved in amber. Such an image portrays this unusual genre as follows: as in the 1960s, Pink films are shot for a budget somewhere in the area of 2.5 to 3.5 million yen, with a production schedule allowing for three to five days of shooting. They are around sixty minutes in length, shot on 35 mm film on location and without sound, and are shown in installments of three films per program in specialized Pink Film theaters.[13] The titles are, in keeping with the mode of consumption they are conceived for, highly stereotypical and often outrageous, only occasionally giving a sense of the film's subgenre, including terms such as *jukujo* (ripe/older woman) or *chikan densha* (train groper).

Production is based on a system of casualized labor, in which the distributor provides a nominal company (actually, the director) with a certain sum after clearing the script, usually 50 percent of the final budget, and the director functions as both producer and director using a very small crew. The directors often, though not always, write the scripts. This practice grants directors great autonomy, and as long as a certain number of sex scenes are included, the director is often free to experiment with form and narrative as he—the directors are overwhelmingly male—likes. It is possible to shoot many films in a short period of time, as the average Pink film might take about one to two months to go from first script stage to finished product; the crew accrues on-set experience quite quickly, and the rule of thumb is that it takes about three years to go from being an assistant director to making a directorial debut. As it was virtually impossible to get an apprenticeship at a major studio from the late 1960s on, Pink Film quickly became one of the sole ports of entry into the film industry. In fact, Pink Film would remain one of the prime sources of directorial and other talent for the Japanese film industry throughout the 1980s and 1990s, and for certain generations it is actually quite difficult to find directors working today that were not involved in Pink Film at some point. A large part of both the most commercially successful as well as the most critically acclaimed names had their first experiences in this industry: Suō Masayuki (*Shall We Dance?*, 1996), Takita Yōjirō (the Oscar-winning *Departures*, 2001), Hiroki Ryūichi (*Vibrator*, 2003), Aoyama Shinji (*Eureka*, 2000), Oguri Kōhei (*Sleeping Man*, 1996), Kurosawa Kiyoshi (*Cure*, 1997), Suwa Nobuhiro (*M/Other*, 1999), and Kobayashi Masahiro (*Bashing*, 2005), and the list goes on.[14] Textual standards include simulated sex scenes at regular intervals, usually around five to seven scenes per film and usually including at least one scene of sexual assault. Genitalia and pubic hair—concealed during shooting with a taped cover called a *maebari*—are hidden on screen by either shooting around them or by using several postproduction masking techniques such as mosaic, dots, or (less often) scratching out. Violence, overwhelmingly against women, has been a mainstay of Pink Film since *Market of Flesh*.

Yet this image of genre stability is also deceiving. For example, as mentioned above, the budget of a Pink film has indeed stayed stable at roughly 3 million yen since the genre's inception, but the value of that amount has of course changed drastically. In 1965 that sum was equivalent to $8,333 in the United States, a minimal amount for a feature film production even at that time. In 2006, when Pink films were still shot almost exclusively on 35 mm film, the same sum adjusted for inflation was worth just about half, and by the 2010s video was making swift inroads into shooting of Pink films.[15] Many of Pink Film's attributes have transformed over time, such as the length of the films (reduced from around eighty to sixty minutes) or the role of sexual violence (much reduced since the late 1990s).

At the same time, the image of stability has itself become an important characteristic of the genre, while in its formational period it was perceived as in constant flux. That approximately ten-year period of becoming Pink Film is the focus of the following chapters, and we might apply to genre what Lisa Gitelman and Geoffrey Pingree write about media: "There is a moment, before the material means and the conceptual modes of new media have become fixed, when such media are not yet accepted as natural, when their own meanings are in flux . . . while they are themselves defined within a perceptual and semiotic economy that they then help to transform."[16] In the case of Pink Film it spurred not only a transformation in the semiotic economy of film in Japan but the very semiotic charge of film and media itself. How, then, was Pink Film identified, named, and recognized as a formation that would proceed to transform film and media in Japan?

Naming Pink Film

In 1960 Iijima Toshio received a special merit award for his decades-long custodianship of the Index of Obscene Films at the Metropolitan Police Department. According to a 1960 article about him titled "Pink Film: 20 Years in the Screening Room," Iijima, as the head of the archive where all films confiscated for obscenity were sent, divided the films into 148 types that recorded name, style, actors, production group, and distribution route.[17] The article emphasizes the theme of historical rupture after 1945, with the ruptural trauma being the forced burning of 216 famous films (not of the obscene variety) by the U.S. occupation forces. Iijima himself emphasizes the differences between pre- and postwar films, saying the prewar films were shot by private clubs and possessed a "Japanese woodblock print beauty." The postwar films were "products of business," shot on cheap 8 mm film, in comparison to the 16 mm and 35 mm films of the prewar period. The theme of the loss of history even enters the discourse on the illegal—by the one who contributes to making them so. In this article detailing Iijima's diligence in elaborately categorizing what was not allowed to be seen, we find a puzzle: how can this article be about Pink Film when the film to be retroactively called the first Pink film would only be released two years later?

Translated Plot Summaries of Pink Films Taken from the Magazine *Seijin Eiga* 10 (October 1965)

Moaning Teens (*Jūdai no umeki*, Kokuei, 78 mins.)
The rebellion of young sexuality in agony over the maturing of its flesh!

A film that describes the gap of sexuality between adolescence and womanhood. Sex without sensation, severe torture, teens overflowing with the energy of youth, the generation in which all of this flows together. A so-called teen rebellion film that strikes against the contradictions and empty existence of a rotting society. Directed by newcomer Umezawa Kaoru. Maki Kazuko in a complementary appearance.

The Cry of Passion (*Aiyoku no sakebi*, Tōkyō Kikaku, 72 mins.)
The inside story of the unhappy passion of a man and a woman and their downfall.

Three years ago Miyuki (Izumi Yuri) was violated on impulse by two wicked youths, but she was helped by a man who happened to be passing by. Having killed one of the youths by accident, he goes to prison, and when he tries to meet her again, the woman has become a call girl. The unhappy story of a man and a woman's love is described with a realist touch. Directed by Takano Taira.

The naming of Pink Film teaches us much about its immediate character as an industrial genre. While the name "Pink Film" (*pinku eiga*) only became an established term in the latter half of the 1960s, the initial common denominators for categorizing Pink Film were budget scale and sexual content, as well as independent production and distribution. Accordingly, the category touted many names, each pointing to a different emphasis, among them *dokuritsu eiga* (independent films), *erodakushon* (an amalgam of "erotic" and "production"), *o-iroke* (sexy films), *sanbyaku-man eiga* (3-million-yen films), *ero-eiga* (erotic films), and finally *o-pinku* (honorable Pink) or simply *pinku eiga / pinku firumu* (Pink films). It is important to note that the two most popular early terms, independent films and 3-million-yen films, do not refer to narrative or stylistic features.

Crazed Instinct (*Kurutta honnō*, **Tetsu Productions, 75 mins.**)
The loss of faith of a girl who gets to know the ugly side of adults!

High school girl Miki (Sakamiki Mayumi) turned her back on life for a certain reason. Returning from school one day, she lost her virginity to three wicked youths, then she learned of the love affair of the mother she trusted, and lost her faith in adults. An elegy to youth and a short life that ends through the experience of the body. Directed by Norimichi Ichirō.

Detestable Skin (*Nikui hada*, **10F Productions, 77 mins.**)
Money or the heart.... A man who weighs women's hearts!

The story of a man who visits four former girlfriends, but each of them shoves him away coldheartedly: "Money is everything!" Is a person's heart important? Is his money important? The story of a man who tests women's hearts with a large amount of money he wins at the bicycle races, and of the women he meets. Directed by Fujita Takashi.

Note: My translation from "Kongetsu no Sukuriin Erotishizumu" (This month's screen eroticism). Most probably all these films are lost. As a great many plot summaries were provided in the magazine, I determined which ones to choose by rolling dice. As some of the names are difficult to determine, here are their originals: 経堂一郎 = Norimichi Ichirō; 藤田尚 = Fujita Takashi; 高野平 = Takano Taira.

There are many possible explanations for the origin of the term "pinku firumu." It may have been used to denote a difference from *burū firumu* (blue films), the more common term for the films that Iijima had painstakingly archived for the police department over decades. These were illegal and hardcore films that had been produced in Japan since at least the mid-1920s, often screened in clandestine events at hot-spring resorts and in urban entertainment centers like Asakusa in Tokyo.[18] It is not exactly clear, however, how common the term "burū firumu" was when "pinku firumu" was coined; and, as in the case of the article on Iijima, the term "pinku firumu" even seems occasionally to have been used with regard to blue film as well. Additionally, some sources trace the term "burū firumu" back to the Japanese translation of Graham Greene's short story "The Blue Film" (1954), in 1955, at the time translated as "Aoi Eiga" (Blue film). There are also explanations that see it as derived from the term *pinku saron* (pink salon), denoting establishments that allowed physical interaction with the hostesses. Additionally the color pink seems to have been associated with erotic media early on, and the political scientist Maruyama Masao is credited with claiming that as a youth in the 1920s one basically had the options of becoming red (leftist) or pink (gravitate toward risqué popular culture such as the *ero-guro* or erotic-grotesque subgenres).[19]

Generally, Murai Minoru is credited as having coined the term "pinku eiga" in 1963 in an article for the *Naigai Times*, a sports newspaper he worked for at the time, although the term was used earlier as well.[20] Sports newspapers such as the *Naigai Times* and *Suponichi* (Daily sports, a paper that also occasionally wrote about Pink Film) catered to a predominantly blue-collar and almost exclusively male readership with sports news and more coarse content; they were highly important for the construction of a certain kind of masculinity in this period. As the legend goes, Murai proposed a Pink Ribbon Award for this emerging new type of film, as a counterpart to the official Blue Ribbon Award that a committee of critics from the sports newspapers gave out annually.[21]

Murai was one of the first to actively report on Pink films, beginning with his set report on the filming of *The Valley of Desire*. In line with the nature theme that its female Tarzan character supplied to the film, it was appropriately helmed by Seki Kōji, a director with experience in animal documentaries. Murai himself subsequently became something of an activist for the cause of Pink Film, and from 1965 to 1973 published the magazine *Seijin Eiga* (Adult film), which covered new films and developments within the Pink Film industry, as well as writing a book on the subject in 1989. The actual driving force and de facto chief editor of *Seijin Eiga* was, however, Murai's (eventual) wife, Kawashima Nobuko. Detailed reports barely entered the established film press or general mainstream press at all, despite film eroticism being a very common subject of discourse in Japanese film periodicals since the late 1950s. The magazine *Eiga Geijutsu* published regular *erotishizumu* (eroticism) specials from around 1958, with an increasing amount of photo illustration after 1960. It appears that film periodicals were feeling the crunch on the movie industry as well and had to find new ways of attracting readership.

Well into the 1960s, this coverage of erotic films was almost exclusively concerned with foreign films. Usually, films from Japan were not featured at all, be it in text or image. There are several reasons for this, and long-standing discourses on sexuality and their entanglement with the question of foreign influence play an important role. For Pink Film, sexuality complexly related the question of self-definition to the nation and the foreign. Ōkura film advertising executive Aoki Masuo proclaimed, "It is said that Japanese women have a weakness for foreigners, but it seems that among journalists there are quite a few that share this female tribe's kind of foreigner-worship. The result is that the type of film called Pink films is silenced to death and not a single article is ever written about it. We can't have that!"[22] Such an angry and cartoonish portrayal tells us much about how Pink Film was framing itself as a site of resistance deeply tied to a gendered national moment.

Pink Resistance I: Bodies

In a 1969 special feature in *Seijin Eiga* titled "Why Is the Lyrical Poem of Resistance Called 'Pink Film' Stagnating?," several contributors, among them Ōshima Nagisa, discuss the role of Pink Film.[23] Ōshima, fresh from shooting *Boy* (*Shōnen*, 1969) at various locations across the country, recounts his surprise at the omnipresence of Pink films in theaters, even in the smallest towns, and emphasizes its political potential.[24]

This is just one example of the widespread theme of Pink Film as political resistance that drew on a number of tropes and discourses that cumulatively circulated since at least the 1920s. To disentangle the strands that helped determine the oppositional image of Pink Film, we can begin by looking at the centrality of the body. Yoshikuni Igarashi has claimed that in the postwar period, "the discursively constructed body becomes the central site for the reconfiguration of Japan's national image."[25] It will be useful then to map the complex connotations this discourse held.

On the most simple level, the idea of Pink Film as resistance can be compared to what Foucault in *The History of Sexuality* called "the speaker's benefit": a suppression of sexuality makes any act of enunciation that concerns the sexual appear as an act of resistance.[26] In the American and European context, pornographic literature in particular has thus been linked to the rise of democracy, to a new focus on individualistic subjectivity and the functional division of public and private space—that is to say, to the emergence of modern culture in general.[27] However, such generalizations are decidedly Eurocentric, not only in the way that they implicitly absolutize a potentially very specific definition of modernity. It is also questionable if they can simply be transferred wholesale to Pink Film's specific history—especially since, as discussed above, the history of Japan is quite capable of confusing such linear models of progress—provided one even decides to adopt a definition of Pink Film as some form of pornography.

Joanne Izbicki has interpreted the appearance of the naked body on Japanese screens in the postwar period as a belated resistance to, and proclamation of freedom from, wartime codes of censorship.[28] However, there are a number of contradictory reasons for the swift rise of a body discourse in postwar Japan, all of which are an expression of the enormous labor of reorientation that Japanese society saw itself confronted with after 1945. This labor called for flexible, potent, and broadly accessible semiotic tools, and the body was immediately at hand.

In Japanese the word "body" can be expressed as *nikutai* or *shintai*, the latter being more common during World War II. Nikutai carries implications of sensuality that were not deemed appropriate to the wartime atmosphere or ideology. The body, especially when figured as nikutai (in which case a more accurate translation would be "flesh"), was used in a variety of ways and with different objectives in the immediate postwar period, but it was certainly used widely.[29] Prominent sociologist and political scientist Maruyama Masao used it conceptually by connecting it to a certain aspect of historic Japanese society that he deemed premodern and is best described as feudal. In his eyes, much of what was problematic in Japan before and after the war was based on feudal concepts of behavior and relations that were inscribed into, indeed existed through, the flesh, what he called "body politics."[30] Society needed to depart from this fleshiness and move toward a less materially based democratic spirit, he argued.

In contrast, the immediate postwar strain of literature named *nikutai bungaku* (literature of the flesh), represented by authors such as Tamura Tajirō and Sakaguchi Angō, saw the body as the only reliable site of departure from the demolished and desperate sense of self the nation was experiencing.[31] As Igarashi has put it, the body was the "sole site" for encountering the "historical reality of defeat and confusion."[32] The *seishin shugi* (spiritism) of the wartime period had manifested in Japanese film quite widely, one prominent example being Kurosawa Akira's *The Most Beautiful* (*Ichiban utsukushiku*, 1944). Spiritism's trust in the power of pure will as a guarantor of victory was, in the eyes of these artists, a manipulative construction that had plunged Japan into war, destruction, defeat, and occupation. Contrary to Maruyama's terminology, for spiritism the spirit was associated with feudal community as much as with the modern idea of nation.

Douglas Slaymaker has explained the pertinence of the body in this reorientation process as a more or less deliberate switch in subject positions, exemplified by a terminological shift. While wartime ideology promoted a national body or *kokutai* (made up of the Chinese characters for "country" and "body"), the end of the war refocused on flesh or *nikutai* (made up of the characters for "meat" and "body," connoting sensuality). This opposition was itself part of official doctrine during the war, one that claimed a binary between Japanese communal austerity and Western individualist decadence. While a switch to the primacy of the flesh is obviously an attempt to break with wartime ideology, in effect it stays firmly within the discursive ground prepared by what it ostensibly seeks to discontinue.

For *nikutai bungaku* (literature of the flesh), the only thing that could be trusted was the flesh, with its unmediated honesty of pain, desire, and subjectivity—ironically to be utilized in the media of print, film, and theater. This resulted in a tense relationship of realism and the stylized use of nikutai as a trope, one I come back to in some of the criticism leveled against Pink Film. It is no coincidence that the major studio Nikkatsu used one of Tamura's best-known works, *The Gates of Flesh*, for its foray into the new territory of more explicitly sexual content in a 1964 film helmed by hyperstylist director Suzuki Seijun, and it echoes the title of the first Pink film, *Market of Flesh*, as well.[33] *The Gates of Flesh* follows a group of prostitutes fighting for survival in the immediate period after the end of the war. To survive in this harsh and desperate environment, they strike a deal to pool resources and renounce any private feelings for men, essentially unionizing and reducing sexuality to its exchange value. The story sets up a brutal conflict between capitalism and different forms of self-determination, and the body becomes the site where contradictory impulses play out; transgressions are punished with torture, which in the films and the play becomes an opportunity for displaying then-provocative amounts of nudity. All of these examples also draw on a lineage within postwar literature, however problematic, of using sexual violence as a trope to express the truth value of eruptive suffering and desire in the social and the political. Literature of the flesh aimed to capture a convulsive transformation, another aspect that carried over into Pink Film discourse along with its highly problematic gender politics. As Tamura himself claimed, "In short, to me, 'the gate of the body' means 'the gate to the modern.'" At the same time, the trope of nikutai became so omnipresent in postwar literature that Maruyama Masao denied that one could delineate a bounded category such as "literature of the flesh."[34]

While Maruyama and Tamura's conceptualizations are almost inversions of each other, they have telling common ground. Both use the idea of a historic discontinuity, the need for or fact of it, and both revolve around the body.[35] They stand in the wider context of a general boom in erotic literature and art, discourses on *sei no kaihō* (sexual liberation) and *waisetsuron* (obscenity discourse).[36] Despite or because of the desolate state of the country, with its capital and other major cities largely destroyed, the body became one of the central concepts for lively debates taking place in the new liberated atmosphere. On a less intellectualized level, from 1946 on, the so-called *kasutori-zasshi*, cheap magazines featuring heavily sensationalist and erotic content, came into circulation.[37] Even more broadly, both of these examples—less respectable popular culture and the high literary experiments—belong to what Masao Miyoshi terms the "discourses of *shutaisei*," or subjectivity, that gripped the postwar imagination. The country was in the turmoil of reorientation, and that turmoil itself was a source of fascination and anxiety, a generator of attractive confusion that was parlayed through the figure of the chaotic immediacy of the body.[38] The national drama of self and other, figured as Japan and the United States, converged on the body as the con-fusion of the self and a set of rules, practices, desires, goods, and bodies from outside. While we need to recognize the extreme simplifications of such a binary, as well as its considerable prehistory, it is also clear that it was, and has remained, one of the main structuring axes of national identity discourse in Japan since 1945.

Thus, flesh—a focus on individual pleasure and desire as represented by the carnal and the corporeal—for contemporary audiences possessed connotations of authenticity, realism, freedom, and resistance, connotations that would eventually pass down to Pink Film. In a 1969 discussion between student activists from Nihon University and Tokyo University organized by the film magazine *Kinema Junpō* on the difference between the political violence (called *gebaruto*, from the German word for violence, *Gewalt*) on the student side and the gebaruto in the films of Wakamatsu Kōji, the body figures heavily. While all of the participants are critical of Wakamatsu, one of them notes that the most important point is not the affiliation via a formulated political statement, but to "feel the other's skin." Another participant agrees, stating that to feel with the body is the most important of all (*ichiban jūyō*).[39] Feeling "the other's skin" and the communal conception of politics is, in fact, a wartime inheritance that was revived in leftist politics in the 1960s and played a role in the establishment of Pink Film spaces. The politicization of the body clearly carried over into the student movement of the 1960s, which in turn felt an ambivalent affinity with Pink Film.

The American occupation at first carried similar ideas regarding the connection of sexual and political liberation. Initially encouraged by the occupation, Pink Film later became one of the sites that used that connection to perform opposition to a U.S.-connoted status quo. Kyoko Hirano has written in detail about how the Motion Picture and Theatrical Branch of the Civil Information and Education Section (CIE) actively encouraged the inclusion of kissing scenes and storylines featuring romantic love in the postwar period. When David Conde, then head of the CIE, famously said to director Sasaki Yasushi, "Japanese tend to do things sneakily. They should do things openly," he was proposing a clear connection between showing and visibility to truth and a deliberative model of democracy.[40] His prescription set off a virtual competition among the studios to release the first *seppun eiga* (kissing film), a race that Shōchiku's *Twenty-Year-Old Youth* (*Hatachi no seishun*, Sasaki Yasushi) won, to much public attention and box-office success in May 1946 (incidentally, in October 1946, the first sexually oriented magazine after the war, a kasutori-zasshi called *Ryoki* [Bizarre] appeared). This success also set the pattern for the confluence of sexual liberation and the capitalist utilization of desire that would be one of the themes of *Gate of Flesh*. It also exacerbated the ambiguity about what liberation, sexual and otherwise, might mean.[41] It is by no means accidental that so many Pink films, especially until the late 1970s but in principle until today, concern themselves with desperate, sexually troubled, and often emasculated men; women as victims of rape; and the impossibility of reacting to a deadlocked politics through anything other than ultimately destructive, eruptive violence. Relatively few of these films seem to offer a utopian, untroubled view of sexuality or society in general. The intense negativity of Pink Film has much to do with its proposed pairing of showing truth and displaying confusion. In the discursive context of the Japanese film, this translated as a negotiation between realism and style.

Pink Film and the Ero-Real

"In Nudity, Let's Go with the Real Thing!"
—Title of an article on Pink Film in *Seijin Eiga* (1965)

"I like eroticism. I despise erotic realism," Kobayashi Masaru of Eirin writes in a 1967 special issue, "Love and Eroticism: Female Charm Screenplays," in the magazine *Kinema Junpō*.[42] He quickly makes clear which films he allots to which category, as he begins his essay with raves about the subtle eroticism in the films of Lubitsch and various other foreign movies, then damns the vulgar realism of Ichikawa Kon's *The Key* (*Kagi*, 1959, Daiei) and Masumura Yasuzō's *Lies* (*Uso*, 1963, Daiei). Kobayashi expounds that the difference lies in the surplus that art supplies in the case of eroticism. In contrast, the "ero-real" is removed from art and largely represented by "adult films by small production companies," a topic he "physiologically can't stand to touch upon," and so wishes "to leave it at the fact that most of them are ero-real [*ero-riaru*]." Although Kobayashi makes allowances for eroticism in the films of a Japanese director such as Mizoguchi Kenji, he obviously situates the standard for art, and therefore acceptable erotic content, with foreign film. This view on foreign film was quite common in the 1910s and 1920s, with the pure film movement one of its most pronounced proponents, and is linked to the larger discourse on the location of modernity and the temporalization of space, in which the West is the perennial future.[43] Indeed, Pink Film was largely excluded from the numerous *shinema erotishuzumu* (cinema eroticism) magazine specials of the 1960s, and the reasons lie with the different connotations attached to sexually themed films from Japan and abroad. As we will see, one of the central points here is clean separability. Eroticism in foreign film becomes a more well-defined category with clear objectives, while Pink Film countered with a bundle of entangled, inseparable discourses that challenged the neatly arranged, high-growth public sphere.

While Pink Film directors sometimes presented it as a question of choice, the Pink Film industry was in a sense damned to the mode of realism that contributed to the physical revulsion Kobayashi felt toward the films. For one, the films were concerned with the flesh, a trope very much connected—if in conflicted ways—to realist traditions. On the other hand, low budgets made on-location shooting, the use of untrained or semiprofessional actors, and a focus on the lower strata of society more probable, indeed often unavoidable. The debates about censorship also contributed to this image, as that-which-is-not-allowed-to-be-seen continued to secure an aura of reality or authenticity. And finally, the oppositional politics of Pink Film (and the need for it to define itself oppositionally) drifted heavily toward a commitment to the portrayal of social reality, in however stylized a filmic mode it may have taken place.

Thus, while the term "realism" is notoriously slippery and historically loaded, here what projects an aura of realism is not necessarily stylistic verisimilitude or an aesthetic strategy. Indeed, many of the extant Pink films are, considering the debates on their realist qualities, surprisingly artificial and stylized, an effect heightened by the soundscape that the characteristic postrecording of sound and the dubbing of all dialogue creates. It is a contextually perceived realism that initially played a defining role for Pink Film's semantic status and contributed to its success. It is based largely on the realist status of the forbidden gaze but also on the idea of nonregulated sexuality as problematic. Pink Film's eruptive and problematic take on sexuality stands in contrast to the 1960s how-to sex manuals that quickly became best sellers in Japan and were often criticized for being in line with (Euro-American) capitalist ideas on pleasure technologies in a burgeoning consumer society.[44] On a basic level, however, realism and the debate around it dealt with questions of positionality and national identity, much as they did in the 1930s. The combination of the forbidden situated within the quotidian (the street, the regional, the working-class environment) multiplied the power of this perceived realism and made it so attractive.

This was a discourse that filmmakers in the Pink Film industry were as aware of as those working for the major studios, yet not all directors agreed with Kobayashi's designation as "too real(ist)." In a 1966 essay titled "Let's Search Our Conscience on the Absence of Humans," one of the prominent Pink directors of the time, Shindō Takae, reflects on the desolate state of the majors and the Pink Film industry. Shindō states that postwar Americanization led to an "aping" of sexual liberation without real human liberation, and erotic films became simple displays of nudity (a statement he could have just as well used for the kissing films of 1946). He likens the Pink Film industry specifically to the Meiji-era realism movement in literature, a movement that in his eyes failed because it never possessed the will to change reality itself.[45] Similarly, Masumura Yasuzō, the very director Kobayashi had lashed out against for his (carnally inflected) vulgarity, rejected realism in an essay in the magazine *Eiga Hyōron*. According to Masumura, who was widely seen as spearheading filmic modernism at the major studio Daiei, realism emphasizes the power of circumstance and is a form of defeatism. In contrast, he argued for liberation of the ego through stylistic exaggerations.[46]

The realism debates with their vague definitions and the political charge that Kobayashi, Shindō, and Masumura are tapping into have a long and tangled history in Japan, and in terms of film they hark back to the 1910s. They dealt with questions of technology, such as the introduction of sound or more mobile cameras, the relationship to literature or to concepts like *shajitsu-teki* (another, differently connoted term for realism), and extended to documentary and feature film.[47] These debates then gained a renewed relevance in the discourse on postwar democracy, and when Pink Film later became associated with realism it was one of the subcutaneous reasons for its condemnation.

The class aspect of this discourse is omnipresent. Director Watanabe Mamoru speaks of the elite mentality of the majors, referring to directors like Ōshima Nagisa and Yoshida Kijū, who stemmed from the generation of major studio directors who could only enter the companies if they had visited elite universities (Yoshida had received his degree at Tokyo University, Ōshima at Kyoto University). Wakamatsu Kōji shot the films *Ecstasy of the Angels* (*Tenshi no kōkotsu*, 1972) and *Sacred Mother Kannon* (*Seibo Kannon Daibosatsu*, 1977) for the Art Theatre Guild (ATG), the most prominent distributor-production company that supported art house cinema from the 1960s onward. Nonetheless, he emphasized, "ATG was a kind of elite to which I didn't belong."[48] The self-image of a supposedly more blue-collar Pink industry, often characterized as a collection of outsiders and dropouts from an obviously different social stratum than the major directors, incorporated such class consciousness into their work and politics (interestingly, Watanabe himself had studied at prestigious Waseda University). Accordingly, the protagonists of early Pink films are often blue-collar outsiders or representatives of rural purity who are set up for betrayal and disillusionment upon their arrival in Tokyo (the former characters were more often figured male, the latter more often female). The sexuality they participated in, for better or for worse, was unwelcome in a sanitized, modernized public Japan.

Despite its almost uncanny success for the first few years, Pink Film was largely ignored by the mainstream press. This continued through a time when Pink films were already highly visible in urban and rural contexts and were a central source of income for a large portion of movie theaters in Japan. However, that silence changed drastically with two decisive scandals in 1965, when Pink Film moved into the public eye and became an open topic of discussion for the regular moviegoer, the established film industry, and the Tokyo Metropolitan Court. This was sparked by the scandals surrounding the inclusion of Wakamatsu Kōji's Pink film, *Affairs within Walls* (*Kabe no naka no himegoto*), in the Berlin International Film Festival, and the charges of obscenity that Takechi Tetsuji's *Black Snow* (*Kuroi yuki*) faced.[49] Before we turn to these, it is important to look at the topography of film that these films exploded into.

The Pink Film Industry Takes Form

Pink films experienced a pronounced and troubling escalation of violence in the latter half of the 1960s, and chapter 2, among other things, attempts to trace the meaning of that development. However, to understand Pink Film's strategies, it is important to recount the genre's early formational phase. It was in 1964–65 that the Pink Film boom built up to a veritable frenzy, and 1965 became the decisive year that a few dozen makeshift production and distribution outfits transformed into an industry. Productions proliferated wildly, and by 1965 over seventy companies were producing an annual total of 213 Pink films, more than triple compared to the previous year. Often Pink films were in the theaters within a month of the first script idea, and could recoup their investment after one week in just one to two theaters. Attracted by the truly astonishing profit margins and quick return on investment, seemingly everyone with money to spare began putting it into Pink Film productions. This led to many instances of fraud and, more problematic for companies thinking of the long term, overproduction and a steep decline in average quality.[50] At this point, production units, usually consisting of a director and maybe one or two business partners, were distributing their own films, usually selling the local rights to local distributors. This practice was basically unheard of in the majors' previously airtight system of national distribution control that saw filmmakers as employees, not free agents.

To curtail the imminent danger of price dumping for distribution, the Pink Film industry began to organize itself. In February 1965, the main production and distribution companies met and discussed plans for a fixed distribution and exhibition network with production quotas. Ōkura Eiga, despite being credited with the "first Pink film," had started regular Pink Film production quite late with Ogawa Kinya's *Female Animal, Female Animal, Female Animal* (*Mesu, mesu, mesu*, 1964). In April, Ōkura managed to assemble one of the large companies, Nihon Shinema, and five smaller outfits—Aoi Eiga, Hiroki Eiga, Kantō Movie, Kantō Eihai, and Meikō Select—to form the Ōkura Pictures (OP) chain. The company would be the single most influential and decisive entity for the consolidation and survival of Pink Film, almost into the 2010s.[51] The OP chain started with ten specialty theaters that were exclusively reserved for Pink Film productions—a seminal step that would have immense repercussions almost ten years later—and a host of other theaters where Pink Film was added as a program supplement. To balance the power that the OP chain held via its national distribution network and specialty theaters, Kokuei, Shintōhō, Century Eiga, and Tōkyō Kikaku formed the Dokuritsu Chēn (Independent chain) in September. Kokuei was unhappy with the arrangement, however, and left the group just two months later to continue distribution on its own.[52] In the midst of these negotiations and the industry's constriction, the media caught on to Pink Film with a vengeance. Fueled by the scandals surrounding the trial of

Black Snow (Takechi Tetsuji, 1965) and the screening of *Affairs within Walls* (Wakamatsu Kōji, 1965) at the Berlin International Film Festival, Pink Film was in the public eye.

The *Black Snow* Trial

Those who are accused of "obscenity" today are being falsely accused. The government is flexing its muscles, and those accused under article 175 are not, in fact, being tried for the crime of "obscenity," but as opponents of authority.
—ŌSHIMA NAGISA, from his plea during his obscenity trial in January 1976

In August 1965, the Tokyo Metropolitan Police submitted the names of forty people to prosecution for the distribution of obscenity according to article 175, among them director Takechi Tetsuji, the manager of the Nikkatsu Shinjuku theater, the head of Nikkatsu's distribution arm, company director Hori Kyūsaku, the production staff, various actors, and, quite sensationally, Arata Masao and Yana Tadashi of Eirin.[53] By December 25, 1965, only Takechi and the head of Nikkatsu distribution, Murakami Akira, were formally charged.[54] The run-up to this conflict sheds light the nervousness about the portrayal of nudity—if it was only that. Takechi Tetsuji repeatedly voiced his opinion that the actual grounds for the police action lay in the story and its intense criticism of the American presence in Japan, even claiming that a police officer involved had told him they were acting on orders from the CIC (Civil Information Center, which he describes as a "branch of the CIA" that was "inside the metropolitan police"). He also illustrated the political relevance of his case by comparing the state's stance toward *Black Snow* with the suppression of sexual imagery by the Nazis or the Tokugawa government of the eighteenth and nineteenth centuries.[55]

Many of the majors' forays into the adult film market were still heavily shrouded in the cloak of art cinema, and they were strategically helmed by respected auteur directors. Takechi Tetsuji, renowned for his albeit scandalous work in theater, should have fit this description as well. However, this did not protect him from having to defend his work in the first court case for obscenity charges against a feature film since the end of the war. The absence of any declarations of solidarity are intricately connected to the establishment of the category and identity of Pink Film.

The chronology of events that led to police action may shed some light on some of the politics involved with this case. Takechi was famously confrontational and had repeatedly come into conflict with Eirin on his previous films. *Black Snow* itself had received revision orders by Eirin from the script stage onward, and the first edited version submitted had to be recut. Nikkatsu complied with Eirin's demands, and on June 5, 1965, opened the film in nineteen theaters, mostly in the Tokyo metroplex area, as a preview with admission fee. Three days later, the metropolitan police warned Eirin that a general release in this form would not be tolerated, and Nikkatsu agreed to further cuts in sixteen scenes, totaling eight and a half minutes. This version received a general release on June 9. One week later, on June 16, the police searched the offices of production company Dai San Pro and Nikkatsu, as well as several Nikkatsu theaters, and seized the print from the previews—different from the one now in circulation—under the charge of distribution of obscenity. Obviously, they were making an example, but opinions differed about what kind of example.

Black Snow focuses on Jirō, who lives in a brothel that his mother runs for American soldiers. After conspiring with a partner to rob his aunt of a stash of dollars, he stabs a black GI on the street and steals his gun. Jirō strikes up a romantic friendship with Shize, but one day slips out of the dark room where they are about to have sex and lets a friend take his place. When the lights go on, Shize dashes out of the building in shock in the most famous scene of the film, running naked along the fence of the American air base with fighter planes roaring above. After Jirō and his friends rob and kill his aunt, he is arrested by a policeman accompanied by the U.S. military police. At the headquarters, Shize and her father visit Jirō and offer their forgiveness. That night a firing squad picks him up from his cell, and as he walks toward his death, he remembers his mother and Shize as she ran naked along the army base. The black and white image becomes inverted, and the snow turns black.

Takechi made numerous statements to the effect that this was a *hanbei* (anti-American) film, and that the persecution he faced was based on political grounds, not on defense of public morals. It is difficult to say now how much the police action was politically motivated, but to many of Takechi's contemporaries, it at least seemed comprehensible, just as it would in Ōshima Nagisa's trial over ten years later.[56] Legal restrictions on the portrayal of the American presence in Japan were commonplace and strict until the occupation officially ended in 1952, and their enforcement was even part of the original Eirin's responsibility. The revised Treaty of Mutual Cooperation and Security (Anpo) between the United States and Japan had been signed to immense public protests in 1960, ultimately leading to the resignation of Prime Minister Kishi Nobusuke. The next renewal was due in 1970, and the Japanese government knew that its policy was not a popular one. It is at least a possibility that in the case of *Black Snow*, two threats to state authority—one political

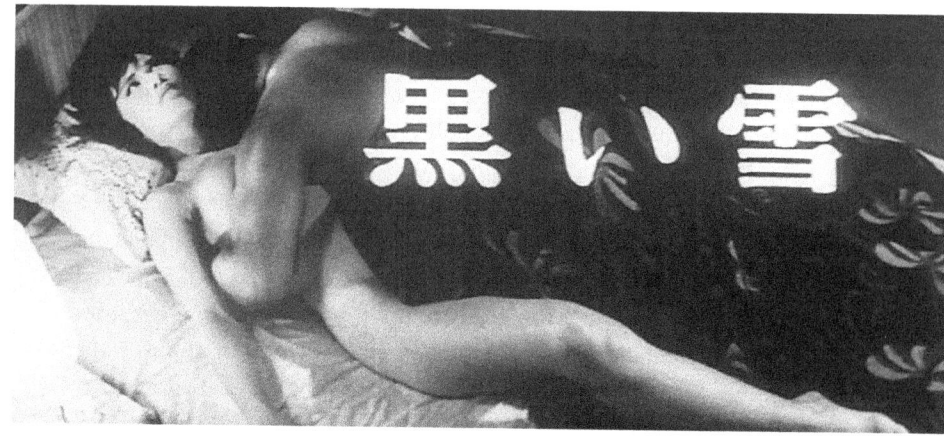

FIGURE 1.1. The opening image of *Black Snow*. The shot shows Jirō's perspective as he peers over a makeshift wall to observe one of the prostitutes with a GI. Possibly following Eirin's suggestion to "pay special attention," the two barely move at all, frozen in position.

and one moral—were being taken care of in one sweep. The revisions Eirin demanded at the script stage give clues to this. Among the usual restrictions on the portrayal of sexuality, such as avoiding full-body nudity, Eirin had demanded the deletion of the lovemaking scene between the black soldier and the prostitute, Yuri, as well as to "pay special attention" when Yuri caresses the soldier. Also to be stricken were any English words the soldier might utter during intercourse, as well as the use of the word "General," as it might imply an individual person. The policeman's statement at the end of the film that the protagonist was being arrested "on order of the occupation army" was also to be stricken.[57]

Reactions to the trial were mixed. The press itself was fairly critical of Eirin and its perceived loose stance on the new brand of erotic films. Indeed, Eirin had been increasingly permissive of nudity, sex, and violent content, possibly because of its closeness to the established film industry, which was experimenting with ways to compete with TV. Now, however, it announced a reorganization and a generally tougher stance, a preemptive move to protect the industry from real legal regulations by the government. The Directors Guild of Japan (Nihon Eiga Kantoku Kyōkai) initially declined any support for Takechi (who was not a member), just as the film world's reaction in general was quite cool.[58] The burgeoning Pink Film industry of 1965, with around 220 films that year, depending on how you count, produced by seventy-one small companies, could well have felt under attack. Yet despite the fact that it was already organizing itself in terms of distribution chains and production agreements, it did not react at all. This prompted scriptwriter and critic Ishido Toshirō to chastise the major directors for not going to the trial to protest, "despite having free time" (an allusion to the difficulties of finding work in the mid-1960s). He also admonished the "masters of the *erodakushon*" for short-sighted ignorance and for not feeling affected since *Black Snow* was distributed by a major company, despite producing "the same erotic films."[59]

The overall lack of support for Takechi, whose politics were quite in line with public opinion and probably those of a great many directors and producers, shows much about the structure of the Japanese film world at the time, and of the burgeoning delineations of identity that were at play. The Pink Film industry was beginning to develop a sense of self, one strongly dependent on the majors as a negative foil, and Takechi simply fell between the cracks. For the majors not to support a move toward more liberal treatment of sexual content, when it was one of the only strategies that seemed to promise financial security, was illogical. For the Directors Guild not to support a filmmaker threatened with (as he saw it) political censorship was strange. And for the Pink Film industry to keep quiet when the very basis of their existence seemed under attack was quite simply verging on self-destructive behavior. But the Directors Guild did not regard Takechi as a proper director; to them he was an amateur. He did not have formal training as a director, or the many years of training as an assistant director that are usually required to climb up the ladder of the paternalistically organized seniority system. Meanwhile, according to the Pink Film industry, *Black Snow* was not a real Pink Film. It had been produced with the idea of distributing it through a major, and Pink Film identity was defined by self-distribution—the stepping-stone to independence from Pink Film's Other, the majors. In contrast, the majors regarded *Black Snow* as a dirty necessity from the outside, far below their still-superior budgets and technical standards, a specimen from the upstart type of sexploitation film that had been stealing the desperately needed audience. In short, nobody involved in the film industry actually perceived *Black Snow* as a Pink film. On the one hand, this shows the relevance of distribution channels for the genre's definition; on the other hand, it demonstrates how a film that participated in both genres was incommensurable with the either/or identity that was beginning to emerge.

The mass media and, consequently, the general public were another story, however. The scandal catapulted sexploitation films into public consciousness, making them even more controversial and, by raising their profile, an even bigger moneymaker. Takechi was acquitted of all charges a year later, though in a verdict he was emphatically not happy with. The court stated that while the individual scenes were to be regarded as obscene, film as a time-based medium had to be seen as a whole, and as a whole it possessed redeeming qualities and could not be labeled as such. Obscene but innocent, *Black Snow* stood at the intersection of several levels of identity negotiations: the national, the film industrial, and the specifically Pink. The court's perspective on the film as a bounded, linear temporal experience foreshadows some of the conflicts that would arise with the appearance of video. For the moment, however, the rupture of scandalous scenes was overruled by the continuity of the whole—itself a kind of confusionist stance.

The *Affairs within Walls* Scandal

The *Black Snow* trial came hard on the heels of another incident, one that may have made the authorities so eager to strike in the first place and that was in a sense Pink Film's grand debut as Pink Film. A scandalous screening at the Berlin International Film Festival clashed with the agenda of an entirely new postwar Japan and further established the oppositional position that Pink Film supposedly held. How, then, did this scandal come about?

Early in 1965, Eiren had proposed several films to the Berlin International Film Festival as Japan's official entries. They were refused, so Eiren submitted two additional films, Daiei's *The Hoodlum Soldier* (*Heitai yakuza*, Masumura Yasuzō, 1965) and Tōei's *Tale of Japanese Burglars* (*Nippon dorobō monogatari*, Yamamoto Satsuo, 1965); these were rejected as well. It is possible that Berlin felt pressure to become a bit more edgy at a time when Bergmann's *The Silence* (*Tystnaden*, 1963) had just received much critical and popular attention, or because the festival was undergoing restructuring that year.[60] In any event, on a business trip to Tokyo, Guenther Maten—of the West German company Hansa Film—stumbled across *Affairs within Walls* (*Kabe no naka no himegoto*, prod. Wakamatsu Productions, distr. Kantō Movie) by Wakamatsu Kōji, proposed it to Berlin, and the festival office agreed.[61] Eiren was shocked, all the more by the fact that it assumed that the official statutes of the film festival at the time ensured that the official Japanese entry would be selected only in mutual agreement with the national producers' organization. This rule did exist, but *Affairs within Walls* had been independently produced, and independent producers were not members of Eiren at this point. The Berlin statutes allowed the interpretation that if a unified national representation, that is, a body representing all producers, did not exist, then the approval of the individual producer was sufficient. The festival saw itself as, formally, on safe ground.⁶² Wakamatsu, then twenty-eight years old, traveled to the festival and soon saw himself enveloped in a national dispute.

After receiving a telegram on June 19 announcing that *Affairs* was in the official selection, Eiren quickly answered on June 22, stating that the film was not fit to represent Japan. The scandal reached diplomatic levels when the Japanese consulate general in Berlin, Tokura Eiji, issued a public statement on order of the Foreign Ministry protesting the screening.⁶³ In turn, the festival and the senator of arts and science, Werner Stein, insisted on the legitimacy of the selection. The film was taken seriously in the German press, even if most reviews were lukewarm, but in Japan the screening was regarded as a blemish on the new and improved image of the Japanese nation that it had presented the world just one year before at the Tokyo Olympics.⁶⁴ The Japanese press raised a storm, with critic Kusakabe Kyūshirō of the *Mainichi Shinbun*, who served on one of the festival juries, famously calling the film a *kokujoku eiga* (national disgrace film), a term that circulated widely at the time. Eiren consequently boycotted the Berlin International Film Festival for the following two years. For Eiren and the majors it represented, the incident challenged its authority in front of the world. The world also played the key role for the political protest when the government appealed to the festival to "not show films that injure national feelings or create a false image of the country of origin."⁶⁵ As in the case of *Black Snow*, Japan's relative position in the world, Japanese identity, and the struggle over the authority to control it were at stake.

In *Affairs*, Makoto's parents are pressuring him to study for a second attempt at the university entrance exams. Isolated and pent up in his tiny room in the apartment housing complex (*danchi*), he spends his time spying on his neighbors with a telescope. Among them is the disillusioned wife of a union lawyer who is having an affair with a former boyfriend from her student movement days, a man scarred by the atomic bombing of Hiroshima who now makes money trading stocks that are rising due to the Vietnam War. Makoto's sexual frustration culminates in him attacking his own sister, but he proves impotent. He seeks out the housewife he has been spying on and attempts to force her into sex, but he again fails. Close to madness, he manically repeats, "Don't look at me! You think I can't do it, but I can! I can do it!" He stabs her with a knife as the radio plays a live baseball game and the sportscaster bellows, "He's in! It's a home run!"

Affairs is a bitter indictment of the new modern postwar lifestyle, with its emphasis on achievement and its partitioning of the public and domestic sphere as encapsulated in "my-home-ism" (*maihōmu shugi*), a popular slogan of the 1960s. Prime Minister Ikeda Hayato had set the trajectory for the 1960s with his "double the national income" plan. The danchi, modern apartment houses promising affluence and a Western lifestyle, represented "my home" and a new emphasis on a consumer culture–oriented domesticity that was transforming the aspirations of a whole society. *Affairs* attacks this sanitized consumer culture with its very existence, as well as in its text. Overflowing with dysfunctional sex, violence, rape, and murder, it is ripe with reference to the political conflicts raging within Japan, and deeply antagonistic to the idea of both a modernized Japan as envisioned by the government, and, by extension, American influence. The danchi portrayed here connect to Pink Film in another sense as well. Ironically, they can be seen as one of the causes of the Pink Film boom, as they are part of the social and demographic changes that moved large parts of the city population to the outskirts and isolated the housewives in the suburbs, which had no cinemas, tipping the scales toward a male film audience. These feminized danchi are an explicit topic in *Affairs within Walls*, with its montages of housewives patrolling the streets and talking high-speed gibberish.

Whether *Black Snow* and *Affairs* accurately reflected the greater part of Pink films produced at the time or not, the two incidents they were identified with in 1965 heavily influenced the public perception of Pink Film and, maybe more importantly, the idea the genre held of itself. Pink Film, in the form of scandal, negotiated identity across the realms of economy, nation, and gender. But the connotations of resistance and Japanese national identity politics came to the fore because they were already rooted in discourses that existed before Pink Film itself did. Pink Film latched onto a number of tropes and themes that were highly important in the postwar era and only went through the slightest of transformations to adapt to the new medium.

Pink Resistance II: The Role of the Independents

Already, a development is beginning in the film world that is exactly like the Soviet invasion of Czechoslovakia.
—From the introduction to a 1968 roundtable discussion featuring the most prominent Pink Film directors of the time, regarding the majors' entry into Pink territory by producing pink series

The second foundation for connotations of resistance inherited by Pink Film lies in its initially abrasive position in the economic system of film production, distribution, and exhibition.[66] More specifically, it was Pink Film's

FIGURE 1.2. Different negotiations of urban space on the same page of the *Asahi Shinbun* in 1968. An article in the middle of the page describes local resistance to the building of a Pink Film specialty theater in the Sumida section of Tokyo. The bottom of the page features an ad with an invitation to a "my-home tour," to take a look at new and modern housing. It was quite unusual for a new theater to be built to show Pink films. In this case, the Keitsū chain was building a theater simply because in the same year this article appeared it founded the Pink Film production and distribution outfit Million Films and wanted to enlarge its Pink Film exhibition arm. "Eigakan Kensetu ni Monoii: Sumida no Rengō Chōkai: 'Pinku Jōei wa Komaru'" [Protests against film theater construction: Sumida's neighborhood association: "Pink Film screenings would create problems"], *Asahi Shinbun*, October 11, 1968, 16.

status as *dokuritsu puro* (independent productions)—ironically, a category that Pink Film would eventually contribute to making defunct. By the end of the 2000s, 90 percent of all theatrically released films in Japan were produced without the involvement of a "major," and 75 percent were distributed by non-"majors." These quotation marks are justified by the erosion of meaning these terms have experienced (just as their relevance has changed several times over in Japanese film history). In the context of late-1950s industrial organization, when independent feature film distribution dwindled to near zero in 1959, such divisions held little practical value.[67] However, they were relevant and even became structuring discourses during times like the immediate postwar period or the mid-1960s, when two systems, majors and independents, seemed to exist simultaneously. If at present these terms have been emptied of meaning, they were highly politically charged in the postwar period when leftist political orientation and independent production were seen as deeply intertwined—connotations that held strong consequences for later Pink Film discourses.[68] This has its roots in industry organization in the immediate postwar years, and was epitomized by the three labor strikes at Tōhō from 1946 to 1948.

The postwar film industry represented less a rupture than continuity with prewar and wartime Japan. In 1942, the ten largest film companies were consolidated into the three large studios of Tōhō, Shōchiku, and Daiei in order to enhance wartime efficiency; film stock was allotted by the state, and censorship, starting at the planning stage, was intense.[69] After the war, several of the top executives of these companies, including Shōchiku's Kido Shiro and Daiei's Nagata Masaichi, were temporarily banned from the industry—only to return after a pro forma time in exile—while filmmakers themselves were not implicated.[70] This brief interruption in tenure for the industry's power players later became an argument for the revision of the 1971 copyright law. This law was partly engineered by Nagata, head of Daiei, who successfully argued, among other things, that since producers after the war bore the brunt of legal responsibility for wartime production, they also deserved all legal rights to the films.

While the major companies and their executives were officially associated with the war, the American occupation at first actively encouraged organized labor in the belief that it would encourage self-determination. By late 1945, all three feature film companies were unionized, and early successes in negotiating with studio management led to widespread enthusiasm for unionization. In the events leading up to the second strike in late 1946, the Tōhō union split into two opposing factions for and against a strike.[71] After the second strike had taken place, Tōhō founded Shintōhō (New Tōhō) for those employees who had not participated in the strike. The third and most spectacular strike, in 1948, was broken up when the U.S. Army appeared with aircraft and tanks at the Tōhō gates; as one person famously described it, "The only thing they didn't send was a battleship."[72] The crushing of the high-profile strike held national import for both sides, and the outcome made the balance of power clear. Subsequently, Tōhō was purged of strike leaders and communist sympathizers.

Unexpectedly, Shintōhō, formed for the strike-opposing and anticommunist employees, now became the troublemaker. After much wrangling about production and distribution deals, in March 1950 Shintōhō became an independent company and, ironically, a haven for leftist filmmakers. That they would need such a refuge was foreshadowed in the American participation in breaking up the third strike at Tōhō. In the wake of the Cold War and anticommunist hysteria, the initial policy of encouraging union activity was all but reversed. The so-called Red Purge of the film industry (among others) commenced. On September 14, 1950, the office of the union section of the occupation summoned the studio heads to a meeting and demanded the expulsion of communist sympathizers from the industry. This eventually led to the firing of 137 employees from the major companies, sixty-six of them from Shōchiku alone (among them, director Imai Tadashi).[73] Already after the third Tōhō strike in 1948, a number of the leftist filmmakers who left Tōhō had entered independent production, and the purged filmmakers quickly joined their ranks. According to Tanaka Jun'ichirō, 1946 saw three independent productions, 1948 thirty-eight, 1949 sixty-seven, and 1950 ninety-four out of a total of 215 that year.[74] Satō Tadao claims that many of the purged filmmakers used their "retirement money" after leaving the majors to self-finance the projects they wanted to realize. Others held strong financial ties to labor unions, whose goals were actively endorsed in the films.[75] For a short time, independent productions drew critical and popular success, and even filmmakers from major companies ventured outside of their mother ships to realize projects that would not have been greenlighted within the studios. Ichikawa Kon, for example, teamed up with the theater group Gekidan Seihai to shoot *A Billionaire* (*Ichiman chōja*, 1954, distr. Shintōhō).[76]

Partially through their low budgets and partially through their ideological stance, these independent films were usually shot on location and aspired to heightened (social) realism. They were also often in conflict with Eirin. At this point, still strongly under American influence and observation, Eirin would caution independent filmmakers about even portraying widespread unemployment, which was frowned upon by the occupation forces. This may be one of the reasons that these political independents only started developing as a force toward the end of the occupation, between 1950 and 1952, and reached their peak of production shortly thereafter. Realism, signaled by a low-budget style and thematic focus on social problems, was thus at this point associated with a specific political stance and a specific mode of production and distribution. This connection largely carried over into discourse on Pink Film, though not everyone accepted the idea of Pink Film as necessarily realist. Takechi Tetsuji complained that the very reason Pink Film powerhouse Ōkura Eiga was experiencing so few problems with the state was their lack of political relevance, partially due to their shoddy sex scenes, which robbed the films of any "feeling of realism."[77]

Consequently, independent production in the early 1950s was so strongly associated with resistance and leftist political inclination that the terms *dokuritsu eiga* (independent film), *shakai eiga* (society/socialist film), and *sayoku eiga* (leftist film) were often used interchangeably.[78] Critics praised many of the early films and sympathized with the often-ambitious productions. Independent production was constructed as inextricably connected to leftist resistance against the status quo embodied by the majors, Eirin, and the now not-so-liberating American influence. This, however, is only partially true.

While the discourse at the time constructed the oppositional image of independent production, the picture seems more complicated. The dubious opposition between majors and independents has held strong in writing on film from Japan, in the case of the postwar independents, or on 1960s' new wave directors and Pink Film. However, much closer to the truth is that they had a symbiotic relationship characterized by occasional upsets in the power balance. The majors actually distributed and exhibited independent productions widely in the late 1940s and strongly depended on them to fill the supply gaps left open by production facilities that could not handle the demand resulting from the theater-building boom. Additionally there were a large number of only nominally independent production outfits that exclusively subcontracted, and often had financial connections, to the majors. Among these were Takarazuka Eiga (Tōhō), Tōkyō Eiga, Fuji Eiga (Nikkatsu, later Shintōhō), Kurosawa Productions (Kurosawa Akira's company, connected to Tōhō), and Junketsu Eiga Kyōkai.

The 1960s saw similar cases. Even if Ōshima Nagisa left Shōchiku in a fight over the short-lived release of *Night and Fog in Japan* (*Nihon no yoru to kiri*, 1960) to found his own independent production company, Sōzōsha, most of his feature films of the 1960s were still distributed by Shōchiku or the Art Theatre Guild (ATG).[79] ATG itself, often heralded as the only (independent) bastion of auteur film against the overly commercial and creatively bankrupt majors, was founded largely with capital provided by Tōhō, which also contributed several theaters to its distribution circuit.[80] Independent production needed the majors, and the majors needed the independents. They were gap fillers, experimentation ground, and cost-efficient suppliers. Yet the power balance in this relationship of mutual reliance was, of course, uneven.

As Aaron Gerow has written, the success of independent production depended "less on artistic or political viability than on overall industry strength."[81] Despite the initial successes of the postwar independents, the majors' grip on distribution and exhibition tightened in step with their financial buoyancy in the 1950s. Tōhō had long emphasized the *hyakkan shugi* (one hundred theater doctrine) of its cofounder Kobayashi Ichizō—one of the architects of consumer culture in Japan—but in general all companies realized the importance of a strong exhibition arm and invested heavily in theaters, buying some and recruiting others to block-booking contracts.

The competition in the film market became fiercer after Nikkatsu reentered film production in 1953. When the fairly new studio Tōei adopted the *nihondate* (double bill) system in 1954, all major companies stepped up production to the degree that there was no need to involve independent production to fill exhibition slates anymore.[82] Independent distribution, the only option left, became increasingly difficult, with fewer and fewer uncontracted theaters available outside of the block-booking system; theaters were under contract to show films for a fixed amount of time, regardless of whether they were successful or not. Additionally struck by the audience's waning interest, independent production began to dry up, and from June 1956 to June 1957, when the majors were still at the peak of their power, the distribution income share of independently produced and distributed feature films was a miniscule 0.32 percent.[83] Critics regularly bemoaned that many independent productions had become intellectually less interesting, often not much more than long commercials for the labor unions financing them.[84]

The onset of high economic growth changed the audience. In a country now in tangible reach of real and widespread prosperity, socially critical messages were less appealing than my-home-ism and the *sanshū no jinki* (three sacred treasures) of the 1960s: the TV set, the refrigerator, and the washing machine. In 1960, Prime Minister Ikeda Hayato proclaimed his goal to double the national income, and on the eve of the Pink Film explosion in 1963, director Shindō Kaneto was writing a nostalgia-drenched regular column titled "Our

Independent Film History" for the magazine *Eiga Geijutsu*.[85] Independent production was, at this point, merely a fading memory—if one that Pink Film soon claimed to revive.

Pink Resistance III: Protest Culture

By the late 1960s, Pink Film developed a considerable fan base among the student population. Chapter 2 discusses the question of Pink Film audiences in more detail, but one important result of discourse on Pink Film oppositionality was, as mentioned earlier, its association with the student movement. In some ways Pink Film was highly suited to this connection; it was young and it was fast. During its boom, Pink Film had an immense demand for staff, and the directors, primarily in their twenties, often shot six or seven films a year. In comparison, the directors at the major studios often worked as assistant directors for fifteen years before being allowed to helm their first film. Because Pink films were produced extremely quickly, they could even react to current news.[86] The demand for staff also made interaction with young artists outside of the mainstream easy, and Pink Film frequently linked into the new urban culture of *angura* (short for *andāguraundo*, or underground), loosely designating nonmainstream arts including everything from certain jazz groups to Matsumoto Toshio's experimental films or Kara Jūrō's Red Tent theater troupe. The students' attention in terms of Pink Film focused most prominently on Wakamatsu Kōji and his stable of assistant directors and scriptwriters at Wakamatsu Productions, among them Adachi Masao, Komizu Gaira, Arai Haruhiko, and Yamatoya Atsushi. Their attractiveness to the student audience is one of the reasons for film scholarship's retrospective overemphasis on Wakamatsu as a supposed representative of Pink Film. Even in 1968, *Seijin Eiga* editor Kawashima Nobuko stated, "Listening to students, one gets the impression that Pink Film consists only of Wakamatsu Kōji."[87]

In fact, the connections between the angura scene and Pink Film ran broad and deep, and a director-producer such as Mukai Kan was much more commercially successful and more influential than Wakamatsu in terms of themes and storylines. Like Wakamatsu, Mukai established his own production company, Mukai Production, quite early, employing four directors and a total of fifty staff by 1969. His later company, Shishi Pro, trained some of the most popular directors working in film in Japan today in mainstream film as in Pink Film. Despite his seminal role in training an entire generation of directors, Mukai is virtually absent from official film histories. In Satō Tadao's multivolume *Nihon Eiga Shi* (Japanese film history), he grudgingly devotes six pages to Pink films, barely mentioning anyone other than Wakamatsu. Yomota Inuhiko's *Nihon Eiga-shi Hyaku-nen* (One hundred years of Japanese film) only mentions Pink Film as an addendum to Wakamatsu, calling him "the King of Pink Film" in the chapter's subtitle. Yamamoto Shinya was certainly the most influential director of the 1970s, and the most popular. He, Mukai, and an entire panoply of influential Pink Film directors have been almost uniformly ignored in criticism and research.[88]

One element of compatibility between angura culture and Pink Film was the way the oppositional stance that was integral to their identities could be commodified. The 1969 special angura issue of mainstream film magazine *Kinema Junpō* features a star portrait of Pink Film director Adachi Masao of Wakamatsu Productions. Complete with pictures similar to pop star pinups, the issue impressively demonstrates how even an experimental and highly politicized director like Adachi—later a member of the Japanese Red Army (Nihon Sekigun)—was part of image commodity culture via the angura brand.[89] Another point of contact between this underground culture and Pink Film was the actors. Many actors in Pink Film were also active in the young theater companies, often founded to counter the established *shingeki* troupes, and identified themselves as members of the *shin-sayoku* (new left), while the established troupes represented a hierarchically ossified old left.[90] The latter sported a strict seniority system, were very difficult for young actors to break into, and often had monopolistic ties to the major film companies. Without membership in one of the established troupes, it was difficult for theater actors to work their way into the majors' films. Pink films offered a much faster, and less constricted, route to the screen. There are many examples: Pink actress Tsuruoka Yoshiko played in Mishima Yukio's short film *Patriotism* (*Yūkoku*, 1966); Kanō Kazuko from Wakamatsu's *Affairs within Walls* later entered the Bungaku-Za troupe; Taniguchi Yuri entered the Ningen-Za troupe; and actress Niitaka Keiko as well as later Pink Film director Ikejima Yutaka were active in Terayama Shūji's avant-garde theater troupe. Kara Jūrō, head of the Jōkyō Gekijō / Red Tent troupe, played in Wakamatsu Kōji's *Violated Angels* (*Okasareta byakui*, 1967), and Butoh dance legend Maro Akaji played in Yamatoya Atsushi's *Inflatable Sex Doll of the Wasteland* (*Kōya no Dacchi Waifu*, 1967).

The students' enthusiasm was of national proportions. University festivals commonly screened Pink films, and later Nikkatsu Roman Porno, as part of their festivities. This included elite universities like Waseda or Tokyo University, and is an indication of the association with resistance to which the highly politicized students of the 1960s and early 1970s were attracted. In 1972 alone, the Underground Film Center (in a later incarnation to become

Image Forum, the prime promoter of experimental film from Japan) distributed thirty Wakamatsu films to thirteen universities (on 16 mm). Gotō Kōichi of Shintōhō mentions that renting films to university festivals was once very common, but the only university still renting films from Shintōhō in the mid-2000s was Okayama University.[91]

Discussions on Pink Film in this period virtually always included the revolutionary potential of Pink Film and its "guerilla style." "'Gebaruto' Pinku Eiga" ("Gebaruto" Pink Film), the 1969 *Kinema Junpō* special issue on Pink Film, featured the discussion mentioned above between several student activists on the role of Pink Film in the protest movements sweeping the country. "Gebaruto," a Japanization of the German word *Gewalt* (violence), was associated with the student movement and was commonly used in reference to violent clashes with the police during political demonstrations.[92] The July 1969 issue of *Seijin Eiga* features a special report on the spirit of *gebaruto kakumei* (gebaruto revolution) that was "rolling over the Pink Film world."[93] Yet this raises the question of how such a supposedly oppositional and radical section of the film industry was able to carry almost half of the entire film output of Japan.

Pink Film, TV, and the Major Studios

In late 1962, a film about a "vampire fly from the Soviet Union" that "provided a woman with an ecstatic death while sucking her blood" became one of the less likely successes of the year. After the female-Tarzan film *The Valley of Desire* had made waves earlier in the year, Kitasato Toshio, a strip-show owner from the Ikebukuro section of Tokyo, employed a Russian actress and set out to make *Lara of the Wild* (*Yasei no Rāra*, 1962) for the production company Naigai films.[94] Since the film is lost, it is now difficult to say how far the narrative may have gone with its anticommunist subtext. What the film teaches us, however, is that Pink Film made the gateway into film production extremely porous almost overnight. Practically anyone, it seemed, could get into the film business and make money. Whether this was true or not, starting in 1962 a virtual rush to set up tiny production companies ensued. As a result, what developed in the early 1960s was a curiously interdependent yet uneasy relationship between television, major film studios, and Pink Film. From the beginning, none could be fully separated from the others.

Pink Film proliferated in what was seen as a very troubled industry; but if that is true, how was it able to secure such immediate success, even for films as unlikely as *Lara of the Wild*? As mentioned above, after the 1958 peak of influence and prosperity, the six major studios—Shōchiku, Tōei, Daiei, Tōhō, Shintōhō, and Nikkatsu—had fallen into considerable financial difficulties.[95] These were exacerbated by the fact that banks were notoriously cautious in dealing with the low-status movie business, with its air of vulgarity, unpredictability, and *yakuza* connections.[96] The capital-poor studios swiftly moved into the red when the income from their films failed to cover the investments.[97] As in other countries, the rise of television was singled out as the main culprit for the losses, although it is probable that a general increase in leisure activities due to rising income was just as much to blame. In 1958, after an initial phase of cooperation with TV broadcasters beginning in 1954, the studios had struck the so-called six-company agreement asserting that no actors or other staff would be shared with, and no broadcast rights for films would be sold to, TV stations. The following year, thirty-four private stations received licenses, creating a spike in demand for broadcast-ready product just when the major studios had instituted a boycott.[98] This demand was partially satisfied with affordable TV films and series supplied by U.S. studios, creating a window into idealized, American middle-class living standards that would help fuel much of the commodity culture of the 1960s.

However, when the major studio Shintōhō was on the brink of bankruptcy in July 1961, it sold the broadcast rights to 559 films from its archives to various television stations to cover its debts. This happened immediately after it left the Motion Pictures Producers Association of Japan (Eiren, which is distinct from the industry's self-regulatory body Eirin), under whose umbrella the anti-TV coalition had been formed.[99] Effectively ending the ban on selling feature films to television, it occurred too late for the majors to really capitalize on it, as TV stations had begun to rely heavily on imported series and feature films. The stations were also getting ready to create their own film production facilities. In fact, the TV production model is often cited as having provided the blueprint for the standard Pink film budget and length, via a recommendation made by a TV producer to Motogi Sōjirō, producer of *The Seven Samurai* (*Shichinin no samurai*, Kurosawa Akira, 1954) and later a prolific Pink Film director.[100] Additionally, the import quota on foreign films intended for theatrical release, introduced after the peace treaty of 1952 officially granted Japan autonomy, was dropped in April 1964 (the quota had initially allowed for 208 films, with each country allotted a certain share) in accordance with Japan's entry into the eight-country system of the OECD, following International Monetary Fund regulations.[101] Pressure on the major studios was building from several sides, both inside and outside of the country. Almost all of the difficulties were connected to Japan's reentry into the global economic sphere, which at the time was often termed modernization.

The characterization of Pink Film as a danger to the majors and a sign of the decline of the movie industry was summed up in typical headlines such as "The 3-Million-Yen Films That Are Threatening the 5 (Major) Companies" or "To What Degree Are They Eating the Majors' Market?"[102] However, the reality was more complex. As we will see, at some point every single one of the major studios inserted Pink films into their programs and theaters. In fact, the majors actually contributed to the rise of Pink Film and, to a certain degree, depended on the product. The key to Pink Film's initial explosive growth lies in the differences between the exhibition structures in the major cities, and what in Japan is called the *chihō*, roughly "the regional/provincial," in reference to everything outside of the nine major cities. From 1960 on, due to the immediate and disastrous effects of lower revenues in their distribution and exhibition businesses, the majors quite swiftly and dramatically reduced their film production activities. The 1968 Nikkatsu-distributed *The Sands of Kurobe* (*Kurobe no taiyō*, dir. Kumai Kei, prod. Ishihara Production and Mifune Production) was a 196-minute extravaganza produced by its stars, Mifune Toshiro and Ishihara Yūjiro. For its first run, the film was shown as a single bill for an entire month, when double bills usually changed weekly. This created considerable problems for the exhibition sector, especially the second- and third-run theaters (*kabansen*) that relied on the so-called nihondate or double-bill system. In this system a double bill switched once a week, or at the very least every ten days, forcing each of the majors to produce an astonishing two films a week to be able to supply their respective exhibition infrastructures, totaling around 104 films a year per studio.[103] The power balance was obvious. In such a system, the production sector was simply a tool to keep the exhibition section—where most of the money was made—supplied. As a consequence of the majors' continual reduction of output, it was the exhibition sector and its omnivorous hunger for product that made Pink Film possible in the first place.[104]

With TV acting as the sword of Damocles and with the reality of sharply declining income, most of the majors ostensibly switched to a strategy of making fewer films with higher production value, the *taisaku shugi* (blockbuster doctrine).[105] However, when the majors began dramatically reducing their output and increasing fixed screening periods, a film vacuum formed immediately.[106] It was a vacuum for which Pink Film was literally ideal. As illustrated in table 1.1, from 1960 to 1962, the number of theaters dropped by less than 10 percent, while the number of film releases dropped by over

TABLE 1.1. Shift in Number of Theaters and Film Production, 1958–65

Year	Number of Theaters	Studio Films	Pink Films
1958	7,072	503	0
1960	7,401	545	0
1962	6,808	364	12
1964	5,366	285	67
1965	4,647	277	225

Source: Takahashi Eiichi, "Go-sha no Shijō o Doko Made Kutte Iru Ka," 192.

Note: The combined production of non-Pink and Pink films in 1965 almost exactly equals the total production of 1958. The discrepancy between the number of Pink films in this table and numbers given elsewhere is due to different definitions of Pink film, as these numbers do not include "(strip) show films" (*shō eiga*).

35 percent. The deafening sound of the vacuum created by the majors' strategy was heard most audibly in the suburbs and the chihō; this had to do with the distribution of theaters. The majors' films had a longer road show phase in which they were released only in designated urban theaters, and then trickled down to the second- and third-run theaters much more slowly than before. These second- and third-run venues comprised about 70 percent of all theaters, and they suffered most intensely from the majors' drop in production.

The exploding demand for Pink films was supported by that fact that the distributors charged a fraction of the screening fee of major studio films, and their racy content often attracted a larger audience. While a major would ask for around 50 percent of the box-office income, Pink films usually took 20 percent or less. In fact, dropping prices due to overproduction would become a problem for the Pink Film industry from 1965 on, with some local distributors charging as little as 4,000 to 5,000 yen ($13.88 in 1965) per booking. Ōkura Mitsugi's OP chain, which would decisively influence the course of Pink Film, refused bookings below 10,000 yen, but could not stop the general trend.[107]

In the early phase of Pink Film there are numerous reports of theaters so crowded that there was not even standing room; in this gold-rush phase, the producer-distributor often (supposedly) made over ten to one hundred times their initial investment. Director Ogawa Kinya boasted that his debut film, *Mistress* (*Mekake*, 1964), went on to make 50 million yen (about $139,000), while the production budget was the usual 3 million.[108] Such claims must be treated with a healthy degree of suspicion, but there is little question that the return on investment was swift and very lucrative.

Pink films filled the holes left by the majors and supplied a welcome audience influx. Exhibitors officially belonging or contractually bound to the majors often included Pink films in their programs clandestinely, thereby indirectly supporting the majors' distribution systems. The major companies even purchased Pink films for use in second- and third-run theaters themselves, with Nikkatsu apparently being the most active.[109] The demand for Pink films was so strong that, again with reminiscences of the early twentieth century—when film production in Japan had sprung from the exhibition sector—a group of theaters banded together to found a company, Dai Nana Gurūpu (Group of Seven), to finance Pink films and ensure supply.[110] Attracted by the spectacular success and the stunning profit margin, companies producing and distributing Pink films proliferated wildly. While just two to three companies had been active in 1962, by early 1964 the number had risen to over thirty, and by 1965 there were around seventy production and distribution outfits churning out films. Eventually, even the majors would dabble in Pink production and distribution—but more importantly, they would soon be swept into a spiral of dramatic structural change spearheaded by Pink Film.

TWO

PINK TIMES AND PINK SPACES

Three years before Pink Film begins to emerge: In Ozu Yasujiro's 1959 film *Good Morning* (*Ohayo*), two neighborhood boys regularly flock to a neighbor's house to watch sumo wrestling on television. Soon their desire for a TV set becomes a major plot point of the film and leads to tantrums, revolt, neighborhood strife, and a multitude of fart jokes. Shot in the year in which movie attendance experienced its first precipitous drop, *Good Morning* presents what was seen, maybe too conveniently, as the main culprit for the decline: TV and the social and spatial reorganization of moving-image consumption. What it does not show is the way television would widely come to be seen as a domestic yet in many ways international medium, deeply connected to a purported "feminization" of the public arena. Connotations of commodity culture, sanitization, and modernity became intertwined with a specific gendering of media, technologies, and practices, and it affected the now old medium of film as much as it did magazines and radio. Pink Film was a central and immensely influential part of the renegotiation of what film was, or could be, in the era of multiplying media channels.

This chapter maps the second half of the period of formation, when the tracks that Pink Film began to lay for the future of film and media in Japan solidified. The industrial genre's plot thickened: Pink Film still experimented on all levels, but it honed its strategies, and its arguments and audiences became more delineated. Pink Film's formational period extends roughly from 1962 to 1972. It is in this phase of becoming Pink Film when all levels of the industrial genre were cohering, yet still enough in flux to stand in direct and volatile interaction with the sociopolitical context of its time. We have seen how Pink Film identity emerged and began to build on older discourses to articulate and commodify the experience of confusion. It was only in the early 1970s that it eventually settled into a relatively stable form, and that stability itself had severe consequences for the political efficacy and the level of connection to mainstream Japan it could still generate. In many ways it is the process of the petrification of Pink Film.

The trajectory of Pink Film during this time tells us much about the entanglement of media and nation. Theater spaces in 1960s Japan, marked by an increase in the themes of sexuality and violence, took on meaning very much in relation to the Other of TV. Pink Film and its emerging specialty theaters especially stood in clear contrast to this domestic medium that for a time seemed dominated by foreign films and series. Critic Yamane Sadao saw the very centrality of representations of sexuality in 1960s film as an expression of a national identity crisis related to this binary: "One can point out that by making sex the main topic, by descending into that circuit of desire, they try to make the search for the nativity of the Japanese, that is to say the image of a native Japanese, the topic of their expression."[1] If Pink Film was—both in broader and more narrow senses than Yamane conceived—part of a national-identity discourse, then the industrial genre of Pink Film, as we will see, by no means offered a clear-cut solution. In fact, it capitalized on the chaos.

Who was the audience for Pink Film? Why do the films couch (presumed) titillation in a tone so pronouncedly dark and pessimistic? Why is sexual violence against women one of the most consistent topoi in Pink Film? Exploring these questions will help us map the adjustments Pink Film went through, and how it slowly, as an industrial genre, became evacuated of the explosive significance it had once held.

Pink Audiences

The 1960s movie industry generally accepted the idea of an intensifying gender axis in moving-image consumption. Despite some exceptions, the most pervasive trend of Japanese film in the 1960s was its increasing attempt to appeal to an assumed male spectator. Pink Film thus intensified a trend of audience segmentation that had been developing for quite some years and was deepening across media. In 1964, the immensely influential *Heibon Punch* became the first magazine to target specifically young (presumed heterosexual, cisgender) men and the first mainstream one to feature a nude spread.[2]

Television quickly learned to temporalize gender and age by positioning certain programs at certain times of day. Eventually the media business explored the commercial potential of the segmentation of sexualities via publications that had previously circulated informally, such as the gay-themed magazine *Barazoku* (Rose tribe) from 1971.

In the latter half of the 1950s, Nikkatsu's sun-tribe (*taiyōzoku*) films had tested the patience of the moral watchdogs but helped solidify a youth audience, and Shin-Tōhō's pearl-diver (*ama*) and erotic-grotesque (ero-guro) titles, as well as the increase in striptease-based show films, foreshadowed the strategy of appealing to more specific (mostly male) audience segments. However, both studios usually still attempted to attract older and female audiences as well. For fear of angering their female fans, Nikkatsu action stars such as Kobayashi Akira and Ishihara Yūjirō were often forbidden to kiss their costars on screen.[3] Even so, splitting up the audience along ever finer lines of gender and age was a general feature of the media landscape in 1960s Japan. Most visibly, Tōhō used Mifune Toshiro and Daiei used Katsu Shintarō (in its *Zatōichi* series), as well as a host of other series and subgenres, for increasingly male-centered action films. However, besides Pink films it was Tōei's *ninkyō* (chivalry) yakuza films and stars like Tsuruta Kōji or Takakura Ken that became the main factor in creating a gendered screen from 1963 until they fell out of favor about ten years later.[4]

But apart from being male, who was the audience for Pink Film? Omnipresent yet largely removed from the public eye, in 1965 Pink Film supplied half of the total film output in Japan, raising the question of how narrowly defined that group could be. Nonetheless it was discussed at length, and the idea of a blue-collar, authentic inflection of Pink Film loomed large in attempts to explain its success. Critic Satō Tadao claimed that the success of Pink films was due to changes in housing patterns that took place because of the migration of young workers and college students from rural areas to the cities, especially Tokyo. Families moved to the suburbs (into the danchi), leaving the cities in the hands of "young bachelors who loved erotic and violent films" and who themselves lived in a climate of "power plays in which violence is not an abnormal effect but part of the main thrust."[5] Two main discursive axes run through this characterization, one of class and one of tension between the regional (chihō) and the urban.

While this narrative fits very well with the idea of the raw, working-class, oppositional, and antimodernization authenticity often attributed to Pink Film, it seems unlikely that only testosterone-loaded young workers from the countryside and politicized students (all presumed to be strictly heterosexual by Satō) were attracted to watching (relative) nudity and violence on screen. Most of the urban exhibitors claim that their audiences were predominantly students and white-collar salary men, as did former Shintōhō studio head and Pink Film power broker Ōkura Mitsugi. In his 1969 essay titled "Contemporary Society's Tranquilizer," he argues that disorientation and discontent—political for the students and existential for the salary men—are the main motivations for what he sees as the escapist frequenting of Pink films.[6] An analysis of ticket sales at the OP chain–related Shinjuku-za theater in Shinjuku, printed in the *Pink Film White Paper* (*Pinku eiga hakusho*) in 1969, at least provides clues to the proportion of students in the audience in an urban center. In a given week, a total of 10,207 tickets were sold, with 6,250 regular tickets, 1,802 student-rate tickets, 1,569 tickets for the morning special rate, and 462 for the late-night rate. Just over 1 percent, or 123 tickets, were sold to female audience members, who only had to pay 200 yen ($0.55 at the time), compared to the regular rate of 450 yen.[7] Though obviously to be accepted with caution, a fairly detailed audience survey in the same theater finds the majority of the audience being predominantly in their early twenties. When asked where they had heard about the film they had just seen, fifty-eight answered, "In a newspaper"; forty-two said, "A poster on the street"; and ninety-two replied, "The poster displayed at this theater."[8]

In addition to the audience structure, the locus of the demand that was driving Pink Film can be debated as well. While several sources claim that the success of Pink Film and its show-movie forerunners was triggered by the theaters in the chihō, others steadfastly claim that the urban centers were the important markets.[9] The truth seems to lie in the middle. While the largest income certainly (and unsurprisingly) came from urban theaters, the demand was larger, and originated in, the chihō. Kokuei producer Satō Keiko claims that demand in the chihō was the spark that set off the flame: theaters outside of the main urban centers, which made up the bulk of second- and third-run theaters, suffered the most from the audience decline and film dearth of the early 1960s, making them the more probable candidates for the initial explosion of demand.[10]

It is an important point, however, that the origin of Pink Film in urban, working-class contexts and politically energized students, both coming from the influx of rural population to the cities, was seen as plausible and became a constitutive part of Pink Film identity. What comes heavily into play here are once again older discourses that associate urban Japan (Tokyo) with modernization opposite the regional, associated with Japanese authenticity and, by extension, realism.[11]

Pink films in the 1960s make the rural-urban tension a frequent theme and plot point, with the pure-hearted rural woman deceived and corrupted by amoral urban ways as a highly typical narrative. Mukai Kan's part-color *Meat Mattress* (*Niku futon*, 1971) is a late example that plays with this divide (if with a different gender division) but cannot take it seriously anymore; the city is a place of monetized sex, fluid costumes, and deceptions, yet these tropes are now played for comedy. In it Gorō and Shinji, two cowboy hat–wielding country bumpkins from Yamagata Prefecture who are tired of tending horses, decide to head for Tokyo, inspired by a nude magazine. Once there, the two suffer serial misfortune as they are robbed by a woman who (in the language of the film) turns out to be a man. They are sexually abused by a trio of housewives who turn out to be dominatrixes when trying to support themselves as callboys, secretly exploited for a blue film production, and ultimately set up for a murder they didn't commit. Intimidated and on the run, the two decide to return to the safety of their rural home.

Part of the abundance of rural settings in early Pink films also has to do with the production practices of the genre. Shooting a Pink film on location in the city was quite difficult in the 1960s, so a great number of productions used *onsen* (hot spring) resorts. Director Yamamoto Shinya remembers using the same hot spring resort in Yabuzuka for nearly every production over a stretch of several years, due to its discretion and proximity to Tokyo.[12] In the 1970s, when budgets became too tight to justify hotel costs for the entire staff, he switched from rural locations to urban ones, creating the immensely successful *chikan densha* (train molester) subgenre, among others. Referring to documentary director Ogawa Shinsuke's move to working mainly in Yamagata Prefecture and to the "Discover Japan" railway ad campaign, the 1970s are often characterized as a time in which attention turned to rural Japan. However, the migration of Pink Film production and its narratives from even partially rural settings to the city is one other important vector of late 1960s and early 1970s media culture. Eventually the opposition of the urban and the rural would lose much of its import for Pink Film, as would the idea of Pink Film as realist and authentic.

Pink Film Spaces

Author Kurahashi Yumiko describes watching *Black Snow*, *Affairs within Walls*, and other Pink films in a theater full of "middle-aged" men and students that emitted the smells of "cheap humans and a specific pomade," as well as the "odor of [lower] class."[13] Literary critic Yajima Midori similarly recounts watching the two films in theaters filled "mostly with men," fascinated by how enraptured they are by a film she deems important but amateurish.[14] In the mid-1960s there were still very occasional articles by female critics on Pink Film, but the screening spaces that Pink Film infiltrated were increasingly, and increasingly hermetically, marked male. By the late 1960s, the tenuous permeability of the Pink Film space had ended. Female editors of *Seijin Eiga* reported on the near impossibility of entering a Pink Film theater without being molested, certainly further decreasing the already miniscule female audience. By 1975, approximately one-third of theaters in Japan screened Pink films either exclusively or as a supplement to the program.[15] Even behind the camera, total male subjectivity was (ostensibly) defended. Occasionally, more often than not, actresses directed Pink films as publicity stunts. One of the few female directors working consistently within Pink Film, Hamano Sachiko, changed her name to the gender-ambiguous Hamano Sachi in the 1970s.[16] A female director's name would have disturbed the appearance of totalized male subjectivity.

Pink Film thus participated in the postwar discourses of domesticity, consumerism, and modernity in a number of complex, often seemingly contradictory ways. It relied on spatialized gender divisions and a clean separation of male and female; yet on that basis, it questioned the separability of history from the present (before and after 1945), of foreign and native, of perpetrator and victim. In concert with TV, the gender-segregated, semipublic space of the Pink theater reinforced the specific kind of division into public, semipublic, and private spaces that was as vital to my-home-ism as a gendered division of labor. Pink Film was both an enabler and a collaborator in the postwar family system, a sanitized public sphere and part of a violent reaction against it. Pink Film performed a masculinist outcast appeal, emitted the whiff of the blue-collar and the rural. It combined this with the auratic authenticity that flesh discourse, an appeal to realism, and the threat of censorship promised. These themes may have been highly attractive to a male audience exposed to a discourse that perceived men—correctly or not—as demoted in the symbolic order, as occupied, emasculated, and supposedly forced to embrace an imposed vision of feminized consumer-culture futurity. Indeed, the emasculated man is a common theme in 1960s film, and Pink Film in particular. As simple as this trope might seem, the processes such images set in motion in the theaters is a complex, and confused, story. Before we explore those processes, however, we need to address the momentous influence Pink Film was developing on the majors.

Intermission: The Major Studios' Pink Film Strategy

"Nikkatsu and Daiei Scheme to Intercept Pink Film"
—Headline of an article in *Seijin Eiga* magazine

Pink Film's success was to have a deep and lasting impact on the Japanese film industry, one of the three largest in the world.[17] The majors were, of course, long aware of the market value of sensational portrayals of sex. By the early 1960s, all of the major studios had been heavily influenced by the success of *seijin eiga* (adult films). Eirin introduced the designation in 1955, and it had been used to attract audiences long before the small, independent productions that would later be called Pink films appeared.[18] By 1963, the major companies probed into incorporating and promoting sexual and violent content much more heavily than before, and initially did so with success. In 1963, seven of the thirty-seven adult films were made by the majors, among them *Lies* (*Uso*) by Masumura Yasuzō at Daiei; Imamura Shōhei's *Insect Woman* (*Nippon konchū-ki*) at Nikkatsu; and *Naked Body* (*Ratai*, dir. Narusawa Masashige), distributed by Shōchiku. The majors more than quadrupled their adult-film mileage in 1964 to thirty-one, with Nikkatsu producing Nakahira Kō's *Monday Girl* (*Getsuyōbi no yuka*) and Suzuki Seijun's scandal-invoking *Gate of Flesh* (*Nikutai no mon*), based on the classic story by Tamura Tajirō of the postwar literature of flesh genre and the first commercially released film from Japan to feature female upper-body nudity. Tōei produced Watanabe Yūsuke's *Two Female Dogs* (*Nihiki no mesu-inu*) and *Evil Woman* (*Akujo*) for their new line of adult-oriented films, while Imai Tadashi shot *A Story from Echigo* (*Echigo tsutsuishi oyashirazu*) for their lineup.[19] Shōchiku had experimented with its brand of Shōchiku Nouvelle Vague films for similar reasons. Now it turned to an outside seijin eiga production, Takechi Tetsuji's *Daydream* (*Hakujitsumu*, prod. Dai-San Productions). Tōhō likewise bought and distributed an independent production, Teshigahara Hiroshi's *Woman in the Dunes* (*Suna no onna*, prod. Teshigahara Productions).[20] In the golden age of the late 1950s, the majors had virtually stopped distributing films that they had not produced themselves. However, Tōhō had extensive experience with the efficiency of subcontracting production in the late 1940s, and it increasingly led the way in reviving a practice that would eventually become the industry standard. Ultimately, Tōhō remained tied to its founder Kobayashi Ichizō's model of a unified mass public through its unique infrastructure of large, centrally located theaters and resisted the general trend toward sex, choosing instead to focus on subgenres such as monster films (*kaijū-eiga*) and comedies.

The encroachment from the majors also created problems for Pink Film. The immense boom and overproduction of 1965 led to a backlash, and many companies that were inexperienced in turning a profit from self-distribution exited production as fast as they had entered it. By 1969, the number of Pink Film companies was back to around thirty-five, halved from the around seventy of the early boom period. But if Pink Film was consolidating, the long-suffering majors were in serious trouble and under immense financial pressure by the late 1960s. Shōchiku had closed down its Kyoto studio in 1965, and in 1968 Nikkatsu and Daiei replaced the greater part of their managerial ranks in response to the more than worrisome developments. While the majors had reduced their production of adult-designated film after the first rush in 1964, increasingly explicit material—in terms of both sexuality and violence—seemed the only guarantor of consistent box-office success.

The majors still handled direct involvement with Pink Film cautiously: Shōchiku famously pulled out of a distribution deal with Wakamatsu Kōji for a film called *Pass the Phone Please!* (*O-Denwa Chōdai!*), in 1966. However, eventually Pink Film was mined quite unreservedly in terms of production ideas, personnel, and films. Daiei released Takechi Tetsuji's *Cruel Woodblock Print Story* (*Ukiyoe zankoku monogatari*, 1968), and Nikkatsu began distribution of Pink films in 1968, as well as producing sex-themed films like *The House of Strange Loves* (*Onna ukiyo buro*, Ida Motomu, also called Ida Tan, 1968). Tōei was continuing its highly successful erotic (*erosu*) lines with shockingly misogynistic, for viewers then as now, degrees of violence against women. Films such as *Lineage of the Tokugawa Women* (*Tokugawa onna keizu*, 1968), *The Joy of Torture* (*Tokugawa onna keibatsu-shi*, 1968), and *Hot Spring Massage Geisha* (*Onsen anma geisha*, 1968) were helmed by Ishii Teruo, who had started as a director at the original Shintōhō studio. Much to the chagrin of the Pink Film industry, the latter film employed eleven of the biggest Pink Film star actresses.

Pink Film was thus under pressure to find new strategies to differentiate itself from the majors' fare, which its existence virtually depended upon. Politically, aesthetically, and in terms of economic structure and sexual explicitness, Pink Film had fashioned itself as the major studios' Other. Now the majors were recapturing the field of screen sexuality on an obviously much higher-budget level. Pink films were still cheap in terms of distribution fees, but this only guaranteed exhibitors as long as the audience showed up to see them. Pink Film needed to define itself against the majors. On the level of economic organization, it attempted to further consolidate and regulate production, distribution, and exhibition.[21] Another strategy was to more closely delineate the specific confusion Pink Film was formulating. In practice, this led to a further increase in explicit sexual violence, but also to the development of styles of confusion.

Pink Film and the Style of Confusion

Seki Kōji shot the first 3D Pink film, *Pervert Freak* (*Hentaima*, 1967, distr. Nihon Shinema), and an invisible-man Pink film, *Invisible Man: Ero Doctor* (*Tōmei ningen ero hakase*, 1968, distr. Shin Nihon Eiga), and later used infrared film stock for *Obedient Belly Kingdom Japan: Intercourse, Birth* (*Zuitai ōkoku nihon: Kōi, shussan*, 1972). Seki was regarded as an idea man in the Pink Film industry, and after his debut with *Valley of Desire*, from the end of the 1960s onward he was extremely active in introducing new gimmicks to capture the audience's attention. These innovations were also a question of necessity; without a doubt, the Pink Film business was slowing down by the late 1960s. Product differentiation was a pressing issue, and experimentation included distribution strategies, narratives, styles, and budget levels, especially from Kokuei. Some of these experiments became, for a time, defining elements of Pink Film, especially those that matched Pink Film's commodity of confusion with a visual or experiential equivalent.

One important aspect of Pink Film's visualization of confusion was its embrace of the aesthetic of part-color, a standard practice after 1965. With part-color, films were mostly shot in black and white; more sensational scenes were shot in color, be they appearances of vengeful ghosts as in Ogawa Kinya's *Pinku kaidan* (ghost) film, *Supernatural Tale [of the] Dismembered Ghost* (*Kaidan bara bara yūrei*, distr. Ōkura Eiga, 1968), or, more commonly, nude scenes. This is often noted as an essential aspect of Pink Film's attraction. Producer Satō Keiko enthusiastically remembers, "When the sexy part begins, the screen lights up like a musical!"[22] Rather than align with black and white and its connotations (by the mid-1960s) of low-budget, nonmajor production or with the all-color glamour of the major studio films, and all the attached discourses of class, realism, and so on, Pink Film fused them to an experience that was both and neither.

The first all-color Pink films were 1967's *Valley of Deep Desire* (*Fukai yokubō no tanima*, Sawa Kensuke), *The Pleasure of a Hussy* (*Abazure no etsuraku*, Kobayashi Satoru), and *New: History of a Love Affair* (*Shin: Jōji no rirekisho*, Yamashita Osamu). It quickly became customary to release prestige, all-color Pink films for the busiest seasons: New Year's Day and Golden Week in late April. However, all-color films would become standard only from 1973 on, when the shock of major company Nikkatsu switching wholesale to the production of sex films, and the restructuring of the Pink Film exhibition system that followed, resulted in pressure to adjust to major studio conventions.

Another important aspect of the performance of confusion was the so-called *jitsuen* (real performance). This was a sexually themed theater performance or show that featured, at least in its later phase, frequent nudity. It was acted out in the movie theater where a Pink film had just been screened, sometimes with the very same actors and actresses that had appeared on screen just minutes before. While regarded as innovative at the time, there had been similar events for some of the *basukon* (birth control) films screened in strip-show venues. In 1951, the Asakusa Shōgekijō offered one strip show and one birth-control film for the price of 40 yen ($0.11).[23]

Performances attached to Pink films began in 1966 at the Cinema RIRIO and Kajibashi-Za in the Ikebukuro section of Tokyo, with a theater group called Aka to Kuro (Red and black) that was formed by several well-known Pink Film actresses in 1965.[24] The performances were instantly popular, so much so that on New Year's Day 1968 they were attached to all the big Pink Film releases. In the same year, the Keitsū theater chain began introducing jitsuen as a standard addition to its screenings, employing four contracted theater groups to keep up with the demand: Baku/Sunahara, Honō, World, and Yamabe Pro. Each was assigned two theaters for one week, with two performances per day. The performances reportedly raised attendance by 20–30 percent, sometimes even 100 percent.[25] This was another strategy to increase the level of reality that Pink Film touted, even if it was reportedly substandard acting and lacking in narrative subtlety, with one audience member quoted as saying, "They think just showing nudity is enough. It lacks in drama and the acting is bad."[26]

Jitsuen became such a popular phenomenon that many specialized theater groups formed between 1968 and 1972, often performing national tours of major cities and the chihō. Some of the more famous actresses like Tani Naomi—who later became the star of Nikkatsu's S&M films and created her stage name out of a combination of her favorite author Tanizaki Jun'chiro and one of his most famous characters, Naomi—formed their own troupes;

in Tani Naomi's case it was the Gekidan Naomi (Theater troupe Naomi). Kokuei even founded a subdivision devoted to the jitsuen, Kokuei Geinō.

The jitsuen boom even sparked a revival of one of the more underresearched phenomena of Japanese film history, the chain drama (*rensa geki*). Chain dramas were early attempts to mix film and theater, combining film sequences with live performances, and were popular for a short time in the 1910s. Pink Film company Nihon Shinema revived the practice for their 1970 New Year's Day release of *Woman from the Secret Club* (*Himitsu kurabu no onna*, Seki Kōji), and Kokuei Geinō followed suit the same year with the comedy *Mansion of the Lewd Snake* (*Jain no yakata*, Seki Kōji), which also toured the chihō.

Part-color, jitsuen, and rensa geki were examples of translating a sociopolitical experience of confusion into technological and formal strategies. As practices, they mixed time layers associated with the opposition of theater and film, or of black-and-white and color film. They combined a now foregrounded degree of mediation with the unmediated power of the presence of the body. Their appearance, at the same time, bears witness that narrative was not enough to uphold the expression of confusion to which the body in Pink Film had been central. Soon significant changes in the Pink screening space would begin to counter the paradigm of confusion in Pink Film: from the early 1970s, Pink Film was in many ways neutralized.

Before that, however, Pink Film attempted to argue for its difference from the majors and from TV through film narratives as well. It condensed the experience of confusion via the highly troubling trope of sexual violence against women.

Narratives of Sexual Violence

From a woman's point of view, the ten years from, say, 1962 or 1963 to 1973 have been the most disheartening in screen history. In the roles and prominence accorded women, the decade began uncompromisingly, grew steadily worse, and at present shows no signs of improving.
—MOLLY HASKELL, *From Reverence to Rape* (1974)

"Throw Away the Rope, Whip, and Knife!" a headline in the November 1967 issue of *Seijin Eiga* demands, lamenting the increase in violence in Pink films. In truth, Pink films had been inextricably bound to violence, overwhelmingly against the female body, from the genre's germination. *Flesh Market* was purportedly based on an actual case of rape and subsequent suicide of a young woman, and a 1964 newspaper ad for the Kokuei-produced film *Tomb of Lead* (*Namari no bohyō*, Wakamatsu Kōji, 1964) reads, "Scenes of violence that will assault the eyes. The assassin business that is staked on sensuality and cruelty."[27] As an immensely disturbing filmic convention, sexual violence against women persists in Pink films to this day, although since the late 1990s to a much-reduced degree. Even in the 1960s there were considerable fluctuations, but they had as much to do with Eirin's periodical loosening and tightening of inspection standards as with the pressures of product differentiation. The July 1968 issue of *Seijin Eiga* features a large article on the "nudity boom" in the products of major studios Tōei and Nikkatsu, leaving the Pink Film industry desperate to find ways of distinguishing their output.[28]

An increase in female nudity and portrayals of violence against women took place at roughly the same time in Western Europe, the United States, and Japan. While there is at least some evidence of specific reception conventions with regard to moving-image media violence in Japan, such a broad and potentially culturalist explanation says little about the case of Pink Film and the specific meanings attached to it.[29] In the documentary *Pink Ribbon*, Pink Film director and former actor Ikejima Yutaka links the Pink Film audience's fascination with rape scenes directly to the war. Ikejima interprets what he sees as a demand for the spectacle of sexual violence as the result of a combination of suppressed sexuality and exposure to both direct and systemic violence, tied to a certain generational cohort's personal experiences.[30] Yet with the broad age spectrum among the 1960s Pink Film audience it seems improbable that the gradual increase in the pairing of sex and violence can be simply reduced to trauma-based psychopathology. Director Watanabe Mamoru offers a more practice-oriented explanation for the pervasiveness of rape scenes. Because Eirin inspectors deemed violence more permissible than sexual explicitness, Watanabe claims that violence was used to elongate these scenes for an audience that knew what was to follow.

However, the disturbing centrality of sexual violence for the genre cannot be explained solely as a filmmaker's trick to cross the censors. The distressingly common trope of sexual violence in Pink films needs to be related to broader social and historical discourses. Pink Film inevitably had to position itself in relation to a Japanese government that posited 1945 as a moment of complete rupture with the past and conceived of the 1960s as exclusively facing toward the future. As I argued in chapter 1, Pink Film disavowed a supposedly clean break with the past by representing the inseparability, or (eroticized) confusion, of past and present. Violence became an important focal point for that representational strategy, and it drew on a number of discourses that connected gender, nation, and geopolitics.

Interwar and wartime Japan had consciously gendered its national body male to support its role as colonizer, defender, and leader on the path toward a Great East Asian Co-Prosperity Sphere. Postwar Japan was positioned differently. Yoshikuni Igarashi has described the various strategies the occupation government used to emphasize a feminized, and therefore presumably submissive, national corpus right down to the body of the emperor.[31] The positioning of Japan as female, colonized, and victim was one that Takechi followed in *Black Snow* and its appeal to anxiety about race.[32] While consistently used to illustrate unhappiness with Japan's geopolitical partnership with the United States, it also distanced the country from war responsibility and gave validity or at least tangibility to the foundational idea of a fundamental discontinuity that begins in 1945. It is telling that both the occupation and its critics utilized this gendering strategy.

The gender reversal of national identity also served another purpose, one more directly connected to rebuilding Japan. Discourses on Japan's *onna-ka* (becoming-woman) have appeared at many points in Japanese history, but never more intensely than since the 1960s. It was then that Japanese intellectuals posited and often bemoaned the nation as supposedly constructed around a matricentric domesticity that provided a foundational model for the family structure and society itself.[33] Tomiko Yoda has added that this image was highly relevant for supporting the heterosexist labor system that assigned women to the home and retained them as a reserve for part-time jobs. Women made up a disproportionate degree of the part-time labor force, where they were essentially an economic buffer of considerable importance for postwar economic success.[34] The redefinition of domesticity in the 1960s was structured around and valorized this gendered national image, while being essentially based on the new consumer culture and fetishization of (mostly Western connoted) lifestyles and consumer goods. All of these are highly strategic discourses that we must by no means accept, but that we need to take into account to understand the semiotics of the Pink Film industrial genre.

The gendering of modern consumer culture was a discourse that swept over several urban centers in the world, Tokyo included, in the first decades of the twentieth century. Early on, Georg Simmel identified woman with the paradigmatic qualities of modernity—the momentary and the fluid—and the discourse around the trope of the modern girl or *moga* in 1920s Japan ran along similar lines.[35] Americanism was also attached to this complex, and most regions of the world regarded it with ambivalence. In postwar Japan this took a particular inflection, connected as it was to rebuilding not only

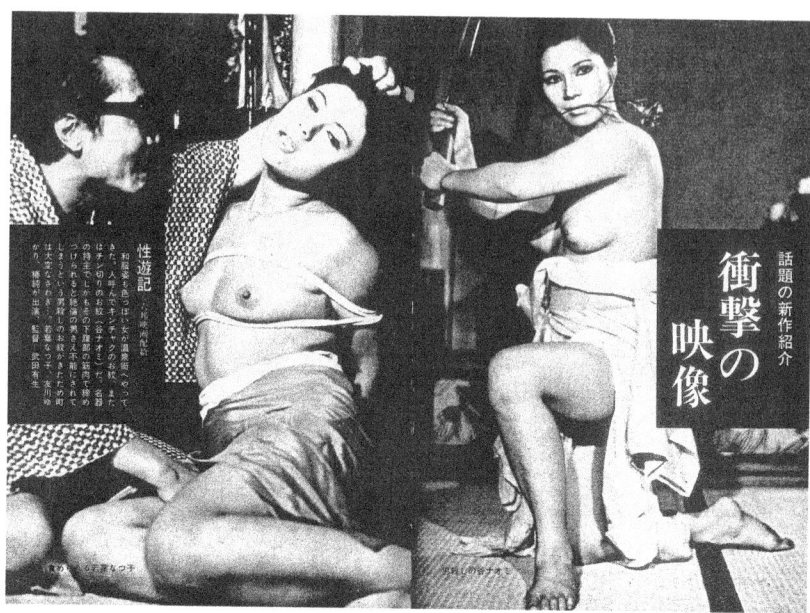

FIGURE 2.1. A typical page spread from *Seijin Eiga* magazine. Two basic types of Pink Film women, victim and aggressor, both supplied identificatory potential for the male audience. The left picture is captioned, "Wakaba Natsuko being tormented," while the right side says, "Man-killer Tani Naomi." Tani Naomi later became one of the biggest Nikkatsu stars and was known for her S&M films. From *Seijin Eiga* 80 (September 1972), 16–17.

the political and economic infrastructure but also a national identity meant to support this reconstruction. In his book *Learning from Akihabara*, Morikawa Kaichirō contrasts the Akihabara and Harajuku areas of Tokyo, with Akihabara (the electronics and manga/anime center) designated as male/Japanese, and Harajuku (the fashion center) as female/Western. Morikawa claims that advertisements in Akihabara feature mostly Japanese models, while in Harajuku Western models predominate. In Harajuku, red, white, and blue colors dominate the neon street signs along with large glass display windows, while Akihabara is dominated by red and white, the colors of the Japanese flag, and windowless spaces.[36] Regardless whether Morikawa's description is empirically true or not, his claims fit into a well-established discursive tradition.

Thus woman was at least doubly signified in a fairly typical way for most industrialized capitalist countries at the time: either as a stable center of the family system around which the new consumer society could develop and find consistency; or as a representative of fluid modernity, a potent image and an almost overpowering feminizing force, always in flux and unpredictable. Pink Film contained and enunciated both images via a confusion that acknowledged their inseparability, and it applied all levels of the industrial genre to achieve this.

Images of Men, Images of Women

The Pink ghost film *Supernatural Tale Dismembered Ghost* (*Kaidan bara bara yūrei*, Ogawa Kinya, 1968) features one of the most ghastly scenes of 1960s Japanese, maybe even international, cinema. The young heiress, Masako, is killed and dismembered in a cave by two couples: her sister and Masako's treacherous lover, along with her stepmother and her lover.[37] Later, Masako will come back to haunt the perpetrators as a collection of amputated limbs visible to only one of them at any given time, driving the group to madness and suicide. Along with Masako's spectral return, *Supernatural Tale Dismembered Ghost* is, in many ways, a metaphor for Pink Film itself. In 1968, Pink Film was similarly a collection of scattered discourses from various strands of the past; it was both spectacular and difficult to ignore, yet somehow only half visible. It was hidden from the public eye, yet invited its male audience into a new all-male, semipublic space, a (not so) private haunting in the dark. With Eirin not allowing the portrayal of full-body nudity or sexual acts on screen, Pink Film cut up the female body into a collection of shots (hands, feet, shoulders, mouths), edited together to create a suggestive if tenuous totality. What runs through these strategies is the question of coherence and ownership, of what once belonged together and how it will belong together in the future—a question of self-possession and (national) identity channeled through stitched-together images of the body.

The female body was then a fragmented cipher both disturbing and promising, one of liberation and a new order of power. It also functioned as a central anchor for the male subjectivity that was formed in the confines of the Pink screening space. What does it mean that violence was unleashed at exactly that level of authenticity or reality that Pink Film itself had connoted with individual freedom, and onto bodies that were portrayed as the victims of the postwar order? It seems plausible to posit Pink Film as offering a vicarious degree of control to an injured male ego, along with arousal and titillation. Such a view would see Pink Film and the abused female bodies that populate it as a crutch for a fundamental insecurity, following Virginia Woolf's famous verdict, "Women have served all these centuries as looking glasses possessing the magic and delicious power of reflecting the figure of man at twice its natural size."[38]

However, along with this function, the films also seem to tell a more complex story. In these narratives, men are rarely strong wish-fulfillment fantasies. They are anxious, insecure, impotent, searching for love, money, for a way out of personal, economic, social, and political despair. Women fulfill the old role of a foil: they are the objects of awe, fear, and desire, the Other needed to define what "male" means in a society changing in ways that women seem—again in just one of the problematic discourses of the time—better equipped for and conceptually more central to.[39] In Kobayashi Satoru's part-color *Impotent Man* (*Funōsha*, 1967), the young Susumu moves to the city with his girlfriend, Mari, but is suicidal due to his difficulty performing sexually. Mari secretly agrees to an affair with her affluent and Westernized boss in order to finance an operation for Susumu. After the procedure's initial success, Susumu's impotence returns when he is ridiculed by an older (again affluent) woman trying to seduce him. Despairing, he flees back to his countryside home, violently assaulting a young woman on the way. Mari, in the meantime, apathetically dances the night away in a nightclub, finally climbing up the wall to stare straight at the camera and proclaim, to a presumably all-male audience, "You are all sentenced to death by hanging!" with the final shot framed by a noose.

As women are associated with exchange and capitalist modernity, the films frequently feature sex workers and temporary lovers. Often the women have been sexually assaulted and otherwise wronged, consequently becoming spiritually empty, cold predators interested only in cash—as in *Blue Film Woman* (*Burū firumu no onna*, Mukai Kan, 1969) or *Virgin Diary of Violence (Female animal)* (*Bōkō shojo nikki [Mesu]*, Mukai Kan, 1968). In *Blue Film Woman*, Mariko is assaulted by her boss while working in a strip club to pay off her hapless (and kimono-wearing) father's debts. She then returns home to find her father driven to suicide by a loan shark. She embarks on a quest to extort money from rich, suit-wearing businessmen by secretly filming their encounters, though ultimately she is assassinated on the order of these power brokers while the stock reports are broadcast on the radio. The theme of rupture, of discontinuity after a traumatic event, is synchronized to the omnipresent questions of nation and capitalism in Japan after 1945.

In the hermetic Pink Film screening space it might seem that everything was about a subjectivity marked male, affixed to male characters on the screen. Yet how did the audience relate to that pessimistic spectacle of social and human failure? We know that identification, most certainly in film, works in much more variegated ways than aligning with simple gender binaries and being fully determined by camera setups. The discussion of identification in film (and beyond) has mainly feminist theory, film theory, gay and lesbian studies, and queer theory to thank for more sophisticated models. Identification has become seen an extremely flexible and multiple mechanism, one that, as Eve Kosofsky Sedgwick emphasized, includes several contradictory, often only partial, and simultaneous processes, and inevitably is always also in some way queer.[40] One important addition to the concept of identification is that of disidentification, the coinciding of identification and simultaneous nonidentification with a dominant, the negotiation of a position that retains a distance from yet works through and ultimately transforms it. José Esteban Muñoz famously defined disidentification as "the third mode of dealing with dominant ideology, one that neither opts to assimilate within such a structure nor strictly opposes it; rather, disidentification is a strategy that works on and against dominant ideology."[41] Judith Butler has touched upon the issue of disidentification as offering a possible "point of departure for a more democratizing affirmation of internal difference."[42] But it is important to note that even for Butler such a mechanism is not necessarily progressive in its larger effects and outcomes. Identificatory confusion as in Pink Film—when the audience identified with victim and aggressor, with both of them overdetermined as Japan and the United States—can be conceived of as one of the more compromising variations of disidentification. Disidentification as a concept was developed as a tool to open up possibilities for minoritarian politics. Yet what happens when the group that participates in these strategies, and indeed perceives itself as embattled, cannot easily (as a whole) be defined as minoritarian or marginalized, and only with many qualifications as embattled? Similarly, Pink Film supports the dominant postwar ideology while still articulating deep discontent with and claiming resistance to it.

When female characters became victims of sexual violence in Pink films, these films were bolstering male subjectivity as much as offering the metaphor of a nation disempowered and violated. They staged a moment of trauma that disrupted a historical continuity that male audiences had deemed central to (male) national identity.[43] One of the most problematic and disturbing aspects of Pink Film, the common suggestion of eventual enjoyment of an assault, provided a tipping point for multiple identifications for the male audience, at the very least both with the violator and the violated. This was able to unfold exactly because it was staged in an all-male designated space. If high-growth Japan of the 1960s reinforced male power in ways that legitimized and supported the use (and literally abuse) of representations of female bodies as overdetermined tropes, the experience of high-growth Japan led to complex engagement with such representations. Victimhood—portrayed as ambivalent or not—was one invitation to identification; the affirmation of male power was another. At the same time, the male audience saw its own nationally connoted masculine desperation, discontent, and fear enacted through the male actors' frantic deeds. Yet even that male power was connoted simultaneously as American (when the focus was on Japanese victimhood) and as Japanese (when the focus was on reestablishing a strong sense of national, masculine self). Pink Film's specific brand of confusion here is, arguably, a double disidentificatory process, the appeal of which built on problematic premises but nonetheless articulated a specific experience of a historical moment. The socioeconomic violence of the high-growth era became reflected in a kaleidoscope of subjectivities, tucked away in seedy, run-down theaters.

Herbert Marcuse has written, "To the degree to which sexuality obtains a definitive sales value . . . it is itself transformed into an instrument of social cohesion."[44] In this case, it is a social cohesion among men that is based on the common experience—consumption—of a multiple identification that heavily relies on moving across genders. Moving closer together in the dark against the free-floating incommensurability of woman and this new nation, that movement allowed tying together experiences and possible futures that the different genders represented. It is a double movement into gender-segregated spaces and across discretely defined gender categories. Possibly we also see here the foundation for the queer space that the Pink Film theater would become from the 1980s onward, a site of differently complex disidentifications, encounters, cross-dressing, and cruising.[45]

Ultimately the male audience supported an increasingly liberalized capitalist system by buying tickets to a space and to films that claimed to oppose it. Pink Film's self-identity relied heavily on independence from the majors, an idea attached to the filmic text, the director, and the distributor. However, this independence was, as we have seen, a precarious one. In fact, from the moment they gave up self-distribution, the independence that Pink filmmakers subjectively achieved by possessing their own production companies, writing their own scripts, and generally having a large degree of control over production was less an avant-garde of self-determination than one of casualization of labor. It prefigured what would become increasingly common practice in the Japanese economy from the 1980s on and the dominant practice in the film industry of the 1990s. It was also reenacting the role of independents in the 1920s and 1940s. Power lay with distribution and exhibition, not the independent filmmakers of the production side. Pink Film as an avant-garde of casualized labor would contribute to wearing down what the films suggested were essential traditional values to be preserved.

Connecting, among others, to discourses of economy, power, and models of history after 1945, the trope of sexual violence was highly polysemic, so much so that it eventually could not contain all the contradictory meanings invested in it and collapsed into convention in the 1970s, dissolving into (even more disturbing) spectacle. While sexual violence was common in the first ten years of Pink Film, it also carried significance, if not a progressive or defensible one. After the early 1970s, the casualization of on-screen violence joined the casualization of labor. It is no coincidence this semiotic collapse occurred at precisely the moment that Pink Film's distribution and exhibition system settled into a stable form in the early 1970s.

The Emptiness of Sexual Violence

On December 2 and 3, 1972, a new kind of studio tour opened on the Tōei studio lot. The 8 mm Porn Shooting Tour provided over fifty participants the opportunity to shoot a *poruno* film with their own 8 mm cameras under the instruction of Pink Film legend Mukai Kan. The magazine *Seijin Eiga* describes the tour as a big success and in high demand. The participants "shot an average of five [film] rolls per person. They could film several scenes such as a rape scene and a lesbian scene, and it was highly popular."[46] This description implies that participants already had an idea of sex film standards and saw them and their staging as detached set pieces independent from narratives. While the Tōei Studios location indicates how deep the connections between the majors and Pink Film had become, it also points to the changing status of sex scenes in Pink Film (and films by the majors). In the early 1970s, representations of rape increasingly became emptied of the multiple meanings they had previously been charged with. What had still raised criticism in the late 1960s transitioned to conventions that were understood by a different set of rules.

The s&m films of the late 1970s were glossy and highly designed visual spectacles. In Takahashi Banmei's *A High School Teacher: Bondage* (*Aru jokyōshi—Kinpaku*, 1978), Keiko is a teacher at a prep school training students for university entrance exams. Once sexually assaulted when she tried to defend a student from bullying, she now is obsessed with elaborate and stylized bondage scenarios. An affair Keiko begins with the nihilistic student Nogami, who is dispirited by the rat race of entering an elite university, ends in violence. As she throws herself naked on him in the middle of class while reciting the lyrics to the Nazareth song "Please Don't Judas Me," Nogami, dejected by his failure in the exams and humiliated by Keiko's boyfriend, stabs her to death.[47] Sociopolitical critique remains a concern in the film, but not in the sexual assault or its consequences. In terms of scripts, sexual violence became less a complex if problematic central trope than a more purely misogynist generic situation. It transformed into an occasion for aestheticization and formal experimentation and increasingly a formalist problem, not a representational one. Audiences had come to understand it as a convention, leading to a disconcertingly casual attitude toward the representation of sexual violence. The magazine *Seijin Eiga*, which just a few years prior had decried the prevalence of violence in Pink Film, now titled an article on actress Aoyama Misa "An Actress So Prim It Makes You Want to Rape Her."[48] A 1978 report on actor Takahashi Akira boasted in its title, "He 'Raped' over Two Hundred Actresses in One Hundred Films!" next to a picture of the beaming Takahashi himself.[49]

If representations of sexual violence retained any level of reference at all, it was transferred to a personal, not political, dimension. This sensibility was very much in keeping with the increasingly depoliticized filmmaking stance of the later 1970s and early 1980s. The S&M Pink films by Ijūin Gō (actually a nom de plume used by Hiroki Ryūichi, Nakamura Genji, and Ishikawa Hitoshi) reduced violence to a completely private event, taking place in closed-off spaces as aesthetic spectacle—even if especially Nakamura's films often retained political overtones. In Nikkatsu Roman Porno, a similar development took place, and films such as Morita Yoshimitsu's *Pink Cut* (*Pink katto—futoku ai shite, nagaku ai shite*, 1983) take place in a postmodern, candy-colored, and carefree story world, almost completely eschewing sexual violence. That same year, Morita would become an international film festival favorite with his best-known film, *Family Game* (*Kazoku gēmu*, 1983).

The specific form and meaning of the representation of sexual violence in Pink Film in the following decades went through a number of transformations. Although it is difficult to measure, the late 1980s seem to have brought a renewed rise in violence to Pink films. This may again have much to do with economic factors, as hard-core pornography distributed on video exerted pressure to differentiate in new ways.[50] In an industry obviously past its economic zenith in the late 1980s, allowances were being made for anything that drew attention. Most visibly, these were the experimental Pink films by the so-called *shitennō*, the Four Devils of Pink Film: Satō Hisayasu, Zeze Takahisa, Satō Toshiki, and Sano Kazuhiro. Their films garnered favorable attention from outside the industry, but Pink Film distributors, exhibitors, and apparently the audience generally did not care much for these dark and difficult films. At the same time, because of their renewed emphasis on sexual violence as a purveyor of meaning and (revived) politics, they were criticized for a conception of filmic politics that remained stuck in male subjectivity and an outsider mentality preserved from the early 1970s.[51] In contrast, the films of the late 1990s decidedly de-emphasized rape and violence, focusing on more quotidian emotional and sexual complications among part-time workers and slackers, even in the more generic fare. Often attributed to the much-touted introversion of the new generation of directors, most prominently represented by the Shichifukujin, or Seven Lucky Gods of Pink Film (Ueno Toshiya, Meike Mitsuru, Imaoka Shinji, Sakamoto Rei, Tajiri Yūji, Kamata Yoshitaka, and Enomoto Toshirō). Yet the decline in extreme violence had just as much to do with the changing media situation. Pink Film began tentatively distributing beyond the theater space. Video rental and especially cable and satellite television channels demanded films that were more compatible with broadcasting and other distribution standards.

A Storm Brews for the Film Industry

Over its formational phase Pink Film had to function within the larger context of the larger film industry, and that was increasingly embattled. Nonetheless, the first boom years were promising for Pink Film. "Independent Productions Now Going for a Blockbuster Strategy Too" the magazine *Seijin Eiga* proclaimed after the release of the Kokuei-produced *Sad Vessel* (*Hiki*, Yuasa Namio, 1966), an extravaganza that included ten of the most popular Pink Film actresses of the time.[52] Just a year earlier Kokuei had produced the first foreign-location Pink Film in Hawaii, *Navel of the Sun* (*Taiyō no heso*, Wakamatsu Kōji, 1965), as well as a coproduction with Taiwan.[53] Pink Film was the site of intense experimentation across systems of production, distribution, and on the textual level, and was proving much more dynamic than the major studios.

However, these experiments by Kokuei also showed the pressures it was under, and that were converging on Pink Film as a whole. Kokuei had canceled its participation in both the 1965 and 1968 attempts to consolidate the Pink Film distribution market, usually because its general strategy called for larger budgets. From an early stage, the company had preferred to produce fewer but more elaborate films that were then intensely marketed. In a distribution system based on fixed production quotas as designed by the OP chain, the returns were largely fixed as well, and Kokuei did not feel it was getting the appropriate share if that meant equal treatment to cheaper, less ambitious productions. Kokuei also did not possess a fixed exhibition circuit (though it did have a large network of regional distribution subsidiaries) and had to push to distinguish its films in a crowded distribution market.

On the one hand, the demand for Pink films was fairly stable during the very late 1960s, and there was even talk of a second boom in 1969. In terms of volume, the industry had established itself as a kind of sixth major, and by most approximations was consistently taking around 10 percent of the annual box office, despite much lower returns per film.[54] However, by 1970, Pink Film budgets were dropping and shooting schedules were getting shorter. The film industry as a whole was on the verge of a deep structural transformation, one that would force Pink Film to retreat into ever more defined and standardized spaces.

Labor relations and conditions were one central aspect of the impending shift to complete casualization, transforming the last director-producer-distributors into contract workers. In late 1971, several Pink Film directors banded to form the Directors' Production Association (Kantoku Prodakushon Kyōkai) to discuss problems such as the constant shrinking of Pink Film budgets and the problem of authors' rights.[55] There was still hope that the structure of the industry could be actively influenced for the benefit of the people it employed. But the flux of experimentation and renegotiation that had characterized Pink Film was already turning toward a more fixed structure with very set power relations. Pink Film's discourse of resistance and independence, it became increasingly clear, had packaged and made palatable both the turbulent contradictions of postwar democracy for the audience and the casualization of labor for the staff in the Pink Film industry.

The majors were in dire straits as well. In 1970, Nikkatsu, Japan's oldest film studio, was forced to sell its studio lot to the Orwellian-named Japan Telecommunications Welfare Association (Zaidan Hōjin Denki Tsūshin Kyōzai Kai), with the option of repurchasing it within two years (production could continue in the meantime). But as the following year rolled around, Nikkatsu was forced to continue selling off much of its remaining real estate holdings. Nikkatsu and Daiei, both on the brink of bankruptcy, had previously decided to further scale down production and distribute their films together through a new company, Dainichi Eihai, that would supply their respective exhibition chains. Dainichi commenced from June 1970, with both companies contributing three films a month. Like Nikkatsu, Daiei was producing more and more films with racy titles like *Cute Devil, I'll Give You Something*

Good (*Kawaii akuma. Ii koto ageru*, Inoue Yoshio, 1970) or *Naked Embrace* (*Hadaka de dakko*, Yuasa Noriaki, 1970), films that were much less explicit than the titles suggested. Despite the sensationalist appeal, Dainichi failed to turn around business, and just sixteen months later the partnership was dissolved. On November 29, 1971, after selling most of its real estate assets, Daiei, the company of Kurosawa Akira, Masumura Yasuzō, Ichikawa Kon, and Mizoguchi Kenji, declared bankruptcy.[56]

Financial difficulties had plagued the major studios for years, and they had already responded by restructuring heavily. All of the majors had intensified their diversification efforts by the late 1960s, when the film business showed little hope of turning around for the better, and all companies had focused largely on real estate development and diversifying within the leisure industry, especially building bowling alleys. Shōchiku and Tōei were, in fact, largely sustained by their bowling business for several years, and even the godfather of Pink Film, Ōkura Mitsugi, had participated in the boom.[57] However, the bowling business took a sharp downturn in 1970, and the companies were forced not only to look for new investments but also to restructure their core business.

In 1970, Tōhō made a historic move with enormous consequences for the future of the film and media industry when it outsourced its recording, art direction, technical, and special-effects divisions to affiliated companies it established, and the entire production division followed in the same year. These changes were the decisive step toward more flexibility in production and an increased casualization of labor, a model that all of the majors would eventually adopt—and one that Pink Film had been following for eight years by then. Tōhō could move more swiftly than the other majors, as it was part of the Hankyū group, an expansive net of affiliated companies with complex interconnections called a *keiretsu* in Japan. As a keiretsu, the Hankyū group was already experienced in creating efficient networks of outsourcing, and it is no surprise that Tōhō was the first to rationalize its structure accordingly. From now on, and with the notable exception of Nikkatsu, the major studios would essentially become distributors in possession of their own exhibition chains. They would buy but not significantly produce films any more.

The benefits of outsourcing were more than just cost-efficient production; it completely circumvented labor unions. While initially the American occupation had made national unions a requirement (when it was still encouraging unionization), in practice in the film industry unions were always company unions and not general unions based on a specific type of labor. If cameramen or -women in the United States belonged to the American Society of Cinematographers, in Japan they might have belonged to the Tōhō or Shōchiku union, depending on the company they were working for. By outsourcing production to much smaller subcontracting companies and thereby reducing the number of actual employees of the main company, the majors were doing away with one potentially troublemaking factor as well as creating more cost-efficient units. Again, it was a type of labor organization that Pink Film had been based on from the beginning.

Nikkatsu alone went a different route among the major studios. Despite its extensive real estate sales, Nikkatsu was on the brink of bankruptcy throughout 1971. By August, production was halted and the company union and management were talking about taking a fairly radical step. The entire production was to switch to sex films modeled on Pink films, but with the production values a studio could provide, to be marketed under the brand name Roman Porno. Thus, in the same month that Daiei announced its inability to continue business, Nikkatsu released the first films from its Roman Porno line.[58] As mentioned above, the films were to be produced for an average budget of 7 to 7.5 million yen, or about two and a half times the budget of Pink films, but with all the merits of a functioning studio lot. For a while Nikkatsu showed double bills of Roman Porno *gendaigeki* (contemporary films) and *jidaigeki* (period films) to make its product competitive; period films were for the most part beyond the budget possibilities of Pink Film. Roman Porno was set to be around seventy minutes long and feature one sexual scene—and this was obviously interpreted broadly—at least every ten minutes. The studio infrastructure and its position as one of the major studios promised tough competition for Pink Film. Nikkatsu counted 109 theaters in its nationwide chain, struck thirty-two prints per film, and had twenty-five directors under contract, along with a constantly working and very well-trained staff and a giant studio lot in Chōfu. It also possessed a very well-oiled public relations machine with access to the more respectable media. The largest Pink Film companies, in comparison, struck a maximum of around twenty prints of a film at their peak at the end of the 1960s. Ōkura was striking ten to eleven prints per film in 1969 and had the largest national exhibition network, with sixteen specialty theaters in the Kantō (Tokyo) region at the time that Roman Porno began. However, Ōkura had far from the 109 theaters Nikkatsu did, and was dependent on free booking for a large part of the theaters it serviced. The only studio lot Pink Film had on offer, Ōkura Mitsugi's small OP Eiga studio in the Setagaya district of Tokyo, closed down in 1973.[59]

Nikkatsu's announcement caused an uproar in the media and within the company itself, as suddenly employees of the oldest studio in Japan found themselves ordered to shoot low-budget sex films. Although Nikkatsu had already been steering toward more titillating themes in the previous two years with titles such as *Shameless School* (*Harenchi gakuen*, Tanno Yūji, 1970, with its manga source material, also an attempt to stay connected to the youth market), the new strategy aimed for a different scale entirely. The company lost over three hundred employees in the month following its announcement and had considerable difficulty securing actors and actresses for its productions. It solved part of the problem by heavily employing young staff, giving assistant directors a chance to helm their first film, and recruiting Pink Film stars, a talent drain that was painfully felt in the Pink Film industry. The first Nikkatsu Roman Porno star actress was Shirakawa Kazuko, who had debuted in Pink Film in 1967 and now entered the mainstream media as a star of national proportions, and others such as Tani Naomi would follow. Nikkatsu immediately applied its public relations machine to the new stars and the new brand of films. Partially due to company strategy, and partially to the young staff it was now employing, the first Roman Porno films often embraced a countercultural stance and were very popular with a young demographic, especially students.

The metropolitan police, however, were not happy with this development. The compartmentalization that Pink Film had inadvertently started—of certain types of films, themes, and audiences into ever more defined spaces—was being disturbed by the entry of practically the same kinds of filmic texts into an at least purportedly more accessible, representative, more public space: the Nikkatsu theater chain. The police had issued repeated warnings against the increase in the "degree of obscenity"; the latest, and the one that prompted Eirin to raise its periodically slackening standards, was in 1970.[60] On October 1 of the same year, police searched the offices of five Pink companies (Ōkura Eiga among them) and seized several prints, leading to strong protests from the Pink Film industry. At this point no one was charged, yet. But only two months after Roman Porno was launched, in January 1972, the police took action, seizing four prints and filing charges against a number of Nikkatsu employees, one Pink Film director, and three Eirin employees for cooperating in the distribution of obscenity over the course of 1972.[61] While the first verdict cleared all the defendants in 1974, the trial marathon continued until the Tokyo High Court delivered a final not guilty verdict in 1980, after a costly and nerve-wracking eight years in court.[62] Nikkatsu, of course, had encountered similar experiences with the *Black Snow* trial and felt it had been unfairly treated. Nikkatsu suspected, as many did in the case of *Black Snow*, that it was not the degree of obscenity of these specific films that had provoked the police action, but politics. Indeed, Nikkatsu had not only taken the Pink Film formula and integrated it into a studio system structure, it also was annexing Pink Film's countercultural aspects to appeal to the youth market. A Nikkatsu producer claimed, no doubt strategically, in an interview, "To show sex [in a film] is antiestablishment; that is why we do it. Another reason is that by using sex as a trigger we can achieve new modes of expression."[63] More importantly, while Nikkatsu continued to produce youth films and non–Roman Porno films as well, the company was moving explicit representations of sexuality into mainstream, more respectable venues. A major studio, with theaters in prime locations of all urban centers, was now unabashedly producing, advertising, and showing sex films with a strong antiauthoritarian, antiestablishment message. It was a breach of the spatial etiquette that had imprisoned and sheltered Pink Film for almost ten years.

Pink Film, then, was in for a rough few years, even if business initially seemed stable. Producers and distributors active at the time often claim that not much changed with the coming of Roman Porno, and indeed the shock waves that passed through the industry were surprisingly small.[64] The new video business began making itself felt from 1970 on and saved quite a few Pink Film companies from financial peril. A sales rush broke out, and spades of archived films were transferred to video for use in love hotels and Japanese inns.[65]

Nonetheless, Pink Film was on shaky ground. Not only was Nikkatsu intruding into its market, foreign sex films were becoming increasingly popular as well. The liberalization of pornography in the United States and European countries had led to an influx of foreign sex films onto the Japanese market, from the German sex education film *Helga* (Erich Bender, 1968, under the title *Jotai no shinpi* [The mystery of the female body]), to increasingly hardcore fare in the early 1970s. These films, heavily cut and with parts of the images blurred and scratched out, possessed a new aura of reality that put Pink Film and Nikkatsu Roman Porno, which relied on simulated sex and focused heavily on narrative, into a different perspective. Foreign nude models and porn actresses like Sandra Julien, Sharon Kelly, and Christina Lindberg became minor stars in Japan; Tōei, in particular, actively distributed their films and employed them in their own productions. Tōei also launched its own line of action films featuring a lot of nudity and sex under the Pinkii Baiorensu (Pinky Violence) label. Directors such as Suzuki Noribumi, Sekimoto Ikuo, and Makiguchi Yūji worked on series such as the *Girl Boss* (*Jobanchō*) and *Girl School* (*Joshikōkō*), or the *Scorpion* (*Sasori*) series featuring stars like Sugimoto Miki, Ike Reiko, or Kaji Meiko in low-budget but often technically accomplished productions filled with nudity, guns, and catfights. Pink Film simply did not have the funds to compete against the action subgenre, and the often campy and sometimes rebellious Pinky Violence films proved a large draw for young audiences. Pink Film was being threatened from several sides. Eventually even Million Films, one of the largest production and distribution companies for Pink films, started distributing lucrative foreign sex films (often hard-core) in 1972 in cooperation with major studio Shōchiku.[66] In 1972–73, one-fourth of all foreign films were designated adult. In comparison, in 1972, of a total of 395 films from Japan, an astonishing 296 were designated adult.[67] Pink Film still provided the bulk of these, but its market was being closed in on.

However, regardless of the ostensibly increasing competition between the majors and Pink Film, the relationship was actually growing much closer, and mutual dependencies were developing. While Nikkatsu Roman Porno was a threat, it was also important for business: Nikkatsu theaters showed triple bills, generally consisting of two Nikkatsu Roman Pornos and one Pink film. For this, Nikkatsu subcontracted to Pink Film companies like Prima Kikaku or Watanabe Productions, which both relied heavily on director Yoyogi Tadashi (later a key person for the development of the adult video genre who found himself ensnared in the obscenity trial against Nikkatsu).[68] These were usually budgeted somewhat higher than regular Pink films, at around 5 million yen. Indeed, all the surviving majors save Tōhō were distributing both foreign sex films and Pink films. They also eventually even moved into Pink Film production, although in a clandestine way. Shōchiku, which was experiencing considerable success with the ultra-family-friendly *Tora-san* series, founded a company, Tōkatsu, in 1972 and mostly employed Pink Film veteran Kobayashi Satoru to produce Pink Film fare.[69] Tōei more openly founded Tōei Central films for Pink Film and B-film production in 1976, relying heavily on veteran director Mukai Kan and production outfits such as Universal Films.

Pink Film reacted to the majors' forays in several ways, but mostly by adaptation and standardization. Ōkura Mitsugi made a last-ditch attempt to redefine the genre's options with a prestige project—a strategy he had been using since his days at the original Shintōhō in the late 1950s—by producing *Sex Manual of Humanity* (*Jinrui no seiten*, Ogawa Kinya) in 1973. Supposedly shot for 100 million yen (about $370,000 at the time), more than thirty times a regular Pink Film budget, the film failed to make any significant impact. Pink films' future form was set. In 1973, with Ōkura leading the way, most companies switched from the standard part-color films to all-color, mostly as a concession to the all-color Roman Porno, and other final modifications would follow. The ever-advancing reduction in output of major films that accelerated in the late 1970s exacerbated the film dearth for the exhibition business and kept Pink films in demand as cheap additions to the program. Often, a complete switch to Pink films became the only means for second- or third-run theaters to stay in business. This was the single most important development for Pink Film after its emergence, one that dissolved much of its articulated confusion and finally settled it into a more or less stable form.

The Spatial Fix of Pink Film

Coaxed by Roman Porno, driven by film dearth, and prodded by audience decline, the Pink Film specialty theater became Pink Film's spatial base and deprived it of its power of confusion. While central to understanding what Pink Film meant, the whole picture of Pink Film exhibition is still unclear, even today. Pink Film advertised in newspapers only to a limited degree, and in the early phase Pink Film distribution was chaotic and not yet systematized. Documentation barely exists or is not accessible. There were also quite a few definitions of what a Pink Film theater actually was, leading to wildly different contemporaneous estimates about the number of venues. Yet it is crucial to attempt to locate the time and circumstances of the establishment of the Pink Film screening space. Historically bound in its meaning and practices, space performs fixity, and as such it was decisive for the way Pink Film transitioned out of politicized confusion and into an orderly, compartmentalized, and standardized commodity.

Because of the variety of definitions and the difficulty of compiling reliable data, estimates on the number of Pink Film theaters are often highly speculative. In 1964, the magazine *Heibon Punch* made the undoubtedly inflated claim that 500 Pink *senmonkan* (specialty theaters) operated across Japan during the previous year at a time when only a comparatively small number of Pink films were actually in existence: 1,500 at the time of the article.[70] Journalist Yamada Keizō claimed to have counted 277 Pink specialty theaters in early 1969.[71] Kuwabara Masae, head of Pink production and distribution outfit Kantō Movie, estimated the number to have risen from 600 to 800 in 1968.[72] In the interviews conducted for this book, heads of production and distribution sections active at the time denied that real specialty theaters even existed until the early 1970s, usually mentioning around 600 nationwide by the mid-1970s.[73] Eiren, in a 1969 survey, claimed that of 3,711 theaters in Japan, 277 showed Pink films exclusively, and 424 showed them in combination with major films.⁷⁴ The usually reliable film journalist Gotō Bin claimed that there were 265 contracted specialty theaters in 1975.⁷⁵

The earliest verifiable example of theaters specializing in sexploitation films made in Japan—what were then only beginning to be called Pink films—was the OP chain founded by Ōkura Mitsugi in 1965, with twelve theaters in the Kantō region. Ōkura remodeled the entrances to his theaters so that large signs advertising the films would block the view from the street to the ticket counter. This made it less embarrassing to purchase tickets, and the idea of a secretive atmosphere supposedly increased the appeal; here we can see the beginning of the gender-segregated, semipublic space.⁷⁶ At this point, however, most theaters played Pink films as additions to regular films. First-run theaters played them if the second week of screenings did not attract enough audience, and second- and third-run theaters played them in combination with rereleases of majors' films, or later in combination with Nikkatsu Roman Porno.⁷⁷ Pink films were cheap, and they were an attractive addition to a program, but their cheapness showed and it was not always enough to attract an audience after the novelty of sex-themed productions had worn off. This dilemma intensified after Tōei and Nikkatsu increased their efforts to recapture the sex film in 1969. Pink Film's public image was not good, and most theaters had opened when cinema meant glamorous, major film fare. Owners were not excited about partially switching to low-budget sexploitation, even if it seemed to promise a steady return, and screening such films exclusively was certainly a last resort.

Today it seems to be commonly held that Pink films were always available only on the Pink Film theater circuit. In fact, until the early 1980s Pink Film would survive on a double tier of specialty theaters and theaters with a more varied program. It is only since around the mid-1980s, and especially after Nikkatu's demise in 1988, that Pink films have been available almost exclusively in specialty theaters.

As Ōkura Mitsugi reasoned when reconstructing his entrances, secretiveness—or rather spatial division—itself was a selling point. The film theaters' specific properties heavily influenced the character of the genre of Pink Film as a whole. The theaters switching to Pink films were, apart from early exceptions, usually small, not in the best shape (due to their financial straits), and outfitted with aging and cheap equipment. These were the theaters that could not participate in the majors' strategy to overcome television by using CinemaScope, elaborate sound systems, and other technological upgrades.

By the early 1970s, theaters all over the country had been going bankrupt at a constant rate for over ten years; they dropped by 60 percent to only 2,673 theaters in 1972 (although the rate slowed down considerably in the urban centers, continuing mainly in the chihō).[78] When bankruptcy became a concern for a theater, Pink films presented a real alternative. The percentages paid to distribution were much lower, and the audience was fairly constant. It is probably around this time, the early 1970s, that the network of theaters that screened only Pink films fleshed out (if it shrank at an accelerated rate throughout the first decade of the 2000s, it was often due to the owners' retirement or death, or the thirty- to forty-year-old projector breaking down beyond repair; the lack of financial resources to repair equipment or buildings is one of the reasons the 2011 Tohoku earthquake and tsunami dealt a further blow to Pink Film).[79] With the second large distribution network in place, the market was now evenly divided between the Ōkura (OP chain) and Shintōhō circuits. Pink Film had transformed its chaotic, dynamic, but volatile distribution industry into a stable supplier of program pictures.

The spatial fixing led to significant transformations in the filmic texts as well. Previously anywhere from seventy to ninety minutes in length, Pink films standardized at sixty minutes to fit the triple bills in which they were shown. Most films could immediately be identified as belonging to a subgenre or series, such as the *danchi tzuma* (suburban wife), *joyū* (women's bathhouse), *sēra fuku* (sailor/schoolgirl uniform), chikan densha (train molester), *sentō-mono* (bathhouse films), *no-pan* (no panty), *jukujo* (ripe/older woman), or *mibōjin* (widow) films. Director Yamamoto Shinya, later active as a well-known TV show host, was the biggest Pink Film director of the decade and the inventor of several of these series and subgenres (most famously the bathhouse and train molester films). He personified not only increased subgenrification, but also a turn away from the darker, problem-laden films of the 1960s to what were perceived as lighter, whimsical urban comedies. Wakamatsu Productions' often political and experimental films worked as individually distributable attractions but were difficult to fit into the standardized form that Pink Film was heading into. More conventional Pink films, which Wakamatsu had continued shooting as well, suffered from the budget pressures prevalent in all of Pink Film. Wakamatsu, always shrewd when it came to money matters, slowly phased out of the Pink Film business in the mid-1970s. Yamamoto, however, moved from the intensely private or political scenarios that dominated early Pink Film's texts and subtexts into the more neutral, quotidian, and in his films decidedly comedic spaces of the train and the public bathhouse. The vector was pointing away from trauma and toward entertainment.[80]

The institutionalization of the Pink Film screening space decisively transformed the genre. It changed the films themselves, the way they were produced and distributed, what they meant, and the audience that went to see them. The production of the semiofficial Pink Film screening space insulated the genre against indignation, scandal, and legal repercussions—at least for a while. It is no accident that it was mostly Nikkatsu—with its ambitions of making sex films accessible for a wider public via a major-studio-type screening space—that bore the brunt of legal action. At the same time, the standardized production of a specific kind of space, which in turn coproduced audiences and meaning, eventually weakened the level of meaning that initially contributed to establishing it.

"The Limits of Pink 'Guerilla-ness'"

"The flower whose blossoms will bear no fruit is in full bloom, but..."
—One of many increasingly pessimistic headlines about the Pink Film industry in 1979–80

By the mid-1970s, Pink Film could only barely uphold the oppositional image it had constructed ten years earlier.[81] The shift of the term "guerilla style" is very telling in this respect. Initially alluding to the on-the-fly realist shooting methods of Pink Film, just as much as to its provocative and political form, it soon became nothing more than a euphemism for the casualized labor organization of the genre. An industrial distinction between majors and Pink Film independents was also dissolving, with three of the four remaining majors now directly involved in Pink Film production and distribution—a fact that the most important annual publication that chronicles the film industry in Japan did not acknowledge. The *Eiga Nenkan* continued to uphold its distinction between Pink films as *dokuritsu puro 2* (independent film 2) and *dokuritsu puro 1*, consisting mainly of ATG films. Yet this distinction of majors and independents was, in reality, quite difficult. The 1979 *Eiga Nenkan* mentions that three distributor-producers dominated the Pink field: Shintōhō, Ōkura Eiga, and Million Film. It fails to mention that they supplied around 50 percent of Pink films, with the other half commissioned and distributed by Tōkatsu (a subsidiary of Shōchiku from 1972 on), Tōei Central (a subsidiary of Tōei from 1976), and Nikkatsu. Though the major subsidiaries centered on certain directors, with Kobayashi Satoru the main supplier for Tōkatsu and Mukai Kan for Tōei Central, all veteran directors still active from the 1960s indirectly worked for the majors at some point. The most popular was Yamamoto Shinya, working for majors such as Tōei directly, in major-contracted Pink films (where he shot a sex spoof starring American porn star Harry Reems) and pure Pink productions simultaneously.[82]

Pink Film's perceived depoliticization and the shift toward entertainment at this time had much to do with the loss of the major studio as Other against which the Pink oppositional identity could establish itself. In many ways the majors had assimilated to Pink Film and the common Other was now TV. It also, as detailed above, had much to do with the standardization of distribution and exhibition. The formation of the Pink Film specialty theater transformed Pink films from a free radical laden with connotations of resistance to an institutionalized program picture, a steady supplier of standardized fare and nudity. Pink Film, in this sense, was part of a larger shift of political discourse into the sphere of commodity capitalism. This is not to say that politics disappeared from Pink Film texts, but that the industrial genre largely lost its political charge. The path to Pink Film depoliticization parallels, in that sense, the development of the student movement. The mid-1970s saw an increasing reluctance to engage with explicit political expression. Film critics such as Hasumi Shigehiko tapped into this tendency with a new form of criticism that focused on film as a primarily aesthetic formation, not to be evaluated primarily by its politics as performed by previous generations of critics.

The (spatial) transformation of Pink Film supported and triggered the attitudinal changes in the audience and the genre practitioners themselves. It also had an effect on the media's treatment of the genre. Around the early 1970s, Pink Film began occasionally receiving more serious attention from critics (as a very early example, the March 1967 issue of *Eiga Hihyō* even included an *O-Pinku* best-of list next to its regular best-of list). On the whole, however, it was treated as part of an increasingly commodifiable counterculture or as legitimate male entertainment, especially after Nikkatsu Roman Porno offered an ostensibly more respectable object of discussion. The air of scandal had diluted to the point that sexually themed film was salable. Several special issues devoted to Pink films began popping up: *Pinky, Kōkotsu no Sekai* (World of ecstasy), *Pinku Joyū Onna Chizu* (Pink actress map of women), and so on were usually more picture than text oriented, and obviously primarily geared toward showing nudity. Regular magazines began covering Pink films as well, with special issues of *Tōseki* or even the women's magazine *Josei Jishin*. Television coverage increased as well, with regular appearances of directors and producers on shows such as *11PM*, and Pink Film actresses featured as talk show guests—unthinkable several years earlier.[83] The new magazine coverage included much less of the political surplus meaning than the first magazine devoted to Pink Film, *Seijin Eiga*, whose attempts to link Pink Film to a societal context were typical for the industry discourse and the films themselves in the early period of Pink Film.[84] By 1973, the year that Pink Film in many ways becomes spatially, aesthetically, and generically fixed, *Seijin Eiga* ceased publication.

The standardization triggered by the Pink Film specialty theater did not eliminate the industrial genre, but it did shift its mechanics. For most members of the audience, this was a movement from Pink Film, the industrial genre, to Pink films, a collection of spatially fixed films charged with less and slightly different contextual meaning. Confusion had been one of Pink Film's main selling points. Where previously con-fused meanings had been commodified and circulated, now seriality was producing controlled and commodifiable difference. Arguably, this development was an early sign of a significant turn in Japanese media capitalism that was already brewing. It was a shift that Kadokawa Film would soon pick up on with a vengeance.

THREE

KADOKAWA FILM

Kadokawa Film holds an iconic status in Japanese film histories, if not always in a positive sense. At various stages, the film activity of the Kadokawa Haruki Jimusho (Kadokawa Haruki Office) itself became part of the narrative that dramatized the developments in film from Japan. Kadokawa Haruki's relationship to the established film world is epitomized in the aforementioned story of how Kurosawa Akira refused to shake his hand at the preview screening of *Kagemusha* (Kurosawa Akira, 1980).[1] No other film industry entity so gripped the attention of critics and spectators alike during these years, becoming the condensed symbol of a new way of producing, marketing, distributing, and watching films. The industrial genre that would redefine how films were made and understood became flesh/meat in the near-mythic figure of Kadokawa Haruki himself. While Pink Film was mostly forced to "bloom in the valley of depression" and was rarely treated in official film criticism at all, there is a virtual plethora of articles on Kadokawa and Kadokawa films.[2] They feature a conspicuous repetition of themes and (mis)conceptions that are as telling as they are informative.

In his article "The Sense of Flesh [*nikutai*] Related to Japanese Film," critic Abe Casio offers his interpretation of the decline of audience interest in theatrical film since the late 1950s:

> Surely the main reason that people went to the film theater was "The joy of witnessing the place [*genba*] where stories become meat [*niku*]." . . .

> But what happened in the latter half of the 1970s was that "story" and "becoming meat" were decoupled.... Around this time, "stories everyone knows" were no longer used in film. Of course, their disappearance is connected to the structural change inherent to the transformation of the general public to fragmented publics.... Kadokawa Film seized the opportunity of this transformation and hammered out a great number of films based on any kind of book.[3]

Abe's disdain is aimed at a number of connected issues of loss: the ebbing of a certain appeal to (social) realism in exchange for spectacle, the waning centrality of narrative, the falling apart of a unified community of spectators, and their ultimate disenchantment with Japanese film. That he names Kadokawa Film as one of the main culprits, or at least profiteers, places his portrayal squarely within the orthodox histories of film in Japan.

At least in some respects, this is a highly unfair assessment of Kadokawa Film, the often reviled genre that catalyzed the next deep transformation in film and media in Japan. When in 1976 Kadokawa Haruki, newly appointed head of Kadokawa Publishing, announced the company's entry into film production, he was ridiculed—or at best perceived as a curiosity and a mere "non-(film) business person." By 1986, he had produced dozens of hits, six of the ten top-grossing films from Japan of all time, and had become the self-proclaimed Other of the established film industry that he had, in fact, helped sustain and transform.[4]

Kadokawa Film was central to a deep and qualitative change in film and media from Japan between the late 1970s and the early 1990s.[5] This chapter and chapter 4 map this transformation, touching upon issues such as the changing role of narrative, the continued relevance of the screening space for imbuing films with meaning, and the central role of the industrial genre of Kadokawa Film in the diffusion of media-mix strategies. It is this last point that most prominently shifted how audiences and the industry thought about media. At the core of these developments stands a fundamental change in how we engage with media and how they make meaning. By looking at the trajectory of Kadokawa Film and its ultimate inability to perpetuate itself as an industrial genre—even making industrial genres less likely in general—we can track this transformation.

Abe's article touches on one of the most visible aspects of that trajectory, especially in contrast with the previous relevance of Pink Film: the question of flesh. Pink Film focused on flesh as a master metaphor, charging it heavily with an "ero-real" political significance and making it the site for negotiating national and social identity via a strategy of confusion. In comparison, Kadokawa Film shifts from the localizable (if confused) Pink Film body toward decontextualized characters, relying on a very specific kind of pop idol as a freely circulating, nearly blank signifier with a reduced corpo-reality. Where Pink Film is pessimistic and problematizing, Kadokawa Film is utopian, and where Pink Film retreated into ever more hermetic cinematic spaces, Kadokawa Film opened up the borders of film and the nation. Many film critics had difficulty accepting the aesthetic changes that Kadokawa Film was seen to symbolize, and Abe distills the position that the many detractors of Kadokawa took: "Kadokawa films are not films."[6]

Two things must be kept in mind when we consider Kadokawa films. First, the public figure of Kadokawa Haruki is a constructed part of the discursive formation of Kadokawa Film, deliberately positioned and deliberately marketed as the embodiment of this industrial genre. In my analysis, I treat Kadokawa Haruki himself as (literally) incarnating a strategic and personalized attempt to cohere media text, production, discourse, and dissemination inherent to industrial genres. It is this attempt to dramatize the discourse of industrial genres by embodying it that is the "becoming meat" that Abe overlooks. Second, Kadokawa introduced the aestheticization and explicit commodification of the business discourses themselves, which formed the basis of the company's success.

Many of the contemporary opinions or ideas about Kadokawa the business entity are factually wrong or strongly exaggerated, precisely because Kadokawa Haruki was so successful in equating himself with Kadokawa Film and in selling a specific image of the industrial genre, not just of the films. These chapters track some of the questions that arise from this: Why was the discourse this genre produced as a commodity so spectacularly successful at this specific time? How did it transform not only what kinds of films were made but how audiences made sense of film and media?

Kadokawa Haruki established and supported his portrayal as a controversial overreacher to his utmost. His public image is that of the savior of Kadokawa Publishing, inventor of the media-mix strategy, instigator of the 1970s blockbuster, revolutionizer of the film business, box-office king, producer of over seventy films and director of seven, a prize-winning Haiku poet, record-breaking sailor, unrepentant eccentric, and head priest of his own Shinto shrine. Kadokawa Haruki constantly reached beyond Japan. He undertook several spectacular sailing journeys, one of them from Japan to San Francisco, sailed around the world to Portugal in an exact copy of the *Santa Maria*, produced the first film from Japan partially set in New York and the first film to be set in Antarctica, deliberated on his experiences with UFOs, headed an expedition to find the wreck of the legendary World War II battleship *Yamato* (and found it), produced musicals on Broadway, and was convicted for ordering one of his staff to smuggle cocaine from Los Angeles to Japan. At the center of the Kadokawa strategy stands the struggle for financially exploitable attention, of which Kadokawa Haruki himself was a constant and provocative part. The cover of his autobiography sees him seated in front of a backdrop of skyscrapers in a samurai uniform and is called *Waga Tōsō*, the Japanese title of *Mein Kampf*.[7]

Many of the discourses Kadokawa Film put forth are based on well-established binaries: spatial, such as those between the Japan and the West or the village and the city, or temporal, such as between the future and the past. While Kadokawa Haruki identified himself and Kadokawa Film with ahistoric agency, internationalism, the urban, and individualism, it is simplistic to say he identified himself with the West, with which these concepts were and are problematically associated in many discourses in Japan. When it came to film, he habitually latched onto oppositional tropes such as Kadokawa versus the established film industry: "I like Japanese films, but I detest the Japanese film world."[8]

Despite the fact that he usually tended to portray himself as located outside of temporal regimes, he and the business strategies of the company he headed are much more part of their times than the visionary enterprise he portrayed it as. Many of the strategies attributed to Kadokawa were widely in use in the mid-1970s, even before Kadokawa officially entered the film business. Yet Kadokawa succeeded in fixing them into a framework of meaning and creating a brand. This brand held implications not only for the economy of the Japanese film industry, but for the larger media ecology of Japan as well.

Kadokawa's Paper Roots

Keiko McDonald stated, "It could well be said that of all the world's cinemas, the Japanese is unique in its closeness, early and late, to the nation's literature." Appeals to uniqueness aside, McDonald is correct in that the two have been extraordinarily intertwined.[9] The fact that films not based on existing works are actually quite rare in certain periods of Japanese film history is important, but this vast field of research lies practically untouched. This chapter does not attempt to fill this void, but it briefly focuses on the specific history of Kadokawa Publishing (Kadokawa Shoten) and its role in developing a more systematic relationship between different media platforms and media systems.

Kadokawa Haruki spent his formative first ten years in business in publishing. Haruki's father, Kadokawa Gen'yoshi, founded the publishing company Kadokawa Shoten in November 1945, immediately after the end of the war. It thrived during the publishing boom of the early 1960s, but its image as specializing in serious national literature and dictionaries, and its lack of magazines, gave it a disadvantage in the emerging pocket book wars of the early 1970s, when small-format paperback editions became popular.[10] Kadokawa Haruki entered the company at twenty-three years of age in 1965 and experienced its growing financial difficulties. According to him, Kadokawa Publishing was constantly recording losses.[11] For his first foray into transmedia marketing strategies he claims to have been inspired by the success of the book, film, and soundtrack of *The Graduate* (Mike Nichols) in 1968.

Encouraged by the low costs of translating books, Kadokawa purchased the publishing rights for Erich Segal's *Love Story* for a mere $250. The book was published half a year before the film's release in 1971, with Kadokawa working with distributor CIC on the advertising campaign. The book sold millions of copies—one of Kadokawa Publishing's biggest successes—although, according to Haruki, it was published with much resistance from inside the company, especially from his father. He followed up the success by publishing *The Strawberry Statement* (*Ichigo hakusho*) by James Kunen to accompany the film adaptation in 1971, while timing the publication of Frederick Forsyth's *The Day of the Jackal* (*Jakaru no hi*) to coincide with the film's release in 1973.[12] He also published an extremely successful line of film novelizations, such as *Le Grand Meaulnes* (*Sasurai no seishun*, Jean-Gabriel Albicocco, 1968), *Me, Natalie* (*Natari no asa*, Fred Coe, 1969), and *Stiletto* (*USA burūsu*, Bernard Kowalski, 1969) in 1970.

Kadokawa published most of these books as small paperbacks, called *bunkobon*, that were growing increasingly popular. Unusual for the time, he gave priority to paperback publishing, decreasing the time between the hardcover and paperback releases. While bunkobon had previously been coverless and black and white, Kadokawa introduced colorful paper covers and, according to his own reports, increased the ailing company's sales by 50 percent a year. He also published books by younger authors and targeted a younger demographic with science fiction, mystery, and what in Japan are called hard-boiled genres, with a heavy emphasis on entertainment. All of this invited strong criticism from the literary establishment for his trivial lineup, prompting literary éminence grise Nagai Tatsuo to state, "Kadokawa Publishing's makeup has changed completely. I have no desire to publish my complete works there." Author Nosaka Akiyuki, who wrote the book that became the basis for Imamura Shohei's film *The Pornographers* (*Erogotoshi-tachi*, 1967), said, "I can't stand selling [books] the same way you sell ramen soup or convenience store goods."[13] The publishing world pejoratively labeled his approach as "cinema books" or even "abnormal."[14]

In 1975, after a much-publicized forty-seven-day canoe trip from Incheon in South Korea to Fukuoka in Japan, Kadokawa began intensifying the coordination of book and film releases.[15] Beginning in 1971, the company had published paperback versions of mystery author Yokomizo Seishi's books, highly popular since the 1950s. In the fall of 1975, it published what was called the Yokomizo Seishi Book Fair, a reissuing of twenty-five of Yokomizo's books, and timed it to coincide with the release of the ATG-produced film, *Murder at Honjin Manor House* (*Honjin satsujin jiken*, Takabayashi Yōichi), based on a Yokomizo novel, to whose advertising budget Kadokawa contributed money.[16]

The project was an impressive success, with 2.5 million books sold in just two months. Fairs would become a staple of Kadokawa Publishing, and other companies soon picked up the method. Its success also probably had a more far-reaching effect, giving Kadokawa Haruki the clout inside the company to embark on a more ambitious endeavor: film production itself. In October 1975 Kadokawa Gen'yoshi passed away, and, in November, Kadokawa Haruki took over as head of the company. On December 4, Kadokawa Haruki gave a press conference announcing his plans to enter film production at the rate of two films a year, and on January 8, 1976, his birthday, the Kadokawa Haruki Office was founded.[17]

The Leap into Media Mix

The idea of a publishing company embarking on active film production was unheard of at the time. It also may not have struck everyone as very wise. The first year since the end of the war in which foreign film achieved a higher distribution gross than films produced in Japan was 1975, making the phrase *yōkō hōtei* (*yōga* up, *hōga* down) one of the most-used expressions of the year in film journalism.[18] Daiei's bankruptcy had happened just five years prior, and Nikkatsu's last refuge in its Roman Porno label seemed like exactly that, a last resort. The number of film theaters was constantly declining and reached a low of 2,443, down about 41 percent in ten years.[19] Maybe surprisingly, however, the picture was not quite as dark as it superficially seemed. The total box-office income of 1975 had been the highest in Japanese history, and all of the major studios increased their profits. Distribution gross for film from

Japan had been rising steadily since 1972, jumping by 54 percent to 22.9 billion yen (at the time about $77,627,000), and there was talk of the film industry rebounding.[20] Still, a publishing company entering film production as an active entity was viewed as an interesting experiment at best, and often enough as "madness."[21] But Kadokawa was not simply planning to embark on film production. It was designing a media-mix strategy that decentered film, even if it retained an important role.

The project that Kadokawa announced at his press conference in December 1975 was the filming of a Yokomizo novel, *Village of Eight Gravestones* (*Yattsuhaka-mura*), in cooperation with Shōchiku. By May 24, he held another press conference announcing the company's retreat from the Shōchiku deal and new plans to produce another Yokomizo-based film, *The Inugami Family* (*Inugami-kei no ichizoku*). The cancellation of the plans with Shōchiku is symptomatic of Kadokawa's relationship to the established Japanese film business, characterized by demonstrations of distrust and antipathy. "I like Japanese films, but I detest the Japanese film world," became one of Kadokawa's oft-repeated phrases, and he consistently characterized the industry as governed by a "village mentality."[22] Conversely, he portrayed himself as a visionary individualist pitted against a fossilized, feudal system—one he associated with dishonesty, lack of transparency, and old Japan.[23] Kadokawa carried over not only certain strategies of intermedia synergy from activities in the publishing world, but also a theme of opposition and individualism that was framed in temporal terms of new versus old. It was a trope the company would use in an increasingly performative way. Kadokawa himself claims that the Shōchiku deal fell through because the company was attempting to milk him for money. It first demanded 400 million yen (about $1,356,000) for the total production and then, when he refused, gradually decreased the sum to 70 million yen, a business practice that made him "unable to trust them."[24]

The Inugami Family was Kadokawa's first attempt at what he called a "media-mix" strategy, a phrase that, despite having been in circulation for quite a while, would become inextricably connected to Kadokawa in the public and the business world's imagination.[25] Originally used in advertising, by the early 2000s it tended to refer less to a centrally planned use of multiple media than to a self-organizing system or network of companies through which narratives and characters spread across media. It is important to emphasize that even within such a definition there is more than one media-mix model.[26] As conceived by Kadokawa, the media mix was a package of print media, film, and music marketed by a single company to the widest possible audience, with each product advertising the others.[27] This strategy necessitated a very specific kind of consumer-public, one as broad and undivided as possible. Generating this level of unification and coordinating the various industry branches required an initial investment of significant amounts of money. In terms of film, it encouraged Kadokawa to move toward a blockbuster strategy. In terms of cross marketing, it went from selling a film to selling something that is much less specific to its medium, which at this stage was a specific narrative embedded in spectacle.

The Inugami Family opened after an intense advertising campaign that, for the first time for a film from Japan, utilized radio and TV commercials in addition to mobilizing unusual synergies, such as inserting theater ticket coupons into 10 million Kadokawa books. The film became one of the most successful of the year. Produced for 220 million yen (about $745,800)—more than seventy times the budget of an average Pink film of the time—and distributed by Tōhō, it opened in October 1976 as an exclusive single-bill road show and had a nationwide release in November. It eventually made 1.559 billion yen (about $5,284,800) in distribution gross, and it stimulated book sales and record sales of the soundtrack, issued by the newly founded Kadokawa Records. Although tie-ins with the music industry using pop stars in films had been common since the 1960s, selling soundtracks was highly unusual in Japan at the time.[28] The influential annual critics' poll in *Kinema Junpō* magazine rated *The Inugami Family* as the fifth best film of 1976, and the readers' poll even voted it into first place. At the same time, as a foreshadowing of attitudes toward Kadokawa films to come, the critics' poll in *Eiga Geijutsu* magazine voted it fourth on its "worst of the year" list.

The Kadokawa Haruki Office was the official producer of the film, while Kadokawa Publishing provided 170 million of the 220 million yen budget. The rest consisted of a bank loan with Kadokawa's private estate as guarantee, one of the rare examples in Japanese film history of a bank loaning such a large sum of money for a single film.[29] For a project of this magnitude, Kadokawa had built in safety stops. The book was by Yokomizo, an established mystery author experiencing a popular revival (the story had been filmed before, in 1954 by Tōei, just as *Village of Eight Gravestones* had been in 1951). Kadokawa asked veteran Ichikawa Kon to direct, and in production they relied on staff trained within the nearly defunct studio system infrastructure. But Kadokawa was quick to underline his opposition to film industry standard practice when he sued one of the producers, Ichikawa Kiichi (one of the few on the staff who was a veteran of independent film, having produced *Woman in the Dunes*), for embezzling 1.11 million yen (about $3,760 at the time) when several bills were charged to fictional addresses.[30] This had been seen as common practice in the film industry, usually to cover unofficial costs such as meals for all-night shoots or protection payments to yakuza, often necessary when shooting on location. However, it seems Kadokawa intended to set off a warning shot against a lack of accountability and the informal industry practices for which the film business in Japan was notorious. Interestingly, Kadokawa's attempt to link certain business practices to an oppositional identity based on the tension between old and new was, performatively, looking for validation through the legal system. By taking judicial action he was also attempting to secure more transparent business practices for future projects.[31]

Eiga Nenkan characterized Kadokawa's success as a "shock for the established film world."[32] In a short set report on the filming of *The Inugami Family*, *Kinema Junpō* still put "Kadokawa Eiga" (Kadokawa Film) in quotation marks.[33] Nonetheless, following the success of *The Inugami Family*, all of the major studios lined up to work with Kadokawa. It was with the next production that Kadokawa fully implemented the media-mix strategies that would become definitive for the identity formation of Kadokawa Film and transformative for the film and media industry. *Proof of the Man* (*Ningen no shōmei*, Satō Junya, 1977) was predictably timed with the Morimura Seiichi Book Fair to stimulate the fairly young author's sales. Kadokawa produced a soundtrack record with a title song fit for a single release, and the following year a television series was based on the book and film. But Kadokawa was seriously set on changing the rules of the industry regarding the handling of film itself. For the first time since the war, Kadokawa divided the majors up to fill separate roles regarding the same film: Nikkatsu would supply the production infrastructure; Tōei's yōga section was responsible for advertising and distribution; and Tōhō would provide the exhibition facilities. Previously, the majors had been able to call all the shots when involved with a film, but Kadokawa put them in a position in which they were forced to compete, and where he could exploit the strengths of each company. This points to the radical shift in the film industry that Pink Film had been so central to initiating. Rather than in-house production in completely separate vertically organized studios, the industry was now a collection of outsourced affiliates that had to compete with each other. While the studios had learned the flexibility of casualized labor from Pink Film and utilized it for their own purposes, they were now trapped in exactly that structure.

The budget for *Proof of the Man* was set high. According to the *Asahi Shinbun*, it was more than double that of *The Inugami Family*, leaving the realm of what one might call a prestige production budget to enter the blockbuster realm.[34] The release strategy would be the centerpiece of the identity politics of early Kadokawa Film. Like *The Inugami Family*, *Proof of the Man* was to be shown in theaters usually reserved for yōga, or foreign films, as a single bill. This not only meant a somewhat more exclusive theater, it also entailed a different kind of distribution. Releases of foreign films are subject to free booking, as opposed to the block-booking system for national films. This means that a yōga-style distribution lets a film run as long as it is profitable before switching to the next film in line. If a film is successful, this means significantly higher profits and longer running times. On the other hand, in the mid-1970s a film released in the block-booking system was guaranteed a running time of usually at least four weeks. This could soften a box-office failure and avoid the financial disaster of having a film taken out of the program after one unsuccessful week in yōga-style distribution. However, even if each screening sold out, the program switched to a potentially less successful film after the designated running time elapsed.

Apart from the different economics of distribution, releasing a Japanese film in theaters usually reserved for foreign titles unleashed a host of implications for the specific interaction of film and screening space. From a marketing perspective, it provided the film with an exceptional and exclusive image, created an additional buzz, and provided a fashionably Westernized aura. It also destabilized the separation of Japanese and foreign films in different screening spaces. This confusion of spatial concerns was at the center of *Proof of the Man*'s strategic position on several levels. Kadokawa supported the aura of the foreign by making it the first Japanese-produced film with location shooting in New York, and by including American stars such as George Kennedy in the cast. The tension between foreign (read, American) and Japanese permeates not only the spectator's locality but the story as well.

In *Proof of the Man*, a young black man travels from Harlem to Tokyo and is murdered in the elevator of the luxurious Otani Hotel. Police inspector Munesue (played by Matsuda Yūsaku, known to foreign audiences for his roles in *Family Game* and *Black Rain*), finds that his own history is entangled in the plot that unfolds. The victim, Johnny Hayward, was the son of Yasugi Kyōko—the fashion designer whose show was staged at the hotel on the night of the murder—and an American soldier stationed in Japan during the postwar years. Munesue had watched his own father get beaten to death and urinated on by American GIs when he tried to protect Kyōko from being raped. When Munesue goes to New York to investigate Hayward's history, he is teamed up with detective Shuftan (Kennedy), whose tattoo he recognizes from the incident with his father. Ultimately, it is revealed that Kyōko murdered Johnny to protect her new career as a fashion designer, which she needed to gain independence from her despised rich husband (Mifune Toshirō). In the final scene, Kyōko jumps off a cliff in front of Munesue and his colleague, clutching the straw hat she had once given to Johnny.

Kadokawa advertised *Proof of the Man* even more heavily than *The Inugami Family*, prompting the magazine *Eiga Jihō* to name the approach the "Kadokawa assault strategy."[35] An independent advertising agency designed the campaign materials to create a stylish feel that would contrast with what the advertising sections of the major studios usually produced. Promotion began in March 1977 with the announcement of an open scriptwriting competition for the film, offering a prize of 5 million yen (about $18,870), an unusually high amount for a script at the time.[36] It was paired with an open audition for the role of Johnny Hayward, the winner of which was also to receive the unusually high sum of 1 million yen for the tiny role.[37] The release was set for October 1977, and the massive advertising campaign began with posters in June. In August, Kadokawa released the theme song, and from September onward targeted broadcasting. Spots featuring the oft-quoted catchphrases, "Should I watch the movie after reading the novel, or read the novel after I have seen the film?" as well as the cryptic, "Mother, what about my hat..." were broadcast 6,500 times on twenty television channels, and 4,000 times via radio.[38] Posters were hung in 21,500 train cars, in 50,000 public baths, and at train stations around the country. The most popular film magazine, *Kinema Junpō*, ran a series with set reports, capitalizing on the spectacle of a foreign location. With an unprecedented (for a film from Japan) investment of 400 million yen (about $1,509,400) for advertising alone, not counting the additional promotion through the hit album, by October supposedly 90 percent of all Japanese knew about *Proof of the Man*.[39] Shot with a budget of, according to Kadokawa, 650 million yen (or $2,452,830, while average production costs at the time were 205 million yen at Shōchiku and 319 million yen at Tōei), the film raked in a distribution gross of 2.25 billion yen ($8,490,600).[40]

The quite impressive total investment—ranging from 1.15 billion yen to 1.37 billion yen, depending on the source (at the time, about $4,339,600 and $5,169,800 respectively)—constituted around 10 percent of Kadokawa Publishing's total turnover in 1977. This was possible only because the once midrange company had expanded its earnings considerably. In the first five years after Kadokawa Haruki took charge of the company, the sales volume tripled, and by 1978 Kadokawa Publishing was ranked ninth of Japanese publishing companies in terms of sales.[41] Despite a troubled book market in which 43.9 percent of books were returned unsold to the publishing companies in

1977, Kadokawa Publishing had actually increased sales.[42] Before the film version of *Proof of the Man*, Morimura Seiichi usually sold around 200,000 units per book. Now, and especially after the next Kadokawa Film, based on his book *Proof of the Wild*, he was selling 1.5 million, prompting his statement, "Kadokawa-san temporarily provided me with 1.3 million additional readers."[43]

The Kadokawa Space-Time Continuum

With *Proof of the Man*, Kadokawa presented a new conception of film to the audiences, critics, and film industry of Japan. It transformed the relationship between industrial structures and practices, and film and media texts, as well as the audience and its consumption practices. Media-mix practice—in which each product advertises another product and the locus of desire begins to shift away from the object and toward a brand or image—had achieved an initial level of popularity with Astro Boy (Tetsuwan Atomu).[44] Kadokawa now employed media-mix strategies deliberately and on a massive scale, but Kadokawa Film also did something else. While, like Pink Film, it was a constellation of discourses with an extensive textuality that included industrial structure and practices, Kadokawa Film marketed its business practices as part of the product. A turn toward a self-referential commodity thus decentered the filmic text and narrative in particular. This was a near-Copernican turn, and it did not sit well with some of the powers-at-large in cinema. Despite the success, or partially because of it, established film criticism virtually loathed *Proof of the Man*. Even more than *The Inugami Family*, it was singled out at as a prime example of the *imēji-ka* (becoming-image) of film that Kadokawa was seen to be implementing. By imēji-ka, these critics were referring not to an increased reliance on visual representation or pictorial appeal, but to what they saw as a shift to surface spectacle away from narrative substance and politics. The idea of the new dominance of the image also indicates the sense of a new temporality: not the guided linearity of narrative, but an instantaneous presence. For critics, Kyōko's fashion show, a full five minutes, was seen as emblematic of the preponderance of superficial spectacle in Kadokawa films.[45] The advertising strategy was called a fraud, as critics claimed that it raised expectations that the films did not fulfill, and was often blamed for Japanese audiences' abandonment of domestic films in ever-greater numbers.[46] Years later on television, the powerful critic Shirai Yoshio would call Kadokawa a "cancer that has eaten away at Japanese film for years."[47]

There is a definite difference between a film's popularity at the box office and its film-historical significance. Yet the fact that a film attracts a large audience does raise the useful question of why. The common claim that Kadokawa films were the root of audience disenchantment is difficult to support. While *Proof of the Man* rated fiftieth on the *Kinema Junpō* critics' poll, it still ranked eighth in the readers' poll, indicating that the audience did not seem to be as disappointed as critics were purporting. Even in the 1990s, many critics' evaluations of Kadokawa Film would claim that it was detrimental to film from Japan because it consistently tricked audiences into the theaters with ad campaigns and then left them perennially disappointed. In fact, however, Kadokawa films continually scored high in annual audience polls, though only occasionally in critics' polls.[48] Indeed, Kadokawa unquestionably succeeded in attracting a young demographic. One poll claims the average viewer of *Proof of the Man* to be 22.6 years of age, with 72 percent of the audience in the sixteen-to-twenty-four age bracket, and a high proportion of female viewers, exactly the audience segment that was supposedly moving to foreign films at the time.[49] Film critics' disdain for Kadokawa almost certainly had less to do with the specific filmic texts themselves than the becoming-image these critics were targeting—and the larger discourses and politics they associated with this process. It must also be noted that while there was an obvious strain of antagonism toward Kadokawa within the film criticism establishment, especially in the first few years, this seems to be overemphasized in later reflections on Kadokawa Film. There were quite a few favorable reviews of most Kadokawa films, but the image of Kadokawa as a despised outsider figure has persisted to this day, a partial success of Kadokawa Film's marketing of Haruki's own persona.

Emphasizing the link between the brand and its embodiment, Kadokawa Haruki made guest appearances in almost all Kadokawa films into the early 1980s. By equating the person with the genre, Kadokawa negotiated a new relationship between the public and the personal, fusing the two and shifting it to imēji, or image.[50] Kadokawa Haruki himself became part of the circulating commodity of the imēji, on par with the filmic product. As scriptwriter Maruyama Shōichi later emphasized, "Speaking of stars, the biggest star was Kadokawa-san [himself]," and Shirai Yoshio stated, "In Kadokawa films, you can't see the face of the director or the actors. To say more, you can't even see the film. All you can see is Kadokawa Haruki's image."[51]

The association of persona and genre also played out as a family drama. For the ad campaign of *Proof of the Man*, Kadokawa appeared on a TV show and made a phone call to his mother, Suzuki Tomiko, from whom he had been estranged for twenty-eight years. Playing on the motherhood theme in the film, the phone call ended with the two of them in tears, arranging a future meeting while the theme music from *Proof of the Man* played in the studio.[52] But it was not only the mother narrative that Kadokawa used for promotion and branding. In countless interviews he spoke about his relationship and opposition to his father, Gen'yoshi. As the venerable founder of Kadokawa Shoten and part of the intellectual literary establishment, Gen'yoshi was representative of the old Japan—albeit a very postwar conception of it—against which Haruki was contrasting himself. He used this relationship again and again to dramatize his emphasis on entertainment and capitalist rationality in his role as an antiauthoritarian rebel. "Be it a boring film or an interesting film, a film that makes money is a good film," is one of his more famous statements, and when he described Kadokawa films as being the antithesis to the belief that film must be art, he used the story of his father to figure his relationship with the film industry.[53]

Kadokawa was drawing on long-established discourses. He pitted his liberalized, capitalist idea of open competition and transparent business models against the feudal business practices based on a village mentality and supposedly characterized by an insular group mentality. Kadokawa was probably the first company in Japan's film industry to regularly use written work contracts, which even in the 1970s were still unusual in an industry that largely functioned on the basis of personal relations and oral agreements. It was, much like the court action against producer Ichikawa after *The Inugami Family*, a conscious and public endorsement of a socioeconomic model that deliberately dissociated itself from the past. Kadokawa Film was implicitly drawing on a discourse described by Marx but also mentioned by Maruyama Masao, who posited "every kind of rationalization and abstraction as adverse to group-oriented practices and customs," when explaining the failure of bureaucratic institutions vis-à-vis Japanese villages in the nineteenth century.[54] Going back also to Maruyama's decrying of the "fleshiness" of feudal structures that had played into the discourse on Pink Film, a vision of antiflesh rationality and a departure from the fleshiness of history suffused Kadokawa Film and attracted the young audience it was trying to reach. Statements such as, "I don't care about culture. Hugh Hefner and the Beatles were doing business first, and became culture later," were provocations against a post-1945 Japan that Haruki's father embodied.[55]

The latent rejection of history in favor of capitalist presentism was exactly the theme that a powerful critic, Ōguro Toyoshi, picked up on when he discounted *Proof of the Man* for its shoddy script, bad directing (citing the famous, extended fashion show scene), and neglect of what he saw as the central point of the story: the exploration of postwar history. For him, Kadokawa Haruki was "nothing more than a manager-like planner," as opposed to an "able film producer." Ōguro also criticized several colleagues for letting Kadokawa use their statements in the advertising campaign. Among them was one of the few prominent female critics of the time, Minami Yoshiko, who defended herself in one of the next editions of *Kinema Junpō*. She stated that her blurb—"This is a human drama that carves out the sadness of love and guilt. The last scene's suggestive sadness will shake your soul"—was in fact referring not to Kyōko but to the American character of Shuftan, who for her stands at the center of the film. He, the likable New York cop who committed a terrible crime during the U.S. occupation of Japan, and now has a sad, faded picture of a Japanese woman in his room, is the character who most expresses a "humanlike weakness."

Tellingly, Minami justifies her statements to an (inevitably male) elder representative of the critical establishment by repositioning it as exploring the historical relations contained in one of the characters. She thereby distances Ōguro's criticism regarding the film's alleged ignorance of history from her own interpretation.[56] This exchange demonstrates how the issue of the right relation to history—the framework of history itself more than a specific history—and of film's role as a signboard of history and politics played a significant role in film discourse of the time, and regarding Kadokawa in particular. Significantly, this is exactly the moment when Hasumi Shigehiko's post-structuralism-influenced film criticism gains a significant following among young film fans increasingly unwilling to accept the primacy of politics over film. Hasumi moved away from the standard reading of film as a direct expression of ideology and instead focused on playful, aesthetically pleasing readings of film as film, indeed making terms such as *tawamure* (play, jest) central to his approach.

How, then, does Kadokawa Film and its discourse negotiate history? While Pink Film played with ideas of historical continuity and rupture, Kadokawa denied history itself. Pink Film had rejected the possibility of a clear separation of past and present, of a clean break between interwar Japan and postwar democracy. It put a spotlight on the painful, attractive, and above all irreversible confusion of victim and victimizer, and the tension of native self and foreign Other. Kadokawa Film, however, had no use even for ideas of rupture or the postwar; instead, it proposed a break of an almost abstract old (historical, Japan) with the new (simultaneous, global), exchanging history itself for an eternal present. Kadokawa worked hard to con-fuse Japan and the world within the horizon of the new, a space of simultaneity of geopolitical speeds, flattened through media. In other words, first Kadokawa Film drew on the classic association of the West with the future in terms of rationalist economy, affluence, commodity culture, and individualism. It then collapsed such colonial ideas of linking geography with different temporalities such as "advanced" and "behind" to position itself in the new, on a playing field with a flattened global hierarchy. For Kadokawa Film, Japan exists only as a residue and as part of a mediatized global now.

Journalist Matsushima Toshiyuki claims that Kadokawa's antiestablishment posture and anti-intellectualism were especially attractive to the student population in the post-student-movement years. Their unease with society at large had not dissipated, but politically formulated opposition was no longer a promising option. Instead, they bought an image of opposition for the price of a book, a movie ticket, or a record.[57] This accessible commodity also suggested a return to an apolitical, unified consumer-public that had been increasingly out of reach in the politically fragmented politics and media of the 1960s. In the case of Kadokawa, it was one that—for a moment—created an imagined global consumer-public. This reflected the dream of a completely level, middle-class Japan in which democracy and equality are achieved via an egalitarian consumer culture, one that the Seibu and Parco department store chains actively promoted and that has been called Seibu culture (Seibu bunka). As Ōtsuka Eiji has written of this image, featured in Seibu's late 1970s and early 1980s advertising campaigns and their slogan of a "delicious lifestyle" (oishii seikatsu), designed by advertising wunderkind Itoi Shigesato: "What Itoi calls delicious and is narrating to the consumers is a situation in which class has been vanquished and anyone can be affluent to an equal degree. At its root it is the leftist affirmation of the middle-class dream. It relates to the specific kind of social democratic nation that postwar Japanese society aimed for by thoroughly redistributing wealth."[58]

Thus Kadokawa, as the instigator of blockbusterism, was in many ways addressing a return to a concept of the public that was not based on fragmentation and subgroups.[59] As we have seen in the previous chapters, from the early 1960s on, film audiences in Japan were separating along lines of gender and, later, age. Kadokawa's concept of a unified audience harkened back to the 1950s, but in his vision it cohered through the media mix. In Kadokawa Film media became deeply interwoven, as Japan became interwoven with "the West." The appeal Kadokawa Film held for the audience lay not only in the intrinsic attraction of the foreign-connoted space of the yōga film theater, but the fact that a "Japanese" film/book/record was being thus contextualized.

Accordingly, the program booklet for *Proof of the Wild* (*Yasei no shōmei*, Satō Jun'ya, 1978, also based on a book by Morimura Seiichi) features whole sections written in English, despite being made exclusively for sale in Japanese theaters. The use of English to suggest a fashionable cosmopolitanism was well established, but Kadokawa's extraordinarily heavy use—for a film partially set in the United States—also suggested that a product from Japan was plugged into a global circuit (defined, typically, as an American circuit).[60] The visible temporal and spatial tension inherent in this strategy was Kadokawa's main asset in his quest for an audience of maximum breadth. Kadokawa Film denied a national identity discourse while simultaneously exploiting it. Similar to Pink Film, early Kadokawa Film, as industrial genre, tapped into a discourse on nation. First, textuality extends into industrial structure and practice. Accordingly, discourses such as Kadokawa's handling of the foreign and of a certain relation to history not only played out in the media texts themselves but were manifest in the way the films were made, marketed, distributed, and seen, just as much as they were attached to Kadokawa's persona. Second, Kadokawa Film coordinated a specific kind of confusion, though Kadokawa packaged this confusion in a much more strategic way than Pink Film had.

Blockbusting History

The first three Kadokawa blockbusters are primarily concerned with family and the destructive power of the past: *The Inugami Family* is a murder mystery about the cabals of a family divided over the distribution of an inheritance, leading to murder and madness that is linked to war.[61] *Proof of the Man* is the story of ambition, trauma, and familial destruction linked to the postwar era and (sexual) contact with the foreign. *Proof of the Wild* features a former soldier (Takakura Ken) who must come to terms with a traumatic event in his past to reconcile with his adopted daughter (Yakushimaru Hiroko). Maybe even more importantly, it featured a dramatic showdown with the Japanese Self-Defense Forces, shot on location in California.

In contrast, the fourth Kadokawa blockbuster, *Virus* (*Fukkatsu no hi*, Fukasaku Kinji, 1980), at the time the most expensive film ever produced in Japan, concerns itself purely with foreign relations, or rather the family of man; indeed, literally, it envisions a society made up almost exclusively of men. An international group in Antarctica, the sole survivors of a worldwide virus epidemic hatched in a Cold War laboratory, must work together to ensure the survival of the human race. Rather than dwelling on past trauma that

FIGURE 3.1. During the grand finale of *Proof of the Wild*, former yakuza film star Takakura Ken takes on the Japanese Self-Defense Forces single-handedly while carrying future idol star Yakushimaru Hiroko on his back. The tanks and grenade launchers were rented from the U.S. Army, and the scene was shot in California. The Japanese forces had declined to cooperate due to a script that portrayed them as authoritarian and corrupt. The narrative overtly falls into Kadokawa's antiestablishment discourse.

tied the previous films to history, *Virus* focuses on future trauma and struggle, moving out of the space of the national and avoiding its fixing into geopolitical time zones.

Kadokawa had continually increased blockbuster budgets in order to keep up with his own strategy of generating and selling attention, until *Virus* reached a budget estimated at 2.8 billion yen (with advertising).[62] The generally accepted distribution-gross yardstick for a big hit film was (and is) around 1 billion yen ($4,545,000 in 1980), which gives an idea of the risk Kadokawa was taking with a production of this magnitude. Kadokawa was obviously aware of this, and decided to go for an unusual (at least for substantial earnings) source of income for film in Japan at the time: foreign markets. *Virus* initially employed an American scriptwriter to ensure palatability for a foreign (i.e., American) audience, but the plan was abandoned after the first meeting between director Fukasaku Kinji, Kadokawa Haruki, and the scriptwriter in Los Angeles.[63] Although Kadokawa paid 20 million yen ($90,909) just for the first draft discussed in the meeting, it was eventually written by Takada

Kōji, with Gregory Knapp doing the English dialogue. The extensive foreign cast, including Glenn Ford, Olivia Hussey, and George Kennedy, was also meant to attract international distributors. Like *Proof of the Man*, *Virus* was reedited for the foreign market using an American editor. Though it amassed an unusual amount of international sales for a film from Japan, it failed to make a box-office impact in any of the markets. Even the (advance ticket–supported) success at the Japanese box office could not compensate for the enormous costs of an international cast, Antarctic location shooting, and the immense advertising campaign—although it probably broke even through Kadokawa's ancillary markets. While a box-office success in Japan, *Virus* was an expensive disappointment for Kadokawa due to its failure to take hold in foreign markets.

The demonstrative disregard for history itself became a selling point for the Kadokawa films, even as the narrative in isolation seems to appeal to history. The films present a collection of tropes that function more as narrative conventions, vehicles for the Kadokawa spectacle, than comments on specific politics of the past. In that sense, it is indeed exactly the becoming-image and discarding of history that leftist film critics feared. Kadokawa Film relied on 1970s literature that still had some interest in history for the source material (*gensaku*), yet neutralized its concerns via the media-mix spectacle of simultaneity. Kadokawa Film took a step toward dehierarchizing media platforms. Spreading the narratives of war-related trauma across media, it applied them as aesthetic tropes that were synchronized to the imagined global circulation of images. In *The Island Closest to Heaven* (*Tengoku ni ichiban chikai shima*, Ōbayashi Nobuhiko, 1984), Harada Tomoyo visits a Pacific island formerly occupied by the Japanese Imperial Army and befriends a boy whose mother was the daughter of a Japanese soldier, all against the backdrop of scenic landscapes and Obayashi's quirky directing style. In *Akuryo Island* (*Akuryō-tō*, Shinoda Masahiro, 1981) the story consists of a memory, triggered by an ex-hippie learning about the death of John Lennon on TV. In his youth he encountered a murder mystery involving a woman who had turned schizophrenic following her twin sister's death in the bombing of Hiroshima. In *Fossilized Wilderness* (*Kaseki no kōya*, Hasebe Yasuharu, 1982), the cop Nishina is entangled in a conspiracy to retrieve a treasure dropped in the mountains during the war. His long-dead father was involved in the plot, and everyone believes the location is locked in Nishina's subconscious, planted when he was an infant. In *At Some Point Somebody Will Be Killed* (*Itsuka dareka ga korosareru*, Sai Yōichi, 1983), the main character played by Watanabe Noriko gets caught up in the search for a computer disc that contains information on a spy ring. The chase is connected to the family history she begins to unravel: her father is half-Japanese, born in the former Japanese puppet state of Manchukuo, and is himself a spy. She eventually finds a safe haven with a group of fashionable illegal residents living a free lifestyle in Tokyo. *Kenya Boy* (*Shōnen Kenia*, Ōbayashi Nobuhiko, 1984) uses its license as an anime to become an exercise in exoticism bordering on revisionism. Wataru, a young Japanese boy, fights to stop the Nazis from developing an atomic bomb in Africa. He befriends the impressed natives along the way, who declare, "As was to be expected, the Japanese child is outstanding."[64]

Thus the tension between literary narratives deeply concerned with history and nation and a genre that claims it could not care less about it weighs heavy in many Kadokawa films.[65] As an industrial genre, Kadokawa Film valorized the new while relying on memory, and represented rebellion while packaging it within a system of commodification. Even more directly than Pink Film, Kadokawa was able to commodify confusion, in this case conceived as simultaneity. It is important to remember that these discourses were deliberately packaged commodities, and that the idea that Kadokawa's strategies were completely new was a product in itself. It is therefore important to take a closer look at these strategies and their specific histories.

Kadokawa Reconsidered

Kadokawa Haruki's reputation as a visionary if divisive genius and solitary pioneer within the film industry must be unpacked as much as Kadokawa Film's discourse of rebellion. At the very least this carefully crafted image must be seen as part of a strategy to produce economically exploitable discourses around the media-mixes the company produced. Kadokawa was indeed credited, or often enough derided, for implementing business principles that would soon become standard in the film industry. Eventually, Kadokawa Haruki would be made responsible for the dominance of the blockbuster mentality, developing the media-mix strategy, destroying the block-booking system, employing massive advertising campaigns, alienating the audience for films from Japan, creating the idol craze of the early 1980s, bringing non–film business money into film production via corporate tie-ups, the financing of films via advance ticket sales, and increased targeting of foreign markets.[66] However, many of these points are connected only to the Kadokawa blockbuster films, the production of which Kadokawa all but halted between 1980 and 1990. In the final analysis, the strategies Kadokawa Haruki was identified with creating were overwhelmingly not innovations he had introduced.

Yet the branding that Kadokawa employed was so strong that it was accepted wholesale and lastingly by the general public, journalists, and even the business world.

Most of the strategies Kadokawa employed were already in practice around the time he entered the film industry, though sometimes in scattered form. The business model of using moving-image media to market other products had a long history, although sweets manufacturer Meiji's sponsoring of Tezuka Osamu's *Astro Boy* (*Tetsuwan atomu*) anime television series in 1963 ushered in a new era.[67] The stickers involved in this sponsorship played a crucial role in the development of media-mix strategies, and in 1972 *Mazinger Z* (*Majingā Z*), based on a manga by Nagai Go, presented the next step. Countless products were marketed around the giant robots of this series, and its influence was immense. In terms of theatrical film, blockbusters and spectacle were certainly no invention of Kadokawa's, and had existed even when the studio system was still intact—Shintōhō's *Emperor Meiji* series is one example—although they were often harnessed by the block-booking system.[68] Even the increasing trend toward reliance on blockbusters in the 1970s had started before Kadokawa's entry into the film business. Tōhō churned out extravaganzas such as *Japan Sinks* (*Nihon chinbotsu*, Moritani Shirō, 1973, based on a book by Komatsu Sakyō, the author of *Virus*) or *The Human Revolution* (*Ningen kakumei*, Masuda Toshio, 1973). Tōei produced *Bullet Train* (*Shinkansen daibakuha*, 1975), helmed by Satō Junya, who later directed the two *Proof of* films for Kadokawa. Nomura Yoshitarō, who later directed *Village of Eight Gravestones*, shot *Castle of Sand* (*Suna no utsuwa*, 1974) for Shōchiku. According to Kadokawa himself, this film was one of the inspirations for the idea that a Japanese book could be made into a large-scale successful film.[69] Additionally, American films such as *Jaws* and *The Godfather* were immensely successful in Japan, as was the soundtrack to *The Godfather*. In terms of the convergence of different media on the business level, Tokuma Shoten, another publishing company, had picked up the production arm of the bankrupt Daiei in 1974. Through Daiei it produced the big-budget *Cross the Funme Bridge* (*Kimi yo funme no kawa o watare*, 1976). The film was directed by the omnipresent Satō Junya and based on a book by Nishimura Jukō, whose *Fossilized Wilderness* Kadokawa would later produce as a film in 1982.

Giving films from Japan a release in theaters specializing in foreign films was likewise a strategy the majors had been experimenting with for quite a while, at least since Teshigahara Hiroshi's *Woman in the Dunes* (*Suna no onna*, 1964), which Tōhō bought as an independent production and gave an initial yōga release before it was block-booked nationwide. The sale of advance tickets was closely connected to the practice of cofunding films with money from nonfilm business entities, usually involving corporations attempting to promote themselves or a certain project. This system, in which the corporate backers involved in production bought a certain number of tickets that they, in turn, forced on their employees and subcontractors, had been in sporadic practice for almost ten years. Blockbuster forerunner *Sun over the Kurobe Gorge* (*Kurobe no taiyō*, Imai Tadashi, 1968), cofinanced by Kansai Electric, is usually named as one of the first culprits.[70] The blockbuster–advance-ticket-sale connection would continue to grow with *Glowing Autumn* (*Moeru aki*, Kobayashi Masaki, 1978), the result of a cooperation between department store chain Mitsukoshi and Tōhō, or the record-breaking *Antarctica* (*Nankyoku monogatari*, Kurahara Koreyoshi, 1983). *Antarctica* was the result of a cooperation between Fuji Television and Gakken Publishing; reportedly, 3.5 million advance tickets were issued to hedge the financial risk. It subsequently held the record for the highest distribution gross for fourteen years.

It is often charged that in many of these cases, although the tickets were sold in advance, the audience did not actually attend the screenings, leading to the strange phenomenon of record-breaking films playing to empty seats. Whether such anecdotes are true or not, the advance-ticket system became essential to creating blockbuster successes, and when in 1996 Sano Shinichi checked the top five earners of all time, he found every single one to have relied heavily on advance ticket sales.[71] Why Kadokawa became so entirely identified with this system is, however, probably more a result of the antipathy that Kadokawa evoked than the company's actual activities. In fact, Kadokawa did not participate in the advance-ticket strategy until *Proof of the Wild* and *Virus*, and barely used it for years afterward. The company did return to it with a vengeance for the epic *Heaven and Earth* (*Ten to chi to*, Kadokawa Haruki, 1990), but it seems that it was simply once again the Kadokawa image that reinforced him as inventor and culprit in the critics' imagination.

For advertising as well, Kadokawa's role as a pioneer must be questioned. Bombastic advertising campaigns had been conducted for *Jaws* (Steven Spielberg, 1975) and *Star Wars* (George Lucas, 1977), and in 1976 even *The Omen* (Richard Donner), distributed by Fox, had an advertising budget of 210 million yen ($711,864), with more than half of the money spent on broadcasting, as compared to the usual 20 percent (Kadokawa would later do the same).[72]

If Kadokawa Film did not invent the strategies it presented as part of its unique identity, what it did indeed achieve was the self-reflexive packaging of a disparate group of business practices. These strategies were then performed for the purpose of marketing not only the films and other media, but the strategies themselves. It fused these practices—rationalized and casualized production and distribution structures, use of yōga theaters, media-mix strategies, an economy of scale, and so on—to sociopolitical and generational discourses that charged them with meaning and created a brand that was centered around a commodifiable character, in this case Kadokawa Haruki himself. What was new was the centrality of the brand.

Kadokawa's legacy is enormous. Years later Horiguchi Toshikazu of the Fuji Sankei media conglomerate, to which Fuji Television belongs, would proclaim, "We learned Kadokawa's way of doing things."[73] While Horiguchi is referring to the strategies of promotion and cross-media marketing and not the packaging of reflexivity, Kadokawa's success and self-promotion immediately provoked emulation, and the genre functioned as a kind of catalyst for the diffusion of a whole host of the above-named practices. The effect set in almost immediately. In 1977 Tōhō spent an advertising budget of 300 million yen (about $1,132,000) for *Mount Hakkodasan* (*Hakkodasan*, Moritani Shirō), and Shōchiku divided the exhibition of *Village of Eight Gravestones* up between Tokyū, Shōchiku, and Tōei. In 1978 a small flood of films from Japan were released via the yōga system, among them *The Glacier Fox* (*Kitakitsune monogatari*, Kurahara Koreyoshi), an animal film and an immense hit for Hello Kitty creator Sanrio, who at that point was also attempting to break into the film business.[74] In the second half of 1978, three of the top five Japanese earners were distributed via free booking: *Proof of the Wild*, *The Glacier Fox*, and *Farewell to Space Battleship Yamato: In the Name of Love* (*Saraba uchū senkan yamato: Ai no senshi-tachi*, Masuda Toshio, 1978).[75]

However, the success of Kadokawa's performative business strategies also created a variety of problems in the long run. This performance was based on an image of opposition as much as on a variety of tensions, such as those between media platforms and between Japan and the world. Once yōga releases of films from Japan became common, it was increasingly difficult to generate publicity or marketable drama via the screening space. In essence, Kadokawa created a stable brand that relied on tension between existing categories, marketing that tension as part of a unique brand. Once these strategies became commonplace, the brand became diffuse. Indeed, Kadokawa Film adjusted its strategy repeatedly to deal with this problem, but even today Kadokawa Film is associated with the blockbuster strategy it all but abandoned after *Virus*.

Rebooting Kadokawa

In 1979, during the production run-up to *Virus*, the Kadokawa Haruki Office produced two films that fell out of the blockbuster grid: *The Adventure of Kōsuke Kindaichi* (*Kindaichi Kōsuke no bōken*, Ōbayashi Nobuhiko, another film with the famous detective created by Yokomizo Seishi) and *The Resurrection of the Golden Wolf* (*Yomigaeru kinrō*, Murakawa Tōru), inevitably based on novels from the Kadokawa lineup.[76] *Adventure* and *Resurrection* were even shown as a double bill (albeit yōga-style) in the chihō, an obvious departure from the single-bill blockbuster strategy Kadokawa was by now infamous for. While Murakawa was an experienced director with roots at Nikkatsu, Ōbayashi was considered a young director (though he was over forty). A star of the 1960s 8 mm film scene and a prominent director of TV commercials, Ōbayashi had only started directing feature films two years earlier and was one of the first major directors to emerge without formal training within the studio system. While he had considerable experience in shooting commercials, his real roots lay in *jishu* (self-produced or "autonomous") film. Ōbayashi was an early example of one of the significant developments of the 1970s: young directors who began shooting film on 8 mm and then switched to the commercial film industry. With the rising popularity of jishu film, an informal national distribution network formed and the Pia Film Festival, specializing in jishu film, was founded in 1976. Young jishu directors such as Ishii Sōgo and Ōmori Kazuki got a chance to direct major studio productions, and a whole generation of film directors and producers emerged from the jishu film scene.[77] Ōbayashi had a reputation for inventive formal experimentation, and he supplied the Kindaichi material with an improvised, parodic, at times surreal speed and incoherence, even including a hectic roller skate race unthinkable in the Yokomizo books.

Kadokawa Haruki claims that at this point he decided to adjust the company's strategy with the new technology of satellite television in mind.[78] Anticipating the increased importance of the media-content business and the financial potential of multiple media platforms, he chose to parallel-produce a large number of smaller productions and fewer blockbusters whose exploitability would not age as fast.[79] While Kadokawa may really have been thinking of ancillary markets, it seems probable that his reference to satellite television is more an a posteriori affirmation of his status as a visionary. Satellite television was still in an experimental phase in Japan in 1979 and would not become commercially exploited until the early 1990s. Home video, then on the verge of exploding as a market, is a much more likely candidate for factoring into Kadokawa's decision. Other reasons may have been the large reservoir of books in the Kadokawa lineup, making it financially and logistically not viable to follow through on a blockbuster strategy with all of them, and the increasingly close ties to Tōei, a company still specializing in the program picture system. In any event, after the financially mixed results of *Virus*, Kadokawa tipped the scale in favor of smaller films that could be produced in greater number. Additionally, Kadokawa created mixed forms where double bills, typical for block booking, were distributed via free booking, yōga-style.[80]

A typical charge leveled against Kadokawa Haruki since the early 2000s is that he employed a stunted version of the media mix. While his brother Tsuguhiko would develop a media-mix model in the late 1980s that was based on variations of a narrative via fictional worlds and user involvement, Haruki simply transferred—so the claim goes—narratives from one media platform to another.[81] While the claim that a narrative can simply be transferred between media is itself problematic, it is also simply not correct—at least for the post-blockbuster phase. Kadokawa Film in fact heavily used the more low-budget releases to continue the thread of textual experimentation that had begun with *The Adventure of Kōsuke Kindaichi*. In contrast to the big-budget blockbusters, the smaller productions were increasingly allowed to veer away from the original novel, often leaving it barely recognizable apart from the title and the very basic elements of the setting. Maruyama Shōichi's scripts for *The Beast to Die* (Murakawa Tōru, 1980) and *Dirty Hero* (*Yogoreta eiyū*, Kadokawa Haruki, 1982) leave virtually only the main characters' names and the books' titles intact. For *W's Tragedy* (*W no higeki*, Sawai Shinichirō, 1984) scriptwriter Arai Haruhiko, formerly of Wakamatsu Productions, inserted a play-within-a-play setting that is nowhere to be found in the novel by Natsuki Shizuko. When Maruyama apologized for the reworking, Kadokawa replied, "I only want the title and your contemporary sensibility," which resulted in heavy criticism from novelist Ōyabu Haruhiko.[82] Thus, while the films nominally depended on the gensaku (original work), in reality they initiated a system that in fact encouraged variation and inconsistency.

In a media business that relied on the marketability of the product across media, narrative was pushed to the margins. Now, other factors needed to be able to function across media and texts. Along with discourses of opposition and global simultaneity, another was a specific type of character, which Kadokawa made the focus of the next and even more influential phase of the genre. The title song for *Sailor Suit and Machine Gun* (*Sēra fuku to kikanjū*, Sōmai Shinji, 1981) by lead actress Yakushimaru Hiroko was a massive hit, but the eponymous song title did not feature once in the song's lyrics, which in turn had nothing to do with the film's story. What held the film, the novel, and the soundtrack together was not the character in the narrative, but the character—or rather *kyara*—of Yakushimaru Hiroko. *Sailor Suit and Machine Gun* became part of a push for ever more fluidity of product, media text, and meaning, while retaining the basic tenet of Kadokawa as eternally different and new. The film became the epitome of Kadokawa's new approach.

FOUR

THE RADICALIZATION OF KADOKAWA FILM

Mobile police units moved in, and the stage greeting was canceled on police orders. On December 20, 1981, around one thousand people had attempted to rush the three theaters of the Umeda Tōei in Osaka, where *Sailor Suit and Machine Gun* was set to screen with idol and main actress Yakushimaru Hiroko in attendance. This exceeded the theaters' capacity several times, and a panic ensued as the crowd outside blocked the street and continued to push toward the entrance. Two years later, at a promotional event for *Legend of the Eight Samurai* (*Satomi hakkenden*, Fukasaku Kinji, 1983) at the Tokyo horse-racing track, a reported 27,000 people showed up to see a stage greeting by Yakushimaru Hiroko and the rest of the cast. Public hysteria on this scale was rare in an environment of proliferating idols, and even the Osaka incident, of course, made for great advertising.[1]

In 1981 Kadokawa turned its production lineup around by shifting production to make a greater quantity of smaller films, as the Osaka incident and others show, again to tremendous commercial success. Kadokawa now decided to tie the media mix together with a new strategy and without resorting to the spectacle of scale that blockbuster budgets provided. This strategy would have significant implications for the future of film and media in Japan. The specific kind of star commodity that Kadokawa created for the media mix to revolve around was initially a spectacular success and became the herald of a new media economy. It was also ultimately impossible to sustain. It provided the foil on which and against which the massive media industry of Japan models its strategies even today. Its eventual failure had momentous consequences for the discourses of a global Japan, a synchronized geopolitical time, and an immediating media ecology that Kadokawa had attached to it.

The number of films the Kadokawa Haruki Office produced rose from three in 1980 to six in 1981, and continued to rise annually to nine films in 1984. Despite the increase in films, the respective films, books, records, television series, and especially magazines were still marketed via the media-mix strategy, extensive ad campaigns, and publicity stunts. In these productions, which still had considerable budgets, Kadokawa experimented with a host of young and less experienced but formally adventurous directors throughout the early 1980s. Almost without exception, these are some of the most recognized directors working today, with Kadokawa Film sharing Pink Film's role as a training ground for young talent, albeit on a more mainstream level: Sai Yōichi shot four films for Kadokawa, Ōbayashi Nobuhiko six, and Sawai Shinichirō three. Kadokawa also recruited heavily from the only place where young directors with a modicum of experience were still to be found: Pink Film and especially Nikkatsu Roman Porno. From the latter, Sōmai Shinji was known to European and American audiences for the film-festival success *Taifun Club* (*Taifū kurabu*, 1984), and Morita Yoshimitsu was known for *Family Game* (*Kazoku gēmu*, 1983); directors Negishi Kichitarō, Izutsu Kazuyuki, and scriptwriters Arai Haruhiko and Tanaka Yōzō were also recruited.[2]

Several issues led to Kadokawa's turn away from the blockbuster spectacle: it was financially risky; this model of production had lost its exclusive attachment to the Kadokawa brand; and the narratives were too unwieldy to carry flexible commodification across media on their own. The media-mix environment demanded commodities that could be exploited across media and that could extend beyond the narrative. The solution was recourse to a phenomenon that was by now widely extinct: The "becoming flesh" of a story that Abe Casio had spoken of, the star—though an entirely different one than the kind known from the major studio's films, imbued with a different temporality and a new flexibility of meaning.

The Unfixed Idol

Yakushimaru Hiroko, along with Harada Tomoyo and Watanabe Noriko, was the centerpiece of the *Kadokawa san-nin musume* (three Kadokawa girls), who attained a feverish level of popularity in the early 1980s.[3] Yakushimaru first gained prominence in her role as Takakura Ken's daughter in *Proof of the Wild* in 1978—or rather she did by winning the national audition Kadokawa had used to promote the film. At fourteen, she received an exclusive contract with the Kadokawa Haruki Office and became the first of the idol stars that Kadokawa marketed.[4] In the first half of the 1980s they acted, sang, modeled, appeared in advertisements, wrote essays, and did many other things, fulfilling the multipurpose job description of what in Japan is called an *aidoru*, or idol.

Idols are a central development in Japanese media culture and are basically stars nonspecific to any medium or function. At various times they may sing, play in television series and movies, and appear on talk shows and in photo collections, but are characterized less for a specific talent than a certain atmosphere. An aidoru is therefore not regarded the same as a dedicated singer or an actor, who is specialized and expected to perform at a much higher level of professionalization, even if the idol sporadically releases a song or a movie. By the late 1960s, the film industry gradually lost its ability to create its own popular stars and began to use popular singers who crossed over into film. While there are multiple precedents, Misora Hibari being the most prominent, one of the foremost examples of deliberately creating a multiple media existence was the female pop duo Za Pīnattsu (the Peanuts), who appeared in the *kaijū* (monster) film *Mothra* (*Mosura*, Honda Ishirō, 1961). *Mothra*, a story about a giant moth, was produced by Tōhō, while Za Pīnattsu were managed by talent agency Watanabe Productions. Both companies would play a decisive role in the development of the cross-media phenomenon called aidoru.

Cooperative deals for aidoru increased heavily throughout the 1960s, with TV taking an increasingly central role. The true power brokers were now the various talent agencies, such as Watanabe Productions, Hori Productions, and Johnny's (an all-male idol agency that became influential in the early 1980s), which became powerful enough to exert considerable influence on the production lineup of the majors.[5] Watanabe Productions' near monopoly on the idol business was broken in the 1970s by the popular Nihon Terebi show *Sutā tanjō!* (A star is born!), which spawned several of the biggest idols of the decade, among them the most famous aidoru of the 1970s, Yamaguchi Momoe. While 1960s idol films had consisted mostly of Tōhō and Nikkatsu *seishun* (youth) films, the 1970s saw a renewed boom of the strategy, this time with Shōchiku and Tōhō at the forefront. Film versions of popular television series proliferated at Tōhō, while Shōchiku integrated idols into the program picture format, with directors like Yamane Shigeyuki specializing exclusively on the subgenre. Idol films quickly gained the reputation of providing a degree of space for auteurist work. Similar to Pink Film, as long as certain conditions set by the talent agency were met (nudity was not tolerated, for example), they often guaranteed a fair amount of creative freedom, as Kadokawa films had in the 1980s. In 1985, the film magazine *Image Forum*, known more for its devotion to experimental and independent film, ran an article titled "Screen Girl: Idol Films Are the Impulse-Providing Line of Films Rushing Along at the Very Forefront of Japanese Film."[6]

Film stars in the studio-system sense of the word had all but disappeared by the time Kadokawa entered production, and the former majors were in no position to create new ones. By the 1970s, the direction of the current was unmistakable. Talent agencies were making stars through television and the music industry, and film was simply another, if important, channel. Aidoru were now the glue that held together a media-mix strategy that was orchestrated by increasingly powerful talent agencies. Given that, it is not difficult to see why Kadokawa was attracted to the idea of marketing his own brand of idols, but to do it in an even more radical and flexible way.

Yakushimaru Hiroko became Kadokawa's first and extremely successful attempt to create an idol star on its own terms. The basis of Kadokawa's strategy was to ensure radical mobility for the idol image. He restricted Yakushimaru's exposure mostly to the media the company itself controlled. In stark contrast to the well-established TV-centric aidoru infrastructure of the time, Kadokawa idols barely appeared on television shows and were instead marketed via Kadokawa films, records, photo books, posters, essay books, and the newly founded Kadokawa magazine, *Variety* (as well as the Kadokawa magazines *Comptiq* and *Za Terebi*, which were under the management of Haruki's brother, Tsuguhiko). Idols were ideal for Kadokawa's marketing strategy as they were decoupled from a specific medium but could still function as a recognizable commodity. Many of the Kadokawa aidoru films were broadcast as television series following their film versions, further exploiting the success and often starring the next idol in line to be launched.[7]

Manga theorist Itō Gō has proposed a division between two types of entities in manga that is useful in thinking about the Kadokawa idols as well. According to Itō, manga and image culture in Japan employ characters that are tightly bound to a specific narrative. Much like Bilbo Baggins from *The Hobbit*, they do not exist outside of that narrative. On the other hand, what Itō terms *kyara* are easily detached from a specific narrative and much more flexible. Hello Kitty, for example, has only the most bare-bones backstory and can flexibly be attached to any kind of product, from cars to drills to makeup. In terms of this binary, the Kadokawa idols skewed much closer to a *kyara* than a character. In contrast to Kadokawa's marketing of the Kadokawa musume, more conventional idols had long been characterized by a high degree of mediatized quotidianity due to their frequent appearances on TV and as part of a deliberate strategy. Series such as *Sutā Tanjō!* functioned like casting shows that broke through the shield of a professional performance. Relatability embedded in a framework of *kawaii* (cuteness) was central to the idol concept, and the first idol film boom of the 1960s prominently featured private scenes of housework and schoolwork, for example in *Let's Meet in a Dream* (*Yume de aimashō*, Saeki Kōzō, 1962), featuring the Peanuts.[8]

The Kadokawa aidoru, on the other hand, were kept deliberately distant. Following Kadokawa's strategy of "becoming image," they were closer to icons than tangible humans, and it proved an immensely successful formula. *Sailor Suit and Machine Gun* became the fourth most successful film from Japan at the time, grossing nearly as much as *Virus* for a fraction of the production cost, and in 1982 a TV-series version was broadcast starring Harada Tomoyo, which also prepared the public for the next Kadokawa idol.[9] On the surface, the over-the-top story is the coming-of-age tale of Izumi, a young girl who suddenly becomes the head of a small yakuza group and must learn to steer it through a dangerous international drug conspiracy orchestrated by a mad villain, all while coming to terms with death, love, and responsibility. Director Sōmai's trademark long and winding takes install Yakushimaru as a perpetually moving kinetic spectacle. She is also constantly in flux between different roles. As Izumi mentions in the film, to her father she was "mother, wife, and daughter," and throughout the film she is schoolgirl and yakuza boss, prepubescent girl and young-adult woman. In the final scene of the film, she strolls around as a schoolgirl, imitates office ladies on a break, pretends to smoke on a street corner, and shoots imaginary guns with children while standing on an air duct that blows up her skirt, quoting Marilyn Monroe in *The Seven Year Itch* (Billy Wilder, 1955). She is in constant imitative play, unbound by history or a fixed sequence, a character that must have been very attractive to a consumer audience for whom the reorientation of identity was now presented to be as easy as a shopping tour. Izumi's free-floating radicalism harmonizes exceptionally well with Kadokawa Film and the various discourses it participated in.

Apart from restrictions on television exposure, Yakushimaru and Harada were only allowed three external advertising contracts at a time to keep them exclusive and to distinguish them from their competition.[10] They were additionally spectacularized by being in films that veered from the cultural and formal verisimilitude that Kadokawa had aimed for with his blockbusters. Thematically and formally, Kadokawa films became increasingly fantastic and sometimes almost experimental in the 1980s, harmonizing well with Kadokawa's specific inflection of the idol strategy. Yakushimaru fought aliens plotting to take over a school in *School in the Crosshairs* (*Nerawareta gakuen*, Ōbayashi Nobuhiko, 1981), inherited the position of a yakuza gang leader in *Sailor Suit and Machine Gun*, and was a princess on the run from an evil sorceress in *Legend of the Eight Samurai* (*Satomi hakkenden*, Fukasaku Kinji, 1983). Harada had her feature-film debut in the immensely successful time-travel mystery *The Little Girl Who Conquered Time* (*Toki o kakeru shōjo*, Ōbayashi Nobuhiko, 1982), and played an adopted girl searching for her mysterious past while aiming to become a musical dancer in *Love Story* (*Aijō monogatari*, Kadokawa Haruki, 1984). As Kadokawa's most successful films in the 1980s, they renegotiated how to capture the public through a specific constellation of gender politics, realism, and spectacle.[11]

Mediatizing the Human

In his article "Monsters/Godzilla and Actresses," prominent leftist theorist and activist Suga Hidemi likens megastar Yakushimaru Hiroko to the Buddha, but also to E.T. for being a "small, fat, ugly ... alien" with a strange walk, all of which contributes to her "undisputable mythical power," something he finds reflected in her roles as a total outsider in *Sailor Suit and Machine Gun* and *School in the Crosshairs*.[12] Considering the mediated spectacle presented by idols, Suga focuses specifically on the Kadokawa musume. Suga finds the move away from humanity toward a media presence that has elements of alien otherness as much as religious devotion both captivating and disturbing. Charting Yakushimaru's change across her filmography, he posits her as a symbol and a part of the nuclear age, describing what he sees as the idol's mutation from a lizard to a weakened, compromised Godzilla—a discombobulated pseudo-maturation—as indicative of the effects of the Cold War system.

On the other hand, Suga claims that directors such as Negishi Kichitarō of *Detective Story* and Morita Yoshimitsu of *Main Theme* (*Mēnu tēma*, 1984) tried to give Yakushimaru the more orthodox role of a thin, cute character, with Morita taking special pains to correct Yakushimaru's walking style, thereby "destroying her mythic quality" and leading to the films' failure.[13] Harada, on the other hand, is defined as "playing a spectacle of masks," with no "persona" of her own. She is "supernaturally gifted" in that such "undistinguishedness ... possesses a thousand faces."[14] Indeed, in films such as *Sailor Suit and Machine Gun*, *The Terrible Couple* (*Tonda kappuru*, Sōmai Shinji, 1980), and *Detective Story*, Yakushimaru is otherworldly as a restlessly performative spectacle, constantly engaged in summersaults, climbing, crawling, and rolling around. Harada, on the other hand, was deliberately marketed as a versatile, ultimately unknowable shape-shifter, with Kadokawa habitually remarking in interviews that he was "looking forward to seeing how she will change next."[15] Suga's contextualization of Yakushimaru's transformations as mutation, not maturation, in the nuclear age points to the way that an ontological shift in mediated imagery of the human was both spectacularly attractive and deeply unsettling. It is not surprising that Suga pinpoints directors such as Morita and Negishi as (unsuccessfully) attempting to counteract the media spectacle of Yakushimaru Hiroko by pushing the character closer to a human presence, defined by stages of maturation. These are directors who were trained in Nikkatsu Roman Porno and indebted to Pink Film and its commitment to fleshy humanist and historicist realism.

Whether one follows Suga's explication of the monstrousness of the Kadokawa idols (and its misogynist undertone) and his unease with the mediatization of the human or not, Kadokawa's idol strategy can be seen as a systematic erasure of reference points. Kadokawa not only placed both Yakushimaru and Harada outside of the usual idol infrastructure and conventional aidoru mold, he also positioned them on the outer limb of distinct gender models, preferring a near-degendered design outfitted with an alien aura. In the meantime, the prepubescent though not necessarily boyish girl idol has become an archetype of Japanese pop culture, though the Kadokawa aidoru are quite different from later incarnations.

Kadokawa claimed that he always avoided fulfilling the needs of the audience, preferring to create "unnecessary needs" and thereby monopolize them.[16] This continues the emphasis Kadokawa placed on creating an eternal present rather than being subject to history. As part of this, Yakushimaru and Harada were devised as distinct but highly artificial phenomena ostensibly placed outside of history, and thereby eminently flexible and exploitable products. Supposedly unbound by sequence or media specificity, they become constantly re-forming constants that enabled simultaneity of media and nations. While the films continued to be distributed to yōga spaces, the aidoru detached themselves from the spatial fixing of the foreign and moved toward the more complete otherness of the alien. When the diminutive Yakushimaru, dressed in a schoolgirl's sailor suit and with her yakuza gang behind her, confronts the aged enemy gang leader and defiantly tells him off before firing a round with her machine gun while mouthing the word *kaikan* (pleasure), she is a fantastically radical outsider of conceivable societal and temporal order, loaded with ironic references to Japanese popular culture.

Here, once again, the entire textuality of the industrial genre was involved. The aidoru and the films participate in the same discourses as the business strategy and its personalization, Kadokawa Haruki. Kadokawa again and again speaks of his fascination for, personal experiences with, and connections to aliens in official interviews and his autobiography. This can be taken both as a performance of eccentricity and as an expression of the drive for an atemporal, open space, populated by aliens not bound to geopolitics or history.[17] Like Yakushimaru the alien and Harada the shape-shifter, Kadokawa Film—and by extension Kadokawa Haruki—marketed itself as the site of total simultaneity and presence, placed outside of history, unbound by space or other liminalities, a singular brand that can contain a confused mix of temporalities and identities within itself.

Youth was central to Kadokawa Film's idol construction for several reasons. For one, the youth demographic was becoming increasingly central to the entertainment industry, a fact that Kadokawa and most everyone else was very aware of. This had changed the aidoru as well, whose job description called for increasingly young performers so they could appeal to their own age group; teenage idol Minami Saori's hit *17 Sai* (*Seventeen*) in 1971 was an early herald of this. At this historical moment, age held a specific sociopolitical significance. Anyone seventeen years of age in 1971 was born in 1954 and had experienced neither the war itself nor the poverty and shock of occupation that followed. They were children raised within the economic boom years of the 1960s and full-fledged residents of a time when, as Igarashi Yoshikuni has phrased it, "memories were quickly disappearing."[18] Youth, especially prepubescent youth, provided a blank slate. It was presentable as not institutionalized, not subject to history, but rather rich with the potential for future transformation. Ostensibly removed from discourses of rupture versus continuity, the young generation became representative of the concept of rupture itself. The Kadokawa idols enhanced the surprise potential and served the increasingly nonhistorical sensibilities of the audience with their mutability and unmarkedness. The question of continuity and rupture and the confusion of reorientation that had been so decisive for Pink Film until the early 1970s dissolved into an eternal ever-changing present in these films. The theme of youth also carried a strong antinarrative connotation. In the mid-1970s, a powerful discourse emerged and claimed a rising resistance against becoming adult, encapsulated in the term "moratorium generation" (*moratoriamu sedai*). This discourse has carried over to discussions of *otaku*, where it has been connected with the fate of narrative in contemporary popular culture in Japan. Ōtsuka Eiji has proposed an intensification in the 1990s that he sees embodied in the character of Ikari Shinji of the anime *Neon Genesis Evangelion* (*Shinseiki evangerion*, Anno Hideaki, 1995). As Shinji rejects going to battle for humanity and taking on adult responsibility, he stands for a rejection of the bildungsroman structure of previous anime based on ideas of personal growth, development, and, ultimately, history.[19]

At the same time, aidoru served Kadokawa in his economic goal to create a universal and completely mobile transmedia vessel. Youth contributed to creating an aidoru that was a largely undesignated cipher, helped make it a commodity for male and female audiences, and gave it as broad an appeal as possible. Watanabe Noriko, the third of the Kadokawa musume, was already nineteen when she first starred in a Kadokawa Film and never achieved the degree of popularity to rival the other two, who began their Kadokawa careers at a much younger age (contemporary comments often explained this with the fact that she fit more conventional contemporary standards of femininity and attractiveness). But neither Yakushimaru nor Harada could occupy nonplace or nontime indefinitely. As they visibly aged, they inevitably exited the semantic vacuum of youth and could no longer fulfill the role of unmarked entities. Yakushimaru's transition "from idol to actress" was discussed in countless articles, usually with mixed reviews.[20] Even the films themselves acknowledged this development, mostly via the theme of sexual maturation. As her characters eventually experienced first kisses (*Detective Story*, 1983), aimed to lose their virginity (*Main Theme*, 1984), and engaged in sex (*W's Tragedy*, 1984), Yakushimaru the aidoru was less and less a free-floating extraterrestrial radical than a narrativizable young woman, and her popularity declined rapidly.

Main Theme, the story of a young woman and her relationship to a magician, and *W's Tragedy*, the story of a young and ambitious actress caught up in a murder case, were Yakushimaru's last two films for Kadokawa. In 1984, her exclusive contract with the Kadokawa Haruki Office was discontinued.[21] Likewise, Harada's box-office results continued to sink from her immensely successful screen debut onward, and in 1986 she only played a bit part in *Cabaret* (*Kyabarē*, Kadokawa Haruki), about a young musician looking for authentic jazz. *Woman in a Black Dress* (*Kuroi doresu no onna*, Sai Yōichi, 1987), about a young woman on the run, cast her deliberately against her aidoru persona as a woman with a past; it was a financial failure.[22] The final scene of *Woman in a Black Dress* has Harada walking down the side of the road recounting the four seasons in an endless cycle. Where she was once the time-traveling girl who could escape sequential temporality, she was now entangled in the narrative of biological and social life. Her contract was not renewed either.[23]

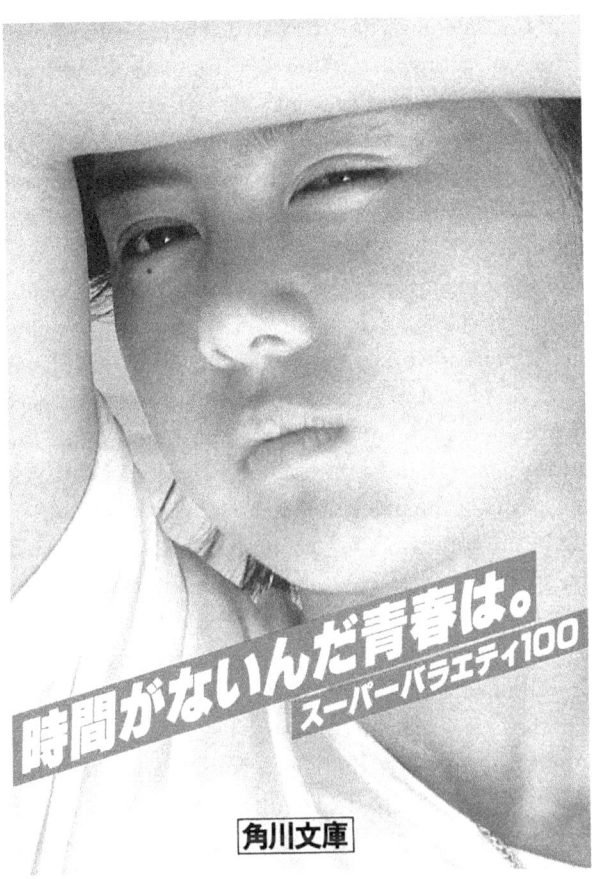

FIGURE 4.1. "Youth has no time." Temporal politics in a promotional image of Yakushimaru Hiroko for the Kadokawa magazine *Variety*. The absence of time was a common theme in Kadokawa's marketing of idols.

Kadokawa's strategy of marketing the controlled indeterminacy of the aidoru had much to do with his distaste for conventional realism. When he states that he wants to "challenge" film criticism's idea that realism is "a 4½ *tatami* room, a teenage boy that likes motorbikes, and national railway tracks," he is echoing Kobayashi Masaru's disdain for the ero-real in Pink Film.[24] Kadokawa was not alone of course in creating fantastic filmic spaces of controlled indeterminacy. In the early 1980s, detachment from the fleshy constraints of realism and history was clearly an idea whose time had come. In the aestheticist and stunning *The Beast to Die* (Murakawa Tōru, 1980), a genius but disturbed outsider figure goes on a crime spree. After convincing his partner to kill his first victim, he gives a dramatic speech telling him how beautiful he is now after becoming "the beast that rejects history." Time-slip films played to the softening up of linear or sequential time and were generally highly popular in the 1980s, and Kadokawa led the way with *The Little Girl*

Who Conquered Time and *G.I. Samurai*. The latter film was possibly the first to use pop music in a period-film setting, as it followed a group of soldiers from the Japanese Self-Defense Forces thrown back into the sixteenth century in an unexplained freak accident. As we have seen, even some Pink films of the early 1980s echoed the general trend of dissolving temporal order (for example, the parallel-world drama of *Bizarre Experience: Wet Dream* [*Ryōki taiken: Musei*], Watanabe Tsutomu, 1985).

Kadokawa began publishing manga and boarded the anime trend with *Harmageddon: The Great Battle with Genma* (*Genma taisen*, Rintarō, 1983). Anime and manga had, by the late 1970s, worked themselves out of the children's market up the age ladder, and the colorful characters with blurred borders of gender and nationality provided a semantically blank canvas, much like the Kadokawa idols did. Indeed, manga and anime would become the basis for a considerably different model of the media mix that Haruki's brother, Tsuguhiko, was developing in the company's magazine section and that would later lead to a rift within the company. Here we begin to see the intricate connection between economic expansion across national borders and the drive for a new relationship to history. Fleshy history was a burden, and a blank canvas promised freedom. Anime and manga in particular became one of the main export successes of the Japanese media industry.

It is difficult to pinpoint a single motivating source for this *ars oblivionalis*. Variably, it must have seemed attractive to the young audience demographic to disassociate itself from a fading and problematic past, both in terms of the failure of empire and the failure of the student movement. It was also practical to renegotiate it for a government interested in renewed (now economic) international expansionism. Kadokawa's turn away from history entailed a renegotiation of the relationship with the foreign, and this expressed itself, once again, on the level of filmic texts as much as on the level of business strategy. In Japan, a general renegotiation of history and identity was very much at hand. *Kokusai-ka* (internationalization) was a national buzzword long before prime minister Nakasone Yasuhiro announced his vision for an "international nation Japan" (*kokusai kokka nihon*) to the Japanese parliament in 1984. At the same time, the newly intensified national discourse on history and identity manifested itself in the *nihonjinron* (theories about the Japanese) boom in books and other media. Essentially, the reevaluation of the status of history, either via exceptionalist identity discourses (nihonjinron) or the creation of blank-slate characters outside of history (aidoru), entailed a strong ahistorical thrust that proved to be very commodifiable. Accordingly, the 1980s saw changes in the extratextual and textual approach to the topic of the foreign, which, as represented by the United States and Europe, had placed Japan in the colonial temporal logic of the always-slightly-behind. Kadokawa films carry obvious traces of this binary, even if they began to deny any such heterochronic tension by the early 1980s. The films that Kadokawa Haruki decided to direct himself give an idea of the complex relations he was maneuvering in his attempt to stay outside of the temporal order while exploiting the tension it had initially possessed. Kadokawa's turn away from history entailed a renegotiation of the relationship with the foreign, and this expressed itself, once again, on the level of filmic texts as much as on the level of business strategy.

Kadokawa's Foreign Affairs

At a preview of rushes of the film *Dirty Hero* (*Yogoreta eiyū*, 1982) organized for the press, Kadokawa famously proclaimed that he would commit hara-kiri if the film did not make over 1.2 billion yen in distribution income (fortunately, it did).[25] This was Kadokawa's first venture into film directing, a development he described as an accident due to the fact that he could find no suitable director in time for shooting.[26] It can also be seen as part of the trajectory to intensify the personalization of Kadokawa Film, to solidify the genre's perceived homogeneity in terms of industry, media text, and discourse. It also made obvious that Kadokawa Shoten was increasingly staking itself on film, which was by now becoming more than simply a means to sell more books. This was not quite as hazardous as it may have seemed at the time. Despite the fact that in 1981 the film industry was a shadow of its former self, Japan still possessed a vigorous film infrastructure. The film industry in Japan at this point was still second only to India in the number of feature films it produced; and with about 55 percent of the box-office income stemming from indigenous productions, Japan was topped only by the (anomalous) United States and India in that regard. Thanks to the world's highest ticket prices and the lowest box-office taxation, the Japanese film industry achieved the highest total box-office income in the world after the United States.[27]

While European and American film critics at the time regarded Japanese film essentially as dead, the industry was abuzz with projects. Much of the apparent revitalization and the very survival of film production in Japan was due to the increased shift of production to smaller, more flexible companies and the majors' increased focus on distribution and exhibition. In fact, direct production by majors was down to a fraction of its former output. From July 1980 to June 1981, a total of 268 films were independently produced, 197 of which were Pink films and 71 of which were regular films. Shōchiku, which had churned out two films a week, produced only seven films in the same span of one year, while Kadokawa, without a studio history, produced six films in 1981.[28] The expansion of independent production and the new business constellations that emerged from it were in no small part due to Kadokawa Film and the changes it helped implement—for better or worse.

Kadokawa Haruki directed five films during his time as head of Kadokawa Shoten: *Dirty Hero, Love Story, Cabaret, Heaven and Earth* (*Ten to chi to*, 1990), and *Rex: A Dinosaur's Story* (*Rex: Kyōryū monogatari*, 1993). Apart from *Cabaret*, all of them were considerable box-office successes, and all of them were fairly high-budget productions, although only *Heaven and Earth* can qualify as a blockbuster-level production.[29] When Kadokawa embarked on a directing career in 1982, the company had just launched its line of smaller films to complement the larger productions, even proclaiming a new art film line at a press conference. The first up was *In the Storehouse* (*Kura no naka*, 1981), whose director, Takabayashi Yōichi, was, like Ōbayashi Nobuhiko, a star of the 8 mm scene of the 1960s. The film portrayed a brother's incestuous relationship with his tubercular sister, who was played by Matsubara Rumiko, one of the first celebrities regarded as a *nyū hāfu* performer.[30]

Kadokawa's directorial debut and the film he claimed he was willing to disembowel himself for, *Dirty Hero*, was the third Ōyabu Haruhiko book Kadokawa Publishing adapted for film.[31] *Dirty Hero* is the story of motorbike racer Kitano Akio's obsessive drive for a comeback after an absence due to a life-threatening crash. There is little character development in the film, as Kitano is simply determined to win, and in the end does exactly that. He seduces several women along the way and declines all offers that might distract him from his goal, effortlessly gliding through luxurious surroundings and glossy images. The very emphasis on affluence and the style that Kadokawa indulges in to the point of parody once again carries strong undercurrents of an internationalist identity politics. In virtually every interview he gave for *Dirty Hero*'s promotion, Kadokawa distanced himself from "Japanese film," stating his approach was "the absolute opposite," that the film expressed his personal sentiment "rather than a Japanese one." According to Kadokawa, films in Japan do not use images to tell a story, just dialogue, and Japanese directors are only good at "mining their own private lifestyle."[32] They are passable at "portraying 4½ Tatami rooms" but "when describing the upper classes, they are helpless." While "Japanese films . . . are like green tea over rice, . . . foreign films have the atmosphere of eating beefsteak."[33] He claims that he gave his utmost "with the intention of creating an international film."[34]

While separating himself from the style and atmosphere of "Japanese" film, Kadokawa drew on well-worn discourses we have encountered with regard to Pink Film, associating Japan with parochialism, poverty, backwardness, and stylistic realism. In contrast, the foreign—virtually always America, which in Kadokawa films almost always means New York—is connected to a modern and affluent future. True to fulfilling his claim of creating an international film, *Dirty Hero* is an inter-national movie that relies on imagined differences between nations, while Kadokawa paradoxically attempts to de-emphasize temporal hierarchy at the same time. He chooses to create an eternal present where nations are temporally synchronized. Differences exist only in traces and allusions, leveled by the total surface of the image commodity. While Kadokawa uses New York as a symbol of affluence, virtually all of the scenes in *Dirty Hero* are set in a Japan that is primarily a nonlocal, transnational space.

Kitano is a superman who, between races set to *Rocky*-style American background songs, glides through a luxurious world where tatami mats are nowhere to be seen—only wide spaces of impressive villas, smooth surfaces, and postmodern architecture. He speaks flawless English, drinks only Perrier, and has two love interests in the film, international fashion designer Kyōko (with stores, inevitably, in New York) and superrich heir and businesswoman Christine Adams. The imagery is so steeped in TV commercial imagery that this would be a classically postmodern film of the 1980s if it possessed any sense of irony. After finally winning the decisive race, Kitano departs on an international racetrack tour. When saying goodbye to his mechanic's small son, the Japanese boy says (in English), "Goodbye, hero." The final credits inform us of Kitano's further string of successes and his eventual death on the racetrack.

Apart from the obvious parallels of this overreaching, tragically lonely heroic figure with Kadokawa's own self-portrayal in the media, Kitano is constructed as a more general wish-fulfillment figure for an internationalizing and increasingly prosperous Japanese audience. The character of Kitano—played by Kusakari Masao, a former model and the son of an American GI and a Japanese woman—radically dispenses with all the (male) insecurities and ambivalences that informed early Pink Film and instead represents a stylish, international, successful, and rich individual who is fearless, virile, and enticing. He seduces the American woman, Christine, with ease, capturing her heart, though he is destined to always be (heroically) alone—a break from the chaste hero rare in film from Japan. Kitano is inextricably bound to the otherworldly, hermetic aestheticism Kadokawa introduces. Christine claims that to her "Japan is like another planet," but the Japan portrayed here will have seemed like another planet to the greatest part of the Japanese audience as well. While drawing on long-established discourses of the relationship between Japan and the foreign, it is no longer an asymmetric relation where Japan is real and the foreign is image. In *Dirty Hero* both have entered the fantastic space of the readily commodifiable image and meet there on, ostensibly, cosmopolitan and equal terms. Mirroring the screening of films from Japan in yōga theaters, however, Kadokawa must still rely on stereotypes of the foreign to produce the fantastic space in which Kitano lives. It is a binary from which he cannot quite escape.

In *Rex: A Dinosaur's Story*, Kadokawa places the tale of a little girl who befriends a freshly hatched dinosaur in the indefinable landscape of Hokkaido. This northern island, tellingly, was the common backdrop to many of the *mukokuseki eiga* (anational films) of the 1950s and 1960s.[35] On her journey with the dinosaur, Chie, played by child star Adachi Yumi, stumbles from the Western-ranch-style laboratory to a town supersaturated with Christmas decorations and toys. After escaping from a group of evil foreigners, all of whom speak flawless Japanese and sport Japanese names, she finally returns Rex to his hidden homeland with the help of an old Ainu shaman.[36] In the conservative family subplot of the film, Chie's scientist mother had left for New York to pursue her career and abandon her family, only returning for the dinosaur. In *Rex*, the personal problem between Chie's divorced parents is linked to the destructive power of the foreign. Even in a fantastic space, the confirmation of difference and hierarchy based on the national is a trope Kadokawa can never fully dispose of.

The paradox of the fantastic is of course that it cannot be attractive without referring to a reality. Anchored in long-standing colonial discourses of different stages and speeds of development, Kadokawa's fantastic spaces are not solely universes of cosmopolitan, free-floating signifiers. Kadokawa suggests a level playing field through a synchronizing aesthetic regime while actually latching on to older discourses of heterochronicity and sequence. It is the spectacle of simultaneity, or rather temporal confusion, that makes the tension inherent in them digestible and commodifiable.

In business strategy as well, Kadokawa initially created a multimedia platform that attempted to do away with temporal sequence; videos, films, and books—even at the time usually released in sequence—were released simultaneously. While the strategy eventually failed, it was an initial attempt at making a completely simultaneous media space.[37] The texts indulged in fantastic transnational spaces while relying on nationally tinted ideas of sequence, and they did so both in their aesthetic strategies and in the way they were distributed. Kadokawa Haruki's self-portrayal follows the drive for simultaneity and a confusion of temporal order as well. Besides performing Shintō rituals before each film's shoot, he constructed himself as a full-blown capitalist entrepreneur who derided so-called village mentality and constantly challenged borders—between media, between the public and the private, and of nationally connoted spaces. He inserts pictures of himself in traditional Japanese garb into his autobiography, and appeals variously to tropes borrowed from romanticism, modernism, and other histories.

Kadokawa films commodified the attractive tension between a lagging Japanese national space bound by history and a supposedly cosmopolitan now; yet that meant it needed what it was supposedly distancing itself from. Haruki himself was not immune to this mechanism. Repeatedly, he used Hollywood as a point of reference for the films he, ostensibly located outside of sequence and history, produced and directed. He likened *The Inugami Family* to spaghetti Westerns, *Love Story* to *Flashdance* and *Rocky*, *Legend of the Eight Samurai* to *Star Wars*, *The Blade of Kamui* (*Kamui no ken*, Rintarō, 1985) to *Raiders of the Lost Ark*, *Cabaret* to *Peggy Sue Got Married*, and *Rex: A Dinosaur's Story* to *Jurassic Park*, thus once again tangling himself in the salience of sequence.[38] As much as he attempted to place himself outside of temporality as a genius, a singular individual, and an associate to aliens, the demarcation lines he chose for the fantastic spaces he created and the village mentality he distanced himself from were provided by the very binary he was trying to avoid. Again, this is by no means to suggest a contradiction inherent in the person, but one in the personalized discourse he came to represent. Like Pink Film, Kadokawa Film allowed for containing a profitable con-fusion of elements, cohering despite their contradictions.

Dirty Hero, *Love Story*, *Cabaret*, and *Rex: A Dinosaur's Story* are not necessarily representative of everything the Kadokawa Haruki Office put out, simply because this output was quite varied in terms of budgets, narratives, and styles. But they are representative of the specific strain of Kadokawa Film discourse that lodged itself in the collective memory of journalism, criticism, and the general public. This image was what the general scorn for Kadokawa hinged on. If 1984 was the most prolific year for the Kadokawa Haruki Office, it became the point where its strategies peaked. It released nine films, among them a prestige animated feature, *Kenya Boy*, the last whole-hearted series of aidoru films such as *Main Theme*, *Love Story*, or *The Island Closest to Heaven*, and attempts at a more sophisticated program picture, such as *Mahjong*

FIGURE 4.2. A Kadokawa ad for the simultaneous release of *Detective Story* and *The Little Girl Who Conquered Time* in theaters (as a double bill) and on video, again emphasizing the absence of temporal hierarchy. On the left is Yakushimaru Hiroko and on the right is Harada Tomoyo. From *Baraeti*, August 1983, 107.

Vagabond Chronicle (*Mājan hōrō-ki*, Wada Makoto) and *W's Tragedy* (the latter two would accord Kadokawa a degree of recognition within established film criticism, but results at the box office were mixed). From 1984 on, Kadokawa would reduce its output annually, with a shift to anime, until in 1989 it produced only three films: *Afternoon When Flowers Fell* (*Hana no furu gogo*, Ōmori Kazuki) and an anime double bill distributed by Tōhō, *Five Star Story* (*Faibu sutā monogatari*, Yamazaki Kazuo) and *Space Prince* (*Uchū ōji*, Yoshida Genji). The latter two were not even produced by the Kadokawa Haruki Office but by Kadokawa Shoten under Kadokawa Haruki's younger brother, Tsuguhiko, who supervised them as synergy projects for the manga magazines he was publishing.[39] While Tsuguhiko was developing a fundamentally different model of the media mix than Haruki, the established film industry was working hard to absorb Kadokawa's strategies, endangering Kadokawa's status as opposition and exception.

The Film World Catches Up with Kadokawa

The deep transformation the film and media industry in Japan went through in the 1980s was heavily influenced by Kadokawa Film and was part of its undoing. By the mid-1980s, the Japanese film industry was entering a curious constellation of recession, restructuring, and living on borrowed time. In 1984, motorboat racing boasted attendance figures twenty-five times the total audience of theatrical film. By 1986, it was up to eighty-nine times the theatrical film audience. Stage theater was suffering as well, but by 1986 it was still generating over twenty-two times more than the total box-office income of theatrically released film.[40] Films from Japan and abroad were about on par in terms of distribution gross. While the box office was at least stable in the early 1980s, theaters were still closing down in spades; in 1986 they numbered 2,109, down from 2,453 ten years earlier.[41] More dramatic were the structural changes in exhibition, as the greatest number of closures occurred in the chihō, and new theaters were actually opening again in the urban centers, partially due to the significant boom in small art house cinemas called minitheaters. This greatly increased the proportion of theaters controlled by the majors and their grip on distribution and exhibition; it also helped turn theatrical film into an increasingly urban phenomenon. In the meantime, production was now mostly handled by independents, which proliferated but suffered under the unequal power relationship. The former majors had shifted to mostly distribution and exhibition, and thereby could retain almost complete control of (supposedly) independent production.[42]

Kadokawa was aware of the problem of being at the mercy of the gatekeepers to the distribution channels. From the beginning, his strategy of dividing functions up among the former majors had been an attempt to reduce their control. Kadokawa immediately switched distributors if disagreements arose, as when Tōhō paired the Yakushimaru Hiroko vehicle *School in the Crosshairs* with its own *Blue Jeans Memory* (*Burū jiinzu memori*, Kawasaki Yoshisuke, 1981), a film starring the male idol group Tanokin Trio and produced with cooperation from the powerful Johnny's talent agency. Tōhō supposedly spent 80 percent of the advertising budget on *Blue Jeans Memory*, so Kadokawa turned to Tōei distribution for the next productions, *Akuryo Island, In the Storehouse*, and *Sailor Suit and Machine Gun*. Kadokawa was in a much more powerful position than most independents; its promotional power made it attractive, and it was not as solely reliant on income from the films themselves. Most of Kadokawa's yōga-style releases took the typical yōga rate of 55 percent of the box-office income, while *Heaven and Earth* even took 70 percent.[43] However, this still had to be shared with the distributor, and as the ability to generate publicity with a certain release strategy, or the Kadokawa brand itself, began to fade, the limits of the free-booking rules for yōga releases emerged. Unsuccessful films were quickly removed from the screening schedules to make way for other films. As less successful films weakened the leverage for the next negotiations, Kadokawa Film found itself in a vicious cycle; in response, it attempted to break the majors' stranglehold on distribution and exhibition in several ways.

In 1984, Kadokawa Haruki met with the head of Tōei, Okada Shigeru, and announced his plans for Kadokawa to partially distribute its own films. The following year Kadokawa indeed jointly distributed the double bill of *Early Spring Story* (*Sōshun monogatari*, Sawai Shin'ichirō), a Harada Tomoyo feature, and *Christian the Second Time Around* (*Nidaime wa kurisuchan*) by former Pink Film director Izutsu Kazuyuki, with Tōhō. This proved more difficult than expected, and Kadokawa refrained from further self-distribution efforts, knowing that it would need many more films to sustain an efficient distribution arm.[44] In the same year, on December 24, Kadokawa opened a 310-seat Kadokawa-run theater in Sapporo, a project that would also quickly fail due to an insufficient supply of films. Initially Kadokawa Haruki had even announced plans to build a theater in each of the nine major cities.[45] Now, even more humble plans were laid to rest.

Both of these attempts were, once again, less visionary failures than consistent with developments within the film industry of that time. Despite the former majors' hold on Japanese film distribution, the minitheater boom had been opening up the market for independent theaters and distribution, especially of art house films. From the early 1980s onward there were a number of promising precedents for successful small-scale self-distribution and exhibition, and Kadokawa merely attempted to amplify this in scale. However, both attempts failed quickly, and Kadokawa's film exploits began seriously losing revenue and steam in the late 1980s. The former majors' domination of the exhibition business would continue to increase until the multiplex building boom of the 1990s, when the winds abruptly turned. Until then, however, attempts to circumvent the oligopoly over distribution and exhibition did not let up. Most famously, Argo Project (producers of *The Cherry Orchard* [*Sakura no sono*, Nakahara Shun, 1990]) and Cine Qua Non (producers of *All under the Moon* [*Tsuki wa docchi ni dete iru*, Sai Yōichi, 1993]) established theaters of their own in Tokyo and Osaka.

Much of Kadokawa's lackluster performance in the late 1980s had to do with the changing film industry environment. Kadokawa had introduced or at least assembled a host of marketing strategies under one roof that it efficiently and self-reflexively used to create a brand, defining itself as new on the levels of media text and business strategy. But by the late 1980s, many of the emblematic Kadokawa strategies had become commonplace. While Kadokawa increasingly employed double-bill releases in the mid-1980s, single-bill screenings, originally a blockbuster phenomenon, were on their way to becoming the exhibition norm. Various media-mix forms were now widespread. Among others, publisher Tokuma Shoten, which had bought what was left of Daiei, had mined the same synergies as Kadokawa between film production, video production and distribution, print media, and music (using the label Tokuma Japan). It was especially successful via its ties to Studio Ghibli, which was setting new standards in animation with Miyazaki Hayao's films.[46]

Numerous media corporations and TV stations were seriously involved in film production, most importantly Fuji Television of the Fuji Sankei group, scoring hits with films such as *Take Me Out to the Snowland* (*Watashi o sukii ni tsurete'tte*, Baba Yasuo, 1987), which starred Harada Tomoyo. The list of corporations practicing what Kadokawa had preached included TV and radio stations, publishing houses, toy companies, and record companies; in fact, there was barely a media-related corporation in Japan that was not involved in feature film production in the late 1980s. All of them made use of cross-marketing synergies: Nihon Terebi (NTV), TV Asahi, *Asahi Shinbun*, Mainichi Hōsō (MBS), Kōdansha, Bandai, Nishitomo, CBS/Sony, Victor, JCI, Gakken, Toshiba Eizō, and the list goes on indefinitely.

Additionally, due to the asset price bubble, excessive amounts of money were in circulation. Companies that initially had nothing to do with the media business were rushing money into film production, a strategy intended to create tax write-offs and promote the company name at the same time. Trading companies such as Tōmen, Nichimen, or Mitsui Bussan (of the Mitsui financial group) were producing films with either the independents or the former majors. This led to a considerable increase in films marketed via the advance-ticket system and to a host of films with bloated production budgets that were unpopular with audiences and shunned by critics. They were produced simply because financing was easily secured; commercial viability or critical success was less emphasized during production, sometimes not even the primary goal of the investors. Examples are legion, among them bombastic historical epics such as *The Silk Road* (*Tonkō*, Satō Junya, 1988) or *The Great Shogunate Battle* (*Edo-jō tairan*, Masuda Toshio, 1991).[47] However, midsized films often profited as well, and the result was a film industry that was supported more by macroeconomic conditions and a media-mix infrastructure than by an audience paying to see films.

Kadokawa had, of course, enjoyed a history of corporate-driven advance-ticket financing, most prominently for *Virus* (with TBS). The company also regularly supported film budgets with product-placement deals and, less frequently, actual corporate tie-ups.[48] For *Afternoon When Flowers Fell*, which was set in Kobe, it mobilized a group of Kobe businesses that each contributed 10 million yen ($78,125) to production costs. For *Our Seven Day War* (Sugawara Hiroshi, 1988), the story of a rebellion by high school students that escalates into a military showdown with tanks, Kadokawa partnered with the burger chain Mosburger. However, with the idol strategy abandoned, it was becoming increasingly difficult to generate publicity and grab attention among the flood of similar approaches—and attention was what the Kadokawa strategy was based on. The Kadokawa business strategy was now so commonplace that it was increasingly difficult to stay associated with the trope of the new. The genre was seriously struggling to stay visible and identifiable; the context had changed, and Kadokawa was fading into it. Kadokawa thus decided to return to its abandoned blockbuster strategy with a vengeance, and in 1990 produced *Heaven and Earth*.

The Return of the Blockbusters and Kadokawa Haruki's Arrest

Heaven and Earth was the film that brought Kadokawa back full circle to the blockbuster strategy of the late 1970s. It also revived certain aspects of the Kadokawa Film discourse that would reinforce critics' and journalists' accusation that he had ruined Japanese cinema.[49] Kadokawa had abandoned the high-risk, high-return method of making films after the various problems he encountered with *G.I. Samurai* and *Virus* ten years earlier.

By the late 1980s, the (so-called) program-picture strategy of a greater number of smaller-budget films that Kadokawa turned to after the *Virus* debacle was obviously not profitable anymore. The yōga-style release of free booking was fundamentally risky, and earnings became increasingly volatile from 1984 onward.[50] With financing easy to secure in the bubble-economy era, Kadokawa saw its chance to revive the blockbuster practice on an even larger scale than before. From around 1988 on, the company began preparations for the production of *Heaven and Earth*, a well-known story of the rivalry between two warlords, Takeda Shingen and Uesugi Kenshin. The story has been filmed many times, even playing a role in Kadokawa's own *G.I. Samurai*, where the character of Uesugi Kenshin appears under his original name, Nagao Kagetora. *Heaven and Earth* was based on a best-selling novel that described the rivalry and had also been the basis for a successful television series on public broadcaster Nippon Hōsō Kyōkai (NHK), or Japan Broadcasting Corporation, in 1969.[51]

For the epic, Kadokawa mobilized thirty-one companies for corporate tie-ups to help finance the film, a cooperation for which they received advance tickets and were forced to buy additional ones. Combined with around 1 million tickets sold to Kadokawa employees, and a significant number that were sold to advance-ticket stores (which led to a steep drop in advance-ticket prices for the film), a massive total of 5.3 million advance tickets were issued.[52] The budget reached the excessive sum (for film from Japan at the time) of around 5 billion yen (about $37,037,000 at the time); Kadokawa proclaimed that it would be the most successful film of all time, as well as reaching a theatrical audience of 10 million.[53] While it did make 5.5 billion yen in distribution revenue, in the end, the film failed to achieve the highest revenue of all time, falling behind *Antarctica* and *The Adventures of Miles and Otis* (*Koneko monogatari*, Hata Masanori, 1986). Both of these animal films were produced with Fuji TV's involvement, attesting to the increasing power of television in Japanese film production as well as the hunger for the blank slates that cats, dogs, and foxes could provide just as well as prepubescent aidoru and anime characters.

Despite its Japanese theme, *Heaven and Earth* still retains traces of the Kadokawa-esque exploitation of discourses of the international. Virtually all of the epic but leaden battle scenes were shot in Canada, utilizing over three thousand extras recruited from the University of Calgary who were dressed in samurai and soldier uniforms. Kadokawa screened special runs of the foreign edition of the film in Tokyo, and of course the film was distributed with yōga-style free booking as a single bill, a fact that in itself no longer created additional publicity.⁵⁴ Rejected by Cannes, *Heaven and Earth* failed to make any impact abroad, and Kadokawa was forced to set up a company in the United States even to have it distributed there.⁵⁵

But Kadokawa did not give up its designs on foreign markets. In the early 1980s, Kadokawa Haruki had attributed the failure of Japanese films abroad to lack of visual interest, therefore leaving them victim to their *gengo no shōgai* (language handicap).⁵⁶ Asian markets were much more forthcoming than the American and European ones, but also much less interesting for Kadokawa. Widespread distribution of films from Japan in Asia had roots in Japan's colonial history, and, after the war, ties between the film industries of Japan and other Asian countries continued along Cold War divides. Most prominent was the connection between the Daiei Studio and Cathay and the Shaw Brothers in Hong Kong, which resulted in the founding of the Asian Pacific Film Festival in 1954, envisioned to strengthen ties in the anticommunist part of Asia and actively supported by the United States.⁵⁷ Kadokawa films had been distributed in various Asian countries as well. However, tangled in the sequential temporality that posits Japan as the future vis-à-vis Asia, but as the past vis-à-vis the United States, for Kadokawa the U.S. market remained the point of reference for success.⁵⁸

Kadokawa attempted to circumvent the handicap with a burst of activity, but none of the projects proved successful. In 1990, the company acquired all rights for *The Adventures of Sir Puss-in-the-Boots*, a half-finished Disney animation featuring the voice of Sammy Davis Jr. that had been shelved in the 1970s. As Davis was now deceased, Kadokawa announced plans to use Michael Jackson and Barbra Streisand to re-record the voices, which never came to fruition.⁵⁹ Kadokawa also cofinanced a Broadway production of *Shogun* in 1991, which met with no enthusiasm and closed after a mere two months. In an international public relations event, Kadokawa Haruki sailed halfway around the world in an exact replica of the *Santa Maria* in the same year, while plans for the company to purchase the broadcasting rights for the Barcelona Olympics eventually failed. In 1992, Kadokawa produced the film *Ruby Cairo* (*Rubii kairo*, directed by Graeme Clifford) in Hollywood, starring Andie MacDowell, Liam Neeson, and Viggo Mortensen, which bombed at the box office in both the United States and Japan.

Again, Kadokawa was less a pioneer than very much following the currents of his time, with his attempts to enter the American market in one way or another. Japanese companies had invested in Hollywood productions as early as the 1970s, when Tōhō Tōwa cofinanced Dino De Laurentiis's *King Kong* (John Guillermin, 1976) or distributor Nihon Herald invested in *The Sailor Who Fell from Grace with the Sea* (Lewis John Carlino, 1976, based on a novel by Mishima Yukio). Later, the record company Victor successfully invested in productions such as *Mystery Train* (Jim Jarmush, 1989) and *Nikita* (Luc Besson, 1990).[60] In 1989, the emphasis shifted away from investing in individual productions when Sony bought Columbia Pictures, and in 1990 Matsushita followed suit and purchased MCA. Encouraged by this shopping spree, Kadokawa had set its sights on finally getting a piece of the American pie.

Kadokawa's *Rex: A Dinosaur's Story* almost seems like a last-ditch attempt after the string of failures that preceded it. Originally conceived as a Hollywood production, financing problems slowed down the project; with the film already block-booked by Shōchiku in advance, Kadokawa eventually had no choice but to go ahead with a scaled-down production in Japan.[61] *Rex* was released hōga-style in 1993, the first Kadokawa Film to be released within the block-booking system since *W's Tragedy* in 1984, a sign that the company was not in a betting mood and preferred to make its income more predictable. But even without corporate-driven advance ticket sales or a massive advertising campaign, the film, supported by its casting of child-star Adachi Yumi and its robotronic dinosaur models, became one of the runaway hits of the year as well as a much-needed success for the financially troubled Shōchiku.[62]

Rex: A Dinosaur's Story was officially produced by a *seisakuiinkai* (production committee), a form of production that had become increasingly common even before the end of the bubble economy in 1991. In this form of film financing, several companies, usually each representing a different ancillary market, invest in the production of a film and in return receive a portion of the rights. Often a film-production company, a television channel, a video/DVD distributor and a publishing company will be involved, dividing up the rights for their respective markets. Kadokawa's participation in the production committee for *Rex: A Dinosaur's Story* was not, however, represented by the Kadokawa Haruki Office but by Kadokawa Shoten itself; this was a detail that would prove a fateful omen.

In 1987, Kadokawa Shoten started officially participating in the production of Kadokawa films. The reasons for this new arrangement are not completely clear. According to Kadokawa himself, it was in preparation for his renewed entry into blockbuster production, making involvement of a larger corporate entity useful for financing (production for *Heaven and Earth*, however, is still credited to the Kadokawa Haruki Office). It is also possible that the Kadokawa

Haruki Office was losing so much money that it was not able to support even smaller productions. Certainly for Kadokawa Haruki's film-centered strategy, the media mix had ceased reaping large rewards. In the meantime, Kadokawa Publishing was making its largest profits in the magazine section headed by Kadokawa's younger brother, Kadokawa Tsuguhiko. However, Tsuguhiko resigned from all his positions in 1992 due to internal strife, probably at least partially about the version of the media mix that the company should employ. In March 1993, the deficit-ridden Kadokawa Haruki Office fused with Kadokawa Shoten, a step that was linked to plans for a public stock offering. It was a decision that would soon cause Kadokawa Haruki no small amount of grief.

The new projects would not be realized. On August 28, 1993, Kadokawa Haruki was arrested on charges of instructing a Kadokawa employee, Ikeda Takeshi, to smuggle cocaine from Los Angeles to Tokyo. An immense media uproar followed, and in early September, Kadokawa Haruki resigned from all positions within the company. On September 19 he was formally charged with embezzling company funds and for inciting Ikeda to smuggle cocaine more than ten times between 1987 and 1993.[63] Upon the arrest, Shōchiku immediately decided to cancel the four-week extension to the ten-week run it had booked for *Rex: A Dinosaur's Story*, despite a desperate need for its success.[64] *Rex* thus ended its theatrical run on the initially planned date of September 10 and was hastily replaced by Wakamatsu Kōji's *Singapore Sling* (*Shingapōru suringu*).[65] The film *Coo* (*Coo: Tōi umi kara kita kū*, Imazawa Tesuo, 1993), coproduced with NTV and released in December of the same year, had Kadokawa Haruki's name stricken from the credits. On October 19, Haruki's younger brother Tsuguhiko returned to the company and assumed the position of head of Kadokawa Shoten. One of the steps taken even before Tsuguhiko took his new position was an official retreat from the film business. While much would fundamentally change in the Kadokawa media-mix strategy, this, at least, was a decision that would not last.

New Kadokawa

The corporation that emerged from the years of restructuring and consolidation following Kadokawa Haruki's departure looked considerably different from the company he left behind. It was structurally much more complex in its involvement with various media businesses and shifted to a very different kind of media mix. Ōtsuka Eiji has argued that Kadokawa Haruki relied on the traditional author model and focused on producing media content, while Tsuguhiko introduced a business model that markets platforms for user engagement and content creation.⁶⁶ While this perspective overemphasizes Haruki's attachment to the idea of an original, there are indeed a number of significant differences between the brothers' media-mix models. Kadokawa Haruki's original business strategy was highly reflexive and personalized and focused on the largest possible public. Since the late 1990s, the company has been much more focused on exploiting a multiplicity of small markets as well as media practices such as fan labor. It is no less influential in business terms, but much less visible and performative. Essentially, with Haruki's departure, Kadokawa Film ended its tenure as an industrial genre. The textuality of the industrial genre broke apart, and the media texts and their arguments became detached from those of the larger structures and practices that bring them into circulation.

Despite its official proclamation of retreat from the film industry, Kadokawa Publishing continued to produce animation in 1995 and 1996, with films such as *Slayers* (*Sureyāzu*, Watanabe Hiroshi, 1995). It now did so via production committees and based on series from Kadokawa manga magazines (in which Tsuguhiko had been heavily involved). But it was only on January 1, 1997, that the major newspapers *Asahi Shinbun*, *Mainichi Shinbun*, and *Yomiuri Shinbun* all featured large ads proclaiming the launch of Shin Kadokawa Eiga (New Kadokawa Films). For production, Kadokawa now teamed up with Ace Pictures, a production company headed by venerable producer Hara Masato (one of the producers of Kurosawa Akira's *Ran*) and connected to distributor Nippon Herald.⁶⁷ The first run of films produced were *Lost Paradise* (*Shitsurakuen*, Morita Yoshimitsu, 1997), an erotic romance that was defined as appealing to a female and older audience; the theatrical version of the anime *Neon Genesis Evangelion* (*Shinseiki evangerion*, Anno Hideaki, 1997); and *Parasite Eve* (*Parasaito ibu*, Ochiai Masayuki, 1997), the story of a mad scientist and an experiment gone terribly wrong. The first two proved to be formidable hits.

The productions were marketed as a shift in the company's strategy. Films were targeted, once more, at increasingly defined audience segments, a return to a fragmented audience. The adherence to films based on Kadokawa books was also initially abandoned (though Kadokawa would quickly establish light novels, or *raito noberu*, as a new centerpiece of a different media mix). *Lost Paradise* had been published in the newspaper *Nihon Keizai Shinbun* and as a hardcover by Kōdansha, with no Kadokawa involvement. The primary goal was obviously to establish a self-sufficient film production that could, but did not have to, profit from media-mix synergies.⁶⁸ After launching its new production division, Kadokawa successively built business structures that would ensure it a much more powerful position within the film industry.⁶⁹

The Radicalization of Kadokawa Film · 147

However, Kadokawa's focus was now on building platforms on which media mixes could unfold and in which users (or audiences, readers, listeners, etc.) could participate. Film was one aspect of a larger strategy that included magazines, light novels, moving images, the Internet, and, importantly, fan production of all of these media.[70] It also focused strongly on engaging ever-smaller compartments of consumers, a definite turn from Kadokawa Haruki's push toward the largest possible public.

Kadokawa under Haruki had failed to establish a distribution and exhibition base. The new Kadokawa, however, made platforms, distribution, and participation the basis of its business model. In terms of film, it was now basically a fourth major with strong international ties, such as its heavy investments in the DreamWorks studio and the Chinese multiplex business. Tsuguhiko initially intended to buy YouTube and in 2014 merged with Dwango, the company behind the online video platform Nico Nico Douga. It is in contrast with the truly multiple-channel media-mix strategy of Kadokawa after Haruki that the degree of his indebtedness to the film industry he claimed to detest becomes clear. Haruki still regarded film as the master medium, and despite the reduction in corpo-reality, the Kadokawa idols still remained attached to the human. After Haruki, the company largely shifted to fictional characters from manga, anime, light novels, and games for the media mix—the *Melancholy of Suzumiya Haruhi* series being one of the prominent examples—avoiding the trappings of aging idols. Barely any trace is left of the aggressive discourse of simultaneity that Kadokawa Haruki had narratively linked to the company and even made a decisive selling point. In the public eye, the antagonistically visionary company Haruki had constructed is now simply another part of a completely transformed film and media industrial landscape.

Kadokawa Haruki was released on 100 million yen ($1,000,000) bail in 1994, and resumed various activities in the publishing and film production field. In 1995, he founded the Kadokawa Haruki Corporation (Kadokawa Haruki Jimusho), and in 1997 directed a remake of *The Little Girl Who Conquered Time*. He also coproduced the first Korean-Japanese coproduction of the 1990s, the animation *War Chronicles of Alexander* (*Arekusandā senki*, Rintarō and Kanemori Yoshinori, 1998). In 2000 he was sentenced to four years imprisonment. The sentence commenced from 2001, although he was released in 2004 and spent part of his sentence in prison hospital facilities receiving treatment for tuberculosis. In 2003 he lost a court battle for the rights to the films produced by the (original) Kadokawa Haruki Office and thereby lost all rights to the films he had produced with the company; due to the merger with

Kadokawa Shoten in 1993, the rights remained with the parent company (for a time DVD editions of the films issued by Kadokawa Shoten appear to have struck Haruki's name from the credits).

In 2005 he established his own film production fund, the Kadokawa Haruki Mirai Fund, with which he produced a successful big-budget war film, *Yamato* (*Otoko-tachi no yamato*, Satō Junya), based on a book by his sister about the legendary Japanese battleship, the wreck of which he had tracked down with an expedition in 1985.[71] He also produced a film on Genghis Kahn, *Genghis Kahn / Blue Wolf: To the Ends of the Earth and Sea* (*Aoi ōkami: Chi hate umi tsukiru made*, Sawai Shinichirō, 2007), which with 444 screens received the widest release ever for a film from Japan. Kadokawa Haruki's relationship to history had obviously shifted, and almost all of the film projects he has been associated with since leaving Kadokawa Publishing have been either remakes or based on historical events that eschewed the distancing from history itself that characterized Kadokawa Film. The drive for the eternal present that dominated his work in the 1980s had been replaced with more conventionally historiographic concerns.

Kadokawa and Genre

Though in a different way, history is still a concern for the new Kadokawa. Kadokawa Film represented a web of practices and discourses that this new corporation has actively attempted to shed itself of, from the proclamation of rupture with New Kadokawa Films in the newspaper ads to the erasure of Kadokawa Haruki's name from the credits of the films he produced. The goal is obviously not just to create a distance from the era before Haruki's arrest, but to gradually construct a version of history that is more appropriate to the goals of the present. It is the attempt to erase genre and replace it with a corporation. While the Kadokawa Holdings website consistently adjusts its version of history, the 2007 version details its corporate history in a particularly interesting way, and the periodization it chooses is quite different from the one presented in this book.[72] The history of the company is divided into five stages. The first one ranges from 1945 to 1975, and is titled the "Period of Publishing Literature." Then follows the "Media Mix between Film and Paperback Books Period" until 1982, the "Period of Magazines" until 1993, then the "On the Road to a Mega Content Provider" period, and from 2005, the period of "Expanding the Publishing Business, the Film and Images Business, and the Broadband Business." Apart from avoiding the commonly used division into a before-and-after Haruki era—one that was still present in the 1997 newspaper announcements—in favor of a focus on business models (especially one in which the new CEO was heavily involved, "Phase 2"), there are also divergent concepts of history itself at stake in comparison to Kadokawa Film's self-fashioning. Kadokawa Haruki puts forth a strongly personalized constant struggle, ahistorically structured by his fits and spurts of genius.[73] The Kadokawa Holdings website depersonalizes this account (though subtly giving credit to Tsuguhiko) and moves toward an evolutionary model of stages. It has given up its status as an industrial genre, and its implicit appeal to corporate rationality is now decoupled from the texts it produces and the product it attempts to sell. It also recalibrates itself into national history: Tsuguhiko has spoken of his attempts to build a highly accessible media platform as an extension of postwar democracy, implicitly accepting the idea of a historical rupture after the war.[74]

How, then, to evaluate Kadokawa Film's legacy? In the 1970s, using a historically specific constellation of sociopolitical trends, film industry economics, and consumer culture, Kadokawa Film helped forge a new relationship between various media. Though the genre played upon heterochronic tensions even within the global space it designed, it rarely aligned itself with them. Kadokawa Film claimed a clean break with an old Japan, while the space of the global was envisioned as one of attractive confusion: of temporalities, geographies, and media. Kadokawa called upon liberal capitalist market principles and their eternally challenging contemporaneity as the driving paradigms of its strategies, and thereby attempted to place itself outside of nationally inflected models of temporal order. The self-reflexive nature of Kadokawa marketing, always referencing the old to differentiate and uphold its brand of the new, profoundly transformed audience sensibilities and surrounding business practices to the degree that the Kadokawa model became the standard. Much as it has been an essential problem for the classical avant-garde, relying on the difference between the old and the new became increasingly difficult.

This also had much to do with the shift of emphasis from singular media texts to relations between media texts that the Kadokawa strategy necessitated. While Pink Film could boast a number of concrete defining factors (be it nudity or the uniform budget level of 3 million yen), Kadokawa Film could not afford this kind of baggage if it wanted to retain transmedia flexibility. This shift entailed a de-emphasis on narrative in favor of characters. Finding it difficult to rely solely on Kadokawa Haruki for personalization, the brand switched to the aliens and shape-shifters of the idol strategy. It employed characters positioned so far outside of quotidian regimes that repeatedly repackaging them as novelty was possible, but only for a time. When the actresses' age became a problem and the kyara strategy was refined by Tsuguhiko via manga and games, this aspect of the Kadokawa Film brand had to be abandoned as well. It entered a crisis that was, to a certain degree, self-induced. *Heaven and Earth* was a last attempt to recapture the formerly successful strategy of a politics of scale. This proved impossible to uphold within a nationally restricted context; no matter how much Kadokawa performed a global, eternal present in Japan, that performance turned out to be of limited exportability. Similar strategies still persist. Categories such as J-pop or J-*bungaku* (J-literature) carry traces of the negotiation of national and temporal status that was so decisive for Kadokawa Film. One pocket of film production in Japan that intensified the reflexive tendency of Kadokawa Film for a completely different and much more nationally inflected temporal strategy was the industrial genre of V-Cinema.

FIVE

V-CINEMA

The police officer Joe and his young sidekick arrest a fugitive called Bruce and load him into an American-style police car sporting the emblem "Little Tokyo." On their way to the station they are ambushed by a group wearing clown masks; Joe is wounded and his partner is killed. Investigating the incident on his own, Joe uncovers a conspiracy between marauding gangs and the police, leading him to team up with an attractive and combative nun named Lily and to a fiery finale that only Joe survives. *Crimehunter—Bullet of Fury* (*Kuraimuhantā—Ikari no jūdan*, Ōkawa Toshimichi, 1989) mixes English and Japanese in written and spoken language and is filled with American police cars, foreign extras, and the use of nationally unspecific locations that reference American B-films as much as Nikkatsu anational (mukokuseki) action films of the 1950s and 1960s and Euro-American straight-to-video films of the 1980s. On March 10, 1989, *Crimehunter* was released to the estimated sixteen thousand video stores of Japan. It would become the foundational myth of a new industrial genre, much like *Flesh Market* had for Pink Film twenty-seven years earlier. V-Cinema, centered on narrative, live-action feature films produced by a specific group of companies primarily for the video market, would explode into the moving-image media ecology in Japan with a momentum unseen since Pink Film had appeared almost three decades earlier.

As an industrial genre, V-Cinema intervened in the trajectory I have been tracing through the film industry from the 1960s onward. If Pink Film and Kadokawa Film were concerned with opposing sociopolitical discourses of nation after 1945, V-Cinema engaged with its time through repurposing media history. Through its narratives, characters, industrial styles, and the very technology of videotapes, V-Cinema operated via a complex interplay of national history and media history. Chapters 5 and 6 outline the film-historical context of the 1980s, the different discursive strands that brought V-Cinema into being and how it hurtled toward its first crisis when the bubble economy collapsed in the 1990s. They then map the basic constellation of subgenres that characterize V-Cinema, each of them contributing to its larger discursive force in a specific way. At the center of this force is a specific relationship to time, at the cost of a defining space. This book uses the most basic definition of V-Cinema: a genre that is organized around narrative live-action film produced for the video market.[1]

Although it quickly became a generic term for all live-action feature films (excluding hard-core pornography) produced primarily for the video market, V-Cinema—pronounced *bui-shinema* in Japan—was initially the title of a new product line that Tōei Video, the video subsidiary of the former major studio Tōei, was experimenting with. While V-Cinema eventually became quite diverse in terms of subgenres, *Crimehunter*'s release set a number of paradigms for this new branch of the film industry, most significantly in its active pursuit of a very distinct relationship to time and history. It was one that would prove immediately successful and that was deeply connected to the technology of videotape. V-Cinema absorbed discourses that had been connected to the technology and social practice of video long before it began to form in 1989. At the center of these discourses stands the question of temporality and its increasing figuration as mediated temporality.

Video Technology Time

Appropriately for a genre that relies on the technology of home video—what Siegfried Zielinski has called a "time machine in two senses"—the issue of a specific experience of time resurfaced with renewed force at the time of V-Cinema's emergence.[2] On the eve of V-Cinema's appearance, star theorists Karatani Kōjin and Asada Akira met to speculate on Emperor Hirohito's impending death and the end of the Shōwa era (although he had already passed away by the time the dialogue was printed). The discussion centrally focused on the question of temporal discourses that run through different parts of contemporary Japanese society. In their complex and erratic exchange they touch on the meaning of historical parallels, questions of continuity and rupture, the danger of patterns of repetition and therefore war, as well as the possibility of change. One aspect they agree on is that there is a biological (*seibutsu-teki*) discourse and a resulting tendency toward system theory that runs through conceptions of imperial lineage, Japanese society, and literature in Japan. According to Asada and Karatani this biologism effects specific practices of memory, continuity, and change, with many troubling consequences. While their discussion treats literature primarily as a symptom, it also grants it prime status as the central medium for understanding the contemporary moment. It does not think about changing media paradigms and the significance of that change, and certainly not about videotape. Nor does it touch upon the problem of a society whose memory is already deeply and inextricably entangled with not only social history but also media history and mediated history.[3]

From its inception, video in Japan was connected to the narrative of postwar reconstruction, with an intensified media ecology, and with the confusion of controlled, linear time. As a technology primarily developed to allow a viewer to manipulate time by starting, pausing, rewinding, stopping, and rewatching at the viewer's convenience, video arguably tapped into experiences of temporality in a different way than cinema with its modern connotations of progress and linearity. In 1956, the Quadruplex videotape system enabled the U.S. television industry to solve various problems it had with time-shift broadcasting between time zones, and in 1958 the Ministry of Trade and Industry (MITI) of Japan had already created a roundtable of companies to coordinate research on videotape recorders. This time-manipulation technology was a central project that promised to become a stepping-stone to economic revitalization. Disrupting a model of linear time, however, arguably held a different connotation in Japan than it did in the United States. It tapped into the complicated temporal frameworks Japan had been locked into since at least the Meiji restoration, when it was forced into the role of being behind the United States and Europe. Disturbing that power relationship by dethroning linear time therefore had immense implications. When Sony advertised its Betamax recorders in full-page newspaper ads in the United States in 1981, they asked, "What time is it?" and proposed the technology as a special weapon in man's "historic battle against the dictates and restraints of time."[4] Sony's chairman, Morita Akio, repeatedly emphasized this discourse while also referencing video's self-definition as the Other of TV: "I noticed how the TV networks had total control over people's lives and I felt that people should have the option of seeing a program when they choose to."[5] Accordingly, video was often connected to utopian projects, and one of the first special issues on video technology by film magazine *Kinema Junpō* in 1971 was aptly titled "Videopia."[6]

Video technology allowed for control over the moment of playback as well as fast-forwarding, pausing, and rewinding. However, it still remained a linear playback medium; time manipulation itself took time and necessitated speeding through the tape and running through the linear order. That tension of time manipulation and its limits runs through V-Cinema as well. All of these functions potentially connected to the confusion of linear, colonial time that Japan itself was caught up in. However, in contrast to Pink Film's fraught relationship to the theme of a clean, historical rupture in the postwar system, or Kadokawa's synchronized, eternal present, V-Cinema had to negotiate the crisis capitalism of postbubble 1990s Japan through what we might call multiple impossible rewinds. Such impossible rewinds both suggested the possibility of replaying past historical moments, or rather fantasies thereof, and made the impossibility of such a replay obvious. The nation on tape—in its form as media history—therefore presented a highly compromised vision of linear historical continuity.

V-Cinema's limited disturbance of linear sequence extended beyond subgenre narratives and styles to its industrial structure and relationship to other media. Kadokawa Film had attempted to abolish temporal hierarchy in a cosmopolitan flash of simultaneity, among other things with its experiments with simultaneous video and theater release dates in the early 1980s. It soon had to return to a sequence prescribed by the market, with successive rollouts across different media: the novel was followed by the soundtrack was followed by the TV series was followed by the film.[7] In an environment characterized by media-mix strategies, V-Cinema was in constant interaction with other media channels. Yet, on the whole, it obstinately refused to become a link in a system that increasingly demanded media products that could multiply or travel across the entire spectrum of media, often in a specific order. While drawing on subgenres and works from different media, it circumvented the pull of sequence via low budgets, historically displaced subgenres, excessive serialization and repetition, an ostensible focus on one media platform, and the very technology of the time machine of video. This disruption permeates the narratives and styles of the genre as well. In large parts designed as a rewind of previous subgenres, narratives, and tropes, V-Cinema textuality is also deeply involved in confusing a media-history model of linear sequence. To what, however, do V-Cinema's temporal politics point?

Disturbance of linear temporal models has, from postcolonial theory to queer theory, increasingly become associated with some kind of resistance. Bliss Cua Lim has provided a lucid analysis of cinematic attempts to "glimpse an 'outside' to the regime of modern homogenous time," which for Lim is largely a structure imposed by colonialism.[8] Among others, Lim proposes temporal multiplicities and anachronisms as tactics that she always frames as resistant. Put differently, any disturbance of what Lim calls modern homogenous time is equivalent to anticolonial resistance. As we have seen, it was not that simple in the cases of Pink Film or for Kadokawa Film; similarly, V-Cinema complicates the easy distinction into oppressive versus resistant or subversive forces. As we will see, V-Cinema navigates a very intricate temporal topography, and while it is to some degree disruptive, it is also, like the other industrial genres, conciliatory and exploitative.

Naturally, despite its own protestations, V-Cinema was historically situated. With the burst of the asset bubble, the country entered a prolonged period of reflection on the Shōwa era and what it had entailed: empire, disastrous war, the detonation of atomic bombs on two cities, the postwar system, and spectacular economic recovery when bitter political unrest eventually transitioned into a culture of affluence and the monetary excesses of the 1980s. As the 1990s began, Shōwa-era nostalgia and increased controversy over the evaluation of the past and its specific models of historic rupture and continuity were soon to be accompanied by economic crisis from the early 1990s onward. According to sociologist Miyadai Shinji, anxiety over perennial stasis and the "never-ending everyday" characterized the decade.[9] V-Cinema offered a response that illustrates the changing role of history in a mediatized world.

Crimehunter

The executive producer of *Crimehunter*, Yoshida Tatsu, repeatedly formulated his prime directive for the film, one that exposes the temporal insecurity and challenge that the new video medium posed: to shoot a film that "would not be fast-forwarded."[10] For Yoshida, this temporal anxiety inevitably entailed a national dimension, as "Japanese films" were deemed "too explanatory, so they have no speed," when compared to *Back to the Future* (Robert Zemeckis, 1985) or Stallone films. This national marking of different speeds was an old theme. It had been discussed from the 1920s onward, perhaps most famously by director Masumura Yasuzō in his essay "On Speed" ("Supīdo ni tsuite"), in which he asked the film industry of Japan to make films more relatable for international audiences by focusing less on personal and internal struggles specific to the Japanese context.[11] Such a discourse was linked yet again to the question of global versus colonial time and the fear of being perennially behind, of being too slow. This fear was felt not only in Japan, but in Western Europe as well, where speed and Americanism were seen as intertwined beginning in the twentieth century. Yet, despite the heralding of a new type of "contents," many of the features of *Crimehunter* can be traced to traditions from the established film industry. The harking back to anational and action-film subgenres already points to a relationship to history that would become definitive for V-Cinema, especially in its curious stance on history. It shows that Yoshida's fear of the fast-forward was answered with the appeal of the rewind.

The specific direction V-Cinema took in its earliest form is partially due to the work experience of the individuals involved. The two producers of *Crimehunter*, Yoshida Tatsu and Kurosawa Mitsuru, were veterans of Tōei and Nikkatsu, respectively. Their presence factored largely in the early dominance of action (a 1960s Nikkatsu specialty) and yakuza (a Tōei specialty) films in the Tōei V-Cinema lineup, and would decisively shape early Tōei V-Cinema projects and the course of the genre in general.[12] Both had also worked for Kadokawa productions and were well aware of Kadokawa's temporal politics.

Crimehunter was also obviously modeled on traditions that are usually only cursorily, if at all, mentioned in writings on Japanese film history in English or Japanese. Throughout the 1950s, the major studios had produced medium-length features to complement their main program. These films were shot with much lower budgets, featured highly generic story lines, and were often used as a first testing ground for young staff and directors; what is usually called B-film in the United States is the closest approximation. Shōchiku was the first to introduce what was marketed under the name SP, for Sister Picture, in 1952; Tōei produced such films from 1954 and named them Tōei Goraku Ban (Tōei Entertainment Edition), which were usually shorter than sixty minutes.[13] And of course, Pink Film by now had a more than twenty-year history of showing how feature films could be standardized at a sixty-minute length. *Crimehunter* was likewise set at sixty minutes, and its narrative is so condensed that more than once it seems as if connecting scenes are simply missing. Well into the early 2000s, V-Cinema followed the tendency toward short feature films, usually around seventy minutes, with occasional longer films around ninety minutes in length. In effect, the new format of *Crimehunter* drew on a large number of predecessors and influences, among them mukokuseki films, the

V-Cinema · 157

B-film tradition in Japan, Pink Film, American straight-to-video and B-films, television series, and the running time of many made-for-video predecessors such as educational videos or short horror films.[14] V-Cinema re-presented aspects of past genres to create a specific model of history.

Crimehunter received considerable attention from the trade press due to the new strategy of producing exclusively for the video market—and again industry textuality interlocked with filmic textuality in defining the industrial genre. The film was a decent hit, selling around sixteen thousand tapes—an average of one tape per rental store—while production costs were reportedly around 60 million yen (at the time about $434,800, twenty times the budget of an average Pink Film).[15] Sales gross is hard to estimate in V-Cinema due to the common practice of discounts and package deals. However, even if the average gross were a reasonable 10,000 yen per tape (it was officially priced considerably higher), the total gross would still stand at about 160 million yen (about $1,160,000).[16] Encouraged, Tōei Video released two more V-Cinema films in 1989, *Crimehunter 2* (*Kuraimuhantā 2*, Ōkawa Toshimichi) and *Sniper—The Shootist* (*Sogeki—The shootist*, Ichikura Haruo). Subsequently, it announced it would go into continuous production of one film a month in April 1990 and increase the number to two to three films a month in October. The first film on this regular release schedule was *Black Princess—Angel from Hell* (*Burakku purinsesu—Jigoku no tenshi*, Tanaka Hideo), the story of a female cop out to get revenge for the murder of her brother. While the emphasis was squarely on action films, several yakuza films were produced as well.

Several of the films from the V-Cinema lineup sold over thirty thousand tapes, which at the time qualified as a huge hit, and due to its well-known profitability, the early Tōei V-Cinema lineup became paradigmatic for the genre on various levels.[17] Most visibly, the action subgenre would exert considerable influence on other companies' approach to the genre. Nikkatsu entered the V-Cinema arena with *Capital City High Speed Trial 2* (*Shuto kōsoku toraiaru 2*, Kataoka Shūji, 1990), a "car-action" film; Tōhokushinsha entered with *Big Breast Hunter* (*Kyonyū hantā*, Watanabe Hisashi, 1990), a "sexy action film"; and Japan Home Video with the "gun-action" vehicle *Blowback* (*Burōbakku—Mayonaka no gyangu-tachi*, Muroga Atsushi, 1990).[18] By 1991, over twenty companies had started producing around 150 films annually for the video market, numbers reminiscent of the first appearance of Pink Film. Meanwhile, 230 films from Japan were being released theatrically, the lowest figure since 1951, and theatrical attendance had sunk to its lowest point since the end of the war.[19] While the appearance of Pink Film had once stabilized the number of theatrical releases at a time when major-studio production was sinking, V-Cinema migrated its productions to a different reception space and a different media technology.

Many of the titles chosen as brand names by the respective producers attest to the influence of Tōei Video's V-Cinema line: Japan Home Video named its line V-Movie; Nikkatsu chose V-Feature; Nihon Video Eiga used V-Theater; while VIP chose V-Picture. V-Cinema, however, quickly became the term of choice for the entire genre, with all other brands subsumed under this generic label. The categories of *orijinaru bideo* (original video) or *bideo orijinaru* designate that a product has been made for the video market and include works that are not strictly narrative, such as idol videos (often set at the beach or in exotic locales), wrestling specials, and how-to golf videos. V-Cinema, on the other hand, is an industrial genre—a recognizable body of films and a connected, specific section of the moving-image industry that is part of a shared discourse.

Besides the action tendency, *Crimehunter* established several additional patterns that exerted a strong influence on V-Cinema. The focus on a male star, often an actor with a background in singing, and one or several female sidekicks to supply various levels of visual titillation for a presumed male heterosexual audience, is an enduring characteristic. Serialization tentatively began with *Crimehunter* and its three installments, and eventually V-Cinema developed an extraordinarily serial nature that is important for its temporal discourse. While early series merely counted three or four entries, later successful series far exceeded this number. There were as many as thirty-plus in *Seriously!* (*Maji!*), a comedic series about a young yakuza; forty in *Code of Conduct* (*Jingi*), a ninkyō yakuza series; or even fifty installments of *The King of Minami* (*Minami no teiō*), revolving around a loan shark in Osaka. While V-Cinema contains a number of fairly unique subgenres—the money-lending subgenre, the pachinko and mah-jongg films among them—most of the films rely on models from subgenres that were popular in the 1960s and 1970s. This, along with the pattern of regular monthly-release quotas, often induced commentators to remark on a rebirth of the program picture.[20]

V-Cinema Practice

"An odd creature has resuscitated the action film: On the set of Tōei V-Cinema's *Akunin Senyō*," critic Yamane Sadao writes in 1990.[21] For an entirely new section of the moving-image industry, the rhetoric of repetition with regard to V-Cinema is striking. The association of V-Cinema with the program

FIGURE 5.1. Jacket sleeve of *Black Princess—Angel from Hell*. The first of Tōei's regular production line for V-Cinema, the marketing follows the model of *Crimehunter*. The cover characteristically features only the name of the main actress—and her commodified body—while the director's name is in the fine print on the back.

picture, which Yamane also touches upon in his article, is closely connected to the supposed reappearance of a specific industrial practice. Yet here V-Cinema is already less a revival than an impossible rewind.

Ostensibly replaying the program-picture production systems of the 1950s studios, V-Cinema in fact shifted away from a studio model toward outsourced competition, casualization, and exploitation to a quite radical degree.

Usually V-Cinema is discussed as a producer-oriented system; in comparison with theatrical film production of the 1990s this is perfectly accurate. V-Cinema granted a small number of directors a degree of freedom, especially with regard to long-running series; however, in comparison to mainstream films for the theatrical market, the director's status was greatly reduced. When V-Cinema appeared in 1989, the marketing value and public profile of a director's name was strongly increasing, partially due to the breakdown of studio production. Where an audience had once gone to see a Shōchiku film, they might now go to see a Yamada Yōji film. Directors increasingly became an additional publicity tool, which also increased the number of so-called *igyō* (non-[film] business) directors, especially for theatrically released film. Igyō directors were often well-known figures from the entertainment or, sometimes, literary world with no prior experience in directing. In 1991 alone, over fifty new directors debuted, and while the greatest number were situated within V-Cinema, an astonishing eighteen were igyō directors debuting in theatrically released film.[22] Usually igyō directors disappeared from directing very swiftly, but several enjoyed extensive film careers as directors, among them comedian Takeshi Kitano, playwright Terayama Shūji, or manga artist Ōtomo Katsuhiro.[23]

V-Cinema has supplied a great number of young and not-so-young directors with the chance to work, but it has rarely released them into the mainstream or even other sections of the industry (the case is somewhat different for other staff involved in production). As an industrial genre, it is highly self-contained, with its own rules of financing, production, and distribution, with a hermetic star system and specific labor relations. In Europe and America, V-Cinema has mainly leaked in through the work of Miike Takashi, one of the few directors who transitioned from V-Cinema into more mainstream success. A small number of examples of V-Cinema films have also entered the international festival circuit, such as Mochizuki Rokurō's *The Outer Way* (*Gedō*, 1998) or Kobayashi Masahiro's *Film Noir* (*Koroshi*, 2000).[24] Several directors now discussed and marketed as auteurs worked in V-Cinema, even if they did not begin there, among them Kurosawa Kiyoshi, Shiota Akihiko, and Aoyama Shinji. But only very few emerged from V-Cinema in the way Pink Film became a training ground for a generation of mainstream directors.

The initial explosion of production activity supplied not only young debuting directors but also many veteran directors with work opportunities, albeit often short lived. Directors such as Konuma Masaru of Roman Porno fame, Jissōji Akio (of ATG and *Ultraman* fame), Kudō Eiichi of Second Tōei, and Nishimura Kiyoshi, known for Tōhō's 1960s New Action line, found much-needed work in the genre. There was a large influx of staff from Nikkatsu Roman Porno and especially Pink Film, as these directors exploited their experience with low-budget shooting techniques and were increasingly desperate for work in their troubled native industry. Kobayashi Satoru, Takahashi Banmei, Mukai Kan, Gotō Daisuke, Tomioka Tadafumi, and Takahara Kazuo (the latter two both of Yū Pro) or Kataoka Shūji shot extensively within V-Cinema, and even three of the Four Devils of Pink Film found refuge in

V-Cinema at times; Zeze Takahisa, Satō Toshiki, and Satō Hisayasu all have worked within the genre, and for young Pink Film directors it became a vital source of meager income. With at times over 250 films released in V-Cinema annually, a substantial number of directors who debuted in V-Cinema either remain there to this day or simply disappear from directing. However, even those directors highly successful within the V-Cinema framework, such as Haginiwa Sadaaki or Matsui Noboru, are virtually unknown by name, though the titles of the series they work on—*The King of Minami* and *Jingi*, respectively—may be quite famous. Technical staff, on the other hand, move most freely across the industry, as they are rarely a part of the discourse that defines genres. V-Cinema has accordingly been an important part-time job and training ground for cameramen, lighting directors, sound editors, and so on, and again supplied many veterans with work. Cinematographer Sengen Seizō, for example, worked extensively for Kadokawa films and later became very active within V-Cinema, while periodically shooting films intended for theatrical release.[25] With time, however, even the mobility of the technical staff decreased, as special skills are required for the extremely tight shooting schedules and ever-decreasing budgets.

This V-Cinema tendency to privilege the producer over the director and the subgenre over the individual film has much to do with the fact that most V-Cinema companies have their roots in video packaging and distribution. This is also part of the reason for the reconstruction of genres such as action, yakuza, or sexploitation, which in turn contributed to V-Cinema's impossible rewind. These companies preferred easily marketable films, which generally resulted in films that conformed to certain subgeneric recipes. Their relative inexperience in production reinforced the adherence to preformed patterns and supported a rewind strategy. When such companies entered production to participate in V-Cinema, they often dispatched employees with no previous experience to the production department and occasionally even let them direct.[26] Indeed, even today it is official policy in many companies to recruit employees from sections unrelated to film to be producers, or to favor new recruits with no formal film education, to ensure a "business perspective" rather than an "art perspective."[27]

One important example of this tendency—with immense consequences for film all over Asia and in Hollywood—took place in 1991 and led to the creation of the J-horror brand. Following the scandal around the supposed horror film collection of child murderer Miyazaki Tsutomu in 1989, video companies were forced to retreat from the production and distribution of explicitly bloody horror films. Horror films of the splatter variety had been some of the first films produced exclusively for the video market, the *Guinea Pig* series or Bandai's *Stolen Heart* (*Ubawareta Shinzo*, Hayakawa Hikari, based on an Umezu Kazuo manga) appearing as early as 1985. Nonetheless, companies were searching for a way to return to the horror film market when Tsuruta Norio, who was working as a subtitle producer for JHV, proposed a series focusing on atmospheric supernatural horror centered on schoolgirls having scary experiences. Tsuruta produced (and directed) the films with only 7 million yen ($51,851, or one-tenth of the Tōei V-Cinema budget) in three days, and this became the immensely popular *True Scary Stories* (*Hontō ni atta kowai hanashi*) series. Years later, scriptwriter Takahashi Hiroshi and director Nakata Hideo, fans of Tsuruta's films, used the series' aesthetics to craft a chilling type of horror for the film version of Suzuki Kōji's novel *Ringu*. The resulting film became the template for what was to be called J-horror, and it influenced horror films throughout Asia and led to Hollywood remakes such as *The Ring* (Gore Verbinski, 2002), *The Grudge* (Shimizu Takashi, 2004), and *Dark Water* (Walter Salles, 2005). Tsuruta was not exactly a stranger to directing; he had been a prominent figure in the Japanese 8 mm film scene of the 1980s with classics such as *Toneriko* (1985). Nonetheless, it was the influence of the production side that made his transition into commercial film directing possible. The complaint that V-Cinema producers don't understand film is common among directors, especially if they come from a Pink Film background where they often experience less direct supervision.[28]

Producers also exert a relatively higher level of control for a number of financial reasons. While eminently low budget, V-Cinema has generally had considerably higher budgets than its Pink Film counterparts have—in the early phase often close to a factor of twenty. This has enabled V-Cinema companies to purchase rights for stories and titles from books, serialized articles, and especially manga, which can occasionally lead to restrictions for the director regarding the treatment of the material. As income from dissemination is less secure than with Pink films and the block-booking system, the individual film has less leeway for deviation from a concept or formula. Also significant is the employment of actresses, singers, models, or idols who are under contract with very powerful talent agencies. Even on the less prolific V-Cinema level, the agencies strictly control the image of their talent stable, and the director is often given certain guidelines for their portrayal in advance, such as the degree of acceptable nudity, if they are allowed to smoke, or which clothes to wear.[29] Nonetheless, intervention from the (executive) producers' side is fairly uncommon in V-Cinema, especially after approval of the script and the casting stage.

Scripts are usually not written by the directors themselves, and scriptwriting has been one of the more permeable areas of V-Cinema with regard to other genres. Many scriptwriters active in V-Cinema (often under an assumed name) also work in television, Pink Film, or theatrical film. Graduates from film schools apparently find work as V-Cinema scriptwriters comparatively quickly, as some production companies deem them easier to control.[30] Scripts are, generally, subject to considerable influence by the production companies, who (from *Crimehunter* onward) have usually demanded highly dramatic conflict structures, with clear delineations of the main character and his or her nemesis, and a narrative leading squarely to the resulting finale. This, as well, is a considerable difference from much of the theatrically released film in Japan during the 1980s and 1990s.

The emphasis on the producer and the relatively weaker positions of the scriptwriters and directors have also been a source of ongoing legal conflict. With few exceptions, it is common practice within V-Cinema for the director and scriptwriter to contractually relinquish all claims on royalties with regard to second use in television or other media. This practice is not viewed as acceptable in theatrical film production, and it has been a source of contention for both the Directors Guild and the Japan Writers Guild since V-Cinema's beginning.[31] This conflict points to the highly casualized nature of labor relations within the V-Cinema industry, which far outstrips even those of Pink Film. While once an avant-garde of casualization, Pink Film still retains a minor level of control for the director, who is also the de facto producer. In V-Cinema this is decidedly not the case. Outsourcing of actual production has always been common, and has increasingly become standard practice. Contracts are issued on a per-project basis, with no further royalties, benefits, or guarantees. This is the decisive flaw within the program-picture analogy that is (falsely) accepted wisdom with regard to V-Cinema: while program pictures such as Pink Film and the studio system created legally or informally binding, long-lasting networks of labor relations and film distribution, V-Cinema, for all the conservative and nostalgic discourses penetrating it, is decidedly of the 1990s in terms of highly liberalized business practice. Subcontractors involved in production have much less security in terms of continuous work, and the videos are rarely guaranteed a spot in the video store; instead each must compete for attention and inclusion on its own.

It is important to emphasize how thoroughly V-Cinema as a genre—with well over three thousand films produced since 1989—has been ignored in critical and academic discourse on film from Japan. The image of a banal, vulgar, artistically underwhelming product churned out for quantity rather than quality is not easily subsumed into frameworks such as auteurism, masterpieces, or radical subversion. And indeed, against the backdrop of the 1960s and 1970s subgenres that V-Cinema references, many of these low-budget films might appear as degraded reruns and anemic shadows of a glorious past. In one of the most reductively business-oriented sections of the Japanese film industry, the garish jacket covers reinforce an image of cheap appeal to sex and violence. This does not appear significantly different from much of the films of the 1960s and 1970s, but these goods are stripped of the stylishness and production value even a dying studio system could provide.

In the early phase of V-Cinema, Yamane Sadao was the only prominent critic to occasionally write on V-Cinema, hoping for a "resurrection of the program picture" and rejoicing at each veteran director who secured a job.[32] From 1991, practically the only person to publish regularly on V-Cinema in a critical, if not academic, capacity was the critic Tanioka Masaki. As even annual roundups of the industry's output disappeared from the various yearbooks from the mid-1990s onward, from the mid-2000s Tanioka found himself writing not for film magazines, but for *Truck King*, a periodical aimed at truckers.[33]

And yet the role of V-Cinema, that genre of retrograde and low-budget fantasies of masculinity, helps us detect the trajectory of media praxis and technology at the cusp of the digital age. V-Cinema never had the overt political relevance of Pink Film, nor did it publicly embody a fundamental industrial and cultural shift like Kadokawa Film did. Yet it fulfilled the fascinating function of bridging a new media ecology and an old film world that was melting into air. *Crimehunter* utilized a collective media memory and linked new media technologies to a specific politics of time in a moment of socioeconomic crisis. To understand the specific relational implications V-Cinema entailed and the context it developed in, it is now necessary to take a look at the history of the home video market in Japan.

Home Video in Japan

"The Age of Bedside Cinema!" was the headline the magazine *Seijin Eiga* chose for its decidedly Pink Film–inflected perspective on the beginning of video rentals to hotels and hot springs in 1970. This headline alone points to the fact that video relied on its relation to other media to define itself to an even larger degree than other "new" media such as games did. Video came into being as both a counter and an extension of cinema and TV. V-Cinema would later exist in occasional if subdued interaction with (primarily) film, manga, and TV.

The first rush to capitalize on video playback technology began at the end of the 1960s, resulting in a much-needed shot in the arm for the Pink Film industry. However, it was not just film companies that were interested in this major business opportunity. The race for a portion of the future market opened with the founding of Fuji Pony in early 1970, a joint venture between broadcasters Fuji TV, Nippon Hōsō, and Pony, a Nippon Hōsō affiliate. Fuji Pony's director, Ishida Tatsurō, famously proclaimed that the video market would be worth 500 billion yen ($1,388,900,000) in ten years, and it quickly became clear that everyone wanted a part in this development.[34] By late 1971, broadcasters, publishers, and film companies had joined the rush and formed well over a hundred new companies with the intention of producing and selling video content. The major studios participated as well. Tōhō created a section for distribution of videotapes mainly to ships in 1969. Nikkatsu sold its action films as well as Pink films from Ōkura and Shintōhō through its sound-recording division. Tōei launched Tōei Video as an affiliate in 1970, the same year the Japan Video Association (JVA) formed to represent the flood of new companies.[35]

At this point, video was still targeted at highly specialized groups and for stringently defined viewing objectives. Educational videos for schools were the largest segment, followed by educational videos targeting businesses, crews working on ships, and finally resorts. The first lineup of seventeen Fuji Pony tapes included educational tapes on ballet, golf, and bowling; a documentary on the Sahara; and two anime films produced by Tezuka Osamu's Mushi Production, episodes of *Astro Boy* (*Tetsuwan atomu*) and *Kimba the White Lion* (*Jangaru Taitei*).[36] Several titles indicate more adult entertainment as well, with *Burlesque in Japan—a Fairytale of the Night* (*Bāresuku in Japan—Yoru no dōwa*) and *Burlesque in Japan—the Fantasy of Woman* (*Bāresuku in Japan—Onna no fantajii*) included. Anime and adult entertainment remained mainstays of the video business to the 2010s, and even in 1971 a special issue of the magazine *Videopia* declared, "What can be sold on video are, in the first place, Pink films."[37] At the time, however, sexually themed material was, as described above, under considerable legal pressure, and those wanting to enter the emerging market felt they needed some security.[38] Following the police action against Tōei Video in 1971 and Nikkatsu (video and theatrical) in 1972, Tōei, Nikkatsu, and Japan Bicott joined to form the Adult Video Regulations Autonomous Round Table (Seijin Bideo Jishu Kisei Kodankai). This was an early incarnation of Biderin, the video counterpart of Eirin, meant to provide independent and voluntary self-censorship of adult films on video (Biderin also calls itself NEVA, the Nihon Ethics of Video Association).

In the early 1970s, high prices still made it difficult for private citizens to partake in the technology on an individual basis. Videos (and screening equipment) could often be rented, but an actual rental business had not yet formed; prerecorded videos were usually only available for sale, and at prohibitively high prices. There were attempts to bundle the rental of video machines and tapes as early as 1972, mostly by department stores, but all of them were discontinued. In 1975, however, Sony introduced its consumer-model Betamax recorder to the Japanese market, and in 1976, JVC/Victor launched its VHS recorder. The immediate leap in dissemination of the technology now made a rental business for individual customers viable. On June 23, 1977, the first video rental store in Tokyo opened in the cellar of the Nichigeki Building in the Ginza district, known as a center of expensive and glamorous shopping.[39] The high prices for sell-through videos and of the machines themselves still restricted the target group to—simply put—people with money. Though the Japan Video Software Association (Nihon Eizō Sofuto Kyōkai, formerly the Japan Video Association) oversaw this pilot project, Tōhō ran the shop under commission as the Tōhō Video Shop. Rental fees were set for four days, according to tape length, from 1,000 yen (or $3.77, for twenty minutes) to 3,000 yen (or $11.32, for over ninety minutes) for members.[40] While rentals hovered at a mere average of two tapes per day from 1977 to 1980, the statistics on what kind of films were rented would have a profound impact on the further development of the video business.

War and desire are often-named culprits for the development of technology, and video does little to disprove this too-easy axiom. Ampex, the company that developed the Quadruplex video system, was in fact extensively involved in developing the technology for the U.S. Navy. On the other hand, one of the main motors for early video-deck use was the desire of a very specific kind of spectator, the young, single, and heterosexual (at least according to industry marketing) male.[41] It was common practice to include adult film tapes as a bonus with video-deck sales to make them more attractive. Sexually themed content could now be viewed in the confines of the home, in an even more private space than the already highly segregated Pink and Nikkatsu Roman Porno theaters. With the dissemination of video decks, the demand for sexually themed video material exploded, and the Adult Video Regulations Autonomous Round Table was unable to cope with the number of films. They reorganized themselves, attained status as a legal entity, and renamed themselves Biderin (Nihon Bideo Rinri Kyōkai / NEVA) in 1977.[42] By the late 2000s, Biderin claimed to check around seven thousand videos and DVDs a year for approval.[43]

According to the statistics the JVA gathered through the Tōhō Video Shop in Ginza, from 1977 to 1980 adult films constituted 40 percent of rentals, and feature films also took 40 percent (it is unclear how this distinction was made and to which degree feature films included sexually themed films). Ninety-three percent of all customers were male.[44] This was the upscale urban aspect of early video rental, and one that captured companies' attention.

Yet around the same time in Nagoya, a movie theater by the name of Endōji Theater would have a similarly large influence on the future rental business. It also presents a fascinating example of the complex terrain of media technologies, channels, and practices that video was navigating in this early phase. The Endōji had launched a rental service, the Nagoya Video Library (Nagoya Bideo Toshokan), around the same time that the store in Ginza opened. Initially a *meigaza*, a theater specializing in famous films and classics, the Endōji's programming leaned so heavily toward sexually themed films that it was almost a kind of Pink theater. The programs consisted of two quintuple bills a day, often films arranged by theme, and usually a combination of Pink films and Nikkatsu Roman Porno. But the Endōji was also experimenting with several other techniques for catching customers. The theater eventually began buying videos that it initially showed on a TV set in the theater and established a manga library.[45] For 500 yen ($1.89), one could decide to either lounge around and read or watch some films; this was a forerunner of the manga library-cum-Internet cafés that now line the streets of Japanese cities.

The Endōji switched to a video rental system fairly soon and offered three days, two nights for a rental price of about 10 percent of its cost to purchase the tape. At the time, buying a ninety-minute tape of a foreign film would cost around 40,000 yen (about $150), while films from Japan were often a bit more expensive at 50,000, and sixty-minute Nikkatsu Roman Porno films and Pink films cut down to thirty minutes would cost 25,000.[46] Though not cheap, these tapes were competing with pricier edited 8 mm versions of feature films that Pink Film companies and the majors had been selling for years. For example, in 1973 OP issued a fifteen-minute version of a Seki Kōji film as *The Blind Spot of Peeping* (*Nozoki no shikaku*), priced at 15,800 yen. Some estimates have listed the proportion of income through adult content as oscillating between 20 percent and almost 40 percent of the video market during the late 1970s and early 1980s.[47] While there were, for supply reasons, not that many Roman Porno and Pink films on offer in Endōji's rental business, the selection was highly influenced by the demographics of the spectators frequenting the theater, which were 99 percent male.[48] When the larger companies decided to design a systematic rental program, representatives of Biderin, Warner (the first in Japan to begin selling tapes expressly for rental), and Pony Canyon all visited the Endōji to inquire about its experience with video rental, which informed their future business strategies.[49]

Video Labels: Space, Gender, and Multiple Media

With the video rental store in the Ginza district and the Endōji Theater in Nagoya, two distinct strains of discourse within the video market come into view. In Ginza, video was marked as a fashionable and expensive high-tech commodity. At the Endōji, it was a working-class, "Japanese," and gender-segregated space, much like the Pink Film screening space. Despite these differences, video was obviously positioned as a male domain in terms of both video-deck sales and tape rentals. This would change somewhat, but even in 1989 Yoshida Tatsu at Tōei saw the reduced but still distinct predominance of male customers as the best target group for V-Cinema. According to the JVA, even in 1993 men held over 70 percent of the video store memberships.[50]

The implications of nation that were so central to Pink Film, and that Kadokawa relied on as well, initially seemed less relevant to video. Videotape had the potential to be a window onto film from Japan and abroad, an outsourced, technologically improved, and accessible memory bank with strong international leanings. However, the overwhelming majority of books published for the new videotape consumer in the 1980s focused almost exclusively on yōga.[51] When the magazine *Kinema Junpō* organized a roundtable discussion on the new rental market in 1984, it only invited representatives of the affiliates of the large American distributors: Warner Home Video, RCA Columbia, CIC Victor, and MGM/UA.[52] Prerecorded video was obviously being marketed as a reference library of foreign, primarily European and American, products.

Yet the reality of usage was quite different, at least in the early stage. According to statistics from the JVA, even in 1986 22.8 percent of all income from prerecorded videotape sales came from Japanese feature films, and only 16.8 percent was from foreign film. Another 13.9 percent came from anime and 13.8 percent from musical performances by Japanese musicians.[53] Without question, there is a hidden gender bias within these figures. While the statistics also mention that an additional 5.2 percent of income is made from adult entertainment, this in all probability designates the new and burgeoning AV (adult video) genre, not subsumed under Japanese films because of its documentary style and disreputable status. However, when compared to other available statistics, the figure seems far too low to account for the total number of sexually themed films in circulation at the time. The 22.8 percent designated as Japanese films would therefore probably include a significant portion of Pink films and especially Nikkatsu Roman Porno and sexually themed Tōei films. Since Tōei had established itself as a large player in the video market fairly early on, Tōei yakuza films were also a large part of the films from Japan on offer.

A decisive shift took place with video that would become a determining factor for V-Cinema. As represented by the Endōji's coordination of a male-designated screening space with a video rental store, the biases that linked gender and genre in the 1960s and 1970s were initially transposed to video (and continued to rely on a naturalized gender binary). They relocated the association of certain subgenres, nation, and gender to the home. Video continued the partitioning of space with a gender bias, yet the home viewing situation arguably transforms the mechanisms of identification and selfhood and works very differently than the communal, semipublic space of Pink Film. In 1985 Hatano Tetsurō claimed that the potential for repetition inherent in video robs film of its essential space, somewhat in the way that reproducibility robbed, according to Benjamin, the artwork of its aura.[54] The word that Hatano uses in Japanese is *ba*, which has an extremely wide and complex range of associations but implies a public aspect, a concept of space as a social discourse. Such a statement stands in interesting conflict with Fredric Jameson's claim that postmodernism is defined by a shift to space, and the "end of temporality."[55] How V-Cinema potentially fits into discussions of postmodernism is a complex topic. However, it is clear that V-Cinema emphasizes a specific temporal politics that at least disturbs modern conceptions of time, and that V-Cinema's lack of its own space weakened its ability to cohere as an industrial genre, eventually contributing to its fading away as such.

Theatrical film in the 1980s, on the other hand, refreshed the division of public media space and charged it with meaning along the axis of gender. While Kadokawa was numbing the general audience to spatial labeling with his yōga-release strategies, video became tied fundamentally to a phenomenon that further deepened the discourse of spatial division. This time, it was a space connoted as female that asserted itself. The proliferation of the so-called minitheaters in the 1980s runs almost perfectly parallel to the video rental boom, and the two quickly developed a near symbiotic relationship.

Minitheaters were theaters that specialized in a certain type of film, usually what in the United States would be designated as American or European art

FIGURE 5.2. A report in the March 1977 edition of women's magazine *Josei Jishin* that figures female anxiety about male-marked screening spaces. The headline reads, "Shock! First-Class Theaters Are Swarming with Mites/Ticks!" The article goes on to say that "fifty-eight types are targeting the soft skin of women." On the eve of the appearance of minitheaters, marketed to female audiences as clean and safe public spaces, the decrepit theaters with their often male-oriented fare were increasingly inaccessible to women. "Nihon Fushigi Banashi: Shock! Ichiryū Eigakan ni Dani ga Uyouyo Desu'tte!" [Strange stories from Japan: Shock! First-class theaters are swarming with mites/ticks!], *Josei Jishin*, March 3, 1977, 145.

house cinema. The films were often screened in a single theater, which was in turn connected to an independent distributor. Minitheaters often had an atmosphere of stylish luxury, a sanitized modernity that was supposed to appeal to a young, female demographic. Minitheaters succeeded, at least in urban centers, in recapturing the female audience for theatrically released film by latching onto the same binaries that had structured Pink Film, although with inverted valences. Again, Westernized, modern consumer culture associated with a "feminized" public sphere was juxtaposed with Japanese male realism.

Video became video via a net of relations to and dependencies on multiple media channels and technologies. On the other hand, to a certain degree it was the video market that even made a critical mass of minitheaters possible. It was the income from selling video distribution rights to video packaging companies that enabled the establishment of the small, at times tiny, distribution outfits that supplied the minitheaters with films. In turn, the publicity generated from a theatrical release—and the general press's enthusiastic

V-Cinema · 171

support for the minitheaters played a large role in this—benefited the video market enormously. Films without a theatrical release were becoming increasingly difficult to sell as the number of video releases rose considerably in the late 1980s. Both businesses relied heavily on each other, and both profited. This went so far that prominent industry figures such as Kawakita Kazuko decried the close connections between the video business and selective minitheaters, claiming that they were often creating alibi releases only meant to boost video sales.[56]

Minitheaters and the video business were so hungry for new films that the supply did not meet the demand. In the mid- and late 1980s, theaters and audience attendance trended downward, and yet the number of films released theatrically was swelling. In 1980, on the eve of the first minitheater boom, a total of 529 films were released theatrically (320 from Japan, 209 foreign); by 1989 the number had risen to 777 films (255 from Japan, 522 foreign).[57] The minitheaters' bias toward foreign film is obvious in these numbers, and the effects trickled down to the video industry. The demand for new product was immense, and in 1988 the trade paper *Nikkei Entertainment* published a special report titled "There Isn't Enough Soft!?" Here, "soft" is an abbreviation for "software," which is what is usually referred to as media content in the United States.[58] The article named three factors that were making films an increasingly sought-after commodity: the emergence of the video rental market, the introduction of cable television (CATV), and the introduction of twenty-four-hour broadcasting.

Different sections of the industry found different answers to the dearth of media content and the resulting rise in prices. Distributors specializing in the minitheater market increasingly searched for niche films, especially in not-yet-established foreign markets, leading to a strong internationalization of the films that were available to the moviegoing public. Encouraged by the enormous money surplus of the bubble economy, media companies (and several with no relation to the media business whatsoever) began investing in production. The television station TBS, beverage manufacturer Suntory, and the Itōchū corporation invested in three MGM/UA films.[59] Fuji TV increased investment in film production as well, resulting in productions such as *1/2 of Eternity* (*Eien no nibun no ichi*, Negishi Kichitarō, 1987) and *Summer Vacation 1999* (*1999-nen no natsu yasumi*, Kaneko Shūsuke, 1988). Sony and Matsushita moved beyond the investment in individual films and put money directly into Columbia and MCA. And finally, companies involved in video packaging were beginning to find that, with prices for video rights rising exorbitantly, producing a film for the same price as purchasing one might be a profitable business alternative—especially since one retained rights indefinitely. Thus Tōei, the major company still most grounded in production and with one of the longest-running involvements in the video market, became the first to embark on regular feature film straight-to-video production with *Crimehunter*.

V-Cinema Genre Formation and the First Crisis

Crimehunter's problematic position as the supposedly first V-Cinema film ignores the fact that there were numerous precursors to Tōei's straight-to-video strategy in Japan. As mentioned, educational videos had been a mainstay of the video rental market for years, while Nikkatsu and Tōei had produced narrative, sexually themed, thirty-minute videos following the success of the first appearance of AV films in 1981.[60] Bandai had started producing original video animation (OVA) as early as 1983, when it released the first OVA series *Dallos* (*Darosu*, Oshii Mamoru). In fact, even Tōei Video itself had been involved with OVA production from 1986 on. There had also been a variety of video horror productions, such as the infamous splatter series *Guinea Pig*, that played to the mid-1980s horror-film boom (itself very much connected to video).[61] Even so, *Crimehunter* did indeed lay the foundation for what was to become the industrial genre of V-Cinema.

As detailed above, *Crimehunter* heavily referenced subgenres, gender models, and themes taken from the archive of 1960s and 1970s media texts. On the level of narratives, themes, and styles, it was a compressed and sped-up compendium of film-historical elements, yet always aware that a simple rewind was impossible. As a genre, V-Cinema relied on the technology of video to mark itself as new while presenting a decontextualized remix of film history. The tendency to performatively deny historicity has remained one of the core attributes of V-Cinema throughout the early 2000s. On the contrary, of course, V-Cinema was very much of its time and founded on historical factors that formed the genre and influenced audience demand.

In fact, the eve of the V-Cinema boom was not one of unblemished promise for the video industry. The appearance of *Crimehunter* coincided quite precisely with the general opinion that the video business had passed its prime—a fact that may have actually encouraged many video packaging companies to invest in the straight-to-video production strategy. According to the JVA's figures, in 1989 video rental stores' average income declined for the first time in the history of the business. From this year onward the number of video rental stores would sink annually from its high point of sixteen thousand. With few new stores being opened, there was less demand for large numbers of tapes to fill an initial stock. Additionally, films were becoming increasingly difficult to sell without a previous theatrical release. Japanese feature film was in worse shape in the video market than in the theaters. In 1989, according to film magazine *Kinema Junpō*, just over 19 percent of all tapes in stock in stores were live-action feature films from Japan, while over 44 percent were foreign—predominantly American. An additional 11.5 percent were anime (mostly OVA) and 17.6 percent were adult entertainment.[62]

And yet video generated immense profits, and the former majors were often only alive because they had diversified across media. Tōei was making 22 percent of its total income with video. Nikkatsu, which had retired Roman Porno production, partially due to pressure from the AV market, relied on video to make up 48 percent of its total income.[63] *Crimehunter* set out to capitalize on the potential that low-budget production could offer, and by 1990, nine of the top thirty films from Japan sold on video were from the Tōei V-Cinema lineup, all selling around thirty thousand tapes.[64] Almost immediately, Tōei and its successful action-film model seemed to be what all other companies were out to emulate.

But another narrative of crisis was to come crashing in, this time one of national dimensions. In 1990–91 the Japanese assets price bubble burst, abruptly ending what is infamously known as the bubble era. The burst plunged Japan from a decade characterized, at least in the public mind, by affluent hedonism and enthusiastic consumerism into years of economic crisis and recession. The start of what was later commonly called the lost decade(s) had a profound impact on the direction of V-Cinema. One was in terms of financing, as businesses from outside the film industry stopped investing in film production almost immediately. What had formerly been a matter of prestige, tax write-offs, and diversification was now deemed unnecessary and dangerous. The theatrical film industry was suffering as well. The former majors and other film-related companies had diversified into other businesses since the late 1950s, but the excessive cash flows of the 1980s had intensified their nonmedia activity to a degree that now became a dangerous handicap. Businesses such as real estate had been attractive as land prices skyrocketed, but now became an extremely risky and potentially dangerous financial burden. Nikkatsu's bankruptcy in 1993 happened in part due to failed investments in golf courses and amusement parks, among others.[65]

Kadokawa Haruki's spectacular arrest exacerbated the perception of the end of an era, while the apparently desolate state of many companies' finances became a serious threat to the job security of countless employees. At the same time, competition became even more intense for the media companies that had secured a powerful position within distribution. With Japan Satellite Communications (JSC) getting ready to launch satellite television in earnest in 1991, prices for media content were as high as ever, and rising. What was needed now was cheap content, and one efficient way of acquiring it was to enter production. However, with the possible exception of period films, action was among the most expensive subgenres, and not all companies had the funds and resources that Tōei boasted. V-Cinema was obviously developing into a genre in which films were distinguished primarily by subgenres, and companies immediately began scrambling to find story patterns and settings that would appeal to the desired audience—still seen primarily as young and male.

The burst of the bubble along with the increased reflection on the Shōwa era brought about a considerable mood shift in the media, in business, and in general public sensibility. The 1990s are often—though somewhat simplistically—described as a time of increasing conservatism during which economic troubles provoked a reassertion of national identity, traditional values, and often reactionary politics. The feeling of ennui and the impossibility of change was epitomized in sociologist Miyadai Shinji's aforementioned concept of the "endless everyday." The gleeful consumerist internationalism of Kadokawa Film and the 1980s disappeared with the onset of large-scale bankruptcies, layoffs, and a general sense of crisis that would deepen considerably by the mid-1990s. V-Cinema was still in its early formational period when the economic bubble burst, giving it enough flexibility to absorb and adjust to the turmoil around it, while denying that it was happening at all.

The exaggerations to which V-Cinema texts are prone tend to be ironic, at least in the romantic sense of irony as radical undecidability. They emphasize how history can be replayed but not repeated, thereby questioning the locus of history. They insist on a media history that can be revisited along with the discourses it was suffused with, but neither are now what they were then. V-Cinema therefore straddles the line between ahistoricity and insistence on a fantastical repetition. We could see it as a revised version of the packaging of temporal confusion that took place in a different form in Pink Film and Kadokawa Film. As V-Cinema waged its first struggle for survival, its films were charged with specific contradictions that allowed it to tame its temporal tensions. Chapter 6 explores the subgenres V-Cinema developed for this purpose.

SIX

SUBGENRES

Violence, Finances, Sex, and True Accounts

If V-Cinema has a face, it is that of Takeuchi Riki: an exaggerated snarl supporting an imposing, meatily loud screen presence somewhere between glam rock and yakuza den. One of the genre's biggest stars, Takeuchi has played in over two hundred films and was part of V-Cinema virtually from the beginning, taking the part of the young sidekick who is killed in *Crimehunter*.[1] It is in Takeuchi that V-Cinema seems to most self-consciously display the performatively impossible rewind function it has assumed.

V-Cinema's brutal seriality and imperfect repetitions defined its temporal politics as much as the technology of video did. More than Pink Film or Kadokawa Film, V-Cinema staked its discursive thrust on the array of subgenres it produced and, more importantly, reproduced. V-Cinema's filmic texts needed to stand on their own more than those of Pink Film or Kadokawa did. One especially important reason for this is the absence of a dedicated space it could rely on to charge the genre with meaning. Pink Film (eventually) had specialty theaters, and Kadokawa played out the confusion of national and international spaces by showing films from Japan in theaters for foreign films. Kadokawa additionally extended the spaces of contact with a narrative or character by spreading them across bookstores, record stores, film theaters, magazines, and television. V-Cinema, located in a corner of the video store and viewed in the living room, had no equally defined spatial weight behind it. Neither store nor home were devoid of meaning, but the lack of a dedicated space drained part of the genre's semiotic strength.

This chapter examines V-Cinema's subgenres to accommodate the shift to filmic textuality that increasingly picked up speed in the 1990s, and not only for V-Cinema. Media theory in Japan has increasingly understood the move toward ever more mobile media texts or objects as one of the main developments since the 1990s. Unfixed from specific industrial structures or media channels, characters such as Hello Kitty or franchises such as Yokai Watch become immensely flexible, located in film, manga, TV, or games but not tied to any of them, or to a specific set of meanings.

V-Cinema countered the multiplication across media taking place, among others, in the world of character marketing with radical serialization. The immense surge in production in 1990–91 created an equally immense pressure to make films that could compete for the audience's attention. This posed challenges for V-Cinema and its tendency toward media hermeticism. Even habitual V-Cinema viewers probably rarely entered a video shop with the expressed intention of renting *Code of Conduct Part 17—the Bastard That Kills Them All* (*Jingi 17—Minagoroshi no yarō*, Matsui Noboru, 1998), and almost certainly no one roamed the rental store in search of *Underworld Police—P.O. Box 39—the Sex Video Woman File* (*Ura keisatsu—Shishobako 39—File: Ura bideo no onna*, Haginiwa Sadaaki, 1998). Instead, similar to Pink Film, V-Cinema films attract attention by their subgenre, star, and exaggerated titles and covers.[2] Serialization became an enormously important basis of the V-Cinema business strategy, and though the effects are wide reaching in terms of how the films are understood and engaged with, there are concrete economic reasons for this on the production side. It enables efficient production management by shooting several episodes at once while at the same time increasing brand recognition. A company such as KSS, which entered V-Cinema production in late 1990 and successively increased its output from twelve films in 1991 to twenty-five in 1992, and then reaching an astonishing forty films in 1993, would have to quickly introduce films that were cheap, recognizable, and attractive to the audience by virtue of their subgenre.[3]

This reliance on subgenre was supported by a larger development that was pushing other genres—even Pink Film—to at least partially shift their emphasis to filmic textuality. Kokuei began marketing the films of the *Pinku shitennō*, the Four Devils of Pink Film, as art house films exactly around this time, moving them out of the Pink Film specialty theater space and into art house theaters, video stores, and satellite TV channels. In the 1990s, the importance of industrial frameworks as overt and performative suppliers and catalysts of meaning was decreasing in the film and media industry, in part because of the decrease in spatial distinction between the genres brought about by the media mix and increased mobility across media platforms. From the early 1990s onward, the annual ten top-grossing films released in the theaters have leaned heavily toward animation based on manga characters or TV animation, or live-action films based on existing TV series. V-Cinema was created in exactly this environment. By constant (serialized) reference to a past archive of subgenres, characters, and tropes—largely from yakuza, action, or 1970s sexploitation films—V-Cinema constructed a tense relationship to sociopolitical history. The world it initially constructed relied on older subgenres, not on any obvious reference to the present. As a genre it claimed to position itself outside of sequence; it was a genre of rewinding and replays. Cinematically, it did this by replaying old subgenres; organizationally, it replayed a form of production that confined itself to serial production in one media channel. And while V-Cinema's strategy was, naturally, by no means decoupled from the recessionary 1990s, as we will see, it utilized a common media memory of tropes, styles, subgenres, and stock characters from the history of film. For that reason it is important to take a closer look at the texts it brought into circulation.

With V-Cinema under pressure to differentiate its prolific output, the distribution and production company KSS, in particular, would become central to introducing new subgenres and repackaging old ones, the two basic strategies that V-Cinema companies adopted. In a later phase, a company aptly named Museum would help preserve this system. Films by KSS were divided into three categories that soon became the standard for V-Cinema films: yakuza, gambling (*gyanburu*, referencing all films that focus on money, often also called *kinyū*, or finance), and eros (*erosu*). Each of these is connected to the new financial and social context in which V-Cinema had to orient itself during the early 1990s.

Yakuza Films

Bloodbath Will Come (*Shūra ga yuku*, thirteen installments), *Code of Conduct* (*Jingi*, currently at forty-three installments), or *The Road to Becoming the Don* (*Don e no michi*, well over twenty episodes) are typical representatives of the most persistent and successful V-Cinema subgenre: yakuza film. The numbers are so high that it is difficult to identify how many yakuza series there are, not to mention the wide variations between respective story lines and style. The majority are heavily oriented toward the ninkyō (chivalry) films produced by Tōei in the 1960s, which focus on heroic outsiders who adhere to a strict code of honor, right down to their bloody end, and *jitsuroku* (true account) films of the 1970s. Many series carry titles that consciously refer to that tradition. By far, the greater part are straight-faced yakuza films, full of infighting, gang wars, honor codes, and the classic storming of the enemy headquarters with a sword in the finale.

Despite their fidelity to certain models from 1960s cinema, these films cannot convincingly reconstruct their aesthetics or their specific concerns. Ninkyō films originally addressed both a nostalgia for the supposed loss of a (near-feudal) world of honor and the rise of fantasies of individualism and resistance. They filled an empty hole left by an imagined historical rupture that was acutely felt in the postwar system, and therefore were able to appeal to conservatives as much as to radical students. V-Cinema repeats these themes without their specific historical context, and the nostalgia is now primarily for the lost media history. This gap is countered often enough with a glaring overemphasis that borders on caricature, stretching to models of masculinity as much as to visions of society. It is an aesthetic of exaggeration that demonstrates V-Cinema's awareness of its impossible rewind as much as its (impossible) claim to operate on the media's terms, not those of broader sociopolitical history.

Significantly, there are also occasional lighter variations on the classic theme. Series such as *For Real!* (*Maji!*, over thirty installments) and *The Don That Calmed Down* (*Shizuka naru don*, over a dozen installments and several spin-offs) combine serious drama and melodrama with more playful, often comedic elements. These series perform more or less subtle manipulations on the subtexts of the 1960s films they reference. In *Don*, Kondo is the heir to a yakuza empire, yet he has a day job in an underwear design company—his dream job. He is, effectively, a variation on the Clark Kent / Superman theme. At night he is a tough yakuza boss, during the day a bumbling pencil pusher who fawns at the girl across the desk. She, however, is in love with his yakuza identity, signified by dark sunglasses that supposedly make him unrecognizable. Unusually strong parodic elements run through the story, slyly validating the images of "traditional" masculinity and the values inherent in the yakuza code while ostensibly poking fun at them. The name of Kondo's yakuza group is Shinsengumi (Fresh group), a homophonic play on the famous police force / mercenary group of the 1860s. The title of the series is also a parody of the novel *And Quiet Flowed the Don* by Mikhail Sholokhov, which has the same title in Japanese as the V-Cinema series.[4]

In the *Code of Conduct* series, the Japanese title, *Jingi*, is both a reference to one of the central terms of yakuza ethics and the names of its two protagonists,

Jin and Giro. Jin is an idealized traditional yakuza character: flamboyant, hypermasculine, good-natured, and always adhering to the honor code. He lives in a *shitamachi* area and is good friends with the *shomin* or "little people," the shop owners in his neighborhood. "Shitamachi" literally means downtown, and always refers to a certain social stratum as much as it holds implications of nation and time. It is usually used in the sense that this is where a supposedly authentic Japan is still preserved and where a degree of authenticity can be found. Giro is a graduate of Tokyo University, the institution that has provided Japan with generations of elite bureaucrats, and he runs the financial operations of the yakuza office he and Jin head. Through their friendship and common adherence to the code of honor, they meld the old and the new yakuza in an acceptable fashion, whereas in traditional ninykō films (and a host of newer ones), the new yakuza are almost always negative figures characterized by greed, amorality, and an orientation toward Western technology and clothing. The lighter variations in particular are among the longest running and most successful series in V-Cinema, although they are actually a minority compared to much straighter yakuza V-Cinema. Their success can be attributed to the relative approximation to the TV format, providing a strongly episodic, soap-opera-like character, which opens up the appeal to a somewhat broader audience. One of the consequences is a comparatively large female fan base, as the series are deemed more appealing for a female audience than the classic yakuza films.[5]

This leads to a basic V-Cinema attribute: the extreme focus on (overwhelmingly male) stars. V-Cinema is arguably the only area of the Japanese media business where a self-contained star system still exists and has stayed more or less functional. In contrast to the transmedia commodity that stars in music, television, radio, and cinema have become, the V-Cinema star system is much more closed off, with actors such as Shimizu Kentarō, Ozawa Hitoshi, Shimizu Kōjirō, Watanabe Hiroyuki, and Nakajō Kiyoshi commanding a large following, though they are mostly unknown outside of the genre.[6] Only in the mid- to late 2000s were Aikawa Shō and Takeuchi Riki, the most prominent of the V-Cinema stars and the only ones with a sizeable degree of exposure overseas, able to find significant work outside of V-Cinema.[7] Due to short shooting schedules and the restrictions on the pay they can receive per film, these actors are highly prolific: Watanabe has starred in close to 100 feature films in V-Cinema, Shimizu Kentarō in over 100, Aikawa in over 150, and Takeuchi in around 200. In the mid-1990s there were years in which Aikawa and Takeuchi respectively held starring roles in over twenty films. All of these actors' names are advertised in large letters on the video jackets, usually next to a close-up picture of their faces, while the director's name is found only in the fine print on the back, if at all—and even then the director usually follows the executive producer, producer, scriptwriter, and story developer.

Yakuza Museum

V-Cinema not only rewound to the ninkyō yakuza subgenre, it also reenacted film history's transition away from it. In the late 1990s, a company named Museum entered the V-Cinema landscape and reenergized the subgenre, which had been faltering since the mid-1990s, with only the most prominent series surviving. Museum had entered the business by selling videotapes directly to the rental market in 1997. The company's strategy was to shortcut the wholesale dealers that, with the exception of Tōei, stood between production companies and the actual video stores. Museum collected rights for films, subcontracted production work in addition to doing the producing itself, and subsequently distributed the films to the rental stores through its own distribution section. By exploiting this widened profit margin, it became one of the most prolific V-Cinema companies at the exact time when the V-Cinema market was generally seen to be in decline.

The initial Museum output focused on ninkyō-style yakuza films, usually of a very straight-faced and gritty nature. While a replay of film history, these films can also be read as an adjustment to the general sense of crisis into which the country had descended. The devastating Hanshin earthquake and the Sarin gas subway attacks by the Aum Shinrikyō cult in 1995 became symbolic of an atmosphere of impending doom, supplemented by the continued worsening of the economy, highly publicized corporate layoffs, and millennial angst. V-Cinema thus provided its audience with a simulated authenticity and recourse to a supposedly stable past that was actually grounded in media images and subgenres taken from film history. The testosterone-saturated outsider heroes and the honor codes of the yakuza protagonists may have provided identificatory potential and self-valorization for a young male audience that felt increasingly disenfranchised. But more than that, the films offered participation in a nostalgically marked image culture. At the same time, V-Cinema as an industrial genre was at the forefront of a renewed push toward casualized labor and the reduction of the legal rights of film workers.

The new yakuza wave threatened to run out of steam very quickly, but around the year 2000, Museum rewound again and secured the subgenre for years to come. The company pioneered the (re)introduction of what was to be one of the most successful and increasingly dominant lines in V-Cinema, the *jitsuroku* (true account) yakuza films. The jitsuroku label was so successful that it crept into other subgenres; jitsuroku pachinko films and occasional jitsuroku *chikan* (true-account groper) films emerged, though it stays primarily connected to yakuza films. The countless jitsuroku films ostensibly depict true stories of actual yakuza gang wars and incidents in a dramatized form, and among the more well-known series are *True Account: Okinawa Yakuza War* (*Jitsuroku: Okinawa yakuza sensō*, directed by Ozawa, 2002–3), *True Account: Hokkaido Yakuza War* (*Jitsuroku: Hokkaidō yakuza sensō*, directed by Ishihara Shigeru, starring Aikawa Shō, 2003), and *True Account: Osaka Yakuza War* (*Jitsuroku: Osaka yakuza sensō*, directed by Ishihara Shigeru, starring Shimizu Kentarō, 2002).

The jitsuroku films present a fascinating example of the ever-intensifying constellation of history, media memory, and realism in V-Cinema. The stories are all based on actual occurrences, and the characters usually carry the same (or recognizably similar) names of the people they are based on. Their obvious cinematic debt is to Tōei jitsuroku films, a line that began with Fukasaku Kinji and Kasahara Kazuo's famous *Battles without Honor and Humanity* series (*Jingi naki tatakai*, 1973–74).[8] These are films that followed the decline of ninkyō yakuza films, and their honorable heroes were played by stars such as Takakura Ken and Tsuruta Kōji. Tōei's jitsuroku yakuza films of the 1970s were already highly self-aware in their countering of the formalized, artificial nature of the later ninkyō films. The *Battles without Honor and Humanity* series confronted these films with a hyperbolic and superstylized filmic approach, one that exaggeratedly simulated realism with, among others, frenzied handheld camera movements. A film such as *True Account: Okinawa Yakuza War* follows the patterns set by *Battles without Honor and Humanity*, yet diverges in subtle ways.

After a feverishly paced introduction to the history of the yakuza in Okinawa, complete with documentary photos and a voice-over, *True Account: Okinawa Yakuza War* explains the complex gang constellations. Following several gang wars, and just when the return of Okinawa to Japan is announced, the two remaining factions, Yambaru and Naha, form an umbrella organization, the yakuza council, to prevent further violence. However, tensions build and eventually escalate between the Uehara group and Shinjō, leading to an all-out war. The crisis of identity and nation is one of the underlying themes in the context of Okinawa, and the movie conveys it in a filmic frenzy. The pounding soundtrack and documentary sequences hark back to Fukasaku Kinji's *Battles without Honor and Humanity* series, but the *True Account* series is more straight-faced and much more violent. While Kasahara Kazuo based his script for *Battles* on Balzac's *La Comédie Humaine*, and Fukasaku took pains to combine the documentary style with illustrations of a yakuza life of cowardice, greed, and incompetence, Ozawa's version retains traces of yakuza romanticism and authority.[9] In comparison to the acerbic 1970s jitsuroku series, V-Cinema jitsuroku yakuza are more often portrayed with compassion, at times as heroic or at least as unironically upright or dangerous individuals, and rarely as the shrieking, greedy bundles of cowardice "without honor and humanity" that Fukasaku put on the screen. The reasons for this lie not only with the appeal they might hold for the audience but for certain constraints on the films' production.

In their reference to this already reflexive 1970s subgenre, the V-Cinema jitsuroku films present a two-pronged historiography. On the one hand, they claim to refer to an authentic (overtly national) history; on the other hand, they reference a cinematic tradition while eliding a whole host of implications connected to 1970s films. If the former strategy represents a claim on history, the latter shifts these films to a history of representation. Media history, mediation, and national history become entwined to a degree that is impossible to disentangle or reverse. This inseparability is one of the main issues V-Cinema deals with in a guise that is both radical and ostensibly conservative, yet is also indebted to the social malaise of a recessionary Japan. What it does most of all, though, is work through a new way of understanding media—less as a space partitioned off from the actual, but rather an instantaneous reservoir that largely overlaps with actuality.

What shape, then, do these films take? Jitsuroku films purport to be accurate depictions of actual occurrences, sometimes as recently as the 1990s. They often utilize various cinematic techniques that mark the films with realism by inserting documentary images, an authoritative voice-over, and the use of handheld cameras and minimal lighting. V-Cinema jitsuroku films are much grittier and often more violent versions of yakuza stories, filled with references to the economic difficulties of the 1990s and supplying the films with a historicizing context that other yakuza films often avoid. The reason for this contextualization becomes obvious when we take the psychology of the 1990s crisis into account. Virtually all jitsuroku films, whether they are set in the 1960s, 1970s, or 1980s, use images of war and postwar chaos as the starting point for the voice-over's introduction to the narrative. The yakuza thus become ciphers for Japan and for a certain historical model. The violent turns their insecure but tragically heroic lives take function as stand-in images of a nation formed by the trauma of rupture, and they appeal to the more diffuse sense of crisis in the spectators' present. V-Cinema's industrial side mirrored this conception of history, with its ongoing rhetoric of crisis and the resultant drive for ever more efficient labor exploitation.

Thus the emergence of jitsuroku films is potentially connected to economic crisis in two ways. For one, their appeal may be partially founded on the economic-psychological insecurity that circulated in Japan at the turn of the millennium. On the other hand, they can be seen as a reaction to economic difficulties within troubled V-Cinema. Jitsuroku films have several advantages in terms of production. Two or three episodes of a series can be shot back-to-back for cost efficiency, and the whole style associated with this kind of realism can be exploited for a minimal cost. While they do not characterize all jitsuroku films, shaky hand camera work, minimal lighting, and a gritty location are conducive to fast and cheap shooting, and at the same time are part of the aesthetic brand of the subgenre. One problem for companies participating in this popular subgenre, however, is that these films deal with events whose protagonists are often still alive and active in the yakuza world, which makes their production a very sensitive matter. All of the scripts for the films must be discussed with the representatives of those involved with the actual events, and they must give their approval. The actual shooting can only be entrusted to very specific scriptwriters and directors to avoid trouble with the yakuza world later on. This is the main reason that relatively few companies have participated in this highly successful subgenre, and those that do often virtually specialize in it.[10] While Tōei Video and several other companies dabbled in the subgenre, Museum had a monopoly on the greater part of its production. Its website catalog alone boasts several dozen jitsuroku films (these series are usually restricted, for obvious reasons, to two or three episodes). While V-Cinema jitsuroku is a subgenre that refracts through various levels of mediation and the mediated past, the films are still synchronized to history (or at least one version of it) because they need to obtain yakuza consent.

The nature of the realism extolled in jitsuroku is almost the opposite of the ero-real that was so loathed and sought after with regard to Pink Film. Ero-real was engaged with a historical present, highlighting fissures opened up by high-speed economic growth. V-Cinema jitsuroku, on the other hand, confuses a media history via the forms of a subgenre from the 1970s, a sociohistorical past as mediated through those films, and a historical present. It is important to note that V-Cinema, true to the videotape technology it originated in, stays bound to the linear structure of history despite its efforts to rewind.

V-Cinema jitsuroku was tied to videotape at precisely the moment that video became outdated as a technology. In fact, for a time it was highly problematic for the production companies that V-Cinema yakuza films were mostly available on video when whole stores were switching to DVD rental. However, the V-Cinema companies believed—based on assumptions about the class, age, and gender of the V-Cinema spectator—that the greater part of their audience had not converted to DVD. This initially led to very few V-Cinema films, especially yakuza films, being released on DVD, while the VHS medium itself was disappearing from the rental stores. The implications of the shift from videotape to DVD for V-Cinema will become clear later in this chapter, but it bears mentioning now that V-Cinema quickly took on an image of inferiority vis-à-vis the rows of DVDs located at the front of the stores—especially blockbusters and foreign films, which were associated with DVD technology at an early stage. Only since around 2005–6 did most companies begin to give yakuza films a DVD release as well as a VHS release.[11] The temporal implications of DVD technology, not to speak of digital video files, are no doubt very different from those of VHS. Yet even after its shift to DVD, V-Cinema continues to stay functionally and discursively tied to the videotape technology for which it was created.

Finance Films

In the initial phase of experimentation from about 1991 to 1993, a variety of money-themed subgenres established themselves, usually subsumed under the label kinyū (finances) or gyanburu (gambling) films. As the bubble economy imploded, economic strife became a popular topic in virtually all Japanese media, including television, magazines, books, and manga. Economic insecurity was a source of great anxiety, and V-Cinema was subgenerically flexible enough to draw on it to create popular dramas. Many of the kinyū films are concerned with variations of gambling, their narratives revolving around the promise of swift and unproblematic resolution of (usually monetary) problems. The pachinko films are the most popular of these subgenres, and a wide variety of companies have shot countless entries. Pachinko, the stupendously popular quasi-gambling game, is one of the largest industries in Japan. Players shoot small metal balls onto a vertical board studded with nails, with the goal of getting as many balls as possible into specific slots at the bottom of the board. The popularity of pachinko is astonishing. According to the Ministry of Economy, Trade, and Industry, while in 1989 total box-office gross in Japan amounted to 166.6 billion yen ($1,207,246,000), the pachinko business made over 16 trillion yen—and this figure would almost double in the following seven years.[12] Taking a hint from popular pachinko manga series, KSS was the first to capitalize on the theme, starting with the *Pachinko*

Story series (*Pachinko monogatari*) as early as 1991. Since then there have been a barrage of single films and a great number of series such as *Pachinko Player Nami* (*Pachinkā nami*, 1993–95), *Wild Touch* (*Wairudo tacchi*, 1999), and *True Account: Ryōzanpaku* (*Jitsuroku: Ryōzanpaku*, 1999–2000).[13]

Early examples of the subgenre are already usually fixed to a blue collar backdrop, but they construct much more fantastic spaces than their more recent counterparts. Strong dramatic plots abound in which, for example, a pachinko professional must align himself or herself with someone who is in dire straits and is forced to compete in a final pachinko battle, for example in *Jack—Pachinko Slot—the King of Darkness* (*Jakku—Pachisuro—Yami no teiō*, Matsui Noboru, 1993). Early pachinko films sometimes have, like other V-Cinema subgenres, somewhat fantastic inflections. *Pachinko Player Nami 2* (*Pachinkā nami 2*, Mitsuishi Fujirō, 1993) features a pachinko finale pitting the heroine, Nami, against the mysterious Taiwanese pachinko master Rin-Tsurin, in an open field on supernatural pachinko machines called "coffins."[14] While the film still features the theme of hard economic times by making this a proxy battle between the local pachinko parlor and the ruthless corporate pachinko chain, combined with over-the-top staging, later pachinko films become much more realistic. In *King of Hitting the Mark* (*Tekichūō—Muteki no WAVE riron*, Hattori Mitsunori, 2000), a group that earns money by selling statistical information on various pachinko machines comes into conflict with a yakuza organization.

Later films also claim to offer practical and genuine knowledge on the technique of pachinko, often even referring to actual machine models and promising the necessary knowledge to milk them. The front cover of *CR—Ginpara Monster—the Surge's Final Attack* (*CR—Ginpara monsutā—Dotō no saishū kōryaku*, Shichiji Yukihisa, 2000), for example, advertises quite typically, "How to win? Find that procedure here!" The back cover notes the pachinko machine models it will address.[15] In *True Account: Ryōzanpaku—Pachislo Life—the Philosophy of Naniwa 2* (*Jitsuroku: Ryōzanpaku—Pachisuro retsuden—Naniwa no tetsu 2*, Monna Katsuo, 1999) the young Hiroshi goes through a tough training regimen with the legendary Ryōzanpaku gambling group. It features extensive explanations of the statistics of pachinko and the microfine coordination needed to hold the lever correctly. An early example of the jitsuroku subgenre spilling over from yakuza to pachinko films, *Ryōzanpaku* is based on an actual gambling group and retains the emphasis on locality by taking place in downtown Osaka; even the title proclaims the film is about the philosophy of Naniwa (Naniwa being the former name of

FIGURE 6.1. The jacket for the video of *Wild Touch 3: Great Pachislo Conquest, Asuteka Edition* (*Wairudo tacchi 3: Pachisuro dai kōryak, Asuteka-hen*, Hattori Mitsunori, 1999) provides an example of the educational appeal of V-Cinema. The back reads, "If you watch this video, you can win like crazy!" It also names the machine models treated in the film: Asuteka, Shiimastā, Biimakkusu, and Wādo obu Raitsu.

Osaka). Monna Katsuo, a specialist in the pachinko subgenre, has directed close to twenty *Ryōzanpaku* films.

Another popular kinyū subgenre is the mah-jongg film. It aspires to shitamachi realism even more than its pachinko counterpart does, and the films often claim to be dramatizations of the adventures of actual mah-jongg legends such as Sakurai Shōichi or Andō Mitsuru. The *Mah-Jongg Demon* series (*Janki*, Konuma Masaru; five installments, 1992–95) or the *Mah-Jongg Wolf Tale—Blow of Death!* series (*Marōden—Hissatsu!*, Hattori Mitsunori; three installments, 2000–2001) are cases in point. Often set in the mah-jongg world of the Shinjuku section of Tokyo, they are structured episodically, leading up to a decisive final game. In comparison with the exaggerated and flashy pachinko films, they usually attempt to evoke the atmosphere of smoky backrooms in dingy mah-jongg parlors where immense sums of money are passed around. The games themselves take up considerable amounts of the films' time and cannot possibly be understood without a more than basic knowledge of mah-jongg rules. The screen is often split into four sections during the game sequences, allowing the audience to (potentially) follow each player's strategy. Occasionally a professional player appears after the film and explains several of the game sequences in a kind of tele-lecture.[16] These films are examples of the extreme specialization in one narrow audience demographic that is only possible within the low-budget V-Cinema context. *Keiba* (horse racing) films similarly use the more or less intricate rules of betting and the personal dramas that a jockey encounters in his career as a backdrop for drama.

A great number of films often subsumed under the kinyū label are more directly concerned with monetary transactions. *The King of Debt* series (*Shakkingu*, nine installments, 1997–2002) is the story of an elite bank manager in Osaka, played by V-Cinema star Aikawa Shō, who has illegitimately speculated with a customer's deposit and must now find a way to repay 1.5 billion yen ($12,295,000).[17] He teams up with a down-and-out police detective and the proprietress of a bankrupt bar to swindle immoral people out of money. Kinyū includes a variety of films that are purely concerned with *sagi* (fraud), and usually demonstrate how a group of professional grifters swindle unsympathetic characters out of their undeserved fortunes, as in *Master of Fraud Ippei* (*Sagi-shi Ippei*, Murata Shinobu; three installments, 1999–2000).

The most popular series in V-Cinema history may be *The King of Minami* (*Naniwa Kinyū-den—Minami no teiō*; almost all episodes directed by Haginiwa Sadaaki), which was started by KSS in 1992 and ended in 2007 after sixty installments.[18] The series is loosely based on a manga and revolves around Manda Ginjirō, played by Takeuchi Riki, a hypermasculine moneylender and semi-yakuza who operates in the Minami section of Osaka. *The King of Minami* chronicles Manda and his assistants' encounters with debtors and their problems, both in repaying him and with other more ruthless moneylenders. Tough and flashy in demeanor but good at heart, Manda often ends up helping the victims, usually common people who are not to blame for their plight, by utilizing a variety of legal and semilegal tricks, very rarely resorting to violence. *The King of Minami* installments are usually structured episodically, with various subplots building up to a decisive finale. Film number twenty-two in the series focuses on Manda's dealings with Fujimoto, the owner of a small transport company who is deeply in debt because he spent large amounts of money on a young Taiwanese woman in a local hostess bar. It is later revealed that the hostess is in fact Fujimoto's daughter, who is forced to work by an unscrupulous human trafficking ring, and he has been buying her time to keep her from prostitution. Manda decides to help and finally is able to free Fujimoto's daughter, as well as receive full debt payments by maneuvering the head of the trafficking ring into a difficult contractual situation related to Fujimoto's debts. The legal details are explained in depth with the help of subtitles, functioning almost like a how-to manual. As *The King of Minami* series progresses, the assistants take up increasing amounts of screen time, periodically conferring with Manda in his office, until he becomes actively involved only in the final conflict. This increasing scarcity of the main character as the series progresses is as much a consequence of Takeuchi Riki's excessive shooting schedule as the TV-like format of the series.

The King of Minami is a distilled version of many of the elements that run through the V-Cinema strain of kinyū films, and is exemplary of several developments in V-Cinema in general. The discourses it taps into on the story level are as relevant as they are typical. The series is strongly anchored in a local spatiality that implies an eternal ordinary people's Japan: the Minami area of Osaka, which carries heavy connotations of an old-town, blue-collar environment. The series takes pains to show street scenes and (debtors') houses that adhere to an image of an old or authentic Japan: small alleys with wooden houses, built in an early Shōwa-era style, and inhabited by a working-class populace. The characters speak in an Osaka dialect that emphasizes the regional aspect, and the original Japanese series title can be translated as *Naniwa Tales of Finance—the King of Minami* (with Naniwa being the old name for Osaka) and further evoking a nostalgic place that is temporally and spatially opposed to modernized Tokyo. The drive for a simulated authentic space is complemented by the detail invested in the financial aspects of the stories, which are heavily didactic. The production company, scriptwriter, and director do research at actual money-lending institutions to inform the subplots involving debtors, debts, and transactions. One of the producers of the series claims, probably rightfully so, "When you watch the series, you learn quite a lot about the legal aspects of debts and redeeming loans. That's one reason the series is so popular."[19]

Indeed, the series taps into a very widespread social issue in Japan. When the economic bubble burst, borrowing money from consumer-lending institutions (which charge close to 30 percent interest) became common practice, as banks were increasingly cautious about granting loans. During the economic crisis of the 1990s, posters and television ads for such companies became commonplace, and the number of registered lenders grew to over 13,700, although large national companies dominate the estimated $174 billion industry.[20] In 2006 the Federation of Credit Bureau of Japan, representing only the largest lending companies, estimated its members had almost 14 million active borrowers.[21] V-Cinema was able to tap into the large number of people affected by the crisis. It gratifyingly positioned the spectator as an inhabitant of authentic Japan, as part of the nostalgic communal victim space of shomin (the man on the street), much as it had been achieved in the shomin films immediately after the war. At the same time, it offered escapist hope, knowledge, and a degree of dramatic entertainment.

The interaction of filmic space and geographic space plays out in other ways as well. There are interesting regional differences in the popularity of the subgenres; while yakuza films are most popular in western Japan, especially the island of Kyushu, kinyū films are most popular in the Kansai region around Osaka.[22] These are the exact regions that are used as reservoirs for constructing condensed shitamachi scenarios. This is a sign of V-Cinema's ability to address very specific audience segments, even those defined by a geographical kind of realism, while at the same time using it as a regionally effective marketing tool.

The didactic aspect so prominent in *The King of Minami* is, as we have seen, typical of large parts of V-Cinema: the mah-jongg films, the pachinko films, the sagi (fraud) films, and even the jitsuroku films. This didacticism is part of a legacy of educational and how-to films that were a prominent part of the medium of video since Fuji Pony presented the very first lineup; at the same time, it connected to an audience attempting to deal with the constant rhetoric of crisis. It also played into attempts to further divide the audience into more predictable and more reliable target groups. Not only was the audience hungry for stability, but the troubled V-Cinema producers were as well.

The kinyū subgenre, then, combined disparate films or series such as pachinko films, money-lending films, and fraud films. While yakuza films index a filmic past and, in the jitsuroku films, double index that past with an actual version of history, kinyū films often avoid explicitly referring to the economic crisis that made them so popular in the first place. The reality of corporate layoffs and the increase in part-time labor is much less explicitly stated in pachinko films than even in 1990s Pink films; it is the big unmentionable that motivates their financial didacticism. The fantastic shomin spaces reduce all conflicts and motivations to personal affairs that find improbable resolution precisely because they are set in such fantastic spaces. Both kinyū and yakuza films retain a precisely calibrated proximity and distance in relation to history, though with different strategies and on different levels. Kinyū appeals to an imaginary and eternal blue-collar, simple man space that is a social fantasy, while yakuza films use media history as a basis for their specific form of confusion.

Pause: Rewind, Play, Crisis

V-Cinema never actually emerged from the difficulties of the early 1990s; it merely continued to find ways to deal with perpetual crisis. One of the strategies was an openness to other media on various levels: staff, circulation, narratives, and others. Albeit reserved for the more successful of the V-Cinema films (and those with higher budgets), by the mid-1990s it had become quite common practice to give certain films an extremely limited theatrical release. This release was usually kept to one week in one theater, often in Osaka, but it allowed the company to write "Theatrically Released Feature Film" on the cover of the videotape, or even *zenkoku kōkai* (national release) if it ran in Tokyo and Osaka. This had, in principle, been practiced by Bandai Visual as early as 1990 with the *Hole in the Pants* series (*Pantsu no ana*; some installments directed by Wakamatsu Kōji); however, it only began to be used as a systematic strategy by KSS, Hero, and several other companies from 1994 on. Television also briefly became an omnivorous market for V-Cinema products, especially as CATV and satellite TV were still trying to fill their distribution channels. Even a specialized satellite channel for V-Cinema, called V-Paradise, went on the air in 1997. A clear exception to the V-Cinema norm, *The King of Debt* went as far as to have special episodes produced for theatrical release and for television, and *The King of Minami* (based on a successful manga) did the same.

These hesitant connections to other media platforms point to the fact that after anime in the 1960s and Kadokawa Film in the 1970s and 1980s, marketing works or textual features (narratives and characters) across various media generally became the standard strategy for the film and media industry in the 1990s; this affected even the largely hermetic genre of V-Cinema. With media works and textuality becoming more mobile across media, the coherent extension of discourse across the textual and the structural-industrial level that helped define industrial genres was slowly dissolving. The increase in cross-marketing V-Cinema films is also a consequence of the fact that V-Cinema was experiencing considerable difficulties by the mid-1990s, as was the video business in general. In 1992 Tōei was still making enough money to expand its Tōei V-Cinema brand with *V-America*, a series of V-Cinema films produced in the United States with partially American casts, including George Kennedy and a young Viggo Mortensen. It followed this up with *V-Erotica* and, in 1993, *V-World*.²³ However, by this time it was already clear that not only had there been an asset-price economic bubble at the end of the 1980s, there had been a video bubble as well.

V-Cinema had indeed established itself at a precarious moment. Video sales were already stagnating, and as early as 1991 the JVA was forced to initiate an assortment of campaigns to increase the attractiveness of video: The Love Video Week spurred customers to collect seals that were given out with rentals, which, in sufficient number, could be traded in for a picnic set. A campaign attempted to convince store owners to periodically exchange jacket sleeves to clean up the store's image. Foreign film packagers RCA Columbia, CIC/Victor, Warner, and Fox introduced a video day with reduced prices.

The changing economic climate directly affected V-Cinema. Many companies from outside of the film industry had invested heavily in video, and now retreated to their core businesses to cope with the aftermath of the burst bubble. Real estate company Espo sold its extensive video store chain, one of the largest in the country, and many others simply shut down operations. Especially on the rental store level, consolidation efforts proceeded rapidly. Small stores went bankrupt in very high numbers, while ever-growing chains opened large stores with massive tape selections in the suburbs, gradually creeping into the large cities as well. This was an unfortunate development for V-Cinema, as chains often aim for a clean and family-friendly image that disfavors including V-Cinema in the lineup. The physical position of V-Cinema within the store changed accordingly, and stores began to move V-Cinema closer to the adult video (AV) section—a development that was interestingly halted when V-Cinema switched to DVD. Additionally, certain business procedures employed by video store chains such as Tsutaya work to the disadvantage of V-Cinema distribution.²⁴ While total store space did not change significantly between 1989 and the mid-2000s, the number of stores had halved to around eight thousand, attesting to a shift toward fewer but larger stores. By the late 1990s, V-Cinema was already seen as a business in decline. One of several ways V-Cinema adjusted to this was an increase in sexual content.

Erosu

The erotic rewind that V-Cinema performed in many ways mirrors the complex strategy of its yakuza films, with a profound difference. Again, films from the early 1970s are the main reference, and again there is a double vision, split between film and media history and a contemporary situation. However, if yakuza films emphasized an impossible rewind and highlighted the tenuousness of history in the age of mediatization, a large part of sexually themed V-Cinema was split between male cinematic gazes that were situated in a variety of decades and historical moments. In 1993, Tōei Video pioneered a host of *fiimēru akushon* (female action) films such as the XX series, launched in 1993 with XX—*Beautiful Weapon* (XX—*Utsukushiki kyōki*, Komizu Kazuo/Gaira; eleven installments, 1993–98), which generated publicity via main actress Miyazaki Masumi's first shower scene in a film.[25] While these films referenced action cinema from the 1970s, they also attempted to tie the films to contemporary media trends. As photo books of idols and actresses in various states of undress were at the height of their popularity, Matsuda Hitoshi, of Tōei's advertising department, developed a media-mix plan to tie female action films to photo books released at the same time. While male stars continued to dominate V-Cinema yet remained largely trapped within it, interchangeable actresses were much more mobile across media and became indicators of the increasingly unfixed media body.

Kurosawa Mitsuru of Tōei Video had, as mentioned, begun his career at Nikkatsu producing both Roman Porno and action films, and this experience no doubt carried over into V-Cinema. Tōei made V-Cinema's status as a genre that utilized a cinematic past even more obvious with remakes of its 1970s Pinky Violence contributions; the classic *Female Convict: Scorpion* (*Sasori*) series was revived just as *Zero Woman* was made into a series.[26] One of the few period-film vehicles of V-Cinema, the *Female Ninja Art Scrolls* series (*Kunoichi ninpō chō*; eight installments, 1991–98) and its numerous spin-offs, were based on Yamada Fūtarō's 1950s book series, which had spawned film versions by Tōei and Nikkatsu in the 1960s and 1970s. Each of these series focused on a female figure and her exploits in an action-film context, outfitted with periodic shower and sex scenes. One of the last female action films, and one of the last big-budget V-Cinema films, was *Sasori in USA* (Gotō Daisuke, 1997), a very loose continuation of Tōei's 1970s *Sasori* series, estimated to have cost around 100 million yen ($819,672).[27]

Due to the image of V-Cinema as a genre produced primarily for the (presumed) heterosexual male spectator, it is unsurprising that the commodified female body was part of the V-Cinema production strategy from the beginning. With the possible exception of horror and some strains of yakuza film, V-Cinema in its first two years can be quite evenly divided between action films and more sexually themed films, with action films providing a certain amount of sexual content as well. The rewinds to various sexploitation subgenres of the 1960s and 1970s result, however, in multiple levels of meaning, even as they are

Subgenres · 193

drained of the resistant confusion so important to early Pink Film. The strong diversification of subgenres from 1992 on reduced the proportion of both of these ur-subgenres, but sexual content as spectacle—and the referencing of a media-historical formation of sexuality on film—remained an important strategy for V-Cinema producers.

As mentioned, around 1993 V-Cinema experienced its first crisis due to overproduction in a crowded environment, very similar to Pink Film twenty-eight years earlier. This led both to an intensified reliance on subgenres of the 1960s and 1970s and to an increase in sexual content. The latter used aidoru of midrange popularity for V-Cinema productions, often advertised with the actress's first nude scene or as a tie-up with photo books. Tōei's Pinky Violence films of the 1970s presented a very similar mix of action and sexual content centered on female heroines. The only series in V-Cinema that, at least occasionally, had central female figures played by the same actress over several installments tended to be female yakuza series, such as *Number 2's of the Underworld* (*Gokudō no ni-gō-tachi*, three installments, 1996–97, Museum), a series indebted to Tōei's long-running *Gang Wives* series (*Gokudō no onna-tachi*, 1986–2001), and its various spin-offs.

In comparison to their male counterparts, V-Cinema's female lead actresses tend to change from film to film, even within a series. Seriality remained an eminently male privilege. However, as a performative rewind of media memory, V-Cinema is explicit about the impossible and grotesque replay of past models of masculinity. Takeuchi Riki (among many others) is expected to repeat his exaggerated posturing ad infinitum. Here we encounter the complexly gendered temporal negotiation that V-Cinema is a part of and that differs from the discourses of Pink Film and Kadokawa Film. Male-gendered V-Cinema time is serial but not linear; it holds no real promise or even a serious ideal, only a compromised return to media images in the past. Ultimately it is a disavowal of a conservative and modern ideal of linear and continuous male time. Female-gendered V-Cinema time is based on moments synchronized across media in the present. In contrast, Pink Film staged an attractive *angst-lust* of scattered identifications, ruptures, and continuities that were tied to a specific historical present. Far from opposing the power structures of the gendered gaze, V-Cinema only very tentatively utilizes sexuality to, in the words of Valerie Rohy, "turn away from the discipline of straight time, away from the notions of historical propriety that, like notions of sexual propriety, function as regulatory fictions."[28] There is no attempt to challenge what Rohy calls "straight time" in terms of resistance, real or imagined. V-Cinema's caricaturesque referencing of media history is a complication and problematization of masculinity in 1990s Japan. It enacts a masculinist temporality as parody and media-historical reference, while the female body is ahistorical spectacle.

Accordingly, the greater part of the films that utilize sexual themes as the main selling point refer to precursors in terms of subgenre, not specific films. Rather than purchase rights to remake a specific film, Pinky Violence, Pink Film, and Nikkatsu Roman Porno were raided for themes, syntax, and semantics. Consequently, V-Cinema produced innumerable *jokyōshi* (female schoolteacher) and chikan (train groper) films and series. Not all of these are of low-budget, high-exploitation character. *Groper Diary: The Man Who Continued Caressing the Buttocks* (*Chikan nikki: Shiri o nademawashitsuzuketa otoko*), a chikan series, is one of the most successful series in the whole of V-Cinema. Directed by Tomioka Tadafumi and produced by Kurosawa Mitsuru, the six installments (1995–98) carry very strong marks of the director's training in Pink Film, with carefully constructed subplots and characters. Building on that tradition, the series uses the framework of sexual titillation and a sexist premise to convey themes of alienation and social disconnection. The story tells of a nameless manga artist who is drawn into a secret society of train gropers. On one of his train-groping excursions he encounters a young woman named Hanako who responds positively to his advances, and they later develop a relationship. However, once he finds out that she is famous in train-groping circles for enjoying and inviting the gropers' activities, they have a falling out in which each accuses the other of perversion. While his manga about train groping proves to be a big success, the young man is unable to mend his relationship with Hanako and they ride off melancholically in separate trains.

The majority of sexually themed films, however, are less refined. While even extremely low-budget films are often ambitious and a site of occasionally outrageous experimentation, the budget (or rather absence of it) is usually highly visible in the films and their marketing. In comparison to the pachinko and yakuza films, the budget span for sex films is wider and leans heavily to the extremely low end of the spectrum, supporting discourses about low culture attached to V-Cinema. Although production companies were aware of this problem, by the mid-1990s V-Cinema was obviously in financially dangerous waters, and no company could afford to ignore the easy marketability of sex. To protect their brand, KSS founded Pink Pineapple, a sublabel specializing in sexually themed films. Even Tōei Video, which had specialized in, relatively speaking, high-budget prestige productions, began to produce cheaper, more obviously sexually themed films such as *Scan Doll* (*Skyan-dōru*, Komatsu Takashi, 1996, again produced by Kurosawa Mitsuru). The film depicts a socially alienated young man's pathological hobby of using surveillance technology on his (equally neurotic) neighbors. This leads to an obsession with a schoolgirl who is apparently involved with an overweight salaryman tenant. While early Tōei V-Cinema was exclusively shot on 16 mm film, *Scan Doll* used video technology and was fitted with a cover that far exceeds the film's actual explicitness—a further sign of budget deterioration that also aggravated V-Cinema's cheap image.

Initially, few productions were able to adjust to or even productively use the lower budget range, with Nakano Takao's films being an exception. In *Flower Petal Ninja—Momokage (Peachshadow)—the Big Ninja Technique Petal Turnaround* (*Kaben no ninja—Momokage—Ninpō hanabira dai-kaiten*), the covert ninja Momokage attempts to prevent the construction of a defective dam and battles with villains such as the bubble princess and the insect ninja. Nakano mixes an almost provocatively low-budget aesthetic with a carnivalistic sense of irony and self-conscious bricolage, filled with quotes and parodies of manga, anime, period films, B-movies, and popular culture in general. Valorizing amateurism with its handmade sets, embarrassing costumes, and outrageous ham acting, Nakano brings V-Cinema's replay mode to its extreme. For all its anarchic playfulness, however, it stays firmly within the parameters of serving the hypothetical male spectator.

While Museum's entry into the V-Cinema marketplace in 1997 reinvigorated the yakuza subgenres, and to a degree the pachinko films, most other producers continued their rapid decline in budgets and increasing reliance on sexual themes. By the end of the millennium, Pink Film rereleases on video were becoming more common and more competitive with quite similar V-Cinema fare. Hitherto, Pink Film on video had been placed within the adult video (AV) section, where they were viewed as inferior because the ero-real so maligned in the 1960s was now not real enough. With the increasing sexualization of V-Cinema, they moved into the areas of the rental store where V-Cinema was displayed and could compete on better terms. Additionally, due to difficulties the AV market was experiencing, many companies from the hard-core video market such as TMC and ENGEL began producing sexually themed films with dramatic elements, in contrast to the documentary style so common in Japanese AV. The borders between V-Cinema and other genres were becoming increasingly blurred.

By 2000, critic Kanehara Ichi estimated that around 50 percent of V-Cinema output was sexually themed, with yakuza film being the most popular subgenre.[29] In the same year, thirty-three companies produced 261 films in V-Cinema. Museum, Anchor Films, KSS, Legend, and Tōei Video alone produced 151 of these, with the rest distributed among the remaining companies, many of them very small production outfits with very limited budget capabilities, most of them relying on sex as a selling point.[30]

One V-Cinema subgenre that did not assume a default male-gendered spectator was horror film. The horror boom that began in the early 1990s—in V-Cinema, no less—and was further energized by the success of the *Ring* series addressed a teen and often female demographic usually not associated with V-Cinema. Though three to four new titles a month fell into this category, it was nonetheless dwarfed by the other subgenres. Ultimately sex and violence became two characteristic themes for the genre's films, with the kinyū films trailing not too far behind. The situation of V-Cinema, in a way, came full circle back to its subgeneric roots in the 1960s, when Tōei ninkyō films and Pink films were the only consistently profitable subgenres. This time, however, it enacted a simulation of its generic and subgeneric forerunners that performed a temporal metaconfusion. As simplistic as V-Cinema narratives and subgenre formulas appear, they play out within a highly complicated network of references and counterreferences of film-historical, technological, and film-industrial natures. They point to a fundamentally different form of spectatorship, characteristic of audiences deeply embedded in a media ecology with an extensive history.

Entrenchment and New Strategies

V-Cinema was already on its fourth birthday when Kadokawa Haruki was arrested for cocaine smuggling, and the media ecology in Japan had already largely turned to media-mix strategies. In such an environment, V-Cinema appeared anachronistic, not only on the level of the narratives and subgenres it packaged but also in terms of its media-hermetic business model. As a result, V-Cinema was under serious pressure on all levels of production and dissemination by the turn of the millennium. The emerging DVD market and its apparent incongruence with the videotape-centered V-Cinema texts was just as problematic as the increasing dominance of large chains with their sanitized inventory and V-Cinema-hostile PPT payment system. In 2002 over 250 films were released in the V-Cinema genre, but the next year that number was down to only around 150. Media-mix strategies were by now becoming standard in the media industry, yet V-Cinema could barely participate, positioning it on the periphery of this emergent media system.

V-Cinema was not the only genre experiencing this problem. In the 1990s the whole of the Japanese (live-action) film industry was under increasing pressure and reacted with a variety of strategies. One was the widespread use of production committees to hedge risks involved with producing films. Another was simply to decrease budgets and use the degree of security this ensured to increase the amount of experimentation—in effect a strategy that focused on the singular filmic text rather than on a genre or subgenre. Sentō Takenori launched a line of low-budget art films at the satellite television channel Wowow, and later at the Wowow-backed Suncent Cinema Works; he was responsible for much of what was perceived as a new and exciting Japanese cinema in the late-1990s international film festival circuit, including the films of his then wife Kawase Naomi. Producer Okuyama Kazuyoshi started a similar experiment at Shōchiku that he called Cinema Japanesque, but both Sentō and Okuyama were eventually ousted from their posts after less than promising returns.[31] The critical success that the artistically ambitious low-budget format was able to secure did not create a sustainable chain of production.

V-Cinema companies were aware of the dangers of succumbing to a downward spiral of film budgets. At least the larger companies such as KSS and Museum reacted by expanding their lineups. In effect, they made themselves less reliant on live-action feature film and initiated a curious shift in the genre. By the late 2000s, Museum increasingly distributed DVDs of documentaries and television series, attempting to make itself a node in the media-mix fabric and becoming more of a distribution platform than a producer. Around the same time, KSS made a profitable business out of becoming a major supplier of low-budget animation on DVD. These often sexually themed thirty-to-forty-minute episodes were aimed at the highly specific but also stable anime fan market. At the same time, KSS attempted to deal with V-Cinema's lack of a dedicated space and began to shift toward widely marketable single filmic texts—films that stood on their own and did not primarily appeal through subgeneric patterns. From around 2000 onward, KSS increasingly participated in production committees for the production of films with a broader appeal, higher budgets, and a distinct director, aiming for theatrical releases, satellite television, and foreign sales. The result were films such as *Flic* (*Furikku*, 2004) by Cannes regular Kobayashi Masahiro, the story of a policeman's descent into hallucination; and *Izo* (Miike Takashi, 2004), a fantasy film about a man on a killing spree propelled through time by the pure force of his rage. Such structurally and narratively experimental films represent a clear departure from the usual patterns of V-Cinema subgenres.

Tōei Video has been the most aggressive in pursuing a multimedia strategy and focusing on fewer, individually marketed releases. The sexually themed

Flower and Snake (*Hana to hebi*, Ishii Takashi, 2005) and *Flower and Snake II* (*Hana to hebi 2: Pari/Shizuko*, Ishii Takashi, 2005) were both produced by Tōei Video. Both films are based on a book by famous S&M writer Dan Oniroku that had been filmed in the 1970s, and they received the usual limited short-term theatrical release. But instead of relying on video rental income, as had been the case in the 1990s, the producers heavily promoted the films in the press, on the Internet, and in satellite television specials in order to increase the media channels through which it would circulate. The films were sold with elaborate DVD boxes and were available as video on demand through the website. Photo books and making-of DVDs were marketed as well, and the film was heavily promoted in foreign sales. Straight-to-video films with their own websites are extremely rare, but Tōei Video succeeded in using it to create a great amount of publicity and considerable sales success. The former role of Tōei Video as a second-use outlet for general (theatrical) releases or a low-budget production house for a very isolated market began to dissolve. With the *Flower and Snake* films, Tōei Video aimed to move beyond the limited V-Cinema audience and into various other media to reach a wider public. It thereby used the illicit image of privatized access that places DVD and Internet downloads out of the public sphere, the idea of hermeticism that helped define V-Cinema, to market the sex theme more efficiently. Visitors to the *Flower and Snake II* website first had to confirm that they were over eighteen years old before entering, even though there was nothing more risqué than a photo gallery of the director and actress onstage at the premiere screening.[32] Thus, by the time it attempted to integrate itself into the media-mix ecology, V-Cinema of the late 2000s had largely dissolved as an industrial genre, and its complex strategy of rewinding or confusing history, media history, and fiction had considerably thinned out. Tōei Video produced its last V-Cinema films in 2006, even if it continued to produce films outside of the genre such as the *Kamen Rider* series, which features its own brand of highly complex temporal complications.[33]

The other strategy the industry employed to survive was an even greater efficiency in terms of production, leading to a kind of distillation and entrenchment. Average budgets had been decreasing continually since the mid-1990s, leading to ever-shorter shooting schedules. While Tōei's films in V-Cinema were shot for around 70 million yen (about $544,000 at the time) in 1989, by the mid-2000s it was very difficult to recoup an investment if a film cost more than 30 million (approximately $255,000), and the upper limit for larger budgets began sliding toward 20 million ($170,000).[34] The larger companies increasingly outsourced production. While in 2000, executive producers at

Museum were still directly responsible for the production of up to seventy films, only five years later that number had sunk to four or five. In 2007, Museum released five to six V-Cinema films a month, of which only one was actually self-produced.[35] Companies such as Excellent, Happy 9 Azabu, and Cinema Paradise became the production hubs that made outsourcing possible, and often specialized in specific subgenres. With the turn to extremely tight budgets, directors consistently worked with the same team or production unit; shooting with such low budgets is, similar to the situation in Pink Film, a technique that only very professional teams well trained in the (sub)genre can execute.[36] This led to a concentration of the same experienced staff, actors, and directors, which in turn increased a tendency toward pattern and formula. While the distributors' new strategy saw them partially retreat from V-Cinema, the further intensification of the casualization of labor paradoxically reinforced the genre's hermeticism.

Astonishingly, until the early 2000s the number of films continually increased. Part of the resurgence in yakuza films in the late 1990s and early 2000s had to do with the fact that a production unit was forced to shoot six films a year, instead of four, to make the same amount of money. At the same time, however, average sales continued to decline. While early V-Cinema occasionally sold up to 30,000 tapes, average sales were closer to 10,000. By the late 2000s, this was a number only the biggest hit series could aim for. In 2005, average sales for larger productions were as low as 6,000 to 7,000 units for VHS and DVD combined, or as low as 3,000 units, depending on which company one asks.[37] Even at the time of V-Cinema's first crisis in the mid-1990s, the annual output rose from around 150 films to around 250—though the increase was restricted mostly to the low-budget and sexually themed end. Thus V-Cinema spiraled from one crisis to the next.

The demise of VHS, so integral to V-Cinema discourse, took a toll on the industry. In 2004, DVD overtook VHS in terms of rental gross, forcing V-Cinema distributors to release a portion of films on both DVD and VHS. In 2005–6, Tōei distributed 691 titles on DVD and only 165 on VHS.[38] Jitsuroku films still dominated the yakuza subgenre, and sexually themed films constituted the other large part, with horror film a distant third. In its special review of the year 1990, the magazine *Kinema Junpō* designated the entry of Shōchiku, Nikkatsu TBS, Toshiba, and others into production for the video market as the second biggest news of the year; by the early 2000s, discourse on V-Cinema all but faded away.[39] There were practically no regular reviews of the films, and V-Cinema was no longer even mentioned in most annual reviews of the film industry. This was due less to the sinking number of straight-to-video films than the fading away of V-Cinema as an industrial genre.

V-Cinema and the Revised Role of History

Today the clunky, large VHS tape feels outdated just by merit of its weight and size. V-Cinema, similarly, has an almost tactile, weighty feel of something that does not belong in the current media ecology of interconnections and constant, immaterial circulation. Despite having a dedicated satellite TV channel, V-Paradise, since 1997, and having shifted to DVDs around 2005, its films and male stars seem stuck in the gravity pull of the tape. Many basics of the video rental market were much the same in the early 2010s as in the early 1980s: the great majority of video store customers were still male. Adult video made up about 20 percent of the average shop's stock, and anime is close to 30 percent.[40] It may seem as if the fading genre of V-Cinema was now limping in the same environment it once thrived in. However, the media context had changed, and V-Cinema's strategy of rejecting linear time and historicity—of impossible rewinds and replays—was itself increasingly outdated in the age of the intensified media mix. While V-Cinema was still producing films, the industrial genre had begun to dissolve as the shared textuality between the industrial structure, the practices, the technology, and the films themselves has faded away. For all its performative cheapness, V-Cinema was a midsized-budget affair, but the uninhabited no-man's-land between big-budget, transmedially and transnationally exploitable products and highly specialized, extremely low-budget products began expanding in the early 2000s. It made certain kinds of narratives, characters, and tropes less viable. What, then, did V-Cinema mean, and what did it still mean at the moment when videotape technology and the videotaped image alike were going out of use, beginning to degrade, and breaking down?

Videotape technology was central for the complex relationship to history and temporal models V-Cinema developed. To say this does not, however, mean relying on techno-determinism or teleology. While video technology was central to how V-Cinema was understood, that technology was understood differently at different times. Through video technology, whole stretches of film history, of film from Japan and other countries, became available. In the early 1990s, Timothy Corrigan could still optimistically claim that the whole medium of video created a "fully mobile viewing position, unburdened by

Subgenres · 201

cinematic history."[41] Such a claim has been upgraded by new media theory and what both Lev Manovich and Azuma Hiroki call a "database logic" of media consumption, a model that assumes that flexible access to a vast reservoir of atomized information fundamentally changes our relationship to narrative, and to media more generally.[42] V-Cinema's method of freely drawing on and simulating subgenres past can be seen as a step in that direction. Yet in combination with the specific historical situation of the 1990s, V-Cinema relied not on a database model but on a model of impossible rewinds and replays that emphasized the gap between the historical model and its V-Cinema version. V-Cinema referred to an imaginary social history through the prism of a shared media memory, presented via a program-picture system, borrowed subgenres, recycled themes, and exaggeratedly reenacted stars. Time, however, could not be turned back. History forbade a simple rewind just as the laws of budget and of product differentiation did. Once-common production and distribution methods, character types, subgenres, narratives, and aesthetic patterns had to be recontextualized, brought into relation to the historicity of the present. V-Cinema appeared in the last year of the 1980s, the first year of the Heisei era, and the final gasp of the bubble economy. Action was the subgenre that allowed V-Cinema to simulate the internationalized, sped-up, spectacular, and ultimately fantastic spaces that the 1980s promoted and that Kadokawa and the minitheaters had capitalized on.

When the asset bubble burst, V-Cinema experienced its first crisis, both financial and narrative. Action was no longer viable for V-Cinema in terms of sensibility or budgets, and a shift occurred that propelled the genre toward the development of highly specific subgenres. Its main sustenance was the sturdy pillar of yakuza film. The shift from mukokuseki action to spatially fixed and nationally signifying yakuza film represented a shift in sensibility within a society that was propelled toward introspection and Shōwa-era nostalgia by the onset of an economic crisis that would last for decades. The reference to subgenres of the 1960s and 1970s argued, however obviously imperfectly, for continuity. Yakuza and the later kinyū films could supply the simulated quotidian style of the common man, a way to ease anxieties and address the everyday while retaining a confused and fantastic difference. As such, their conservatism was supported by the compromised temporal confusion that the medium of video itself supported. Pachinko, moneylending, and fraud subgenres attempted to generate pipelines to the everyday by taking on pedagogic and didactic functions. In contrast to the historicism of Pink Film's gender-confusing ero-real, V-Cinema's obsession with the male-gendered, ahistoric, media real increased as the recession continued. It culminated in the fever pitch of the jitsuroku excesses, mixing realism, stylization, and fantasy in bloody dreams of eruptive violence. This was a metanostalgia for a mediated fantasy and V-Cinema aesthetics were always artificial and codified enough to acknowledge this.

Thus, for much of its existence, V-Cinema was in performative but playful denial of a contemporary history that was so obviously inscribed into it. Its attempt to marry media history to atemporality was imprinted in its economic and technological fabric. From its very beginning, the denial of second-use rights for the V-Cinema filmmakers within a system of casualized, post-Fordist labor was congruent with a basically hostile relationship to history. Legal guarantees (i.e., royalties) resulting from a sequence of economic exploitation were denied. The extreme serial nature of V-Cinema denied progression, creating eternal (or at least up to fiftyfold) and gendered repetition—which itself is an imperfect replay of patterns that disappeared with the studio system. To become economically viable, V-Cinema consistently relativized history with its time-shifting tape while—unavoidably—cleanly operating within its paradigms.

Although V-Cinema's outsider image may suggest that this was an act of temporal delinquency, it is by no means performed dissent in the way that Pink Film or Kadokawa Film presented themselves. Neither V-Cinema's films nor its industrial organization are oppositional in any sense, nor do they claim to be. Much as the shitamachi spaces and sexual interactions are simulated, so is the 1960s male-centered outsider mentality; so are the discourses of gender, nation, and public space that V-Cinema references. They are not, however, what Fredric Jameson calls "effectively a way of satisfying a craving for historicity, using a product that substitutes and blocks for it."[43] The ghosts of 1960s and 1970s film are conjured up from within a strictly rationalized and casualized labor system that enables forgetting by producing streams of media memories that stand in for continuity. These memories are historical in the sense that they reference the experience of certain historical moments. Instead of satisfying a craving for historicity, they proclaim its absence, a claim that paradoxically only works at a certain historical moment. As with Pink Film and Kadokawa Film, this did not impede V-Cinema's functionality as a genre. It is coherence of a certain textuality, not the absence of contradictions, that made V-Cinema recognizable as an industrial genre. Yet the fundamental difficulties that all three of the genres treated here experienced in the 1990s, with different outcomes, tell us much about the timeline of an extraordinary shift in film and media culture. It is to some of the consequences of that shift in Japan since the early 2000s that we turn now.

The question of fiction is first a question regarding the distribution of places.
—JACQUES RANCIÈRE, "The Distribution of the Sensible: Politics and Aesthetics"

CONCLUSION
Present Histories

Imaoka Shinji's Pink Film *Lunch Box* was a different film when it was shown on the Pink Film specialty theater circuit compared to its later run in the legendary Tokyo minitheater, Eurospace. The title was adjusted to accommodate this move between spaces, indeed to signify it. While the literal translation of the Pink release is *Mature Woman in Heat Ball Licking* (*Jukujo hatsujō tamashaburi*), for its minitheater release it was called *Blessing* (*Tamamono*), and on the international festival circuit *Lunch Box* (*O-Bento*). In each of these cases, audiences viewed the film in a different context, with different expectations and different assignations: sex film, indie-art house film, world cinema. Imaoka's film is representative of a new kind of Pink film—if it can still be called that—that is more mobile across various spaces and media channels, and is compatible with distinct audiences and different viewing frameworks. It adjusts to a media ecology that demands a high degree of flexibility of moving-image works across different kinds of screens, and of characters and narratives across media. Though it cannot completely shed its Pink Film origins, it nonetheless is not quite a Pink film anymore; it is not strictly bound to the set of meanings and spaces that the industrial genre of Pink Film organized. Within the new media ecology, industrial genres cannot form in the same way they previously did. This points to a number of questions: What is the future of media objects in a new media ecology that emphasizes mobility across media? How does our relation to these texts, and to textuality and fiction in general, transform when we find them spreading throughout our lifeworld? How does it transform when they become not bounded and isolated works for consumption located in specific spaces but always-accessible parts of the larger ecology in which we are embedded? Where is this system heading that has little use for the frameworks of meaning that industrial genres (and cinema more generally) relied on and organized, and how can we grasp it conceptually?

This final chapter outlines three basic shifts connected to the new media ecology. All of these are shifts away from the frameworks that made industrial genres possible in the first place. First, the chapter tracks highly consequential spatial renegotiations by looking at how the film industry has attempted to adjust by creating the nonspace of the *shinecon*, or multiplex. Second, it examines the way in which media industry rhetoric has begun to focus on the term "platform" in order to accommodate a set of utopian yet nostalgic fantasies about new media ecologies. And lastly, it looks at how these shifts have led to a vigorous state interest in popular media culture not only in Japan, but all over East Asia and Southeast Asia—an interest that relies partially on an older media model and a willfully tenuous understanding of new media ecologies. As we will see, these three shifts understand themselves as aligned along a common trajectory from one media model—transmission—to that of the platform. Put differently, we will find a movement away from delivering temporally organized and bounded narratives to participating in utopian spaces of unbound simultaneity.

The Space of the Shinecon

The industrial genres of Pink Film, Kadokawa Film, and V-Cinema all used specific spaces and their attached practices to make their arguments about their historical times. Industrial genres performed complex negotiations concerning a position vis-à-vis dominant temporal discourses such as colonial time, sequential time, straight time, and homogenous time. However, from the late 1990s onward, when V-Cinema's formational period was drawing to a close, the reorganization of space became less a means than an end for the media ecology in Japan, one that claimed to siphon off any specific temporality, ostensibly introducing a kind of universal simultaneity.

In April 1993, Warner-Mycal, a joint venture between Warner Brothers International Cinemas and the Japanese retail group Mycal, opened a *shinema konpurekkusu* (cinema complex), or shinecon, what in the United States is called a multiplex.¹ The shinecon is highly representative of a model of spatial practice that complements the now-dominant media-mix system, enacting a specific model of media, sociality, and control. Supposedly, the first shinecon in Japan opened in Ebina, Kanagawa Prefecture, about 50 kilometers from Tokyo. Soon a chihō location (outside of the major urban centers) would become standard for the shinecon, which usually feature more than ten screens, the newest screening technology, and sleek interiors. They stood in stark contrast to the deteriorating and ailing theaters outside of the major cities, which had often been operating since their construction after the war. Shinecon sprang up rapidly in locations such as the Aichi, Aomori, Mie, and Niigata prefectures, areas of Japan that had seen little or no investment in theaters for decades. The first building boom was limited to rural and suburban areas; urban locations of sufficient size were difficult to find, and only available at considerably higher costs. Nonetheless, in 1996 AMC built the first urban shinecon in Fukuoka, and several others were soon to follow. By the early 2010s, about 85 percent of all screens in Japan were located in shinecon.²

These multiplexes were revolutionary. They did not discriminate between hōga (domestic) and yōga (foreign) films, eliminating screening venues that only played domestic films, which had been gradually shrinking. In 1993, 31 percent of theaters showed only films from Japan; 39 percent showed only foreign films; and 30 percent showed both.³ By 2006, 88.5 percent of all theaters mixed hōga and yōga screenings, largely due to the general shift to shinecon.⁴ All of the films screened in shinecon are free booked (yōga system), enabling the swift replacement of unsuccessful entries. To retain maximum pricing flexibility, these theaters abstain from the advance-ticket system—often seen as one of the scourges of the 1980s film industry—and instead offer their own discounts on certain days or for late shows. And, to the disadvantage of often capital-weaker hōga distributors, shinecon do not split advertising costs with the distributor, leaving it up them to generate publicity for the films.

As always, the narrative of origins has to be questioned. Eiren, the producers' association, defines a shinema conpurekkusu as a building combining five or more screens. Under this definition at least, multiplex theaters have been in operation in Japan much longer.⁵ Regardless, the glossy shinecon of the 1990s required considerable investment, and Japanese film companies were initially wary of this capital-intensive type of theater. The first thrust of investment was eager to capitalize on the Japanese market, driven by the earlier success of such concepts in France and the United States: Warner-Mycal entered in 1993, AMC and UCI in 1996, Virgin somewhat later in 1999. But soon the model's success, and the disastrous effects it had on the older theaters surrounding them, drove larger Japanese exhibition companies to participate lest they lose the strong hold they had on the business. Shochiku Multiplex Cinemas launched its first theater in 1997, as did Sasaki Kōgyō and Kokuba Gumi.[6] In 1998 Tōhō, Tōkyū, and the minor exhibition chains Musashino Kōgyō and Kinei followed; and in 1999, Herald and Eon opened their first shinecon. In 2000 alone, 362 new screens opened at thirty-eight sites, and the first shinecon opened within Tokyo itself.

The shinecon-building rush completely transformed the film exhibition landscape. In 1993, the year Japan's supposedly first shinecon opened, there were 1,734 screens, the lowest figure since 1946. By 2004, just over ten years after this theater type's first appearance, the amount of screens supplied by the shinecon alone—1,766—exceeded that number.[7] As early as 1999, the exhibition gross in the chihō was more than that of the nine largest cities for the first time in ten years, again mainly due to the spread of shinecon.[8]

The rearrangement of space brought on by the deep changes in the exhibition industry had consequences for the spectator and the industry. They transformed the constellation of discourses that had, until recently, regarded space—space not just as place but as an activity and framework for meaning—as part of and a determinant factor of filmic textuality. For the spectator, a new kind of space opened up that was, ostensibly, highly inclusive. Shinecon privileged neither the major cities nor the chihō. Through the (apparent) combination of a great variety of filmic texts, freely mixing hōga and yōga, they did away with a nationally marked spatial branding that implied a temporal or social hierarchy that had been so important for Pink Film and Kadokawa Film, and indeed for the history of film in Japan. Though dispersed across subgenres, this new spatiality ostensibly constructed a mediasphere of reduced national, gender- and class-based associations.

The previous chapters mapped industrial genres that established specific links to exhibition spaces that were fixed in their relation to specific temporal discourses. The large buildings housing huge shinecon began to replace these, ironically, with simultaneity and the claim of less space. As outlined earlier, Harry Harootunian has criticized the comparative tendency of area studies to position different places as living in different times, essentially spatializing temporality. Shinecon are almost a popular culture countermodel, denying any temporal difference and de-emphasizing spatial particularity.[9] As Pink Film theaters continued to fade away and V-Cinema had a harder time finding its way into the large video rental chains from the early 2000s onward, the minitheaters that survived the transition to digital projection in the 2010s increasingly became sites for highly niche films from the extremely low-budget section of film production.[10] Minitheater film as a distinct type of movie started to fade away quickly in the process, as did the many magazine specials that helped construct it.[11]

The shinecon dissolve the concrete marriage of space and film-textual discourses that Pink Film and the other industrial genres relied on; in exchange, they offer a supposedly free flow of subgenres, narratives, and characters without discernible borders. Indeed, the borderless shinecon were initially transnational on the business level, evidenced by the foreign capital that initiated the building boom in Japan and investments by Japanese companies in the Chinese exhibition market.[12] Yet shinecon are neither borderless nor free of national discourses, even if they perform as much. While distinctions collapsed within the shinecon spaces themselves, the sudden influx of foreign capital raised the Japanese film industry's anxiety level and, in contrast to the spectator, actually heightened perceptions regarding the foreign/Japanese binary within the industry. The *Eiga Nenkan* even began including a pie chart illustrating the number of screens controlled by foreign capital in its annual roundup of the state of the industry.[13] Eventually, Japanese companies began buying out the initially foreign-owned chains.

Shinecon claim a detachment of subgenres and texts from concrete spaces, a free space of flow determined only by audience interest. This detachment is only ostensible, as certain subgenres and texts are emphatically excluded. Occasionally Pink films such as Imaoka Shinji's *Lunch Box* will play in a minitheater, but not in a shinecon. Occasionally V-Cinema will play in theaters in Tokyo's east Ginza or in Osaka, but never in a shinecon. Yet the aroma of utopian, transnational, unlimited mobility it promises has a very real appeal for film audiences. For the spearheads of the wider media industry in Japan that idea crystallized around the concept of the platform.

Idyllic Platforms

This blurring of all the temporal boundaries made possible by a unity of place also contributes in an essential way to the creation of the cyclic rhythmicalness of time so characteristic of the idyll.
—MIKHAIL M. BAKHTIN, "Forms of Time and Chronotope in the Novel"

Mikako and Noboru are in high school and, although they do not acknowledge it, they are in love. There is a problem, however, as Mikako must head off to outer space in a *mecha* military-robot combat suit to defend the earth from attacking aliens. Over the following years, she and Noboru exchange longing text messages that, due to Mikako's increasing distance from earth, take years to arrive. The two experience a conflict that became one of the most-discussed narrative tropes of popular culture in Japan in the early 2000s: if you follow your most personal feelings and stay at home, the world will be destroyed. Thus the fate of the entire world and one's most intimate emotions are both inextricably at odds and directly causally linked. This story setting from Shinkai Makoto's twenty-five-minute *Voices of a Distant Star* (*Hoshi no koe*, 2002) is prototypical of a transmedia subgenre named *sekai-kei* (world type).

Voices was scripted, directed, drawn, and produced by a single individual working outside of the established animation industry. Its appearance seemed to herald the breakthrough of the individual, noncorporate production of animation, the rise of the citizen-consumer-producer. Ōtsuka Eiji wrote an entire book on the monumental change he felt this work heralded, called *Hear the "Voices of a Distant Star."*[14] This example of successful noncorporate production of moving images that at the same time could compete in the marketplace made *Voices* seem like an upset in power relations was on the horizon. It symbolized a renegotiation of labor relations, of business models, of the role of narrative and characters, and of basic media models. The site of that renegotiation, by some of the central players in the industry, was seen to be the space of the platform.

It is important to examine the term "platform" here, as it is has gained considerable currency in the rhetoric of the media industry and points to how it would like to define itself. Tarleton Gillespie has analyzed the recent history of the term in English, which is by no means used consistently and has many connotations. Gillespie analyzes YouTube's corporate prose to find that its "use of 'platform' leans on all of the term's connotations: computational, something to build upon and innovate from; political, a place from which to speak and be heard; figurative, in that the opportunity is an abstract promise as much as a practical one; and architectural, in that YouTube is designed as an open-armed, egalitarian facilitation of expression, not an elitist gatekeeper with normative and technical restrictions."[15] Gillespie's taxonomy is joined by a number of additional, specific uses, such as in platform studies (the study of specific software-hardware configurations such as game consoles) or in management studies. With regard to anime, Ian Condry has used the term "generative platform" to help explain how characters and worlds, rather than narratives, help provide a system that creates highly mobile media objects.[16] Overall, however, we can see usages that branch out from the term "platform" as a physical, elevated space, such as a speaker's platform for political speech that took place in the United States in the 1840s. It is here that a certain model of politics becomes as intertwined with the term as its older, more technological meaning.[17]

The term "platform" has a slightly different career in Japan than in the U.S. context. Marc Steinberg has importantly pointed out that the initial central term for industry and policy makers in the wake of the diffusion of digital media and the government's Cool Japan initiatives was "contents," not "platform."[18] Only around 2010 did Kadokawa Tsuguhiko emerge as one of the main proponents of the term "platform." What Kadokawa claims to aim for is a platform that is completely open and allows equal access, use, and modification or production of media objects.[19] In such a model production and consumption meld, and the media object itself is no longer at the center of corporate interest—it is the activity that is generated around it that is monetizable. If, as Maurizio Lazzarato has famously claimed, "The corporation does not generate the object (the commodity), but rather the world in which the object exists," then ownership within that world is of reduced significance to the corporation.[20] The de facto weakening of copyright generates activity and investment that in turn benefit the corporation; it is not the user-generated video that makes money for the corporation, it is the user interactions and site visits that are at the center of this business model. Ownership is transferred from the micro to the macro: from owning the commodity to owning the world in which the commodity exists and that generates commodifiable activity. Pink Film, Kadokawa Film, and V-Cinema's confusions and the politics of compromised disruption that they allowed for have little place in such a world based on constantly moving targets, or at least they lack the power to define it. On a platform there is even less fixed meaning to navigate, and ownership itself becomes ambiguous, further dissolving the basis for a coherent politics of confusion.

In other words while industrial genres used confusion to amalgamate the critique of, expression of, and collaboration with the dominant contradictions of Japan after 1945, this confusion relied on a modern conception of politics. Problematic as a confusionist strategy was, it pointed to a specific model of politics with specific possibilities. Like a canary in a mining tunnel, with the loss of a politics with differentiated, formulated reference points, a unified public, and linear transmission channels, confusion lost its oxygen and industrial genres withered away.

In books such as *The Age of the Cloud and the "Cool Revolution"* and *A Copyright Law That Won't Lose against Google and Apple*, Tsuguhiko has outlined the need to build a platform, essentially the "world in which the commodity exists" that Lazzarato describes.[21] Tsuguhiko explicitly contrasts his highly permeable model with platforms such as YouTube, which arranges itself with copyright holders, or iTunes, which is a closed ecosystem. Tsuguhiko's fondness for Lawrence Lessig and his copyright-critical books on remix culture is well known, and Kadokawa has been an active supporter of organizations such as Creative Commons, the organization cofounded by Lessig to allow more flexibility in the use of copyright. Yet the exact specifications of Tsuguhiko's envisioned platform have considerable political implications, and we will return to them in a moment.

The framing of the platform as introducing entirely new media rules in concert with digital technology must be taken with a grain of salt. The idea of the rise of so-called amateur media production that *Voices* encapsulated is a case in point (not only because Shinkai would go on to a highly successful career in the established animation industry): Both live-action film and animation have a long history of noncorporate production by groups and individuals in Japan. Film produced and distributed by individuals and groups outside of a corporate context has existed in Japan since the 1920s. More recently, Gainax, the company that produced the seminal *Neon Genesis Evangelion*, began as a group that called itself Daicon Film and produced several now-famous and influential animations such as the opening films for the Daicon III and Daicon IV fan conventions in the early 1980s or the 16 mm live-action monster film *Yamata no Orochi no Gyakushū*. And this is not to speak of the rich history of magazines, novels, film, and manga, often called *dōjin mono*, produced in noncorporate contexts. Terms often used in English such as "amateur" media or fan production carry various problematic connotations, and the Japanese terms *jishu*, or "autonomous," and *dōjin*, or "group (of like-minded people)," arguably raise more interesting questions. However, despite the history of such production, it is only since the 1980s that the encouraging of consumer participation in the corporate production of media objects has stood at the center of the new media ecology and has been an active business strategy in Japan. The horror series *Higurashi When They Cry* can serve as one of the best known examples of the interreliance of corporate and noncorporate production in the early 2000s. Originating in a dōjin game distributed at the Comic Market, it became wildly successful and rapidly proliferated across media, spawning a whole host of separate manga series, anime series, straight-to-video animation, live-action films, games, music albums, radio drama, and endless dōjin works. Its mix of a loop structure and a parallel world structure that repeats variations of a basic narrative constellation allows fans to easily add on their own version of the events, some of which are then collected and published by large media companies. Time loops and parallel worlds quickly proved themselves to be one of the most efficient ways to design storytelling structures that produced not singular narratives but an assortment of versions that those formerly known as consumers could add on to. And again the path leads to Kadokawa.

A useful way to outline this phenomenon is the different media-mix strategies Kadokawa Haruki and Kadokawa Tsuguhiko pursued. While Haruki was attempting to produce and sell connected films, novels, magazines, and soundtracks on a large scale, Tsuguhiko was focused on smaller audience groups and creating spaces where their participation could be integrated into production to thus generate commodities—an activity that is itself commodifiable. One of the well-known early experiments was the media-mix series *Record of Lodoss War* (*Rōdosu tō senki*). *Lodoss* originated in a session of the role-playing game Dungeons and Dragons (called a replay) that was printed in the Kadokawa magazine *Comptiq*, which was under Tsuguhiko's purview.[22] Replays are actual game sessions presented in story form, and Lodoss proved so popular that one of the participants in the game sessions, novelist Mizuno Ryo, expanded the storyworld. This eventually resulted in an array of *Lodoss* media, from novels to video games, manga, and anime. Using replays commercially is one technique that commodifies not (only) the game, but the act of playing itself.[23] The massive Comic Market (Komike), held twice a year in Tokyo and attracting well over half a million visitors, is a more prominent example of the unparalleled level of jishu and dōjin activity in Japan. Over 35,000 groups and individuals offer their dōjin manga, music, novels, and many other media, making Comic Market one of the primary sites for blending production, consumption, and corporate attempts to make use of this astounding level of activity set free within this self-organizing system. Some of the most popular media franchises of the early 2000s emerged from the Comic Market, and the industry has already built a pipeline for integrating those media that prove most successful within the dōjin scene.

The momentous and massive interpenetration of corporate and noncorporate production has been widely noted, in both academia and the business world, and approached with many different terms. "Fan labor" or "immaterial labor" (the latter used by postoperaismo theorists such as Lazzarato or Tiziana Terranova) are two important terms, while "playbor" (a hybrid of play and labor) is another. This development is often seen as unquestionably linked to the spread of computer technology and digital culture.[24] There is a strong determinist view of technology at work here that the context of Japan is well suited to complicate. The explosion in popular-culture production by individuals and groups not aiming for a corporate context took place in the 1960s and 1970s, and while it has increased steadily since, this growth curve cannot easily be solely attributed to the spread of computer technology.

Despite its centrality, Kadokawa Tsuguhiko's strategies go beyond the integration of fan labor into a lineup of corporate products—often to the unease of other media companies in Japan. They extend to rethinking the role of copyright and of fundamental business models. Kadokawa created waves when it tacitly approved fan-created subtitles of the series *The Melancholy of Suzumiya Haruhi* (*Suzumiya Haruhi no yūutsu*) and actively encouraged fan-produced videos that often reedited portions of the anime—usually regarded as a problematic breach of copyright law.[25] Kadokawa attached advertisements for Kadokawa series to the fan videos on YouTube and even included fan videos on the official Kadokawa site, where they again function as advertisements. The 2014 merger of Dwango, a media company running the video-sharing site Nico Nico Douga, and Kadokawa is a further step in this development. While the popular press described the merger as the marriage of a "content producer" (Kadokawa) and media infrastructure (Dwango), Ōtsuka Eiji derided this portrayal as a complete misunderstanding of the way Kadokawa positions itself and this business deal. Rather, for Ōtsuka, this was a fusion of Kadokawa distribution/rights business infrastructure and Dwango's net-based infrastructure.[26] A similar misinterpretation of the role of content vis-à-vis structure arguably underlies one of the most visible reactions to the new media ecology in Japan, the attempt by the state in the early 2000s to appropriate the massive energy set free by the emergent set of media practices.

Platforming Politics

When Prime Minister Abe Shinzō resigned from his post on September 15, 2007, the very same day saw a curious economic development. Despite the American subprime loan crisis that was affecting global markets, the stocks of manga, anime, and game-related companies rose considerably. Manga store chain Mandarake's stock rose 13 percent; card-game specialist Broccoli rose 71 percent; video game company Koei Net rose 17 percent; and even animation giant Toei Animation and media-corporation juggernaut Kadokawa Holdings each rose 3 percent.[27] The financial press immediately attributed the stock surge to speculation about Abe's succession. Foreign minister Aso Tarō, one of the most outspoken voices on the political and economic potential of manga and anime, was regarded as a good bet to be Abe's successor, and analysts expected favorable legislation for what in Japan was called the "contents business" if he took office.

Popular media culture gained a new status as governments all over East and Southeast Asia reimagined its possibilities throughout the 1990s and early 2000s. As a growth sector, as an instrument of the state's soft power, and as an opportunity to reimagine the nation, "contents" had gripped the imagination of policy makers in the region. These initiatives were deeply connected to the changing media ecologies and perceptions of their new reach and new working principles. Often enough the fantasies about the uses of media content stood in tension with central aspects of the emerging media systems. Seeing in them new ways to channel and control meaning and emotions, they rarely considered how the workings of media engagement themselves were changing, and didn't always easily align with the purported goals of national or nationalist policy.

Although policy changes concerning media had been gestating in the 1990s, it was Prime Minister Koizumi Junichirō who oversaw a virtual flurry of activity beginning in the early 2000s. Koizumi initiated and chaired the Strategic Council on Intellectual Property himself in 2002, and that same year the Agency for Cultural Affairs launched the Committee on Film Promotion. In 2004, the Ministry of Economy, Trade, and Industry (METI) revised several regulations regarding financing media content. Copyright regulations were extended from fifty to seventy years in 2003—just in time to retain the copyright of several classic directors' most famous films before their centennial, most notably those of Ozu Yasujirō—and the Content Promotion Law was passed in 2004. Government agencies such as METI, the Ministry of Export and Trade, and the Ministry of Internal Affairs and Communication worked together with the Japanese Business Federation (Keidanren) to form the Visual Industry Promotion Organization (VIPO). In 2005 the Ministry of Foreign Affairs of Japan formed the Overseas Exchange Council (counting the presidents of Tōei and media publisher Pony Canyon among its members). The Japan External Trade Organization started a number of projects to enhance the presence of Japanese companies in international content markets, and in 2006 METI launched a series of workshops and seminars at international film festivals to stimulate international coproduction.[28]

In January 2007, the Government Council on Intellectual Property recommended that the government further increase measures to promote entertainment content abroad and implement programs to provide the legal training necessary for such international deals.[29] In September 2007, VIPO organized the first edition of the forty-day Japan International Contents

Festival (CoFesta). This combined seventeen separate festivals and events under an umbrella brand to "create new possibilities" and "make a broad appeal to overseas."[30] Most prominently, and repositioning it as one element in a larger media strategy, the Tokyo International Film Festival was also subsumed under the CoFesta label.[31] Government bodies invoked the slogan of "Cool Japan," modeled on Tony Blair's Cool Britannia campaign, to encapsulate this larger bundle of activity, and the term "content" began to summarize works from the vague range of media the campaign targeted. In response, the Agency for Cultural Affairs promoted *media geijutsu* (media art) as a counter to the business-oriented term "content." As the business connotation of "content" seemed to place the term outside of its purview, this rhetorical switch allowed the agency to speak about popular culture and the media mix, thereby opening a channel of access to the increasing funds available for Cool Japan purposes.[32]

The surge of activity and spending that accompanied the Cool Japan campaign shows an anxious attempt to adjust to a deeply transforming media and information ecology, as well as its position within the larger political and financial economy. It is a transformation we have seen brewing in the trajectory from Pink Film to Kadokawa Film to V-Cinema. While many of the arguments and negotiations these industrial genres performed are specific to the context of Japan, that trajectory is not. The policy push to adjust to these transformations took place globally, although East Asian governments have invested more energy than many others in the rush for national branding through popular culture and what Joseph Nye termed soft power. Soft power has been defined differently at different times, but it roughly refers to the ability to persuade negotiation partners through means other than economic or military pressure. That is not to say that economic calculation is irrelevant here. It is quite clear that recent concerted state support for popular culture in East Asia first took off under Kim Dae Jung in Korea in the 1990s, fueled by a now infamous government report counting the number of Hyundais that needed to be sold to equal the global box office of *Jurassic Park*.

Michael Curtin framed the policy rush in East and Southeast Asia as competition for "media capital," the combination of infrastructure, trained professionals, and content that becomes a potentially powerful resource. Curtin emphasizes the spatial discourse underlying such competition when he points out, "Media capital is a concept that at once acknowledges the *spatial* logics of capital, creativity, culture, and polity without privileging one among the four."[33] The emphasis on space is echoed in Fredric Jameson's previously mentioned insistence on the "End of Temporality."[34]

The idea that a new kind of media spatiality is becoming paradigmatic thus underlies the arguably dysfunctional attempts by the state to utilize contemporary media ecologies. To understand the trajectory discourses have taken here, and the problematic assumptions behind them, the following examines three different stances on the pairing of nation and media: one from the 1920s, one from the early 2000s, and one from the 2010s.

Levels of Spatiality

Captain Tsubasa was in a war zone, and on April 28, 2006, the aforementioned Japanese minister of foreign affairs, Asō Tarō, gave a speech to explain why. "A New Look at Cultural Diplomacy: A Call to Japan's Cultural Practitioners" was the title of his talk at the Digital Hollywood University in the Akihabara section of Tokyo.[35] When expounding on Japanese culture, Asō fleetingly mentioned the traditional arts of puppetry and pottery. The speech then quickly focused on what he called popular culture. Asō spoke of his love for manga and anime, and how widely disseminated they are in the world, mentioning the global status of Miyazaki Hayao's anime and the iconic *Astro Boy*. He urged the students to "join with us in polishing the Japan 'brand.'" He proceeded to tell how in the Al-Muthanna Governorate of Iraq, where the Japanese Self-Defense Forces were stationed, the water supply vehicles Japan had provided through its Official Development Assistance made their rounds with large images of Captain Tsubasa on them, the main character from a soccer-themed anime series known in Iraq as *Captain Majed*. Asō reported that just one month earlier, the Japan Foundation had sealed a deal to provide the largest Iraqi television station with the third season of *Captain Tsubasa* dubbed in Arabic free of charge. In a sweeping connection of aesthetics and politics, he concluded, "In Iraq, a country now struggling to create a political system, we are showing the children the promise of a bright future."[36]

Almost eighty years earlier, in 1927, the author Naoki Sanjūgo had outlined the state of Japanese film and the film world and his ideas on how to improve it. In his text, he drew up a list of issues to discuss, number one being "the common points and differences between America and Japan." His goal was a film industry that was a "real business," free of connections to organized crime and "upstart swindlers." After a succinct analysis of the situation of the Japanese film industry, complete with detailed budget calculations and an account of systemic faults, Naoki's answer to the, in his eyes, dismal state of the vertically organized industry was the free market. An independent distribution business and freely accessible rental studios would lead to fair competition and a rise in production that would result in "many more times the failures and masterworks."[37] He contrasted the "differentiated business" structure of America that in his opinion divided production, distribution, and exhibition with the "unified business" structure of Japan that was "defective" in that it was "not yet developed." Naoki stated that Japan must make up its hundred-year time lag in one-third of the time, fully subscribing to the idea of Japan being temporally behind Europe and the United States; film was centrally "a part of this," and he estimated it would take another two years to achieve parity on the cinematic level, "apart from financial power."[38]

Seventy-nine years lie between these agendas. They entail decisive differences but also considerable common ground. The commonalities in particular show how, despite the often-promoted idea of rupture and the attempt to adjust to a completely transformed mediascape, discourses from the past and the present coexist in a warped overlap. Both Aso and Naoki are at the most basic level in the thrall of the idea of global temporal sequence. The relation to the foreign Other and the question of temporal hierarchy—and a specific futurity—thus almost naturally take center stage and are married to a specific media model. Naoki is explicit about the race to catch up and surprisingly concrete about the estimated amount of time it will necessitate. And while Naoki does not mention it in his text, Joanne Bernardi has shown how the "rhetoric of export"—the idea that film from Japan, if synchronized with an imagined global standard, might help portray Japan in a positive light to the world—was a common accompanying notion in the 1920s.[39] Ultimately, Naoki sees the reduction of temporal distance as a means of improving film from Japan. While nation plays a fundamental role in his argument, he is more concerned with an industry that will produce texts of a higher quality.

Aso takes a slightly more acrobatic position, and one with more wide-reaching motives. He raises the examples of *Popeye* and *Blondie* as serials that helped shape Japanese perceptions of America and the future it stood for, projecting a model of justice, strength, and modern(ized) domestic affluence. Aso, however, formulates his account with confidence that the American future is an anecdote from the past. For him, Japanese content has already caught up and spread throughout the world, has emancipated and proven itself, and is necessarily tied to a politics of nation in which Japan can now show the children of other countries the future. Here the foreign minister is explicitly linking what he calls the content industry to international trade and its concrete effect on the exercising of official foreign policy, specifically the first deployment of the Japanese Self-Defense Forces outside of Japan since the end of World War II.[40] In calling for the "practitioners of the content industry" to help create a popular culture that can "be our ally in diplomacy," he calls for a "partnership" that can only condense on the basis of nation and a unified public sphere—a space entailing few or no borders between the state, economy, and aesthetics.

Here we see the continuity between Naoki's and Aso's conceptions of media, one that dovetails with Aso's insistence on speaking through the framework of "contents." Both Naoki and Aso apply a traditional transmission model of mass media, with centralized senders and a multitude of receivers. In this model bounded works are industrially produced, centrifugally disseminated, and then consumed—and it is at the point of passive consumption where influence is exerted. Production is deeply tied to national contexts, even if distribution beyond them is possible. Such a specific model of centralized and nationally marked control exerts a strong attraction for state policy makers.

While Naoki Sanjūgo could arguably employ such frameworks with some justification in the Fordist film production environment of the 1920s, Aso Tarō must bend the emerging media system to the breaking point to uphold such a temporalized transmission model. Essentially, it caters to a certain nostalgic fantasy of how the state can exert power, tied to a nostalgic fantasy of how the new media ecology is organized.

For one, Aso's media model is built on the premise of a clear distinction between producer and consumer, with the media text delivering a message between them. This is the mechanism by which Japan would be able to communicate itself to the world via popular culture. It is a simplified transmission model of media, one that might have seemed self-evident in the 1920s but that appears significantly less obvious in the present media ecology. This is not only because reception is now conceived of as an active process that heavily depends on the specific audience or reader. More importantly, theorists of media have pointed out the dissolving border between production and consumption even outside of "amateur" media production cultures. Users who take part in the Japanese video-sharing site Nico Nico Douga will add comments that become part of a video, create and upload their own remixes, or create their own live streaming channel. Tracing such developments backward, Jonathan Beller has argued that cinema is at the root of a trajectory that turns spectatorship into labor, mainly in the form of value-productive attention: "In accord with the principles of late capitalism, to look is to labor."[41]

Why then must Aso partially rely on a simplified transmission model of media to justify the logic of short-circuiting nation and popular culture? If the state is eager to harness the new media ecology's considerable power to generate productive and commodifiable activity on the side of what was until this point defined as a consumer, if it wants to argue with a logic of influence, it must ignore the working principles that set this energy free. It is exactly the new media ecology's ability to induce connectivity, to mobilize—or euphemistically, to encourage participation—that generates enormous activity. And it is that activity that is economically exploitable regardless of the "contents" it entails. The new media ecology emphasizes mobility and connectivity rather than a transmittable and consumable narrative. From a media-technophilosophical standpoint, Mark Hansen has pointed out, "What is mediated here, in other words, is the technical capacity to connect on a massive, many-to-many scale. . . . This is a truly McLuhanesque moment in the precise sense that, over and above any content that happens to be transmitted, what is involved in Web 2.0 is a widespread mediatic regime change—nothing less, I would suggest, than a change in the vocation of media and mediation themselves."[42] Similarly, the sociologist Kitada Akihiro has analyzed what he calls the "connective sociality" (*tsunagari no shakaisei*) of media culture of the early 2000s through a case study of the messaging board 2channel. Kitada, deeply influenced by the systems theory of Niklas Luhmann, regards the nationalist sentiments frequently voiced on this extraordinarily influential website as ironically oscillating between naively sincere and cynically disparaging statements. The trope of nation appears to supply a specific charge that enables this oscillation efficiently. However, the oscillation, and the activity it entails, is only a means to the end of connectivity, of interacting with others. It is structure and movement that take primacy, not the content. According to Kitada then, the politics of the new media ecology therefore do not require or even encourage, in the vulgar sense of the word, ideology. And while the right-wing rhetoric that can be found habitually on 2channel sounds ideological, Kitada sees it as a mere epiphenomenon. This is where Aso's fantasy of a Japanese employment of the mechanisms of postwar education by the American occupation and a usurpation of its soft power—based on exactly the transmission model of media—exposes itself as unable to embrace the emerging media principles.

However, it is again critical to emphasize that this new media ecology and the primacy of connectivity do not spontaneously spring from the well of the digital in the early 2000s. In the mid-1970s, prominent leftist critic and activist Matsuda Masao discerned a similar development in Japanese media culture. After a long career trusting in the power of transmitting the right message via film (as, for example, a collaborator on the state-critical film AKA *Serial Killer* [*Ryakushō renzoku shasatsuma*, 1969]) and print, Matsuda began to see the transmission model of leftist media as a failed one. Instead, he initially began to call for ways to introduce self-organizing networks, strangely using the European railway system as one of his initial examples. By 1976, however, Matsuda pinned his hopes for such connectivity on the exploding "autonomous film" (*jishu firumu*) scene. Describing the unique perspective of the new generation as "image thought," Matsuda to some degree mourned the absence of explicitly transmitted politics in the massive number of films this new movement produced. However he also saw it as containing the seeds for a new "principle of collectivity" that arises from within the "circuit of producing and viewing" that was establishing itself on a massive scale.[43]

Both Matsuda's and Kitada's models see a weakening of the content and narrative level of the text, or maybe even a transformation of what textuality itself entails. It is here again that the project of national branding attempts to harness something that seems to fundamentally counteract a narrative notion such as nation. On the most simple level, if the Vocaloid software Hatsune Miku allows any user anywhere to create their own version of a Hatsune Miku song, then the attached character of Hatsune Miku inevitably becomes less clearly locatable as "Japanese." Beyond that, the fundamental discourse of the new media ecology is one of simultaneous presence across a homogenous media space; and while this demands serious scrutiny, it stands in stark contrast to a nation-based vision of the dissemination of bounded commodities, narratives, and ideology. The fantasy of soft power, of one-way influence channeled through or supported by the state, thus denies a tension between the concept of nation or the idea of politics as narrative, and the workings of the new media ecologies. Nation does not disappear, but its quality and function change.

There is, however, a third conception of the political character of media that has emerged in Japan. It is one more attuned to the new media ecology yet still in many ways appealing to the nostalgia of Aso Tarō's conception and develops its nostalgic impulses into a utopian, not a utilitarian, proposal. It is Kadokawa Tsuguhiko's model of an open platform inclusive of all kinds of producers, consumers, formats, and hardware that presents a third model of politics in the new media ecology—ostensibly a democratic and transparent one. In his own words, his completely open platform, part of an "ecosystem 2.0," will flatten the playing field, allowing equal access to corporate content and applications and to "consumer-generated media," with no restrictions on formats or devices, and with no restrictions on the type of media objects to be uploaded (i.e., with no approval process necessary). Tsuguhiko's platform is a space of constant interaction and repurposing, designed to generate maximum activity. The space of this platform is so open that it becomes characterized as a nonspace and generates a temporality that is ostensibly without hierarchy or linearity. The utopian aspect of the model is one that Kadokawa explicitly emphasizes when he speaks of it as an extension and further development of the fruits of postwar democracy.[44]

Tsuguhiko's model is a radicalization of Haruki's quest to control a massive consumer base with global simultaneity and to spread Kadokawa products across an array of media. It is also a radicalization of the shinecon model, which presents a supposedly open, competitive space for all kinds of films. Compared to the platform model, both Haruki and the shinecon rely on a one-way transmission model, in which corporate-produced media objects (films, novels, etc.) are transmitted to consumers. Simultaneity relies on access granted in a top-down system. Tsuguhiko, in comparison, claims his platform to be an egalitarian space of total access and exchange. It is a characterization that, like Aso's, references postwar democracy and the results of occupation education. Yet it understands the result of this education less as an assortment of narratives or ideologemes than, in accordance with Tsuguhiko's model of an ecosystem, a processual framework of access and activity. Yet when Tsuguhiko calls his project alternatively the *hi no maru* (the sun symbol, also used as a name for the Japanese flag) cloud or the Eastern cloud, it is clear that despite its adjustment to new media ecology principles, this framework as well cannot fully detach itself from a national framework, from colonial projects and Cold War anxieties, or think outside of the long shadow of post–Cold War American Internet hegemony. This is of course no specifically Japanese problem, and the universalist rhetoric of Silicon Valley and the U.S. government has always accommodated a national politics.[45] While various national ghosts thus haunt Tsuguhiko's platform model, they do not leave the conception of nation untouched either. Nonetheless Tsuguhiko ties the success of this platform to a unification of nation and platform: "The true greatness of the Japan Content Platform will be in the value it gives birth to when the customer ID evolves into a 'certification system' on the level of citizens. With all content holders taking part in ecosystem 2.0, within three years the majority of citizens will become users."[46] It is the subtle shift from citizen to user that points to the inner tension that even Tsuguhiko's appeal to postwar democracy and nation elicits in its realization through new media ecology capitalism.

After Industrial Genre

Transformation, not death, has been the premise of this investigation. The "end of Japanese cinema" points not to the disappearance of long-form (or other) moving image works as art *or* industry. But it does point to deep changes in the way these works and the attached practices are understood and engaged, across their functions as art, commodity, and social actant. As we have seen, the emergence of or at least the increase in industrial genres from the 1960s onward seems to have coincided with the breakdown of a Fordist system of production and of an industry tightly controlled by a small number of studios. With the increasing interconnection of media and the emergence of systems such as media mixes the role and meaning of media—or rather how media make meaning—has changed. The necessary frameworks for industrial genre—more or less bounded media channels, reception spaces, and media-industrial formations—are dissolving. Film and its passage through this form of organization has been a highly useful constant (of sorts) to track the trajectory of that change. The fantasies, hopes, and anxieties around film have changed as much as the greater social function it can fulfill in its increasing interdependence with other media objects. Industrial genres represented but one of the ways that film organized and negotiated meaning, both as symptom and as intervention.

It is in film's materiality that we find it as perhaps particularly suited to the transitional phenomenon of industrial genre. With its ability to accommodate both basic sequential linearity and the possibility of juxtaposing different times—through editing, through the making present of a temporal absence via the projected image itself—film leaned toward the contrapositioning and combination of times that industrial genres performed. "Confusion" was how this investigation figured the specific constellations of temporalities that industrial genres arranged in attempts to cope with and synthesize a complex array of experiences, expectations, and emotions. Industrial genres' increasing difficulty in managing this, and sustaining themselves, points to a number of disintegrations. First and foremost, it is driven by the weakening of clearly distinguished historical times, if we follow Koselleck, or of historicity, if we follow Fredric Jameson. It is Jameson who has most forcefully argued "that it is most productive to grasp this development in terms of the death of historicity; or to be more precise, the weakening of our phenomenological experience of the past and future, the reduction of our temporality to the present of the body."[47] Here, we might add, it is the present of the platform. And with sequential, linear, and historical time it fades out connected cultural techniques such as narrative and ideology. The increasing centrality of characters that are detached from narrative and media channels, what manga theorist Itō Gō calls kyara, may be one symptom of this.

Narrative played a central role in industrial genres' project of extended textuality, on the level of both grand temporal narratives utilized for confusion and the filmic narratives that helped express them. If the role of narrative changes, then, so does the possibility for designing a specific confusion and the very basis of an industrial genre. As we have seen, industrial genres structured complex, often contradictory discursive, temporal constellations to fashion very specific modes of confusion. This confusion nonetheless communicated a certain positionality, a constellation of politics and subjectivities. Contradiction is a slippery term with a long history of theorization, and it is worth considering at least roughly what it might mean here. While Louis Althusser saw ideology as the prime tool for containing contradiction, Claude Lévi-Strauss has claimed that myth serves to embody the contradictions inherent in a specific society via narrative. Industrial genres did something slightly different. Pink Film, Kadokawa Film, and V-Cinema all operated with confusion by packaging it, commodifying the common experience of confusion, and making it attractive. Yet they remained within the force field of narrative and ideology, even if it is a commodified one. On the other hand, the platform, or at least the fantasy of the platform, promises unadulterated activity and connectivity.

What form of structuring force does film participate in after industrial genre? Or rather, what kind of structuring force does film participate in after the demise of the conditions that made industrial genre possible? Does it find other ways to mediate between industrial organization and its politics, the points, forms, and practices of reception, and the texts and objects it channels? Will we find platformed variations of industrial genre in the future, or do we need to propose something akin to a postindustrial genre? These are questions that, like industrial genres themselves, are not only tied to future analyses of factual film and media situations, but also to the way they discursively organize themselves. They will make claims about themselves that often stand in tension with their own working principles—we have seen this at play in all three of the above ideas, voiced by Naoki, Aso, and Kadokawa, about the connection of film and nation.

Nation then remained one of the foci of the politics of new media ecologies. Despite this, the analysis of media in the early 2000s often centrally assumed the rhetoric of world. Depending on the context, the application of this rhetoric is slightly differently placed. In the U.S. context, world creation became the battle cry of the media industry and a quickly expanding branch of (trans)media analysis. In Germany, a more technology-centered approach stemming from media philosophy posited a shift in the role of that technology, or, as Sybille Krämer put it, "Technology as a tool spares us labor; but technology as an apparatus [*ein Apparat*] creates artificial worlds; it opens up experiences and makes possible procedures that don't simply exist in weaker form without these apparatuses, but that without them don't exist at all. Not the enhancement of performance [*Leistungssteigerung*] but rather the creation of worlds is the productive purpose [*Sinn*] of media technologies."[48] And finally, in Japan the above-mentioned world-type fictions such as *Voices from a Distant Star* became a central axis for discussing media culture of the early 2000s. The self-aware character of these fictions is mirrored in the opening monologue of *Voices*: "There is a word, 'world.' When I was in middle school I vaguely held the idea that the world is the place where the electric waves of my mobile phone reach." The fact that media strategies that focus on the construction of worlds or platforms, theoretical discourse on the concept of worlds, and the *sekai-kei* (world-type) media-mix subgenre all appear in concert around the same time in Japan points to a fascinating intersection that is in some ways similar to an expanded industrial genre.[49] How narrowly future discourses define the new media worlds in relation to frameworks such as nation, how they delineate themselves through other forms of collectivity and community, will centrally define their politics and possibilities.

NOTES

INTRODUCTION

1. Japanese names will be given in the name order conventionally used in Japan, family name first and given name second.
2. Director Ōbayashi Nobuhiko recounts this story in "Boku no Kadokawa Eiga-Dansō."
3. See, for example, Barad, *Meeting the Universe Halfway*.
4. The emphasis is here on an emergent media ecology that functions according to a new set of principles, not an ecology of new media.
5. See Neale, "Melo Talk." Theorists such as Christine Gledhill criticized Neale's position as reifying genre categories and returning to the "taxonomic trap," while Gledhill prefers to focus on the reasons genres have been constructed. See Gledhill, "Rethinking Genre," 221.
6. Genette, *Paratexts*, 2.
7. Genette, *Paratexts*, 410.
8. Gray, *Show Sold Separately*, 39.
9. Gray, *Show Sold Separately*, 26.
10. Altman, "A Semantic/Syntactic Approach to Film Genre."
11. Caldwell, "Para-industry."
12. This conceptualization draws on neocybernetic ideas of emergence, which differ slightly from older, classical cybernetic ideas of emergence. As Bruce Clark and Mark Hansen mention, this means that "in contrast to the technosciences of emergence, it proceeds not (like some latter-day Herbert Spencer) from the simple to the complex, but rather by way of system-specific and system-internal reductions of hypercomplexity to ordered complexity. This is the meaning of von Foerster's statement that it is we who invent the environment that we perceive." See Clark and Hansen, "Introduction: Neocybernetic Emergence," in *Emergence and Embodiment*, 13.
13. Williams, "Is a Radical Genre Criticism Possible?" In Europe, there are naturally more investigations into non-Hollywood genres such as the Italian *giallo* or the German *heimatfilm*. These mostly follow the usual fixation on the text, however.

14 Sarah Berry has called for looking at how (Hollywood-originated) film genres spread to other national cinemas as part of a system of glocalization, when transnational genres assume specific significance in a local context; see Berry-Flint, "Genre." David Desser has attempted exactly that in his article "Global Noir," chronicling the transnational dissemination of a film noir style and certain character relations.
15 Yoshimoto, "Melodrama, Postmodernism and the Japanese Cinema," 32.
16 The term "intra-act" here draws on Karen Barad's usage.
17 Bazin, "The Western."
18 Wright, *Sixguns and Society*.
19 Altman, "A Semantic/Syntactic Approach to Film Genre"; also Altman, "Reusable Packaging."
20 Nakamura, *Eizō/Gensetsu no Bunkashakaigaku*, 68.
21 Changes to the structure of the Pink Film industry and the films themselves, incremental until the early 2000s, have sped up considerably since then.
22 For an excellent outline of Wakamatsu Productions' work in this regard, see Furuhata, *Cinema of Actuality*.
23 A type of production that Yuriko Furuhata sees as one form of the "cinema of actuality." Furuhata, *Cinema of Actuality*.
24 Crom, "Porno und Apokalypse."
25 The notable exception for Pink Film is the writings of Roland Domenig and a volume dedicated to the genre: Nornes, *The Pink Book*.
26 For the paradigmatic example of a structuralist approach, see Burch, *To the Distant Observer*. For an impressive and exhaustive formalist approach that veers away from finding "Japaneseness," see Bordwell, *Ozu and the Poetics of Cinema*.
27 See, for example, Gerow, *Visions of Japanese Modernity*; Nornes, *Forest of Pressure*; Miyao, *Sessue Hayakawa*.
28 For example, see Lamarre, *The Anime Machine*; Steinberg, *Anime's Media Mix*; and Furuhata, *Cinema of Actuality*.
29 Satō, "Nikkatsu Eiga Zenshi."
30 Takamura, "Japanese Film World Rises Again."
31 The gross for domestic films in 2006 was $884.48 million. These are the statistics as published by Eiren, the Motion Picture Producers Association of Japan, Inc. They can be downloaded at Eiren, "2006-nen Zenkoku Eiga Gaikyō" [The national general situation of film], Eiren, accessed June 2014, http://www.eiren.org/toukei/index.html.
32 Richie, *100 Years of Japanese Film*, 208.
33 Tanaka, *New Times in Modern Japan*, 1–2.
34 Anderson, *Imagined Communities*, 52.
35 Harootunian, *History's Disquiet*.
36 Rosen, *Change Mummified*, 108.
37 Freeman, *Time Binds*, xvi.
38 Jameson, "The Aesthetics of Singularity."
39 Rosen, *Change Mummified*, 107.

40 Quoted by Jordheim, "Against Periodization," 161.
41 Koselleck, *Zeitschichten*, 331.
42 Jameson, "The Aesthetics of Singularity."
43 Casetti, *The Lumière Galaxy*. David Rodowick similarly sees the term "film" as connected to the technology of (nitrate, celluloid, etc.) film, and therefore prefers "cinema" as the term more suited to thinking about contemporary forms of moving images; see Rodowick, *The Virtual Life of Film*. I will follow a nuance more common in European languages, where "cinema" or its equivalents often imply space, whereas space is associated with practices. Barthes, for example, in his essay "Leaving the Movie Theater," states, "Whenever I hear the word *cinema*, I can't help thinking *hall*, rather than *film*." See Barthes, "Leaving the Movie Theater," 346.
44 Yoshimoto, *Kurosawa*.
45 Furuhata, *Cinema of Actuality*.

ONE. ESTABLISHING PINK FILM

1 The film now exists only as a fragment of about twenty minutes in the archives at the National Film Center in Tokyo. In my research I have not found any account of someone who has actually seen the entire film. Suzuki Yoshiaki has recounted the novelization of the real story that was printed in *Bessatsu Naigai Jitsuwa*, and on which the film is based. In it, Tamaki investigates a gang of four men and finally realizes the culprit was a boy named Kenji. The story ends with her apology to her dead sister for not being able to take revenge, and reveals Tamaki as preparing to perform an abortion of Kenji's child. There is no way of knowing how much license the film took with the story. See Suzuki, *Pinku Eiga Suikoden*, 38. The title of the book references one of the most famous works of classical literature from China, *Outlaws of the Marsh* (also often called *Water Margin*). It is the story of a bandit who resisted corrupt authority with his band of 108 outlaws in the Shandong Province of the twelfth century, and functions as an allusion to the oppositional image Pink Film would soon acquire. Also see the interview with the lead actress of the film, Tamaki Katori, "Nihon Sekusupuroitēshon Eiga Kōbō-shi 1."
2 There were several cases in which prints of films without an Eirin mark had been seized. In 1952 the films *Farewell to Youth* (*Wakōdo e no hanamuke*, prod. Makino Masami), a sex education film, and *Mark of Love* (*Ai no dōhyō*, prod. Ōsaka Eigajin Shūdan) screened in theaters and strip-show venues, were seized on grounds of exhibition of obscenity. Screening films without an Eirin mark was never actually illegal, though the national exhibitors association, Zenkōren, officially forbade its members to do so from 1962 on. For two examples from 1952, see Haruhiko, *Nihon Eiga Posutā-shū*.
3 Regarding the form of the term "Pink Film": it refers to the genre, while "Pink film" refers to a film situated within that genre. In general, genres are capitalized, and subgenres lowercased. Exceptions are the cases in which a (potential) subgenre is also a trademark label, such as Roman Porno.

4 For details on some of the coverage, see Domenig, "The Market of Flesh and the Rise of the Pink Film."
5 From *Eiga Nenkan 1963*, 35–36. These figures are for a period of one year, from August to August, so they are not strictly calendar years. The precise number of audience attendance was 1,127,450,000.
6 In 1962, ticket sales totaled 662 million (*Eiga Nenkan 1964*, 35–36).
7 The films released in 1962 were *Market of Flesh* (*Nikutai no ichiba*, prod. Ōkura Eiga, dir. Kobayashi Satoru), *Free Flesh Trade* (*Nikutai jiyū bōeki*, prod. Kokushin Eiga, dir. Motogi Sōjirō), and *Incomplete Wedding* (*Fukanzen kekkon*, prod. Junketsu Eiga, dir. Kobayashi Satoru and others). Exact release numbers for Pink films at this phase are difficult to determine accurately. There are differing definitions of Pink films, and due to a very chaotic and do-it-yourself style of distribution, rereleases under various titles were common. Most accounts give roughly the same figures, however, and the proportions to major film releases mostly stay the same. These figures are taken from Gotō, "Pinku Eiga Fūzoku-shi."
8 When not stated otherwise, I always give the rates in U.S. dollars according to the exchange rate at that time.
9 Bataille, *Eroticism*, 18.
10 Freeman, *Time Binds*, 3.
11 Langford, *Fiction and the Social Contract*, 135–36. MacKinnon's comment was seen as too simplistic even at the time.
12 Berry, "The Postdigital Constellation," 45.
13 Since the early 1990s, occasionally Pink films have also been shown in minitheaters, where they are presented as art films.
14 Another, much smaller group of directors who came to prominence in the 1980s and 1990s also came from an adult film background, having received training working for Nikkatsu Roman Porno. This includes directors such as Somai Shinji (*Taifun Club / Taifū kurabu*, 1984), Kaneko Shūsuke (the *Gamera* Series), Sai Yoichi (*Blood and Bones / Chi to hone*, 2004), or Morita Yoshimitsu (*The Family Game / Famiri Gēmu*, 1983). Television, documentary film, and the advertising industry were also possibilities, and although not many directors were able to take this more indirect route, they count among some of the most prominent. Ōbayashi Nobuhiko initially worked in 8 mm film and advertising; Kuroki Kazuō worked in the documentary company Iwanami Productions (like Pink Film director Yamamoto Shinya); and Jissōji Akio of *Ultraman* fame emerged from TV station TBS to become one of the most prominent ATG directors of the 1970s.
15 This calculation is based on the fixed exchange rate of 360 yen for one dollar, as set by the U.S. government in coordination with the Bretton Woods system and in place from 1949 to 1971. In 2006 dollars, the 1965 budget would have stood at $51,600; in 2006 it was around $26,300.
16 Gitelman and Pingree, *New Media, 1740–1915*, xii.
17 "Pinku Eiga: Shishashitsu no 20 Nen" [Pink film: 20 years in the screening room], *Nihon* 12 (1960): 146–48.

18 Though hard to estimate accurately, several articles around 1960 claim that blue film was experiencing a boom. Previous to the formation of Pink Film, *Shūkan Shinchō* reports an extensive blue film racket exposed at a tuberculosis clinic in Hirakata, close to Osaka, that was supplying the convalescing patients with indecent films. The article mentions 150 confiscated films and three projectors. See "Kussuri Yori Kiita Kamo Shirenai" [It may have had more effect than the medicine], *Shūkan Shinchō*, October 23, 1961, 90–91. For detailed information on the blue film boom, screening rooms, and prices, see "Misshitsu no Naka no Hitto Eiga" [Hit films behind closed doors], *Shūkan Bunshun*, December 18, 1961, 98–99. None of these articles actually uses the term "burū firumu." Many thanks to Roland Domenig for his information on the various genealogies of burū firumu.
19 Quoted in Silverberg, *Erotic Grotesque Nonsense*, 29.
20 Roland Domenig has found examples of the term "pinku" referring to Okura's films in 1962, and described the genealogy of the term's usage. See Domenig, "Market of Flesh and the Rise of the Pink Film."
21 See Murai's own version, in which he only mentions that the name was conceived to contrast with burū firumu, in Murai, *Boku no Pinku Eiga-shi*, 17–20.
22 Aoki, "Ryoshiki Yajiuma Zoku to 'Yūgai Eiga.' "
23 "Why Is the Lyrical Poem of Resistance Called 'Pink Film' Stagnating?," *Seijin Eiga* 41 (June 1969): 4.
24 Since the early 2000s the scarce English-language scholarship on Pink Film as well has tended to frame it as radical political resistance, usually via a fairly narrow focus on the films by Wakamatsu Productions and their retrospective move to the art house.
25 Igarashi, *Bodies of Memory*, 13.
26 Foucault, *The History of Sexuality*, vol. 1, 6.
27 See, for example, Hunt, "Introduction."
28 See Izbicki, "The Shape of Freedom."
29 The word "body" can be expressed as *nikutai* or *shintai* in Japanese, the latter being more common during World War II. Nikutai carries implications of sensuality that were not deemed appropriate to the wartime atmosphere or ideology.
30 See especially Maruyama's essay on the relationship of these body politics to both aesthetics and concrete politics: Maruyama, "Nikutai Bungaku kara Nikutai Seiji Made." See also Igarashi Yoshikuni's excellent discussion of Maruyama's attitudes toward the trope of the body, in Igarashi, *Bodies of Memory*.
31 The literature of the flesh was constructed around a fairly well defined group of authors in the immediate postwar period, all of whom focused strongly on tropes and themes centered on the body and unmediated physicality—often explicitly sexual. The term is supposed to have been derived from Tamura Tajirōs's 1946 short story, "Devil of the Flesh" (Nikutai no akuma). For a detailed discussion of literature of the flesh, see Slaymaker, *The Body in Postwar Japanese Fiction*.
32 See Igarashi, *Bodies of Memory*, 56.
33 *Gate of Flesh* has been filmed several times, the first being in 1948 in a version directed by Makino Masahiro and produced by the Tōhō-connected "independent"

production company Yoshimoto Eiga. Nikkatsu produced a film version in 1977 (dir. Nishimura Shōgō) and Tōei in 1988 (dir. Gosha Hideo). Before the first film, however, there was a stage version that garnered much publicity for its explicitness. This high degree of mobility across media itself merits more attention than is possible here.

34 Igarashi, *Bodies of Memory*, 61–62.

35 Maruyama, it must be emphasized, did not accept the end of the war as a date of historical rupture. He saw premodern elements still in existence and hampering the development of political institutions in postwar Japan. He did, however, subscribe to the need for such a rupture.

36 Critic Abe Casio uses an interesting variation of the theme, discussed in chapter 4, when he connects a specific engagement with narrative with the *nikutai-ka* (becoming-flesh) of the story.

37 These magazines were named after a very cheap self-distilled type of sake called kasutori, after two glasses of which one supposedly collapsed, much like these magazines after two issues.

38 See Miyoshi, *Off Center*.

39 From a discussion between anonymous activists from Nihon University and Tokyo University, "'Gebaruto' Pinku Eiga," in Shimaji, *Pinku Eiga Hakusho*, 117. Zenkyōtō was the umbrella organization for self-administrating student protest groups from various universities, in which the students were participating. In *Nikutai no Jidai*, Ueno Kōshi writes of the violence of the student movement as a sign of its nikutai (flesh) betraying their *ishiki* (consciousness—although Ueno also uses it in the sense of "official knowledge"), and sees their emerging nikutai as connected to the nikutai of capitalist society in general. See Ueno's aforementioned *Nikutai no Jidai* (The age of flesh).

40 See Hirano, *Mr. Smith Goes to Tokyo*, 155. Hirano gives a detailed and excellent account of the discussions around the kissing films. There are reports of kissing scenes shot before the war that never reached the screens because of the censorship.

41 Ueno Kōshi has written about how the national project of economic progress, exemplified by prime minister Ikeda Hayato with his "plan to double the national income," led to an absorption of an achievement mentality, or a *gijitsu shugi* (technology/technique doctrine), into the erotic sphere. As an example, Ueno uses the new how-to educational books on sex that began appearing after the phenomenal success of *Sei-seikatsu no Chie* (Knowledge/wisdom of sex life) in 1960. *Sei-seikatsu no Chie* introduced positions and techniques using chairs and beds, a sign of a new ideal lifestyle oriented toward the modern/Western household, epitomized in the new Western-style danchi that became the focus of aspirations for upward mobility (and were not outfitted with the "backward" Japanese style of sitting and sleeping on the tatami-matted floor). This almost Foucauldian position connects capitalism to a burgeoning technology of pleasure. See Ueno's aforementioned *Nikutai no Jidai*.

42 Kobayashi, "Erotishizumu to Ero Rearu Eiga." The epigraph to this section is from "Pinku Eiga Tsūshin," 18.
43 For details on the pure film movement and its attempts to improve film in Japan by applying methods used in foreign film production, see Bernardi, *Writing in Light*.
44 See Ueno, *Nikutai no Jidai*, 106–17.
45 See Shindō, "Ningen Fuzai o Hansei Shiyō,"
46 As recounted in Barrett, "An Interpretive Biography," 266.
47 For an excellent description of these debates, see Yamamoto, *Realities That Matter*; and Hayashi, "Traveling Film History."
48 See the interview with Watanabe Mamoru in the documentary *Pink Ribbon*, dir. Kenjirō Fujii, 118 min. (Uplink, 2004), DVD. Interview with Wakamatsu Kōji conducted by Gō Hirasawa, "I Didn't Care about Movements," MINIKOMI *Informationen des Akademischen Arbeitskreises Japan* 70 (December 2005): 60–68.
49 For a careful look at the historical circumstances of the trial regarding the scandal around the screening of Wakamatsu's film and the trial around *Black Snow*, see Cathers, *The Art of Censorship in Postwar Japan*.
50 Just as sinking (actual) budgets were a constant source of complaint inside the industry, the sinking level of quality was a constant source of concern. From about 1967 on, distributors, producers, and critics regularly complained that "nudity is not enough." See, for example, the interview with Kokuei executive Yamoto Teruo in *Seijin Eiga* 23 (November 1967): 12; or the interview with Nihon Shinema executive Washio Hidemaru in *Seijin Eiga* 24 (December 1967): 12.
51 The postwar independents had made attempts to create their own distribution chain in 1953. Shinsei Eiga, Kindai Eikyō, and eleven other dokuritsu puro negotiated with the exhibitor side, but as the majors would not allow their contract stars to play in independent films and were consolidating their influence on the exhibition side, nothing came of the project in the end.
52 Kokuei was one of the few companies in the position to go solo, as it possessed a national distribution network with offices in Hokkaido, Kyushu, and various other regions. In Pink Film as in the majors, distribution and exhibition were the key to survival. Importantly, the Shintōhō mentioned here is an entirely different company from the Shintōhō that Ōkura Mitsugi had headed in the 1950s. During Shintōhō's dissolution in 1961, some staff from its Kansai region distribution arm bought the rights to several Shintōhō films and the right to use its name, and proceeded to distribute old Shintōhō films (that were still quite popular due to the majors-induced film dearth) as Shintōhō Kōgyō from 1964. Later they became one of the major forces in Pink Film distribution, especially in Kansai, in western Japan, the second largest film market after Tokyo. The company relocated its headquarters to Tokyo by fusing with another splinter of the original Shintōhō, Tōkyō Kōei, in 1972, renaming itself Shintōhō Eiga. My thanks to Jasper Sharp for helping to clear up the puzzle of Shintōhō's history.
53 The epigraph for this section is as quoted in Bornhoff, *Pink Samurai*, 589.
54 The character for Murakami's first name can also be read Satoshi or Tadashi.

55 See the discussion between Takechi and critic Izawa Jun, "Ningen Kaihō no Senpei Toshite," in Shimaji, *Pinku Eiga Hakusho*, 70–84.
56 Again, see the discussion between Takechi and critic Izawa Jun, "Ningen Kaihō no Senpei Toshite."
57 Kuwahara, *Kirareta Waisetsu*, 111–12.
58 The Director's Guild finally issued an official statement of protest against the prosecution's demands toward the end of the trial almost two years later, in mid-1967, at their eighteenth assembly. For the complete wording, see *Seijin Eiga* 18 (June 1967): 13.
59 Ishido wrote scripts for Ōshima Nagisa and Immamura Shōhei, and later co-wrote the script for the blockbuster animal film *Antarctica* (*Nankyoku Monogatari*, Kurahara Koreyoshi, 1983), one of the most successful films of all time in Japan. See Ishiro, "Memeshiki Eizō Ronsha-tachi," originally printed in *Eiga Geijutsu*, November 1966.
60 This year brought a new partitioning of the program into three sections, and a new two-tiered selection system that was supposed to ensure more independence from city administration; it included, for the first time, a critics' jury along with a selection committee. Some statements by members of the critics' jury indicate that a certain amount of controversy was intended with the selection. See Roland Domenig's article in the DVD booklet for *Affairs within Walls*: "Shikakerareta Skyandaru: Kabe no Naka no Himegoto to Dai 15-kai Berurin Kokusai Eigasai" [An installed scandal: *Affairs within Walls* and the 15th Berlin International Film Festival], included in *Wakamatsu Kōji Shoki Kessaku Sen IIII* (Kōji Wakamatsu selection from the early works, vol. 4), dir. Kōji Wakamatsu, 204 min. (Kinokuniya, 2006), DVD.
61 While the German newspapers reporting on the scandal claim that a Swiss distributor proposed the film to the Berlin office, Suzuki Yoshiaki explicitly speaks of Maten and Hansa Film. Roland Domenig found that Maten had previously imported Watanabe Yūsuke's *Two Female Dogs* to Germany and was in Japan to negotiate a coproduction when he was introduced to *Affairs within Walls*. For Suzuki's version, see Suzuki, *Pinku Eiga Suikōden*, 28–33. Roland Domenig's research was presented at the Wakamatsu Kōji Symposium at Maiji Gakuin University in June 2006.
62 See "Film und Diplomatie—Eine Erklaerung des Kultursenators Prof. Stein" [Film and diplomacy—a declaration by senator of culture Prof. Stein], *Telegraf*, July 9, 1965.
63 Tokura's official statement of protest printed in "Geschichten hinter Wänden" [Secrets behind walls], *Der Kurier / Der Tag*, July 7, 1965. For the reply by the senator for art and science, Werner Stein, see "Film und Diplomatie—Eine Erklaerung des Kultursenators Prof. Stein" [Film and diplomacy—a declaration by senator of culture Prof. Stein], *Telegraf*, July 9, 1965.
64 See, for example, "Nachmittag eines Voyeurs" [Afternoon of a voyeur], *Rheinischer Merkur*, January 6, 1967; or "Japanische Wahrheit" [Japanese Truth], *Muenchner Abendzeitung*, July 7, 1965.
65 My translation from German. From the official statement by Tokura Eiji in "Geschichten hinter Wänden," *Der Kurier / Der Tag*.

66 The epigraph for this section is from "'Go-sha no Pinku Kōgeki' Kusokurae!"
67 *Eiga Nenkan 1964*, 39.
68 Dokuritsu puro (independent production) is now rarely used in public or industry discourse to define a film (though industry publications like the *Eiga Nenkan* still use it). *Indīzu* (indies) and *independento eiga* (independent film) are more popularly used, though in different ways. Indīzu is often used as a self-definition in the *jishu eiga* (independent/autonomous film) world, where extremely low-budget films are often self-financed and self-distributed.
69 Shōchiku and Koa became one unit (Shōchiku); Tōhō, Takarazuka, Otaguro, Nan-o, and Tōkyō Hassei became another (Tōhō); while Nikkatsu, Shinkō, and Daitō formed Daiei (originally Dai Nihon Eiga). See High, *The Imperial Screen*, for an excellent account of prewar and wartime film-industry interactions with the government bureaucracy.
70 One of the few who publicly demanded self-reflection of filmmakers' conduct during the war was Itami Mansaku, father of later actor and hit director Itami Jūzō and codirector of *Die Tochter des Samurai* (*Atarashiki tsuchi*, 1936) with Arnold Fanck. Strictly speaking, Itami and Fanck were not codirectors, as each ended up directing separate versions after disagreements on the style of shooting. It is Fanck's version that is in circulation.
71 See Hirano, *Mr. Smith Goes to Tokyo*, 205–40, for an excellent and detailed account of the situation at Tōhō and the unfolding of the successive strikes.
72 Hirano, *Mr. Smith Goes to Tokyo*, 229 and 312. There is evidence that the communist-oriented unions selected Tōhō as a high-profile testing ground for a strike strategy. The occupation army certainly suspected as much and gave an equally high-profile response. As a testament to the enthusiasm around unionization, the Tōhō union even shot a film promoting unionization, *Those Who Create Tomorrow* (*Asu o tsukuru hitobito*), codirected by Sekigawa Hideo, Yamamoto Kajirō, and Kurosawa Akira, who later had his name stricken from the credits.
73 See Yamada, *Nihon Eiga no 80 Nen*, 156. Another very interesting portrayal can be found in Shindō, *Tsuinōsha-tachi*.
74 Tanaka, *Nihon Eiga Hattatsu-shi III*, 345.
75 Examples are Zenkinren (Zenkoku Ginkō Jūgyōin Kumiai Rengyō, the union of bank employees) and Kindai Eikyō's production of *Young People* (*Wakai hitotachi*, 1954, dir. Yoshimura Kōzaburō, distr. Shintōhō); also Zentei (the Japan Postal Workers' Union, Nippon Yūsei Kōsha Rōdō Kumiai) and *Red Bicycle* (*Akai jitensha*, 1953, dir. Fujiwara Sugio, distr. Zentei, prod. Dai-Ichi Eiga), and Nikkyōso (the All Japan Teachers and Staff Union, or Zen-Nihon Kyōshokuin Kumiai) and *A Wall of People* (*Ningen no kabe*, 1959, dir. Yamamoto Satsuo, prod. Yamamoto Pro, distr. Shintōhō). The companies were often centered around directors, such as Yamamoto Satsuo's Yamamoto Pro or Shindō Kaneto and Yoshimura Kōzaburō's Kindai Eiga Kyōkai (Kindai Eikyō). Companies such as Hokusei Eiga-sha—later Dokuritsu Eiga (KK)—hitherto involved in distributing Soviet films, became active in the new independent production scene (the Chinese characters for Hokusei

Eiga-sha are 北星映画社). After Hokusei Eiga's demise in 1954, the Dokuritsu Eiga company continued its activities. Both were led by independent producer and ex-Tōhō man Itō Takeo. To ensure the company had decent production infrastructure, Itō founded the company Chūō Eiga to run a studio lot for independent productions in the Tokyo suburb of Chōfu. Another independent company active after the Tōhō strike was Studio Eight Productions, founded by Gosho Heinosuke with fellow Tōhō refugees like Toyoda Shirō, cameraman Miura Mitsuo, and several writers. There was also Eiga Geijutsu Kyōkai (1948), founded by producer and later Pink Film director Motogi Sōjirō and directors Yamamoto Kajirō, Kurosawa Akira, and Taniguchi Senkichi. The Kindai Eiga Kyōkai was founded in 1950 by Shindō Kaneto and Yoshimura Kōzaburō and joined by communists from Shōchiku and Tōhō. Shinsei Eiga-Sha (founded in 1950 by ex-Tōhō unionists) shot the legendary independent film *City of Violence* (*Bōryoku no Machi*, dir. Yamamoto Satsuo, 1950). See Satō, "Dokuritsu Puro no Eiga."

76 Gekidan Seihai's kanji characters read 劇団青俳 and derive from the full name of Seinen Haiyū Kurabu, which launched the careers of Kanie Keizō and Ishibashi Renji, among others, both of which were later active in Nikkatsu Roman Porno. The story of the connection between theater and film in Japan still remains to be told satisfactorily. While relevant in a number of ways, in the case of *A Billionaire* it shows how independent film has consistently recruited and teamed up with shingeki troupes. Pink Film was heavily involved with theater troupes as well, to the point that troupes like Cemento Macchi were regarded as breeding grounds for Pink Film actors.

77 Again, see the discussion between Takechi and critic Izawa Jun, "Ningen Kaihō no Senpei Toshite."

78 See, for example, Satō, "Dokuritsu Puro no Eiga."

79 Ōshima's films *Violence at Noon* (*Hakuchū no torima*, 1966), *A Treatise on Japanese Bawdy Songs* (*Nihon shunka-kō*, 1967), *Japanese Summer: Double Suicide* (*Murishinjū Nihon no natsu*, 1967), and *Three Resurrected Drunkards* (*Kaette kita yopparai*, 1968), and even his last film for now, *Gohatto* (1999), were all distributed by Shōchiku. *Manual of Ninja Martial Arts* (*Ninja bugei-chō*, 1967), *Death by Hanging* (*Koshikei*, 1968), *Diary of a Shinjuku Thief* (*Shinjuku dorobo nikki*, 1968), *Boy* (*Shonen*, 1969), *The Ceremony* (*Gishiki*, 1971), and *Dear Summer Sister* (*Natsu no imōto*, 1972) were all distributed by Tōhō-funded ATG.

80 Although originally founded in 1961 for the purpose of distributing foreign art film, ATG moved into actual production activity in 1968 with Ōshima's *Death by Hanging*. It started with a small chain of ten theaters, which quickly declined to three, making ATG more dependent on free distribution. See interview with Kuzui Kinshirō, "I Think It Was My Life," MINIKOMI *Informationen des Akademischen Arbeitskreises Japan 70* (December 2005): 49–59.

81 Gerow, "From Independence to Detachment in Recent Japanese Film."

82 Tōei's step was an answer to the growing trend, especially in the chihō (rural) regions, of double and triple bills. This was not at all to the liking of most of the majors and even the government, as the Ministry of Social Welfare issued a state-

ment demanding a retreat from the triple-bill system; see *Eiga Nenkan 1956*, 245. It fit well with Tōei's strategy of mass production, however, and Tōei was the company that would profit the most from this development.

83 *Eiga Nenkan 1958*, 46.
84 See Satō, "Dokuritsu Puro no Eiga."
85 The Japanese title was *Waga Dokuritsu Eiga-shi*.
86 For an analysis of this aspect with regard to Wakamatsu Productions, see Furuhata, *Cinema of Actuality*.
87 Kawashima, "Desuku Nikki," 29. Another reason is that Wakamatsu, a shrewd businessman, retained copyright for all of his films. While other filmmakers' films disappeared in company vaults, Wakamatsu was able to control distribution and eventually releases on VHS and DVD himself.
88 The Chinese characters used for Shishi (獅子) literally mean lion but are also a play on the homophonic word for four, expressing founder Mukai Kan's ambition to bring forth four × four = sixteen directors. The company accordingly has rules that ensure the trainees' education. After a Shishi Productions director's debut, he is allowed to employ assistant directors only from Shishi Productions and must pay a certain percentage of his income to the company for a fixed period of time. Another director who ran a very successful production outfit was Kimata Akitaka, whose wife, Tama Rumi, and son, Izumi Seiji, also were prominent Pink Film directors. His company, Taka Productions, also was heavily involved with television production, and Kimata received awards from the TV industry and the script writers' guild. He was also active in cultural exchange programs with the Soviet Union and Eastern Europe in the late 1970s.
89 Adachi wrote a variety of scripts for Wakamatsu and directed a number of highly cerebral and Brechtian Pink films. Predictably, they were not very popular among distributors. With his strong antiestablishment stance, Adachi seems a very unlikely candidate for the glamorous pop-star treatment he is given with these pictures.
90 Shingeki is a form of theater that emerged around the turn of the twentieth century as a reaction to the highly stylized theatrical forms of kabuki and *shinpa*. It consciously emulated Western acting styles and aspired to realism, just as it was eventually associated with leftist politics. By the 1960s, however, shingeki had the image of fairly authoritarian troupes with dogmatic structures. A new wave of theater troupes founded by young playwright-actors, called "small theater," attempted to break away from the politics of the old left and explore more stylized forms of expression.
91 From "Daigakusai de Hippari-dako no Poruno," *Seijin Eiga* 82 (November 1972): 27; and my interview with Gotō Kōichi of Shintōhō, November 2004.
92 Besides gebaruto, another variation of Gewalt would become a central term for the student movement. *Uchigeba* (inside gebaruto) referred to the violence between several competing factions within the student movement. See "'Gebaruto' Pinku Eiga," in Shimaji, *Pinku Eiga Hakusho*, 111–17.
93 "Pinku Eiga-kai ni mo Oshiyoseta Gebaruto Kakumei no Namikaze!"

94 His name can also be read as Kitazato. Like Kokuei, which was to become one of the dominant production and distribution companies in Pink Film, Naigai Films had been involved in shooting so-called *shō eiga* (show films). These were usually documentaries about strip shows, often unofficially included in programs in less visible rural areas or shown in private screenings. An ad for *Lara of the Wild* can be seen in *Eiga Nenkan 1963*, 32.

95 These difficulties were of course not distributed evenly; Tōei had even founded a "sister studio," Dai-ni Tōei (Second Tōei), in 1960 to accommodate its relatively successful system of highly generic mass production. This attempt failed, and Dai-ni Tōei (by now renamed New Tōei) closed down in late 1961. While most studios reduced their output from 1959 on, Dai-ni Tōei's activity briefly led to an overall rise in features produced in 1960.

96 This is actually true only with regard to direct investment in production. Banks had been involved with the film business from the moment it became profitable. Ōkura Mitsugi had been pushed out of Nikkatsu in the late 1930s because his opponent, Hori Kyūsaku, the later chairman, had secretly bought up company stock with the help of the Bank of Chiba (Chiba Ginkō). Tōhō had only been able to follow its hyakkan-shugi (one hundred theater doctrine) of assembling a strong exhibition arm because its position as part of the Hankyū group empire gave banks a degree of confidence in lending money. But banks stayed extremely wary of directly participating in the funding of films until the late 1990s.

97 The studios had, however, diversified their businesses to other regions of the leisure industry during the income boom of the mid-1950s, and have continued to do so to the present, with mixed results. While their dabbling in the bowling and real estate business at times brought them considerable income, and even sustained the companies, Nikkatsu famously filed for bankruptcy in 1992 not because of its ailing film department, but because of failed investments in golf courses.

98 The introduction of private TV broadcasting was possible after heavy lobbying by Shōriki Matsutarō, an important figure for the history of media in Japan. After making the *Yomiuri Shimbun* newspaper one of the most successful print publications in Japan, Shōriki was the first to dedicate pages in newspapers to radio programs. He later orchestrated the establishment of a professional baseball league and then was instrumental in introducing private TV broadcasting (a useful synergy with the baseball business). Of course, TV sets need electricity, and Shōriki became the central figure for the introduction of nuclear power in Japan, in terms of both the public image—as organizer of the "Atoms for Peace" exhibitions—and policy.

99 *Eiga Nenkan 1962*, 328. The move was possible because Shintōhō had exited Eiren and Eidanren, the Federation of Japanese Film Industry, the previous year, when the initial agreement had been struck. Eiren actually purchased the television rights to a number of Shintōhō films to prevent them from being broadcast. Shintōhō was reorganized into three companies in 1961: the Shintōhō core; a distribution arm, Daitō; and a production arm, NAC (Nippon Artfilm Company). This

did not go well, and in 1962 Daitō was dissolved, while NAC changed its name to Kokusai Hōei. It used the lot as a rental studio for television work and is still active today.

100 In fact, the official antagonism of the movie industry toward television belies the actual involvement of the film and TV industries. While Eiren implemented its boycott of TV stations in 1956, in 1957 Tōei provided much of the founding capital for a new channel, Nihon Educational Television (NET). Shōchiku, Daiei, Nikkatsu, and Tōhō all invested in the founding of Fuji Television in the same year. By 1962, all of the major studios maintained TV production departments within their organization. The television stations, however, were not intent on becoming dependent, and in 1962 TBS, NTV, and NET all founded their own film-production divisions. For a good history of the relationship of the film and television industries in Japan, see Kubo, "From Film to Video." While the Pink films of the early 1960s could often be budgeted as low as under 2 million yen, the archetypal budget of 3 million yen (until 1971 equivalent to $8,333), named then as now as standard for a Pink Film production, is supposedly another legacy from educational film. It apparently was suggested by producer Ōi Yūji from the TV section of Iwanami Eiga (the educational film company that Hani, Kuroki, Tsuchimoto, and Ogawa sprang from, just as star Pink Film director Yamamoto Shinya did) to Motogi Sōjirō: thirty-minute features for television were shot in four days, so 3 million yen and ten days should be fine for a feature film with just over one hour running time. Before eventually shifting to directing Pink films, Motogi had produced, among others, probably the most well-known films from Japan of all time: Kurosawa Akira's *The Seven Samurai* (*Shichinin no samurai*, 1954), *Yojimbo* (*Yōjinbō*, 1961), and *Rashomon* (*Rashōmon*, 1950). From his first Pink Film, *Free Flesh Trade* (*Nikutai jiyū bōeki*, 1962, prod. Kokushin Eiga) on, he stayed with the low-budget formula and is listed in the Japanese Movie Database as having directed 105 Pink films before his death fifteen years later. Motogi directed Pink films under various names, among them Takagi Takeo, Kishimoto Keiichi, and Fujimoto Junji. He also had his own production company, Shineyunimondo.

101 From *Eiga Nenkan 1965*, 78.

102 Murai, "5-sha o Obiyakasu 300 Man Yen Eiga"; and Takahashi, "Go-sha no Shijō o Doko Made Kutte Iru Ka."

103 Tōei introduced this system in 1954. The studio had been mass producing certain types of subgenres (focusing on *jidaigeki*, or period films) and had been able to win a broad base of independent and contract exhibitors, especially in the chihō, where the double-bill system had been establishing itself virtually on its own. This system had popped up around 1950, and the majors were initially unwilling to enter such a high-pressure production arrangement; eventually they had to follow suit to curb Tōei's overwhelming success.

104 There existed, of course, a continual power struggle between exhibition and production/distribution. Traditionally, the exhibition side had been in the dominant position, but the golden age gave distributors a better negotiating position.

According to Eiren, in 1958, production and distribution was taking an average of 54.4 percent of box-office income. By 1967, the exhibition side was taking an average of 59 percent. These figures need to be handled with care, as Eiren is hardly impartial in this matter; however, at least the tendency seems plausible. Also, the significantly lower shares that Pink distribution took of the box-office gross factor heavily into shifting the average figure. The Eiren figures are quoted in Takahashi, "Go-sha no Shijō o Doko Made Kutte Iru Ka."

105 If one analyzes the changes in average production costs, however, only Tōhō actually followed through with the strategy. All other companies merely cut down production, indicating that the blockbuster strategy at this point in time was more a justification strategy than anything else.

106 In 1960–61, Nikkatsu fixed the screening period for the main film of the double bill at ten days, switching the additional, less prestigious film more often. Tōhō even fixed periods of three weeks for their largest productions, often resulting in sudden drops in attendance after the first week.

107 According to Gotō Kōichi of Shintōhō (the Pink incarnation of Shintōhō, not the original major studio), there were two types of distributors of Pink films in the early phase: those from small production outfits like Aoi Eiga or Kantō Eihai that had little experience in distribution, and would hand out the films to local distributors at prices that were much too low, and more experienced distributors whose staff had previously worked for the distribution sections of major companies, such as those at Ōkura Eiga or Shintōhō. While small distributors for Japanese film became common in the 1980s and 1990s, this was a totally new phenomenon in the context of the early 1960s. From my interview with Gotō Kōichi, November 2004. For Ōkura's comments on booking fees, see Takahashi, "Haikyū Men wa dō Natte Iru ka," 177.

108 The Japanese system usually refers to *haikyū shūnyū*, or distribution income, which already has subtracted the exhibition share from the total box office. As described above, while for a Japanese major film, the exhibition share would be about 50 percent of box-office gross, for Pink films it was often 20 percent or less. It is unclear if Ogawa is referring to box-office or distribution income; were it distribution income, the box office would have been approximately 250 million yen ($694,445). Suzuki, *Pinku Eiga Suikoden*, 83.

109 The magazine *Seijin Eiga* estimates that Nikkatsu "and others" bought around sixty Pink films (Nikkatsu is later specified as having bought forty-four) between 1964 and 1970 for inclusion in programs for second- and third-run theaters. It also mentions that another rumor speaks of up to two hundred films for Nikkatsu alone, probably a very inflated number. See *Seijin Eiga* 54 (December 1969): 31. A different source mentions that Nikkatsu entered Pink Film distribution in May 1968 with *Hateful Good Spot* (*Jōen no anaba*, Matsubara Jirō). See Takahashi, "Haikyū Men wa dō Natte Iru ka," 171.

110 The company employed ex-Shintōhō (the major company, not the Pink Film incarnation) man Miwa Akira to direct. This is another example of how previous Shintōhō staff dominated the early Pink Film industry. See Gotō, "Pinku Eiga Fūzoku-shi," 137.

TWO. PINK TIMES AND PINK SPACES

1 Yamane, "Taishū no Yokubō to Eiga no Hihan," 554.
2 While female-oriented magazines and male-oriented magazines had of course existed for quite a while, this was a new attempt at aiming for a much more specific demographic in terms of age and class, similar to the attempts of Condé Nast some years earlier in the United States.
3 Tanaka, *Nihon Eiga Hattatsu-shi IV*, 283.
4 The series that started the ninkyō film boom was the *Jinsei Gekijo* (*Theater of Life*) series, with the first film being *Jinsei Gekijo—Hishakaku* (*Theater of Life—Hishakaku*, Sawajima Tadashi, 1963), starring Tsuruta. The film was based on the series of stories by author Ozaki Shirō, which first began serialization in the *Miyako Shinbun* newspaper in 1933. Multiple film versions of the *Theater of Life* series already existed, beginning with the 1936 film shot by Uchida Tomu.
5 Satō, *Currents in Japanese Cinema*, 234, 236.
6 Ōkura, "Ōkura, Mitsugi."
7 These figures must obviously be cited with caution. Shinjuku was a primary hangout for students during that time; as a center of underground culture it was a decidedly atypical space. At the same time, the Kabuki-chō section of Shinjuku is one of the entertainment centers in Tokyo, catering to a broad variety of activities and venues, including film theaters, bars, bathing parlors, and bowling alleys. Yamada, "Kōgyō Men wa dō Natte Iru no ka."
8 Forty-two of the 232 surveyed alone were twenty years of age exactly; seventy-one of the 232 were students, and eighty-six were office workers. The dominant role of public posters would cause problems for the Pink Film industry from 1984 on, when the public display of posters was discontinued under pressure from the police and the revision of the law regarding businesses affecting public morals. This survey, while being very detailed, has some obvious methodological problems, the main one being that participation was voluntary and therefore highly selective. Furthermore, this survey was taken only in one central urban specialty theater, while the majority of Pink films at this time played in rural theaters as a supplement to a more mainstream program. For the complete survey, see *Seijin Eiga* 36 (January 1969): 18.
9 Author Suzuki Yoshiaki and producer Satō Keiko (of Kokuei) on the one hand, Gotō Kōichi of Shintōhō on the other. From my interviews with Satō Keiko (Tokyo, February 2005) and Gotō Kōichi (Tokyo, June 2004).
10 My interview with Satō Keiko (Tokyo, February 2005).
11 See Sharon Hayashi's extensive discussions about the 1930s, when filmmakers, due to the increased mobility of camera technology, discovered the countryside. Entwined with discourses on realism (much like Pink Film) that the new farm films genre had inherited from rural literature, the constructed opposition was basically identical. The countryside or the character embodying it functioned as "a repository of morals which can purify the wayward morals of the big city." A great number of early story lines follow the opposite trajectory, chronicling the ill effects

the urban environment exacted upon the rural newcomers, usually women eventually forced to sell their bodies. By the time this discursive opposition had arrived in Pink Film, purification of the urban was not an option. See Hayashi, "Traveling Film History," 79.

12 See Yamamoto Shinya and Kurihara Kōji's *zadankai* (discussion), "Yamamoto Shinya Kantoku no O-Pinku Eiga Jūnen-shi," *Eiga Hyōron* 31, no. 9 (September 1974): 120–33.

13 *Seijin Eiga* 9 (September 1965): 40.

14 Kurahashi Yumiko, "Ero Eiga Kō," 499–507, and Yajima Midori, "'Kuroi Yuki' no Orime Tadashii Morarizumu," 507–12, in Gendai Nihon Eigaron Taikei Henshūiinkai, *Gendai Nihon Eigaron Taikei* 4 (Tokyo: Tōjusha, 1971).

15 *Pink Ribbon*, Fujii Kenjiro, 2004. Also Aida, "Asakura Daisuke Interview."

16 Female directors of Pink films are few and far between, and some directed only one or two films, often as publicity stunts. The first woman to direct a Pink Film was Ōgimachi Kyōko with *Yakuza Geisha* (Ōkura Eiga, 1965), who was, at the time, charged with belonging to the publicity stunt category. In general, most of the female directors were former actresses, with prominent director Hamano Sachiko, who began at Wakamatsu Productions but left in indignation at how she was treated as a female assistant director, being an exception to this rule. Other female directors include Hama Keiko, Satsuki Mari, Fuji Hiroko, Arisugawa Keiko, and Aoi Marii, all of them actresses who directed only one to three films each. Tama Rumi is, together with Yoshiyuki Yumi, one of the few actresses who became a prolific director. She acted in her first Pink film in 1965 and directed over eighty films since 1980. A new development is the increase in female scriptwriters in the industry. The presence of women inside the Pink Film industry is elaborated in greater detail in Domenig, "Women in the World of Pink Eiga."

17 The epigraph for this section is from "Pinku Eiga o Yokodori Shita Nikkatsu / Daiei no Kontan," 4.

18 The designation introduced in 1955 was *seijin-muke*, or "adult oriented." It was changed to *seijin eiga*, or "adult film," in 1957.

19 The title, *Echigo tsutsuishi oyashirazu*, is also a play on erotic expectations. Echigo is the old name for the current Niigata Prefecture, and Tsutsuishi is a city in Niigata. Oyashirazu, or "the parents don't know / unknown to the parents" refers (at least directly) not to any illegitimate activity but to a very fast current on the coast, so called because anyone caught in it will disappear without the parents ever knowing what happened to the victim. Oyashirazu can also refer to any immoral activity, and it is the common name for wisdom teeth.

20 Almost all of these films were distributed in Europe as well. In Germany, *Insect Woman*, *Gate of Flesh*, *Naked Body*, *Evil Woman*, *Daydream*, and *Woman in the Dunes* as *Frau in den Dünen* all received an eighteen-and-older rating.

21 In 1968, the OP chain again assembled eleven of the main Pink production and distribution companies to form a single large distribution network for the Kantō region (Tokyo and surroundings). After only three months, Kokuei, Tōkyō Kōgyō,

and Nichiei left the agreement and continued loosely linked but independent distribution. While the OP chain released ten to eleven films a month, the three independents together supplied around three films a month.

22 Aida, "Asakura Daisuke Interview," 82. Asakura Daisuke is a male name and has been used by several producers at Kokuei, although Satō has used it exclusively since 1984.

23 See Kuwahara, *Kirareta Waisetsu*, 25.

24 See, for example, "Pinku Joyū no Butai Shinshutsu!!"

25 See the jitsuen special "Nama no Hakuryoku! Pinku Jitsuen."

26 "Nama no Hakuryoku! Pinku Jitsuen," 6.

27 My translation: "Me o osō bōkō shiin. Kannō to zankoku de shōbu suru koroshiya no kagyō," quoted in "Ninja Shōhō: 300 Man-en Eiga no O-Iroke Sakusen" [Ninja methods: The sex strategy of the 3-million-yen films], *Heibon Punch*, August 31, 1964, 40–43.

28 Tōei had been immensely successful with *Lineage of the Tokugawa Women* (*Tokugawa Onna Keizu*, 1968). Directed by ex-Shintōhō director Ishii Teruo and starring a number of Pink Film actresses, earlier in the year it had started the trend of dipping into Pink Film's workforce. See "Nugi Nugi Būmu de Kasegimakuru Tōei/Nikkatsu."

29 See empirical studies that compare Japanese and American TV programs and claim that in Japanese TV it is usually the hero or positive protagonist who suffers the most violence. For example, Iwao et al., "Japanese and U.S. Media."

30 Ikejima began as an actor in the avant-garde theater troupe of Terayama Shūji, in the 1980s appearing regularly in Pink films. He made his directorial debut in 1991 with *The Masturbating Lesbian* (*Za onanie rezu*). He is currently one of the most popular directors working in the industry. See *Pink Ribbon*, dir. Kenjirō Fujii, 118 min. (Uplink, 2004), DVD.

31 Igarashi, *Bodies of Memory*, 28–35. A particularly illustrative example Igarashi puts forward is the popular actress and singer Ri Koran / Li Xianglan. Born to Japanese parents in the Japanese-controlled state of Manchukuo, she specialized in the role of the indigenous girl in the (Japanese) colonies, often saved by falling in love with a Japanese man who gives her stern but affectionate direction, an image of obvious political significance. After the war she shed the Chinese name and identity, and was known under her Japanese name, Yamaguchi Yoshiko, or even Shirley Yamaguchi for her appearances in American films like Samuel Fuller's *House of Bamboo* (1955). As Ri Koran, she played the role of the occupied who learns to be grateful to the occupier in, for example, *China Night* (*Shina no yoru*, Fushimizu Shū, 1940) and *Sayon's Bell* (*Sayon no kane*, Shimizu Hiroshi, 1943). After the war, she was one of the few members of the film community to openly repent her work in the wartime film industry. She continued to work under the name of Yamaguchi Yoshiko in Japan, then in Hollywood as Shirley Yamaguchi, and even in Hong Kong as Li Xiang Lan, the Chinese reading of Ri Koran. After her retreat from acting she became politically active, both with regard to Japanese politics and, later, with

regard to Palestinian rights. Eventually she met Yassir Arafat, who gave her the name Jamira (which she occasionally used afterward). She later became a member of parliament. For an interesting chronological comparison of Yamaguchi/Ri/Li/Jamira's life with that of Japanese star Hara Setsuko, herself a star in several wartime propaganda films, see Yomota, *Nihon no Joyū*.

Yamaguchi effectively embodies the reversal of gender positions entailed in the switch from Japan as occupier to Japan as occupied, from colonizer to colonized, from male to female. In the context of the popular and anxiety-ridden idea of hordes of oversexed GIs flooding the country, such a gendering strategy and its utilization for assuming a victimized position was highly relevant for, and contested in, Japanese society then as it is now. The impending rape of Japanese women was one of the greatest fears spread among the Japanese population upon surrender, and it belongs to some of the most persistent and widespread iconographies of the postwar period.

32 The American occupation obviously realized the relevance of such deep-seated fears in Japan, and diligently censored any reference to the fraternization of American soldiers and Japanese women. The image stayed powerful in the public consciousness, however, and even in the 1970s films regularly used it as a trope for characterization and trauma. See, for example, Fukasaku Kinji's *Battle without Honor and Humanity* (*Jingi naki tatakai*) series or Kadokawa Haruki's second film, *Proof of the Man* (*Ningen no shōmei*, 1977).

33 For two of the standard texts on Japan as a matricentric society, see Eto, *Seijuku to Sōshitsu*; and Doi, *Amae no Kōsō*.

34 Yoda, "The Rise and Fall of Maternal Society."

35 See the chapter on "weibliche Kultur" in Simmel, *Philosophische Kultur*, 254–95.

36 Morikawa, *Shuto No Tanjō*.

37 There is no official English distribution title for the film, and the title has been translated differently in different sources. The Internet Movie Database gives the English title *The Dismembered Ghost*, while Jasper Sharp calls it *Ghost Story Dismembered Phantom* in Sharp, *Historical Dictionary of Japanese Film*.

38 Woolf, *A Room of One's Own*, 43.

39 It goes without saying that the fundamentals of this discourse are highly debatable, not only but certainly in economic terms. The female labor force was continually coaxed to work part time, with significantly lower wages and a lifestyle associated with the so-called M-curve (where women enter the workforce in their twenties, leave it for marriage and child rearing, and then return when the children have left the household). In the mid-1990s, women accounted for 79 percent of temporary workers and 75 percent of day laborers in manufacturing. The temporary workforce has been growing intensely, increasing 70 percent between 1982 and 1987, while full-time jobs increased fewer than 5 percent in the same period. In a sense, women actually are on the forefront of capitalist modernity, participating heavily in the restructuring of the workforce along lines of casualization. It is another matter, however, whether they are profiting from the development. See, for example, Tabb, *The Postwar Japanese System*.

40 See, for example, Sedgwick, *The Epistemology of the Closet*. There are of course countervoices such as Anne Friedberg, who sees identification as always fundamentally a "denial of difference." See Friedberg, "A Denial of Difference."
41 Muñoz, *Disidentifications*.
42 Butler, *Bodies That Matter*.
43 The only person to die in the protests of 1960 was also female: Kanbu Michiko died on June 15, 1960, after violence due to police intervention at a demonstration.
44 Marcuse, *Eros and Civilization*, ix–x, quoted in Ellis, "Disseminating Desire," 39.
45 As anyone who has been to a Pink Film theater in recent decades can attest, a considerable amount of activity takes place in the audience area, with frequent seat switching, negotiation, and exchange of sexual favors. For one of the few written accounts, see Markus Nornes, "Introduction," in *The Pink Book*, 1–17.
46 "Hitori heikin firumu 5 hon o torimakutta ga."
47 Nazareth's song is used repeatedly in the film and points to one of the issues that contributes to the inaccessibility of so many Pink films today. Playing only in Pink specialty theaters, the films ignored copyright and used popular music freely, making it extremely difficult to sell the films later on VHS, laser disc, or DVD.
48 "Okashitakunaru yō na 'sumashita joyū.'"
49 Murai, *Dokyumento Seijin Eiga*, 94.
50 Hard-core pornography in Japan is visually censored, as blurs, mosaics, and dots are used to conceal any explicit portrayal of the genitals. Hard-core, then, often only means that it is unsimulated sex that is being filmed, though not necessarily seen.
51 Director and scriptwriter Yamazaki Kuniki, for example, opines that the films of the shitennō (Four Devils) feature the same old portrayal of sex unified by a male subjectivity that is connected to a classic *naimen shugi* (internalism). As quoted in Kiridōshi, "Poruno Eiga ga Sekai o Koroshitai Nara," 121–22.
52 "Dokuritsu Puro mo Taisaku Shugi de Iku," 12.
53 *Haha Arite Inochi Aru Hi* (1966), to be directed by Yuasa Namio; the film does not show up in any of the databases or Yuasa's filmography, but it is mentioned in *Seijin Eiga* 13 (November 1966): 19.
54 This according to calculations by Takahashi, "Haikyū Men wa dō Natte Iru ka."
55 A major legal revision of authors' rights took place in 1970, after a film industry commission headed by Daiei director Nagata Masaichi had recommended (unsurprisingly) that all rights to a film lay with the producer, not the director, scriptwriter, or any other involved party. The recommendation was followed. In Pink Film the situation was even more complicated, as, increasingly from this time on, a film was often formally produced by a front company belonging to the director, who then sold the film to the distributor that had provided the production money in the first place.
56 What remained of Daiei was bought up by Tokuma Shoten, one of the largest publishing companies, in 1974, and continued sporadic production of theatrical films and later V-Cinema. In 2002 it changed hands to Kadokawa Shoten, which fused it with its film subsidiary to form Kadokawa-Daiei. In 2004, the name was

changed to Kadokawa Eiga. This was fused with distribution arm Kadokawa Herald Pictures and renamed Kadokawa Herald Eiga in 2006, but in early 2007 was renamed Kadokawa Eiga. The Daiei name is only preserved in the name of the original studio lot in the Tokyo suburb of Chōfu, called Kadokawa Daiei Satsueijo (Studio lot).

57 See, for example, *Eiga Nenkan 1974*, 78.
58 Actually, Nikkatsu also continued shooting films targeted at children and some youth-oriented films outside of the Roman Porno line. This partitioning of strongly defined audience groups was a further sign of the fragmenting of the audience that had begun in earnest with Pink Film.
59 Interview with Gotō Kōichi of Shin Tōhō, November 2005. Also see Takahashi, "Haikyū Men wa dō Natte Iru ka."
60 See "Seijin Eiga no 'Erosu' ni tsuite Kongo dō arubeki ka," *Seijin Eiga* 58 (November 1970): 4–8, for a collection of voices from the film industry regarding the warnings issued by the police and Eirin's subsequent tightening of standards, with Ōshima Nagisa, among others, participating.
61 The police first arrested several employees of the Nikkatsu Kansai branch for distribution of obscenity via videotapes in Tokushima Prefecture on January 21. One week later, the metropolitan police searched the offices of Nikkatsu-connected theaters and Pink subcontractor Prima Kikaku on suspicion of distribution of obscenity. Three films were the target of this action: *Love Hunter* (*Ai no kariudo: Rabu hantā*, Yamaguchi Seiichirō), *Office Lady Diary: Smell of a Female Cat* (*OL Nikki: Mesu neko no nioi*, dir. Fujii Katsuhiko), and the Prima Kikaku–produced *High School Student Geisha* (*Jokōsei geisha*, Watanabe Teruo).
62 Tōei was also charged with the distribution of obscene material, but with regard to sex films the company had distributed on video. For a detailed account of the trials, see Cathers, *The Art of Censorship in Postwar Japan*.
63 My translation from the quote in Tanaka, *Nihon Eiga Hattatsu-shi V*, 283.
64 This was the most common opinion in the interviews I conducted.
65 *Seijin Eiga* even ran a special called "The Age of Bedside Cinema!" (Beddo saido shinema jidai!), explaining the details of the new business branch. The video's prices are claimed to be around 200,000 yen ($555) per film, a very attractive prospect for films that could not be sold to television and were lying around, more or less useless. According to the article, companies such as Nihon Yūsen Terebi Eiga, Teichiku, Victor Geinō, Hikari Enterprises, and Ōkura Shinema were buying the rights to the films, transferring them to video, and renting them to hotels and hot spring inns for around 25,000–35,000 yen (at the time $70–$97) a month. One month earlier, the magazine reported that Wārudo (World) Eiga alone had sold fourteen films for transfer to video. See *Seijin Eiga* 54 (July 1970): 30–31; and *Seijin Eiga* 53 (June 1970): 33.
66 Million Films, the Pink distribution subsidiary of the Keitsū exhibition chain (later it created the Joy Pack film distribution-exhibition powerhouse in 1976, renamed Humax Pictures in 1989), began a cooperation with Shōchiku for Shōchiku Porno Road Shows in several theaters in Ginza, Shinjuku, and Shibuya. The screenings were apparently highly successful. See *Eiga Nenkan 1974*, 103.

67 *Eiga Nenkan 1974*, 67.
68 Yoyogi's original name was Watanabe Teruo; however, he began using the name Yoyogi due to the Nikkatsu Roman Porno trial. Yoyogi later split off to form his own production company that worked to supply Nikkatsu, Watanabe Productions.
69 Tōkatsu, slyly enough, is written 東活, using characters in 東映 (Tōei) and 日活 (Nikkatsu), but none from 松竹 (Shōchiku). It seems that in 1972, Tōkatsu was actually still only buying films from productions like Gorudo, Tasono Productions, and Wakō Eiga for distribution. It started regular production of three films a month in 1976, which is why that year is mistakenly often given as its founding year.
70 "Ninja Shōhō," 40–43.
71 Yamada, "Kōgyō Men wa dō Natte Iru no ka."
72 The characters for Kuwabara Masae are 桑原正衛. "Ero Guro Kara no Dappi o Hakarau."
73 Interviews with Gotō Kōichi (November 2004) and Satō Keiko (January 2005).
74 Quoted by Takahashi, "Go-sha no Shijō o Doko Made Kutte Iru Ka."
75 Gotō, "'76' Pinku Eiga Sōkatsu."
76 Interview with Ōkura Mitsugi in Murai, *Boku no Pinku Eiga-shi*, 28.
77 In his book on programming his second-run theater in Kanagawa, Fujioka Shinami gives examples of the programs he ran, one being from 1964, when he programmed a triple bill made up of Imamura Shōhei's *Insect Woman* (*Nippon konchū-ki*, Nikkatsu, 1963); Takagi Toshio (高木才夫)'s Pink Film, *The Other Side of a Love Affair* (*Hanmen no jōji*, G Pro); and a show movie called *Sexy Vacation* (*Sekushii bakansu*). See Fujioka, *Eigakan Bangaichi*, 41.
78 From 6,808 in 1962. *Eiga Nenkan 1968*, 48; see also *Eiga Nenkan 1976*, 36.
79 These were named as the most common reasons for Pink Film theaters closing down in several interviews I conducted with distributors (for example, Gotō Kōichi and Fukuhara Akira of Shintōhō).
80 That is not to say that Yamamoto was not also at times connected to a resistance theme. In protest of the Roman Porno trial, he famously shot the film *Molester 365* (*Chikan 365*, prod. Tōkyō Kōei, 1972), in which a policeman perpetrates a long chain of molestations. The film received a special report in *Seijin Eiga* titled "The Melody of Resistance against Police Power." See "Keisatsu Kenryoku e no Hangyaku no Merodi."
81 The section heading is the title of an article on the year's Pink productions. Oda, "Pinku no Guerilla-sei no Genkai," 134. The epigraph is from Oda, "Adabana wa Mankai da ga . . . ," 128.
82 The film was *The Sacrificing Women* (*Ikenie no onna-tachi*, 1978), produced by Tōei Central films. It was executive produced by Kurosawa Mitsuru, the man who would become instrumental to the formation of V-Cinema from 1989.
83 See *Seijin Eiga* 54 (July 1970): 26, for several examples. The *Tōseki* issue is from May 1972, and the *Josei Jishin* issue is from April 22, 1972.
84 *Seijin Eiga*, it must be noted, had a marked increase in pictures and decrease in written text toward the end of the magazine's run.

THREE. KADOKAWA FILM

1 A story recounted in Obayashi, "Boku no Kadokawa Eiga-Dansō," 34.
2 Oda, "Fukyō no Tanima ni Saku Pinku Eiga." There was, however, quite strong coverage of Nikkatsu Roman Porno films, indicating that it was not the foregrounding of sex that kept critics away from Pink Film.
3 Abe, "Hōga ni Matsuwaru Nikutai-kan," 8–10. (Note: Abe usually transcribes his name as Casio, while the book itself gives Kashou, and the usual transcription would be Kashō). In the same chapter, Abe claims that the "becoming meat" of stories, which film critics of the 1970s especially were missing, was still in practice in Pink Film and Nikkatsu Roman Porno. However, according to Abe, these films flew under the radar of most critics, who held Ozu, Mizoguchi, and Kurosawa as their ideal. Abe uses the terms "meat" (*niku*) and "flesh" (*nikutai*) interchangeably, but I have upheld the distinction in my translation of the quote.
4 The *Eiga Nenkan* calls the fact that a "publishing-business person" was successful with a film production a "shock" for the established film companies. See *Eiga Nenkan 1978*, 98.
5 "Kadokawa films" refers to the films produced by either the Kadokawa Haruki Office or Kadokawa Publishing. "Kadokawa Film" refers to the industrial genre in which Kadokawa—the man, the legal entities of the company, and the films—participate.
6 Abe, "Hōga ni Matsuwaru Nikutai-kan," 10.
7 Annie Leibovitz took the picture.
8 This is a quite famous and oft-quoted statement; see, for example, a *zadankai* (round table discussion) in *Eiga Geijutsu*, "'Kadokawa' Tataki, Soshite Yurimodoshi," 12. See also Nomura, "Eiga-kai o Kassei-ka Saseta Oni-ko ni Jujitsu."
9 McDonald, *From Book to Screen*, ix.
10 The image of Kadokawa as a serious, literature-minded company has to be supplemented by Gen'yoshi's considerable tolerance for mixing established, canonical works and more popular literature in the Kadokawa lineup.
11 Kadokawa, *Waga Tōsō*, 132.
12 *The Strawberry Statement* (*Ichigo hakusho*, Stuart Hagmann, 1970); *Day of the Jackal* (*Jakaru no hi*, Fred Zinneman, 1973). Kadokawa also published Forsyth's books, *The Odessa File* (as *Odessa fairu*) in 1974 and *The Dogs of War* (as *Sensō no inutachi*) in 1975.
13 "Zakka Shōhō to Hanpatsu mo" [Convenience store strategy and those it repels], *Asahi Shinbun*, January 10, 1979, morning edition. Nagai Tatsuo was an important figure of the literary establishment. He had been a successful author, editor of literary magazines, and collaborator with Kikuchi Kan before the war and helped establish the venerable Akutagawa and Naoki literary prizes.
14 Quoted in Yamakita, *Kadokawa Haruki no Kōzai*, 45.
15 See, for example, "Ningen Tōjō" [People's appearance], *Yomiuri Shinbun*, August 6, 1975.

16 Kadokawa, *Waga Tōsō*, 137. The sum was actually an unimpressive $1,695, but in his autobiography Kadokawa Haruki emphasizes the payment, presumably to give proof of how his cross-marketing ideas developed.
17 According to all accounts of the time, the office was founded with capital of 15 million yen (at the time, $50,675); however, Kadokawa himself later claimed that it started with a capital of 6 million yen, 2 million of which he borrowed from friends. It is a little-known fact that besides film production, the Kadokawa Haruki Office was also seriously involved with the business of importing the Queen Elizabeth/Asuka whiskey brand (which also appeared in quite a few Kadokawa films). By the late 1980s, the Kadokawa Haruki Office employed a staff of around ten people who were responsible for film-related activity, while six or seven people worked on the whiskey import business. For information on the founding of the company, see "Hi wa Kyōchū ni Ari" [A fire in the heart], *Asahi Shinbun*, November 8, 1987, morning edition. For the press conference, see "Kadokawa Shoten ga Eiga Seisaku ni Shinshutsu" [Kadokawa Shoten enters film production], *Hōchi*, December 5, 1975.
18 "Yōga" is written with the Chinese character for (Pacific) ocean, and the character usually implies "Western" as much as it does "foreign." For a time this presented something of a conundrum for distributors when Hong Kong films became popular. It apparently did not seem quite right to categorize a film from Asia as yōga, but for lack of alternatives they eventually were.
19 *Eiga Nenkan 1980*, 36.
20 As audiences had been declining since 1959, exhibitors very consistently increased ticket prices to compensate for the losses. Thus, exhibition income has constantly risen to new record numbers over the course of the years, practically until today, while ticket prices climbed as high as over 1,800 yen (around $13 at the time) in the late 1990s. This was initially beneficial to the majors, who had an increasingly tight grip on exhibition and distribution—until the early 1990s, when the first multiplex cinemas began appearing.
21 Minobu Shiozawa, "Kadokawa Shoten to Yokomizo Seishi no 'Yattsu Haka Mura,'" *Ryūdō*, November 1979, 260–72.
22 From my interview with Kadokawa, March 2005.
23 For an excellent review of the multiple ideological implications of the term "village" in Japan, see Hayashi, "Traveling Film History."
24 From my interview with Kadokawa, March 2005.
25 For a very detailed retracing of how the term was introduced in advertising, see Steinberg, *Anime's Media Mix*.
26 Michael Raine has even argued for a media mix that predates the Astro Boy anime and is specific to the era of high economic growth. Symposium at International Research Center for Japanese Studies, Kyoto, 2014.
27 Kadokawa has also claimed that his inspiration for the media-mix strategy was in large part born from reading Hitler's *Mein Kampf*. This is probably one of his habitual provocations and an attempt to associate himself with another overreaching figure. See Yamakita, *Kadokawa Haruki no Kōzai*, 48.

28 The soundtrack for *The Inugami Family* was not as successful as Kadokawa had envisioned, however. He later attributed this to the fact that there was no actual song on the album, only the instrumental score. For *Proof of the Man*, Joe Yamanaka contributed a pop song, and it was significantly more successful. From this film onward, Kadokawa would employ theme songs in each film, many of which became substantial hits and strongly increased record sales.

29 From my interview with Kadokawa, March 2005. There were precedents of producer-directors of 1960s independent film taking out bank loans, but the sums were much smaller. An example is Okamoto Kihachi's *Nikudan / Human Bullet* (*Nikudan*, 1968).

30 "'Inugami-kei . . .' Seisaku Staff o Kokuso" [Legal proceedings against the production staff of "Inugami Family"], *Asahi Shinbun*, November 25, 1976, evening edition.

31 Kadokawa stated this in my interview with him (March 2005), and as much was widely suspected at the time.

32 *Eiga Nenkan 1978*, 98.

33 "'Kadokawa Eiga' Stāto."

34 The budget figures mentioned in the *Asahi Shinbun* article were supplied by the Kadokawa Haruki Office. Kadokawa himself has mentioned significantly lower figures, often by half. The best explanation for this is that the *Asahi Shinbun* article's figures include the advertising costs (or that Kadokawa simply adjusted the figures according to the interviewer). In any event, the budget for *The Inugami Family* is set at 500 million, *Proof of the Man* at 1.26 billion, *Proof of the Wild* at 1.9 billion, and *Virus* at 2.8 billion. See "Geijutsu Tsugu 'Kadokawa Eiga,'" *Asahi Shinbun*, June 13, 1981, evening edition.

35 "Ryūdō Suru Eigakai—76' Nen o Kaiko Suru—Kawakita Kaichō no Jitsugen kara Kadokawa Shoten no Nagurikomi Sakusen made" [The fluid film world—looking back on '76—from the realization of chairman Kawakita to Kadokawa Shoten's assault strategy], *Cinema Times Eiga Jihō* 294 (December 1976): 4–14.

36 Eventually the prize money went to Matsuyama Zenzō, a veteran scriptwriter.

37 Open and heavily publicized auditions would become one of the main promotion instruments for Kadokawa films. Some of them seem to have been actual open auditions, some of them staged. All three of the famous Kadokawa idols (see chapter 4) were selected at what seem to have been actual open auditions. Specifically, Watanabe Noriko and Harada Tomoyo were chosen from an audition in which supposedly over 57,000 young women participated. There was even an audition for kittens for the film *Play It, Boogie-Woogie* (*Surō na bugi ni shite kure*, Fujita Toshiya, 1981).

38 The Japanese versions are "Yonde kara miru ka, mite kara yomu ka" and "Ka-san, boku no bōshi dōshita deshō ne." In a magazine published by Kadokawa Shoten, the English version of the latter appears as "Mama, I wonder what happened to that old straw hat," which is not a very literal translation. See "Ningen no Shōmei" [Proof of the man], *Baraeti Bessatsu Kadokawa Daizenshū*, June 1986, 29.

39 Shiozawa, "Kadokawa Shoten to Yokomizo Seishi." The article portrays it as if the advertising costs themselves had been 1.1 billion yen, but Kadokawa claims that production costs were 650 million and advertising costs 400 million, adding up to 1.05 billion total. See "Hi wa Kyōchū ni Ari" [A fire in the heart], *Asahi Shinbun*, November 8, 1987, morning edition.
40 For official average production costs, see *Eiga Nenkan 1980*, 99 and 104. Kadokawa himself has claimed a somewhat higher gross for the film, 2.35 billion. Also see "Hi wa Kyōchū ni Ari." Other sources claim a budget of 670 million yen for production and 700 million for advertising. See Yamakita, *Kadokawa Haruki no Kōzai*, 27, 82.
41 Yamakita, *Kadokawa Haruki no Kōzai*, 107.
42 Yamakita, *Kadokawa Haruki no Kōzai*, 33.
43 "Zakka Shōhō to Hanpatsu mo."
44 For an excellent description of this history, see Steinberg, *Anime's Media Mix*.
45 See, for example, Higuchi, *Suna no Utsuwa to Nihon Chinbotsu*.
46 "'Kadokawa' Tataki, Soshite Yurimodoshi," 19.
47 Mentioned in "'Kadokawa' Tataki, Soshite Yurimodoshi," 4.
48 With regard to the *Kinema Junpō* polls, *Proof of the Wild* scored number eight on the readers' poll and number forty on the critics' poll. *Virus* scored number six on the readers' and twenty-four on the critics' poll. *School in the Crosshairs* scored number thirteen on the readers' poll and thirty-eight on the critics' poll. Between *The Inugami Family* (1976) and *Kamata Kyōshin Kyoku* (1982), none of the seventeen feature films Kadokawa produced entered the annual critics' *Kinema Junpō* ten-best list. Moderate critical success would appear in the mid-1980s with films such as *Mahjong Vagabond Chronicle* (*Mājan hōrō-ki*, Wada Makoto, 1984) and *W's Tragedy* (*W no higeki*, Sawai Shinichirō, 1984), but their success at the box office was usually moderate as well.
49 Quoted in Yamakita, *Kadokawa Haruki no Kōzai*, 28. The origin of the poll is not mentioned, however, and it must be taken with a certain amount of caution.
50 This renegotiation may have been particularly vexing for the many leftist film critics that associated the fusing of the public and the private spheres with the government of the 1930s. See Maruyama Masao's thoughts on the importance of creating a valid public sphere (i.e., separating it from the private sphere) after the war as a means of guaranteeing a working democracy, in Maruyama, "Denken in Japan."
51 "'Kadokawa' Tataki, Soshite Yurimodoshi," 22; Yoshio Shirai in the *Sunday Mainichi*, September 19, quoted in Suga, "Imēji Tsuijūsha-tachi no Gukō," 27.
52 For detailed descriptions of the scene, see "Kadokawa Haruki ni Okeru 'Ka-san no shōmei'" [Kadokawa Haruki's "Proof of the mother"], *Shūkan Asahi*, December 30, 1977, 22, morning edition; and "Zakka Hōhō to Hanpatsu mo" [Convenience store strategy and those it repels], *Asahi Shinbun*, January 10, 1979, morning edition.
53 My translations. Quoted in Hiroyuki Shinoda, "Media Mikkusu Kushi Shita Sofuto Bijinesu no Jittai," *Tsukuru*, February 1991, 98–111.
54 My translation from German. Maruyama, "Denken in Japan," 62.

55 My translation. Quoted in Noda, "'Zen media e Shinshutu' o Gōgo Suru Kadokawa Haruki no Yabō," *Tsukuru*, January 1983, 59. Years later, when this variant of dramatization had become much less effective in a business sense, Kadokawa would write, "Ultimately, I definitely feel I didn't lose against my father." My translation; see "Hi wa Kyōchū ni Ari" [A fire in the heart], *Asahi Shinbun*, November 8, 1987, morning edition.

56 Minami's criticized statement in the original is "Ai to kanashimi o kizumukonda ningen dorama desu. Rasuto ni hirogaru aizetsu no yojō ga, anata no tamashii o yurugasaburu deshō." See Toyoshi and Yoshiyuki, "Satō Junya Kantoku no 'Ningen no Shōmei.'" For Minami Yoshiko's answer, see Yoshiko, "Ōguro Toyoshi Sensei e," 58.

57 Matsushima, "Sengo no Dokuritsu Pro, Soshite Kadokawa Eiga," 144–46. Matsushima was the film journalist for the *Mainichi Shinbun* during the late 1970s and 1980s, and one of the few to take Kadokawa films seriously in their overall meaning for the industry and in terms of socioindustrial meaning. Zenkyōtō, or the All-Campus Joint Struggle Committee (Zengaku kyōtō kaigi), was founded during the events leading up to the protests at Nihon University in 1968, as a more inclusive way to politically mobilize the student body. Zangakuren, the All-Japan Federation of Students' Self-Governing Associations (Zen-nihon gakusei jichikai sō rengō), which had been the national political representational organization, was by that point divided into several feuding suborganizations of various leftist political colors. Zenkyōtō was able to create a platform around which students could rally for political action against the renewal of the Anpo security treaty, the Vietnam War, the building of Narita Airport, and university-specific issues. It was also loosely associated with the radical left that turned to violence, which led to great disillusionment with political activism in general, and Zenkyōtō in particular, in the mid-1970s. This is referred to as the post-Zenkyōtō generation.

58 Ōtsuka, *Otaku no Seishin-shi*, 70.

59 So called in the introduction to a *zadankai* (public round table discussion) between Matsuoka Isao, chairman of Tōhō; Okada Shigeru, chairman of Tōei; and Kadokawa Haruki: "Yatte Kita Eiga Ōgon Jidai," *Zaikai*, March 11, 1980, 104.

60 It is important to note that cosmopolitanism is deeply connected to the establishment of the nation-state as much as it is, in slightly different form, to contemporary national-identity discourses.

61 Despite the fact that its budget positions it only as an upper-range regular production, or prestige production, I count *The Inugami Family* as part of the blockbuster strategy because of the way in which it was marketed.

62 The question of budgets is a continually difficult one to resolve. Basically, the only sources available are Kadokawa's own comments or articles that base their figures on information provided by the Kadokawa Haruki Office. Even these numbers often vary considerably, and Kadokawa of course may have had a vested interest in spinning his official claims. While the *Eiga Nenkan* at the time stated that *The Inugami Family*'s budget was 300 million yen, to me he claimed a figure of 220 million yen, and an *Asahi Shinbun* article from 1981 uses numbers from the Kadokawa

Haruki Office to claim production costs of 500 million yen. One possibility is that the numbers in the *Asahi Shinbun*, which seem inflated with regard to all of the films listed, include public relations and marketing costs, which were immense, probably around double the production costs. The article also claims 1.26 billion yen ($4,754,717) for *Proof of the Man*, 1.9 billion ($8,837,209) for *Proof of the Wild*, and 2.8 billion ($11,764,706) for *Virus*. See "Geijutsu Dzugu 'Kadokawa Eiga'" ["Kadokawa Film" awakening to art], *Asahi Shinbun*, June 13, 1981, evening edition. For figures on *The Inugami Family*, see "'Inugami-kei . . .' Seisaku Sutaffu o Kokuso" [Legal action against the staff of "Inugami . . ."], *Asahi Shinbun*, November 25, 1976, evening edition. See also *Eiga Nenkan 1978*, 99.

63 According to Okada Yutaka, it was the scriptwriter for *Capricorn One* (Peter Hyams, 1978), and although Peter Hyams himself is officially credited with the script, it is possible this was a different, uncredited writer. See "'Kadokawa' Tataki, Soshite Yurimodoshi," 4–26.

64 The Japanese quote is "Yappari, nippon-jin no ko wa erai."

65 The fact that this was a common theme in Japanese literature undoubtedly made it quite easy for Kadokawa to find appropriate material.

66 For a discussion of these positions, specifically that of critic Shirai Yoshio of Kadokawa as a peddler of "empty" films deceiving the audience via advance ticket sales, see "'Kadokawa' Tataki, Soshite Yurimodoshi," 4–26.

67 Again, see Steinberg, *Anime's Media Mix*.

68 The first and most successful being *Emperor Meiji and the Great Russo-Japanese War* (*Meiji tenno to nichiro dai sensō*, Watanabe Kunio, 1957).

69 Kadokawa, *Waga Tōsō*, 137.

70 As mentioned earlier, this film was infamous for being block-booked for four weeks, excessive for the 1960s. It was also a scandal in the film industry because it paired Mifune Toshirō and Ishihara Yūjirō, stars from different studios—a move that was forbidden under the five-company agreement between the majors. Other examples are *Sky Scraper!* (*Chōkōsō no akebono*, Sekigawa Hideo, 1969), meant to promote the building of a skyscraper by Kashima Construction (Kashima Kensetsu); *5,000 Kilometers to Glory* (*Eikō e no 5000 kiro*, Kurahara Koreyoshi, 1969), which had an advance-ticket deal with Nissan; and *The Human Revolution* (*Ningen kakumei*, Masuda Toshio, 1973), partially funded by the religious movement Sōkka Gakkai.

71 Sano, *Nihon Eiga wa, Ima*, 226.

72 "Ryūdō Suru Eigakai," 13.

73 My translation. "Kisoi-atta Eigakai no 'Soto-zama'" [Competing and meeting film world "outsiders"], *Asahi Shinbun*, September 4, 1993.

74 Other Japanese-film yōga releases for 1978 include *To the Edge of the White Glacier* (*Shiroi hyōga no hate ni*, Kadota Ryūtarō, distributed by Tōhō Tōwa); *The Mouse and His Child* (*Oyako nezumi no fushigi na tabi*, Fred Swenson and Fred Wolf, another Sanrio production distributed by Herald); and *Gatchaman Science Ninjas* (*Kagaku ninja tai Gatchaman*, Toriumi Hisayuki, distributed by Fuji Eiga).

75 *Farewell* was the sequel to *Space Battleship Yamato / Star Blazer* (*Uchū senkan Yamato*, Masuda Toshio, 1977), the hit film that demonstrated the viability of animation for theatrical release.

76 *The Adventure of Kōsuke Kindaichi* was from one of Yokomizo Seishi's novels; and *The Resurrection of the Golden Wolf* was a novel by Ōyabu Haruhiko. *G.I. Samurai* was written by Hanmura Ryō. Kadokawa himself produced two more films for Tōei that year, *The Demon Comes and Blows a Flute* (*Akuma ga kitarite, fue o fuku*, Saitō Mitsumasa) and *Blind Spot at Noon* (*Hakuchū no shikaku*, Murakawa Tōru), but these were not official Kadokawa Films productions.

77 There are too many to name, but notable among them are Ogata Akira, Kurosawa Kiyoshi, *Ring* producer Ichise Takashige, Sono Shion, and *Neon Genesis Evangelion*'s Anno Hideaki.

78 My interview with Kadokawa, March 2005.

79 My interview with Kadokawa, March 2005.

80 While program pictures actually entailed churning out films within a fixed production structure and a constant and regulated dissemination by means of hōga-style block booking, Kadokawa films of course did not fulfill these criteria. Nonetheless, journalists, critics, and Kadokawa Haruki himself refer to this as Kadokawa's turn to program pictures, in effect simply for differentiation from the blockbuster strategy. Keeping this in mind, the same terminology is used here.

81 See, for example, Steinberg, *Anime's Media Mix*, or various writings by Ōtsuka Eiji.

82 "'Kadokawa' Tataki, Soshite Yurimodoshi," 12. See also Maruyama Shōichi, "Yajū Shisubeshi—Deai Ikasubeshi" [The beast must die—the meeting must be made to take place], *Baraeti Bessatsu Kadokawa Daizenshū*, June 1986, 46–47. For a Japanese producer, Kadokawa was unusually focused on scripts. He was willing to invest considerably more than was usual at the time, and to spend more time on the script stage. As mentioned, Kadokawa paid 5 million yen as the main prize in the scriptwriting competition for *Proof of the Man* and commissioned an expensive American screenwriter for *Virus* (then did not use the result). His greatest investment in scripts was probably *Rex: A Dinosaur's Story*, which had two American script versions, five versions by Maruyama Shōichi, and eight versions by Kadokawa himself. He additionally used TV scriptwriter Uchidate Makiko specifically for the dialogue, something very unusual for film in Japan even today.

FOUR. THE RADICALIZATION OF KADOKAWA FILM

1 For various examples of the events used to promote the idols, and the scale they sometimes reached, see "Dai Ibento Monogatari 1976–1986" [Big event story 1976–1986], *Baraeti Bessatsu Kadokawa Daizenshū*, June 1986, 84–90.

2 Many of the Nikkatsu directors and scriptwriters, as well as scriptwriter Maruyama Shōichi, were introduced to Kadokawa by Kurosawa Mitsuru (also sometimes called Kurosawa Man). Kurosawa had begun work at Nikkatsu but later switched to Tōei Central Films, where he also produced films by Pink Film director Yama-

moto Shinya. Kurosawa also played a decisive role in the creation of the V-Cinema genre when he headed the production arm of Tōei Video in the late 1980s.

3 *Kadokawa san-nin musume* (three Kadokawa girls) is a reference to the san-nin musume trio of Misora Hibari, Chiemi Eri, and Yukimura Izumi, who starred in a series of films together in the 1960s, although there have been many other units of three girls in Japanese film and music history.

4 There was one moderately successful attempt at creating a male idol. Nomura Hironobu was selected in the highly publicized open audition for *Main Theme*. He later played in other Kadokawa films such as *Cabaret*, but he never achieved the degree of identification with the Kadokawa label that the Kadokawa musume did. Sanada Hiroyuki, known to audiences outside of Japan for his role in *The Last Samurai* (Edward Zwick, 2003), was also connected to Kadokawa for a short time in the early 1980s, but he was already a popular actor before Kadokawa employed him.

5 Interestingly, the history of talent agencies is connected to the American occupation period. The archetypal and immensely powerful talent agency of the 1950s and 1960s, Watanabe Productions, grew out of the jazz scene that formed to cater to the GIs.

6 Kawasaki, "Sukuriin Gyaru."

7 Following the film version of *Sailor Suit and Machine Gun* in late 1981, the TV *dorama* (limited TV series) version started in July 1982. It starred Harada Tomoyo, who would have her film debut as a Kadokawa aidoru in *The Little Girl Who Conquered Time* in 1983. Harada also starred in the TV dorama version of *School in the Crosshairs* later in the same year. The dorama version of *Detective Story* (1983) was broadcast in early 1984, starring Watanabe Noriko, the next Kadokawa musume in line. Several "making of" specials were also broadcast on TV, although most of them were named after the idol they focused on, and merely inserted "making of xxx" in the subtitle.

8 The somewhat evasive (and since the 1990s, omnipresent) term "kawaii," roughly translatable as "cute," is highly relevant to Japanese pop culture but cannot be elaborated on here. For an interesting overview, see Yomota, *Kawaii-ron*.

9 *Sailor Suit and Machine Gun* was shown in a double bill with Tōei's *Burning Brave* (*Moeru Yūsha*, Dobashi Toru, 1981), but it was clearly Kadokawa's film, and Yakushimaru's excessive popularity, that carried the program. While the double bill with *Sailor Suit and Machine Gun* made, as mentioned, almost 2.3 billion yen in distribution gross, *Virus* made 2.37 billion yen. These figures are taken from the *Eiga Nenkan 1986*, 50.

10 My interview with Kadokawa Haruki, March 2005.

11 According to data supplied by Kadokawa, the double bill of *Love Story* and *Main Theme* made 1.885 billion yen ($7,854,167); the double bill of *Sailor Suit and Machine Gun* and *Burning Brave* (*Moeru Yūsha*, Dobashi Tōru, 1981) made 2.288 billion yen ($10,400,000); and the double bill of *The Little Girl Who Conquered Time* and *Detective Story* (*Tantei Monogatari*, Negishi Kichitarō, 1983) made over

2.8 billion yen ($11,764,705) in distribution gross (so box-office gross would be almost double). See "Kadokawa Eiga Zen Sakuhin Haishū Seiseki" [Kadokawa Films distribution income of all films], *Baraeti Bessatsu Kadokawa Daizenshū*, June 1986, 83.

12 Suga, "Kaijū (Gojira) To Joyū."

13 While Suga does not mention it, their roots in flesh-committed Roman Porno may play a role in their treatment of the idols. In fact, both films were highly successful at the box office, although this was arguably attributable to the relatively higher popularity of the films that they were paired with in double bills, *The Little Girl Who Conquered Time* and *Love Story*.

14 Suga, "Kaijū (Gojira) To Joyū."

15 Wakita, "Kadokawa Haruki Intabyū," 49.

16 Interview with Kadokawa, March 2005.

17 For an extensive report on Kadokawa's experiences with aliens, see Kadokawa, *Waga Tōsō*, 47–58. Also for an example of how this near obsession was perceived, see Shigemasa, *Katte ni Eiga-shō/kō*, 20–22.

18 Igarashi, *Bodies of Memory*, 194.

19 Ōtsuka, *Otaku no Seishin-shi*, 403.

20 For example, "Eiga Topics Journal," *Kinema Junpō* 892 (August 1984): 160–61.

21 *Main Theme* played with *Love Story* in a double bill distributed by Tōei and grossed 1.85 billion yen ($7,708,333) in distribution income. *W's Tragedy* played with Harada's *The Island Closest to Heaven* (*Tengoku ni ichiban chikai shima*, Ōbayashi Nobuhiko, 1984, Tōei distribution), earning 1.54 billion yen ($6,416,666) in distribution. See "Kadokawa Eiga Zen Sakuhin Haishū Seiseki," 83.

22 *Cabaret* played with *His Motorbike, Her Island* (*Kare no ōtobai, kanojo no shima*, Ōbayashi Nobuhiko, 1986) (starring Harada's sister, Kiwako) on a double bill distributed by Tōhō, and earned a somewhat disappointing 950 million yen ($5,588,235). Tōhō also distributed the double bill of *Woman in a Black Dress* and *Time of Lovers* (*Koibitotachi no jikoku*, Sawai Shinichirō, 1987) to a very disappointing 230 million yen ($1,642,857) in distribution income.

23 Both Harada and Yakushimaru have had fairly successful subsequent careers, with Yakushimaru more active as an actress and Harada better known as a singer. Yakushimaru played a version of herself as a former idol star on the hit drama *Amachan* in 2013.

24 The tatami refers to the smallest standard size for a Japanese room, in this case packed with connotations of kitchen sink realism. For the Kadokawa quote (my translation), see Wakita, "Kono Eiga Wa Zen-Enshuttsu-ka," 94.

25 Noda, "'Zen Media e Shinshutsu' o Gōgo Suru Kadokawa Haruki no Yabō."

26 Wakita, "Kono Eiga Wa Zen-Enshuttsu-ka."

27 See *Eiga Nenkan 1980*, 43. It is quite telling that in the *Eiga Nenkan* only Japan and Western film industries are compared, showing where Japan situates the norm to be measured against. India, for example, another country with a strong film industry, is not mentioned.

28 From *Eiga Nenkan 1982*.

29 As listed earlier, according to Kadokawa, *Dirty Hero* cost 420 million yen ($1,714,285), *Love Story* 500 million yen ($2,083,333), and *Heaven and Earth* an amazing 5 billion yen ($37,037,037). For his statement on *Heaven and Earth*, see "'Kankyaku Dōin 1000 Man-nin' ni Jishin" [Confident of a "10 million audience"], *Asahi Shinbun*, July 2, 1990, evening edition. For his statement on *Love Story*, see Wakita, "Kadokawa Haruki Intabyū," 48. For his statement on *Dirty Hero*'s budget, see Wakita, "Kono Eiga Wa Zen-Enshuttsu-ka," 94.

30 Nyū hāfu is a broad category of performers who were assigned male at birth and perform as women, but can include a variety of gender identities. Matsubara was an important figure in popularizing the now very common term in Japan.

31 Shot for 420 million yen ($1,714,286), this was not a blockbuster-scale budget; by comparison, *Virus* cost 2.4 billion yen ($10,909,091).

32 Wakita, "Kono Eiga Wa Zen-Enshuttsu-ka," 94.

33 Noda, "'Zen media e Shinshutu' o Gōgo Suru Kadokawa Haruki no Yabō," 59.

34 Wakita, "Kono Eiga Wa Zen-Enshuttsu-ka," 94.

35 Mukokuseki films were popular in the late 1950s and early 1960s. Usually set in Hokkaido, in a landscape that was not instantly recognizable as Japanese, these films featured characters, plots, and sets highly reminiscent of American Westerns. Some of the most popular mukokuseki films were shot within the *Wataridori* series, featuring Kobayashi Akira in the main role.

36 The masks and motorized movements of the dinosaur were designed by famous special-effects master Carlos Rambaldi, a fact used in marketing the film. The Ainu are the indigenous people of Hokkaido, regarded as ethnically and culturally different from "real" Japanese.

37 Kadokawa initially released films to the video and theatrical film market on the same day, for example in the case of *Dirty Hero* and *Black Magic Wars* (*Iga Ninpūchō*, Saitō Mitsumasa, 1982), released on a double bill by Tōei. As the importance of the video market increased, Kadokawa discontinued the practice and stopped selling the video rights, preferring to distribute the films via Kadokawa Video, beginning with *Kenya Boy* (*Shōnen Kenia*, Ōbayashi Nobuhiko, 1984).

38 Kadokawa, *Waga Tōsō*, 139; Wakita, "Kadokawa Haruki Intabyū," 45–46; *Flashdance* (Adrian Lyne, 1983); *Rocky* (John Avildsen, 1976); Kadokawa, "Satomi Hakken-den," 204; *Star Wars* (George Lucas, 1977); Kadokawa, "Kamui No Ken," in *Shisha Shitsu no Isu*, 266–75; *Raiders of the Lost Ark* (Steven Spielberg, 1981); "Taidan Kadokawa Haruki to Yamane Sadao"; *Peggy Sue Got Married* (Francis Ford Coppola, 1986); *Jurassic Park* (Steven Spielberg, 1993).

39 For details on Tsuguhiko's strategies with regard to magazines, again see the important Steinberg, *Anime's Media Mix*.

40 From statistics supplied by the National Tax Agency, quoted in *Eiga Nenkan 1988*, 40.

41 The release of the Italian-Japanese coproduction *Dedicated to the Aegean Sea* (*Ēge-kai ni sasagu*, 1979) provides an early example of the dynamics at work in the industry. Produced for 120 million yen ($545,455) it generated publicity for being based on a best-seller by Ikeda Masuo, who also directed, and for including nudity

and racy scenes in the Mediterranean. Due to its foreign cast, including Italian porn star Ilona Staller, it was released by Tōhō affiliate and foreign film distributor Tōhō Tōwa with 151 prints nationwide during Golden Week. It went on to become one of the biggest hits of the year with a box office income of 2 billion yen (or $9,090,909) according to director Ikeda. Very little of this money, however, arrived at the production end, as Tōhō / Tōhō Tōwa found several ways to increase its stake in the profits. Outside of Tokyo the film was shown as a double bill with *The Legacy* (David Foster, 1978; released in Japan as *Regashi*), cutting the income allotted to the production company in half. Ikeda was angry, as *The Legacy* had proved an underperformer in Tokyo, and *Dedicated to the Aegean Sea* carried the double bill. Again according to Ikeda, of the 2 billion yen grossed, 1 billion was subtracted as the so-called top-off, for financing the advertising campaign. Of the remaining money, half went to the exhibition side (made up heavily of Tōhō theaters), and after subtracting costs for the prints a mere 200 million yen were left for the production side to cover all their costs. *Eiga Nenkan 1995*, 34; *Eiga Nenkan 1980*, 36.

42 While these figures are from Ikeda himself and must be accepted with caution, the basic thrust is accurate. See Maruyama, *Sekai ga Chūmoku Suru Nihon Eiga no Henyō*, 22–39; see also *Eiga Nenkan 1980*, 111–13.

43 From my interview with Kadokawa, March 2005.

44 From my interview with Kadokawa, March 2005.

45 See the interview with Kadokawa Haruki by Shinji Yamagiwa, "Kinmirai-gata Kadokawa Eiga" [The shape of Kadokawa Film in the near future], *Baraeti Bessatsu Kadokawa Daizenshū*, June 1986, 168–71.

46 *Kiki's Delivery Service* (*Majo no Takkyūbin*, Miyazaki Hayao, 1989) made an estimated total of around 10 billion yen (almost $72 million), with over 4 billion in box-office gross, 2.5 billion with video and laser disc markets, 1.3 billion with merchandising, 1.2 billion with publishing, and 700 million with other ancillary rights (television, etc.). See Shinoda, "Media Mikkusu Kushi Shita Sofuto Bijinesu no Jittai," 98–111.

47 Interestingly, *The Silk Road* managed to win the Japan Academy Prize for best film despite being unpopular.

48 *Rex: A Dinosaur's Story* has a list of corporate partners that is almost comically long. It also diegetically features a full TV commercial starring Rex for Kadokawa Bunko, the Kadokawa pocketbook line.

49 For a discussion of many of the charges leveled against Kadokawa, see the *zadankai* on Kadokawa, "'Kadokawa' Tataki, Soshite Yurimodoshi," 4–26.

50 To illustrate the trajectory toward less and less profitable returns: in the Kadokawa magazine *Baraeti*, though with numbers taken from *Kinema Junpō*, the double bill of *Fair Weather Sometimes Murder* (*Hare tokidoki satsujin*, Izutsu Kazuyuki, 1984) and *Cursed Village in Yudono Mountains* (*Yudono-sanroku noroi mura*, Ikeda Toshiharu, 1984) is listed as having made but 390 million yen, certainly a financial failure. The following double bill of *Love Story* and *Main Theme* then was successful with 1.855 billion yen ($7,854,167) but was followed by the double bill of *Sometime Somebody Will Be Killed* and *Mahjong Vagabond Chronicle*, which only made 510

million yen ($2,125,000). Further signs of deterioration appeared in 1985, as the double bill of *The Blade of Kamui* and *In Love with Bobby* (*Bobii ni kubittake*, Rintarō, 1985) only made 220 million yen ($936,170), and the double bill of *Marriage Invitation Mystery* (*Kekkon annai misuterii*, Matsunaga Yoshikuni, 1985) and *Sleep Well, My Friend* (*Tomo yo, shizuka ni nemure*, Sai Yōichi, 1985) only reached a distribution gross of 130 million yen ($550,847). See "Kadokawa Eiga Zen Sakuhin Haishū Seiseki," *Baraeti Bessatsu Kadokawa Daizenshū*, June 1986, 83.

51 The series was part of NHK's *Taiga Dorama* series. The *Taiga Dorama* is an annually changing year-long TV series broadcast on NHK. *Taiga Dorama* always has a period setting and regularly scores some of the highest ratings among Japanese TV series.

52 From my interview with Murata Nobuo, a former employee at the Kadokawa Haruki Office, August 2006.

53 See "'Kankyaku Dōin 1000 Man-nin' ni Jishin."

54 The international version of the film was edited by Robert C. Jones, who also worked on *Shampoo* (Hal Ashby, 1975) and *Days of Thunder* (Tony Scott, 1990). It was completed in a month and the print had English subtitles, which had been made for the (unsuccessful) submission to Cannes.

55 This company, Triton Pictures, later distributed another Kadokawa film that failed to find distribution, *Ruby Cairo* (Graeme Clifford, 1993). It also distributed other films, such as *Toto the Hero* (*Toto le héros*, Jaco van Dormael, 1991).

56 Kadokawa speaks of a "gengo no shōgai" in Wakita, "Kono Eiga Wa Zen-Enshuttsu-ka," 91.

57 There had also been multiple production cooperations between Korean, Taiwanese, and Hong Kong companies in the 1960s. Nishimoto Tadashi had even achieved relative fame in Hong Kong as a cameraman and director; he handled the cinematography for classics such as *Come Drink with Me* (*Da zui xia*, King Hu, 1966) or Bruce Lee's *Return of the Dragon* (*Meng long guojiang*, Bruce Lee, 1972).

58 Actually, Kadokawa films were exported mainly to Asia. The only Kadokawa films that had farther-reaching international distribution success of some kind were *Virus* and *G.I. Samurai*.

59 "Mikansei de 20-nen kan Kura-iri Dizunii Anime Seisaku, Haikyū-ken Kadokawa Shi Baishū" [Production and distribution rights for an unfinished Disney film that lay in the vaults for 20 years is purchased by Kadokawa], *Asahi Shinbun*, October 31, 1990, morning edition.

60 Victor is connected to electronics giant JVC (Victor Company of Japan), which in turn is connected to Matsushita Electronics.

61 See "'Kadokawa' Tataki, Soshite Yurimodoshi."

62 This is not to suggest that advance tickets for the film were not available. However, the tickets on sale were ones given out according to agreements between the distributor and the exhibitors. This is regular procedure for the greater part of films released in Japan as a means of measuring the degree of public interest in a film prior to its release and securing an initial audience. However, *Rex* was not driven by advance ticket sales forced upon the employees or subcontractors

of the film's corporate sponsors, as had been the case with many of the previous blockbusters.

63 "Kyō ni mo Sai-Taihō" [Rearrested again today], *Asahi Shinbun*, October 8, 1993, evening edition. See also "Kadokawa Zen-shachō Kisō" [Former Kadokawa company president charged], *Asahi Shinbun*, September 20, 1993, morning edition.

64 Prompting scriptwriter Arai Haruhiko to the wry criticism that this showed a "TV mentality" and that "Mishima Yukio's books weren't specially taken out of print" after his failed military coup. See " 'Kadokawa' Tataki, Soshite Yurimodoshi," 6.

65 Despite *Rex* certainly being a financial success for Shōchiku, it was not necessarily for Kadokawa, at least not in the theatrical release. Reportedly shot for a budget of 2 billion yen ($18,181,818, of which Shōchiku shouldered 100 million), and saddled with advertising costs of 450 million yen, the film made an estimated 2.2–2.5 billion yen in distribution revenue. This is a considerable hit, but must have failed to cover Kadokawa's costs by far. See Nomura, "Eiga-kai o Kassei-ka Saseta Oni-ko ni Jujitsu," 62. See also "Eiga 'Rex' Uchikiri" [Film "Rex" closed down], *Asahi Shinbun*, August 30, 1993, morning edition.

66 Ōtsuka, *Mediamikkusu-ka Suru Nihon*.

67 Originally, it had been incorporated into Nippon Herald as Herald Ace Pictures.

68 Under Kadokawa Haruki, only one of over sixty films had not been based on a preexisting book or comic: *The Two Called the Shame of the Metropolitan Police—On a Detective's Strange Journey* (*Nippon keishi-chō no haji to iwareta futari—Dekka chindō-chū*, Saitō Kōsei, 1980) was novelized but made from an original script. Novels from other companies were also filmed under Kadokawa Haruki, as in the case of *Time of Lovers* (*Koibitotachi no jikoku*, Sawai Shinichirō, 1987; script by Arai Haruhiko). But while the hardcover version was published by Shinchōsha, Kadokawa still published the bunkobon version after deciding that it would be filmed.

69 In 1998, Kadokawa entered a joint venture with the Sumitomo Corporation by merging Ace Pictures with distributor Asmik to form Asmik Ace Entertainment. In the same year it scored a hit that would have international implications with the double feature of *Ring* (*Ringu*, Nakata Hideo) and *Spiral* (*Rasen*, Iida Jōji). In 2002 Kadokawa purchased the remainder of the Daiei studios from Tokuma Shoten to form Kadokawa Daiei, thus earning an entry ticket to Eiren, the Motion Picture Producers Association of Japan. Eiren, traditionally the most powerful film-industry lobby group, was originally composed of the major studios and at present counts Shōchiku, Tōhō, Tōei, and Kadokawa Herald Pictures as its core members. In 2004 Kadokawa bought 43 percent of distributor Nippon Herald, thereby also gaining access to several important minitheaters and multiplexes that Nippon Herald co-owned via its affiliate Cineplex. It additionally established Kadokawa Holdings as a holding company for Kadokawa Publishing and the other affiliate companies, and renamed Kadokawa Daiei as Kadokawa Pictures. To tap into new financing methods, Kadokawa Pictures established a fund called the Japan Film Fund Co., a form of financing that was becoming more attractive due to regulatory changes. In 2005 they finally invested in Nippon Herald and merged it with

Kadokawa Pictures to form Kadokawa Herald Pictures. In March 2007 the name was once again changed to Kadokawa Pictures.

70 The 2014 merger of Kadokawa with Dwango, the Internet company that created the Nico Nico Douga site, one of the main centers of fan production in Japan, is another step in this direction.

71 *Yamato* was produced by the Yamato Production Committee. Kadokawa's stake in the production committee is taken from the Kadokawa Haruki Mirai Fund. Half of the rights of the film stay with Kadokawa, and of the share of earnings Kadokawa receives for the film, 90 percent go back into the fund while 10 percent stay with the Kadokawa Haruki Corporation. From my interview with Kadokawa, March 2005.

72 "History of Kadokawa," accessed May 20, 2007, http://www.kadokawa-hd.co.jp/history.php.

73 See Kadokawa, *Waga Tōsō*.

74 In Kadokawa Tsuguhiko's presentation at the Kadokawa Summer Seminar at Tokyo University, July 2014.

FIVE. V-CINEMA

1 While nonfiction film and original video animation have been a sizeable component of the straight-to-video market, they will figure less here.

2 Zielinski, *Zur Geschichte des Videorecorders*, 318. Zielinski sees time manipulation as inscribed in both the vertical-scan technology utilized in the recording process and what it is used for, enabling the spectator a much larger degree of (temporal) manipulation over the viewing situation. There is an extensive amount of literature on the relationship between the medium of video and the dimensions of time and space. Most of it can be traced to ideas formulated by Harald Innis that each medium tends to lean toward privileging either time or space (itself based on Lessing's *Laocoon*). Others disagree and see video as the first medium to facilitate spatial and temporal diffusion. See, for example, Marlow and Secunda, *Shifting Time and Space*.

3 Asada and Karatani, "Shōwa Seishin-shi o Kenshō suru."

4 Marlow and Secunda, *Shifting Time and Space*, 128. The ads were actually a response to the lawsuit that had been brought against Sony for copyright infringement.

5 Quoted in Wasser, *Veni, Vidi, Video*, 72.

6 "Bideopia," *Kinema Junpō Bessatsu*, August 1971.

7 Here the difficulties with an imperfect term such as "media" come into play. As Manovich has pointed out, while film and photography can still be defined as different media according to models of time-based versus spatially based media, TV and video shift the definition to the level of the device. Manovich, "Postmedia Aesthetics."

8 Lim, *Translating Time*.

9 The year 1989 was when three of the Four Devils of Pink Film made their directing debuts, as did Kitano Takeshi, Tsukamoto Shinya, and Sakamoto Junji. For Miyadai's influential theory of the never-ending everyday, see Miyadai, *Owari Naki Nichjjō o Ikiro*.

10 See, for example, "Yoshida Tatsu-shi ni Kiku" [Asking Yoshida Tatsu], *Gekkan Shinario* 507 (October 10, 1990): 5–8.

11 "Yoshida Tatsu-shi ni Kiku." Also see Masumura, "Supīdo ni Tsuite."

12 Yoshida had worked under Shundo Kōji, the legendary Tōei producer credited with single-handedly creating the successful *ninkyō* (chivalry) line of yakuza films. The ninkyō subgenre dominated Tōei's output from about 1962 until the *Battle without Honour and Humanity* series by Fukasaku Kinji in the early 1970s. Accordingly, Yoshida's entire career had been heavily aligned with yakuza films. Kurosawa began his career at Nikkatsu, which specialized in action films, the other staple of early V-Cinema. He later switched to Tōei Central Film, through which he came into contact with Kadokawa, for whom he produced nine films. (Yoshida was, for example, also involved with the production of *Proof of the Man* for Kadokawa.)

13 These films garnered much less attention from established film criticism for their lower production values and reduced narratives, but some of them, such as Tōei's *Yukinojo Henge* series, attained considerable popularity. Their introduction was highly contentious among the majors in the 1950s, as they were closely tied to double-bill screenings, which the majors (apart from Tōei) were wary of. The history of these B-films basically ended with the founding of Second Tōei in 1960. For an excellent rendition of the history of these films, see Masubuchi, *B Kyū Eiga*.

14 The gang in *Crimehunter* seems to be taken straight from the reactionary portrayals of demented youth gangs in the *Death Wish* or *Mad Max* series.

15 "Yoshida Tatsu-shi ni Kiku."

16 Success in V-Cinema is not always easy to measure. Initially, most companies sold their films to wholesale dealers, who then traveled the country and sold the tapes to video stores. While the amount sold indicates a certain success for the producer and the wholesaler, it says nothing about how often the film was actually rented or seen. If 10,000 tapes are sold, and each is rented once, that results in (at least) 10,000 viewers. It is also possible for a tape to sell 5,000 times and be rented an average of ten times per tape, resulting in (at least) 50,000 viewers. Figures on actual rentals are very sparse, and only very occasionally made public by larger chains like Tsutaya. As far as available figures, however, they indicate that on average V-Cinema films were on the lower end of actual sales but had fairly good rental rates, often making first place in terms of rentals while not even appearing in the top twenty for sales. This has to do with the store practice of stocking only one tape per V-Cinema film and several tapes of potentially more popular films, decreasing the rentals per tape for these. For example, according to Culture Convenience Club (which runs the Tsutaya chain), in December 1990 *Tales of a Golden Geisha* (*Ageman*, Itami Jūzō, 1990) was the most-rented film in their chain, accounting for 61,923 rentals. However, with an average of 8.9 rentals per tape, it only achieved eleventh place on the rental-rate chart. Number one was *Pachinko Story* (*Pachinko*

monogatari, Tsuji Makoto, 1990), with 12.8 rentals per tape. In terms of total rentals, it was not even listed within the top forty. (*Pachinko Story* is not, however, V-Cinema.)

17 According to producer Yoshida Tatsu, *The Shootist 2* (*Sogeki 2—The Shootist*, Ichikura Haruo, 1990) and *Neo Chinpira—the Bullet Goes Zoom* (*Neo Chinpira—Teppōdama pyu*, 1990), by former Pink Film director Takahashi Banmei, sold well over thirty thousand tapes. Yoshida also mentions that *Crimehunter* was broadcast on television in early 1990, achieving a considerable rating of 15.7 percent. See "Yoshida Tatsu-shi ni Kiku."

18 Car action even had a (small) section of its own in the Tsutaya video store at Shibuya Station when I was there in the summer of 2004. Yamane Sadao gave the designations "sexy action film" and "gun-action" in Yamane, "Tōei V-Shinema no Kanōsei."

19 *Kinejun Eiga Bideo Iyābukku 1992*, 330–31.

20 See, for example, Yamane, "Tōei V-Shinema No Kanōsei." See also Yamane, "Kimyō na Ikimono ga Katsugeki o Yomigaeraseta."

21 Yamane, "Kimyō na Ikimono ga Katsugeki wo Yomigaeraseta," 154–68.

22 Igyō, however, can also designate directors from the advertising world, and does not always refer to celebrity directors. For a complete list of the igyō directors from 1991, see Ōtake Hirō's interview with Okuyama Kazuyoshi, "Kitano Takeshi ga Kuruma kara Dete Kita Toki." Also see Ōtake, *Nihon Eiga Gyakuten no Shinario*, 227–28.

23 The practice was occasionally used even in the studio system, where it generated much controversy due to its circumventing of the seniority system. One of the famous examples that created much trouble among the assistant director ranks at Tōhō was writer Ishihara Shintarō directing his own script in *Young Beast* (*Wakai kemono*, 1958). Ishihara had achieved prominence as a founder of *taiyōzoku* (Sun Tribe) literature, which in turn spawned the controversial *taiyōzoku* films. Still controversial, though in a different fashion, Ishihara later became the governor of Tokyo.

24 *The Outer Way* was shown among others at the International Film Festival Rotterdam, and *Film Noir* was shown in the Directors Fortnight section of the Cannes International Film Festival.

25 For Kadokawa, Sengen worked on *Dirty Hero*, *Detective Story*, and *W's Tragedy*, among others.

26 From interviews with Ōno Seiichi of GP Museum, Fukumaki Taizō of KSS, and Tsuruta Norio, in 2004–5.

27 Interview with Fukumaki Taizō.

28 Interviews with various Pink Film directors, some of whom did not wish to be named on this point.

29 Interviews with Takahara Hidekazu and Gotō Daisuke, September 2004.

30 From an interview with a V-Cinema producer who wishes to remain anonymous on this point.

31 Kamoi Tatsuhiko, head of the Japan Writers Guild, warned of such a development as early as 1990. See Kamoi Tatsuhiko, "'Orijinaru Bideo' ni Kan Suru Sakka

Kyōkai no Tachiba" [The Writers Guild's position concerning "original video"], *Gekkan Shinario* 507 (October 10, 1990): 14–15.

32 See, for example, Yamane, "Tōei V-Shinema no Kanōsei," or Yamane, "Kimyō na Ikimono ga Katsugeki o Yomigaeraseta."

33 Tanioka has published several books on V-Cinema that are a necessary starting point for any research on these films, partially because virtually nothing else was written on V-Cinema when it was still an active genre. For the most informative overview of the genre, see Tanioka, *V-Shinema Damashi*.

34 Shiozawa, "Ugokihajimeta Bideo Sangyō no Genjō Sōtenken," 146.

35 The JVA (Nihon Bideo Kyōkai) received status as a legal entity in 1978, when video sales began in earnest. It changed its name to Japan Video Software Organization (Nihon Eizō Sofuto Kyōkai) in 1996.

36 The tapes were almost all thirty minutes in length and priced at 30,000 yen ($83), a considerable amount at the time. The full lineup can be seen online on the Japan Video Association's page, "Nihon Eizō Sofuto Kyōkai 40-nen no Ayumi," accessed January 2017, http://jva-net.or.jp/history/index.html#11.

37 My translation. The original says, "Bideotēpu de ureru no wa, mazu Pinku eiga de aru." In "Ima Bideo de Nani ga Mirareru Ka" [What can currently be seen on video], *Kinema Junpō Bessatsu*, August 1971, 7–24.

38 According to the JVA's website, by summer 1970 around 2,500 resorts had installed video machines for adult entertainment.

39 According to Tanioka, *Kingu obu V-Shinema*, 38.

40 At the time, 1,000 yen was $3.88.

41 This was not restricted to Japan, of course. In 1979, 75 percent of all prerecorded videotapes sold in the United States were X-rated. See Klopfenstein, "The Diffusion of the VCR in the United States," 21–39.

42 The actress usually named in connection with the bonus adult tape strategy is Aizome Kyōko. She achieved notoriety starring in Takechi Tetsuji's remake of his own *Daydream* (*Hakujitsumu*, 1981), the first theatrically released film from Japan with hard-core, not just simulated, sex scenes. As the legend goes, her tape was attached as a bonus to VHS recorders, which gave the technology the critical push to increase market share over Sony's Betamax system. Aizome has gone on to direct several films in V-Cinema since the turn of the millennium.

43 Biderin merged with the Contents Soft Association's internal review body, the Media Rinri Iinkai (Mediarin), to form the Eizō Rinri Kikō. This then merged with two additional review bodies to form the Nihon Kontentsu Shinsa Sentā (Japan Contents Review Center) in 2016. There are, however, still several other organizations that offer the same services, and companies such as Museum didn't submit their films to any organization, so the actual number of videos and DVDs released is most certainly higher.

44 Quoted on the homepage of the Japan Video Association, "Bideo Sofuto no Rental Shisutemu ni Kan Suru Hōkokusho" [Video software rental system inquiry written report], accessed January 12, 2007, http://www.jva-net.or.jp/jva/history/6-4.htm (the website is now defunct).

45 Actually, Maeda was the owner of a company called Shinehausu, which primarily created flyers and pamphlets for film. It was Shinehausu that ran the Nagoya Video Library, even if it was situated within the Endōji Theater.

46 These are figures given from memory by one of the employees of the Endōji, Ōno Wataru, in an interview in February 2005. Nakamura Hogaru gives other numbers that seem to conform better to official pricing figures. Video films were, and are, rarely sold to rental shops for the listed price, however. The numbers Nakamura gives for a 60-minute and 90–120-minute film (respectively) are for 1977, 19,000/60,000 yen ($72/226); 1979, 15,000/60,000 yen; 1981, 9,800/30,000 yen; 1982, 9,800/20,000 yen; 1983, 7,800/17,800 yen. See Nakamura, *Nihon Bideo Sofuto-shi*.

47 The figures Nakamura gives for the years are, respectively, 1979, 21.5 percent; 1980, 19.4 percent; 1981, 33.9 percent; 1982, 39.7 percent; 1983, 21.7 percent. See Nakamura, *Nihon Bideo Sofuto-shi*.

48 Interview with Ōno Wataru.

49 The Nagoya Video Library was closed in October 2005.

50 The figure of 70 percent is taken from the annual statistics collected by the International Image Software Promotion Council (Kokusai eizō sofutouwea suishin kyōgi kai), quoted in *Kinejun Eiga Bideo Iyābukku 1993*, 360.

51 While the four-part book series *Asa Made Bideo* [Video until morning], published by Yōsen-sha, devoted part two to *hōga*, or films from Japan, the others were exclusively foreign films. Also see Nomura, *Kaikan!*; Itō, *B-kyū Bideo Hakkutsu Kataroggu*; the book by director and actor Mizuno Haruo, *Bideo de Miru Hyappon No Yōga*; or the most prominent TV critic for almost thirty years, Yodogawa Nagaharu, *Yōga Bideo De Mitai Besuto 150*. See also *Video Club Xanadeux*. The latter is concerned exclusively with yōga, or foreign, films; the Xanadeux in the name of the club that published the book is another indication of the utopian attitudes toward early video.

52 Significantly, three of these companies (Warner, CIC Victor, and RCA Columbia) were not even members of the JVA, which at that point had fifty-two member companies. "Zadankai—Sutāto Shita Bideo Rentaru Jidai."

53 Other larger categories were sports (3.0 percent) and business education (5.8 percent).

54 Hatano Tetsurō, "Bideo ga Eigakan o Shisha Shitsu ni Suru," in *Nihon Eiga 1985*, 121.

55 Jameson, "The End of Temporality."

56 "Minishiatā: Nankai Eiga mo Shareta Hoteru Kankaku Nara" [Minitheaters: If difficult films (are shown) with the sense of a fashionable hotel (they will be watched)], *Shūkan Asahi*, August 25, 1989, 125. Throughout the late 1990s, the Cinepatos theater located near Ginza was a typical outlet for V-Cinema that was looking for a theatrical-release label. It was used heavily by KSS, especially for its *King of Minami* releases; from summer 1995 to summer 1996, KSS released ten films theatrically, all of them at Cinepatos. Gaga was another company involved with V-Cinema that used Cinepatos for films like the *Eko Eko Azarak* series.

57 *Kinejun Eiga Bideo Iyābukku 1991*, 364.

58 My translation from "Sofuto ga Tarinai!?" [There isn't enough soft!?], *Nikkei Entertainment*, October 5, 1988, 6–12.

59 Suntory's director, Saji Keizō, actively sponsored cultural institutions and events for many years, building the Suntory Hall and the Suntory Museum, among others. It is an interesting fact that Torii Shinichirō, who was instrumental in Suntory's entry into the media business (and was director of the company from 1990 to 2001), was not only the grandson of Suntory founder Torii Shinjirō, but also of the cofounder of Tōhō and founder of the Hankyū group, Kobayashi Ichizō. Kobayashi is a central figure in the creation of a mass consumer culture in Japan; he was the head not only of the Hankyū railway empire but also founder of the Takarazuka musical troupe and the Hankyū department stores. His strategy of strategic theater building is one of the foundations of Tōhō's current dominance of the distribution and exhibition market. Suntory was involved in founding the Argo Project; in 1989, a group of well-known independent producers joined to create a production company with its own exhibition outlet, one theater in Shinjuku and one in Osaka. Films such as *No Life King* (*No raifu kingu*, Ichikawa Jun, 1989), *The Cherry Orchard* (*Sakura no sono*, Nakahara Shun, 1990), and *Original Sin* (*Shinde mo ii*, Ishii Takashi, 1992) resulted from this company. It renamed itself Argo Pictures in 1993, and though near bankrupt, it continued production of films such as *800 Two-Lap Runners* (Hiroki Ryūichi, 1994) or *Tokarev* (*Tokarefu*, Sakamoto Junji, 1994). In 1995 it was forced to close its theaters, and later only functioned as a production outfit.

60 Nihon Bideo Eizō's *Vinyl Book Woman: Total Peep View* (*Bini-bon no onna: Hiō nozoki*) and *Office Lady Confession: Ripe Secret Garden* (OL *warume hakusho: Jukushita mitsuen*) are usually named as the first AV films, or rather the forerunners of what was to become the category of AV.

61 The series became well known in the United States when Charlie Sheen contacted the FBI after seeing the film and assuming it was an actual snuff film. It was produced by Orange Video House from 1985 and Japan Home Video from 1988.

62 *Kinejun Eiga Bideo Iyābukku 1990*, 297.

63 In 1985 Nikkatsu launched a series called Roman X to recapture the market share that AV had annexed. The series was shot on video (though blown up to 35 mm film for the theaters) and featured hard-core (i.e., not simulated) sex scenes, though it conformed to the regular standards for visual censorship. *Woman in a Box—Sacrifice of a Virgin* (*Hako no naka no onna—Shojo ikenie*, Konuma Masaru, 1985) was the first Roman X film. The series was not very successful in turning around the trend, and Nikkatsu finally declared its retreat from Roman Porno in 1988.

64 *Kinejun Eiga Bideo Iyābukku 1991*, 358. These figures are biased in the sense that only very few companies released exact sales figures. Also, as discussed above, they give no indication of how often the respective films were actually rented and ultimately seen.

65 Nikkatsu reported debts of 71.4 billion yen ($649,090,909), 8 billion of which were due to investments in golf courses, 5 billion from investments in new media, and 3.5 billion to its failed Movieland project. *Kinejun Eiga Bideo Iyābukku 1994*, 354.

SIX. SUBGENRES

1. Interestingly, Takeuchi, now completely identified with V-Cinema, is somewhat of a bridge figure between genres. He had his feature film debut starring in Kadokawa's *His Motorbike, Her Island* in 1986.
2. While surveying several video stores in Tokyo, it became clear that the smaller stores all used categories that were fairly broad and referred to subgenres: *akushon* (action), *gyanburu* (gambling—everything concerned with money, not just actual gambling), or ninkyō. Larger stores such as the Tsutaya chain branches in Shibuya and Shinjuku, with a large stock of older films and often frequented by film fans, additionally used many categories devoted to various V-Cinema actors and specific series. The Shibuya branch, for example, stocked forty tapes (with thirty-eight installments) of the *Code of Conduct* (*Jingi*) series. While there was no spelled-out V-Cinema category, tapes belonging to the genre were usually shelved in one spot in the store, not mixed with the other films.
3. Originally, KSS was named Nihon Soft System. The current name is an abbreviation of Kansai Super Station, a radio station the company used to run.
4. *The Don That Calmed Down* had twelve installments from 1991 to 2001, all directed by Kashima Tsutomu. It is also unusual within V-Cinema for its degree of transmedia expansion. Besides the manga and V-Cinema versions, one theatrical version has been released, and in 1993 Nihon Terebi produced a television series. In 1997 a V-Cinema spin-off, *New: The Don That Calmed Down* was produced with six installments.
5. This is according to my interviews with producers Fukumaki Taizō of KSS and Ōno Seiichi of GP Museum in February 2005. Both referred to their market research to support this idea and estimated the female audience to be sometimes as high as 30 percent.
6. Shimizu Kentarō is known for his role in the original *Mah-Jongg Demon* series (*Janki*, Konuma Masaru, 1992–95), and later became one of the main actors involved in the various jitsuroku films. Shimizu Kōjirō played in the highly successful early Tōei V-Cinema *Like a Beast* (*Kemono no yō ni*, 1990–92) films; later well-known films are the eight-part *The Road to Becoming the Don* series (*Don e no michi*, all directed by Ishihara Shigeru, 1998–99) and various jitsuroku films. Nakajō Kiyoshi is also active as a producer and has most prominently starred in the *New Third Underworld* series (*Shin dai-san no gokudō*, thirteen installments, 1995–2000, the first two of which were directed by Miike Takashi). Watanabe Hiroyuki has divided himself between yakuza, pachinko, and mah-jongg films. His more recent work has concentrated on the jitsuroku films. Ozawa Hitoshi has been active in producing, directing, and acting, with his acting work concentrating on various jitsuroku films (far over twenty in the early 2000s). He directed all three installments of *True Account: Okinawa Yakuza War* (*Jitsuroku: Okinawa yakuza sensō*, 2002–3). Virtually all of the V-Cinema stars had some occasional acting experience in the mid-1980s and later became popular (and very busy) within the V-Cinema framework.
7. Aikawa and Takeuchi achieved some degree of international visibility through Miike Takashi's *Dead or Alive* series. Aikawa has recently been working on television

and starred in Miike's *Zebraman* (*Zeboraman*, 2004), and Takeuchi played parts in *Battle Royal II* (Fukasaku Kenta, 2004) and *Yo-Yo Girl Cop* (*Sukeban deka*, Fukasaku Kenta, 2006). Takeuchi is best known for his popular series *Code of Conduct* (*Jingi*, 1991–) and especially *The King of Minami* (*Minami no teiō*, 1992–). Takeuchi runs his own fashion label specializing in his flashy yakuza style, advertised at the end of some of his series' installments. Aikawa had successful runs in much of the early V-Cinema work of Kurosawa Kiyoshi, most prominently the *Revenge* (*Fukushū*, 1997) series and the *Suit Yourself or Shoot Yourself* (*Katte ni shiyagare!*, 1995–96) series. He also was highly popular in the *King of Debt* (*Shakkingu*, four installments and two theatrical films, 1997–98) moneylender series, and the ninkyō-oriented *Bloodbath Will Come* (*Shūra ga yuku*, thirteen installments, 1995–2000). He has also starred in some of the most popular V-Cinema films, among them *Neo Chinpira—the Assassin's Bullet Goes Zoom* (*Neo Chinpira—Teppodama pyu*, Takahashi Banmei, 1990) and *Ley Lines* (*Nihon kuro-shakai—Ley lines*, Miike Takashi, 1999), two of the rare V-Cinema films to garner critical attention from the general film press.

8   Actor Matsukata Hiroki, who starred in a variety of the Tōei jitsuroku films in the 1970s, returned to the subgenre when V-Cinema began to pick it up around 2000.

9   Director Ozawa is the aforementioned Ozawa Hitoshi, who also plays a major part in the film.

10 From several interviews with producers involved with jitsuroku production, who want to remain anonymous.

11 Interview with Fukumaki Taizō, February 2005.

12 Modern pachinko machines are combinations of slot machines and the pinball-like game itself, and are outfitted with intricate sound and light effects (sometimes referred to as *pachisuro*). Pachinko parlors are virtually omnipresent in any Japanese city, especially in front of train stations, the space that film theaters once occupied in the 1950s. For figures on box-office gross, see *Eiga Nenkan 1995*, 33. For the Ministry of Economy, Trade, and Export's figures on the gambling industry and pachinko specifically, see Ministry of Economy, Trade, and Export (METI), "Rejā / Yoka Katsudō no Dōkō ni tuite," accessed January 2017, http://www.meti.go.jp/statistics/toppage/report/bunseki/pdf/h17/h4a0506j3.pdf.

13 The script for the first installment of *Pachinko Player Nami* was written by Shiota Akihiko, who later achieved international film festival prominence as the director of films such as *Moonlight Whispers* (*Gekkō no sasayaki*, 1999), *Harmful Insect* (*Gaichū*, 2001), and *Canary* (*Kanaria*, 2005), and later directed the big-budget spectacle *Dororo* (2007). There are a few quasi-antecedents to these subgenres. Tanioka Masaki names Tōhō's program-picture *In Front of the Train Station* series (*Ekimae*, twenty-four installments, 1958–69) as one for the pachinko films. The Kadokawa-produced *Mah-Jongg Drifter* (*Mah-jongg hōrō ki*, Wada Makoto, 1984) could be seen as an influence on the V-Cinema mah-jongg films. However, there is no example that makes gambling itself so central to the film or the basis of a whole subgenre.

14 The films are also a good example of how permeable early V-Cinema was for staff. Director Mitsuishi received training in Pink Film under several of the Yū Produc-

tions directors, such as Ishikawa Hitoshi and Hiroki Ryūichi, as did scriptwriter Ikawa Kōichirō. *Pachinkā Nami* was even shot by Film Kids, Hiroki Ryūichi's production outfit, which was subcontracted by Tokuma Japan Communications.

15 My translation: "Ika ni katsu ka, sono purosesu wa koko ni aru!" Director Shichiji was a frequent assistant director for Aoyama Shinji (among others) on *Shady Grove* (1999) and *Eureka* (2000).

16 For example, in *Mah-Jongg Wolf Tale: Blow of Death! Subspace Deadly Strategy* (*Marōden: Hissatsu! Akūkan sappō*, Hattori Mitsunori, 2000).

17 The Japanese title combines the words *shakkin* (debt) and "king" to make shakkingu.

18 Since then there have been a limited number of TV specials with a different cast, *New King of Minami* (*Shin Minami no teiō*, 2010–).

19 Interview with Fukumaki Taizō, February 2005 (my translation).

20 "Japanese Consumer Finance," *Economist*, August 10, 2006, 15.

21 Peter Alford, "Acceleration Clause Speeds Money Lenders' Demise," *Australian*, September 13, 2006, accessed December 2006, http://www.theaustralian.com.au/business/acceleration-clause-speeds-money-lenders-demise/story-e6frg8zx-1111112202746 (no longer available online).

22 From interviews with Fukumaki Taizō and Ōno Seiichi.

23 *V-America* launched with *Distant Justice* (*Fukushū wa ore ga yaru—Distant justice*, Murakawa Tōru, 1992), a production that was set in the United States and costarred George Kennedy, a veteran of Japanese productions since *Proof of the Man*. *V-Erotica* was launched with the fifty-two-minute *Manila Emanuelle—Bewitching Paradise* (*Manira Emanieru fujin—Mashō no rakuen*, Niimura Ryōji, 1992). And *V-World*, which was meant to be first of a series of international coproductions starring Jacqueline Bisset, was launched with *Crimebroker* (*Kuraimuburōkā—Kamen no yūwaku*, Ian Barry, 1993). None of these efforts was very successful, although thanks to costar Viggo Mortensen another production, *American Yakuza* (*Yakuza vs. Mafia*, Frank Cappello, 1993), has had a long shelf life.

24 The Culture Convenience Club conglomerate that operates the largest chain store, Tsutaya, had introduced pay per transaction (PPT) to its stores in March 1990 with Sakamoto Junji's debut film *Knockout* (*Dotsuitarunen*, 1989). In this system, video stores only pay a small sum to the production company or distributor for royalties, and then pay out a certain percentage for each respective rental transaction. This transfers all of the financial risk to the producer or distributor, which makes it potentially dangerous for the smaller and more capital-weak V-Cinema companies. Companies such as KSS therefore rejected the PPT system, but had to deal with the powerful position of chains such as Tsutaya.

25 Gaira is another prominent Pink Film director who would find occasional work in V-Cinema. The first of the female action V-Cinema films is probably another Tōei film, *Black Princess—Angel from Hell* (*Burakku purinsesu—Jigoku no tenshi*, Tanaka Hideo, 1990).

26 *Zero Woman* was originally a manga by Shinohara Tōru that Tōei made into a film as *Zero Woman: Red Handcuffs* (*Zeroka no onna: Akai wappa*, Noda Yukio, 1974).

27 The film was also not the norm for V-Cinema in terms of financing, produced by a production committee consisting of Wani Books, Vision Sugimoto, and Fuji Television, according to an interview I conducted with Gotō in 1994.
28 Rohy, "Ahistorical," 70.
29 Kanehara, "Orijinaru Bideo Mūbii."
30 Figures extracted from film lists given in *Eiga Gaidobukku 2001*, 383–401.
31 The Cinema Japanesque series included films such as *The Eel* (*Unagi*, Imamura Shōhei, 1997) and *Cure* (*Cure/Kyua*, Kurosawa Kiyoshi, 1997). With Suncent Cinema Works, Sentō produced such films as *Eureka* (Aoyama Shinji, 2000), *Firefly* (*Hotaru*, Kawase Naomi, 2001), and *Electric Dragon 80,000v* (Ishii Sogo, 2001). He had begun the strategy at Wowow (at the time called Nihon Eisei Hōsō, with only the channel called Wowow) with the *J Movie Wars* series, a collection of thirty-minute films produced primarily for broadcast, but eventually distributed in theaters as well (along the lines of the Kadokawa strategy, Sentō insisted that the films be shown only in yōga theaters). One of the films from this lineup was *J Movie Wars: All under the Moon* (*J Movie Wars: Tsuki wa dotchi ni dete iru ka*, Sai Yōichi, 1993), which was reshot as the very influential feature-length *All under the Moon* (*Tsuki wa dotchi ni dete iru ka*, Sai Yōichi, 1993).
32 See the website, *Flower and Snake II*, http://www.hanatohebi-movie.com/.
33 In 2014, Tōei Video produced a film to commemorate the twenty-fifth anniversary of V-Cinema, simply titled *25* and starring Aikawa Shō.
34 These estimates are from my interviews with Ōno Seiichi of GP Museum and Fukumaki Taizō.
35 Interview with Ōno Seiichi.
36 V-Cinema is now practically exclusively shot on digital video.
37 Interviews with Ōno Seiichi and Fukumaki Taizō.
38 This figure includes general films and rereleases of old films. However, it still illustrates the change in power relations between VHS and DVD. The figures are taken from *Eiga Nenkan 2006*, 95.
39 The top news item of the year was Matsushita's purchase of Universal. "90-nen Eiga-kai 10 Dai-nyūsu Senshutsu."
40 These are average figures taken from data on four video stores published by *Video Insider Japan* magazine. See "Mansurii Repōto: Rentaru Mise-jo Hōkoku-sho" [Monthly report: Rental stores], *Video Insider Japan*, April 1, 2005, 202–5.
41 Corrigan, "Glancing at the Past," 37.
42 See Manovich, *The Language of New Media*; and Azuma, *Otaku*.
43 Quoted in Corrigan, "Glancing at the Past," 35.

CONCLUSION

1 The reasons for this joint venture are not hard to fathom. Shinecon are often situated near shopping malls to enhance each other's appeal and present a common consumption space. This development did not begin with the shinecon. In 1992 Tōei began restructuring a number of its real estate holdings and theaters as

mini malls-cum-movie theaters, not primarily theater spaces. See "Eiga Topikku Jānaru."

2 According to the Motion Picture Producers Association of Japan (Eiren), in 2013 out of a total of 3,318 screens, 2,831 were at shinecon. See the statistics page on Eiren's website, "Statistics of Film Industry in Japan," Eiren, accessed September 23, 2014, http://www.eiren.org/statistics_e/.

3 *Eiga Nenkan 1995*, 35.

4 Kawabata and Kawachi, "Nihon Eiga," 186.

5 Possibly the earliest example is a seven-screen theater that the Korona enterprise, for a long time running the largest independent shinecon chain in Japan, opened in Komaki in 1980.

6 Shōchiku had actually tentatively entered the business a year earlier, when it opened the Mycal Shōchiku in Kanagawa.

7 *Eiga Nenkan 2006*, 20. In 2006, the total number of screens in Japan climbed above 3,000 for the first time since 1970 to 3,062, with 73 percent of all screens attributed to shinecon. See Kawabata and Kawachi, "Nihon Eiga," 178.

8 See *Eiga Nenkan 1999*, 129.

9 See Harootunian, "Ghostly Comparisons." It also relates to Fredric Jameson's argument that recent decades, especially with the influence of postmodernism, have seen a weakening of temporality and a privileging of spatiality. See, for example, Jameson, "The End of Temporality."

10 Many minitheaters in fact attempted to adjust to the shinecon threat in the late 1990s by dividing their existing space into several smaller screens to show more films. One of the most important minitheaters, Eurospace, has even opted to create a kind of minitheater-shinecon, closing down its previous location and opening two screens in a building it shares with the Minitheaters Cinema Vera and Q-AX Cinema, for a combined five screens. The new theater is in the Shibuya section of Tokyo, the uncontested minitheater capital of Japan.

11 There were countless specials like these, especially in the leading film magazine *Kinema Junpō*. See, for example, Abe and Hayashi, "Ima Ki ni Naru Mini Shiatā"; see also, "1992 O-shōgatsu Mini Theater Eiga Tokushū."

12 Kadokawa Holdings struck a joint deal with Hong Kong–based Sun Wah group in 2005, agreeing to cooperate on building and managing twenty shinecon sites in mainland China.

13 See, for example, *Eiga Nenkan 2004*, 20.

14 See Ōtsuka, "*Hoshi no Koe*" o Kike.

15 Gillespie, "The Politics of 'Platforms.'" It should be noted that this usage of the term "platform" is very different from the one put forth in platform studies—a field promoted by theorists such as Nick Montfort and Ian Bogost. Platform studies focuses on computing systems that include a specific set of hardware and software and how they work together to produce certain experiences and forms of production, and interact with the larger culture they are embedded in.

16 Condry, *The Soul of Anime*.

17 Cambrosio and Keating, *Biomedical Platforms*.

18 For the most thorough discussion of the issue, see Steinberg, *Naze Nihon wa 'Media Mikkusu Suru Kuni' na no ka*. In English, see Steinberg, "Converging Contents and Platforms."
19 Presentation by Kadokawa Tsuguhiko at the Media Mix Summer Program 2014, Tokyo University, July 16, 2014.
20 Lazzarato, "Struggle, Event, Media." Lazzarato's work has become an important reference point for media studies–inflected work on the Japanese context. See, for example, Steinberg, *Anime's Media Mix*.
21 Kadokawa, *Kuraudo Jidai to "Kūru Kakumei"*; Kadokawa, *Gūguru, Appuru ni Makenai Chōsakuken-hō*.
22 See Steinberg, "Platform Producer Meet Game Master."
23 See Ōtsuka, *Kyarakutā Shōsetsu no Tsukurikata*.
24 For example, while many of the contributors to an important volume on the topic emphasize that the spread of certain forms of labor and productive activities on the Internet are only extensions of earlier practices, the volume itself is still titled *Digital Labor*, implicitly claiming a special quality for the tools used to perform these activities. See Scholz, *Digital Labor*.
25 See, for example, Kenji Hall, "Japanese Anime Studio Embraces YouTube Pirates," *Bloomberg Businessweek*, August 5, 2008, http://www.businessweek.com/stories/2008-08-05/japanese-anime-studio-embraces-youtube-piratesbusinessweek-business-news-stock-market-and-financial-advice.
26 Ōtsuka Eiji, "Kigyō ni Kanri Sareru Kaiteki na Posutomodan no Tame no Essei" [An essay for the cozy postmodern(s) controlled by corporations], *Saizensen*, May 17, 2014, http://sai-zen-sen.jp/editors/blog/sekaizatsuwa/otsuka-%20essay.html.
27 "Manga-Related Stocks Rise Due to Abe's Resignation," *Japan News Revue*, September 13, 2007, http://www.japannewsreview.com/business/stocks/20070913page_id=2131; Prerna Mankad, "Abe's Resignation Triggers Manga Boom," *Foreign Policy*, September 13, 2007, http://foreignpolicy.com/2007/09/13/abes-resignation-triggers-manga-boom/; "Manga Shares Gain on Leader Hopes," BBC *News*, September 12, 2007, http://news.bbc.co.uk/2/hi/business/6991720.stm.
28 The workshop and seminar series initiated by METI began with a coproduction seminar at the 2006 Berlin International Film Festival and continued at several international film festivals throughout the world.
29 Even by the 2010s, Japan had, in comparison to the United States and many European countries, a dearth of entertainment lawyers. In this sense, the formalization of business relations that Kadokawa attempted to introduce through insisting on complex business contracts and litigation has not fully penetrated all of the media industry. The chairman of the Government Council on Intellectual Property, Ushio Jirō, is the head of a prominent lamp-making company.
30 "About Cofesta," CoFesta, accessed July 2007, http://www.cofesta.jp/english/whats/about.html.
31 Douglas McGray's article about the global reach of Japanese popular culture, "Japan's Gross National Cool," is often credited with triggering these developments after it appeared in *Foreign Policy*, exposing many Japanese policy makers to it. While the

article seems to have been widely read, the buildup to this explosion of activity is visible in the trail of government white papers addressing the question with increasing force throughout the 1990s. See McGray, "Japan's Gross National Cool."

32 The Agency for Cultural Affairs (ACA, the Bunkachō) had, however, been changing its position toward film, a development that began in the late 1980s. Until the wider government developed its interest in content, the ACA had been the main official source of cultural policy on the film industry. It was here that slight attitude changes were the most visible over time. Since the late 1960s, it had annually awarded monetary prizes to select films, organized screening events, and was involved in the affairs of the National Film Center (part of the National Museum of Modern Art). In 1988 it published a document titled "Promotion of Film Art" ("Eiga geijutsu no shinkō"), which for the first time spoke of the necessity of protecting film more generally, not just particular works. In 1994 it published a similar essay that outlined various fields in which such activity should take place. In 2004, however, picking up a number of recommendations from the Committee on Film Promotion, it released an article titled "Plan for Promoting Japanese Film and Image Media," which changed the wording entirely. Previous publications had only spoken (although increasingly so) of the importance of supporting select culturally or artistically valuable films. This article outlined very concrete measures of promoting Japanese film, a project that was seen as inextricably tied to both business and cultural aspects. The plan now spoke not only of promoting culturally valuable film, but of creating a "self-controlled production cycle" and of "increasing the number of Japanese film releases and the box office gross for Japanese films" (at the same time the budget the agency assigned to film was raised from 1.8 billion yen [$16,822,429] to 2.5 billion yen [$23,364,485]). In the original, it reads, "Jishukuteki na sōzō saikuru no kakuritsu" and "Eyō to suru kōka ni tsuite wa, (8) ni kijutsu shita dōri, Nihon eiga no fūgiri honsū, kōgyō shūnyū sōka." The document can be downloaded from the Ministry of Export and Trade website, interestingly not from the ACA itself: "Nihon Eiga-Eizō Shinkō Puran" [Plan for promoting Japanese film and image media], Ministry of Export and Trade, accessed May 10, 2007, http://www.mext.go.jp/component/b_menu/other/__icsFiles/afieldfile/2015/04/07/1356615_054.pdf.

33 Curtin, *Playing to the World's Biggest Audience*, 23.

34 Jameson, "The End of Temporality."

35 Digital Hollywood is one of the many film schools that appeared during the 1990s to capitalize on the training gap left by the waning of on-set training and the seniority system.

36 The entire speech in its English translation is accessible from the Ministry of Foreign Affairs website. See Aso, "A New Look at Cultural Diplomacy: A Call to Japan's Cultural Practitioners," Ministry of Foreign Affairs of Japan, April 28, 2006, http://www.mofa.go.jp/announce/fm/aso/speech0604-2.html.

37 There were virtually no pure distribution companies in Japan at the time; production companies had evolved mainly from exhibition companies, and distribution was usually linked to them.

38 Naoki, "Nihon Eiga Oyobi Eigakai." Naoki provides many calculations of the cost of studios, film prints, and so on that are invaluable for anyone researching film of that time period.
39 Bernardi, *Writing in Light*.
40 In April 2007 the Foreign Ministry under Aso continued with its efforts to utilize the aesthetics of manga and anime when it issued a sixteen-page pamphlet featuring the popular manga and anime character Detective Conan visiting the Foreign Ministry, alongside a multitude of similar tie-ups with the manga-anime industry.
41 Beller, *The Cinematic Mode of Production*, 2.
42 Hansen, "New Media," 180–81.
43 Matsuda, "Media Kakumei no tame no Akushisu"; see also Matsuda, "Wakai Sedai no Eiga Shisō."
44 Presentation by Kadokawa Tsuguhiko at the Media Mix Summer Program 2014. See also his subchapter, "Net Democracy," in Kadokawa, *Kuraudo Jidai to "Kūru Kakumei,"* 86.
45 Marc Steinberg has, in this connection, warned of a "platform imperialism" that simply displaces the geopolitical power imbalances found in more traditional transmission models of media onto the level of platform principles. See Steinberg, "Converging Contents and Platforms."
46 Kadokawa, *Gūguru, Appuru ni makenai chosakuken-hō*, 187.
47 Jameson, "The Aesthetics of Singularity," 128.
48 Krämer, "Das Medium als Spur und Apparat," 85.
49 In this vein, Marc Steinberg has analyzed the anime *Tatami Galaxy* as a metacommentary on the media-mix world-creation model. Steinberg, "Condensing the Media Mix."

BIBLIOGRAPHY

Abe, Casio. "Hōga ni Matsuwaru Nikutai-kan" [The sense of flesh related to Japanese film]. In *Nihon Eiga ga Sonzai-suru* [Japanese film exists], 8–18. Tokyo: Seido-sha, 2000.
Abe, Susumu, and Hayashi Kanako. "Ima Ki ni Naru Mini Shiatā" [The minitheaters that are on everyone's mind]. *Kinema Junpō* 892 (August 1984): 40–61.
"The Age of Bedside Cinema!" [Beddo saido shinema jidai!]. *Seijin Eiga* 54 (July 1970): 30–31.
Aida, Toji. "Asakura Daisuke Interview." In *24th Pia Film Festival Catalog*, edited by Kataoka Mayumi, 82–87. Tokyo: Pia Film Festival Office, 2002.
Altman, Rick. "Reusable Packaging: Generic Products and the Recycling Process." In *Refiguring American Film Genres: History and Theory*, edited by Nick Browne, 1–41. Berkeley: University of California Press, 1998.
———. "A Semantic/Syntactic Approach to Film Genre." In *Film Genre Reader II*, edited by Barry Keith Grant, 26–40. Austin: University of Texas Press, 1995.
Anderson, Benedict. *Imagined Communities: Reflections on the Origin and Spread of Nationalism*. London: Verso, 1983.
Anderson, Joseph, and Donald Richie. *The Japanese Film: Art and Industry*. New York: Grove, 1960.
Aoki, Masuo. "Ryoshiki Yajiuma Zoku to 'Yūgai Eiga'" [The commonsense crowd of onlookers and "harmful films"]. In *Pinku Eiga Hakusho*, edited by Shimaji Takamaro, 152–54. Tokyo: Kinema Junpō-sha, 1969.
Aristoteles [Aristotle]. *Poetik*. Stuttgart: Reclam, 1982.
Asada, Akira, and Karatani Kōjin. "Shōwa Seishin-shio Kenshō suru" [Inspecting the psychological history of the Shōwa era]. *Bungeikai*, February 1989, 72–101.
Azuma, Hiroki. *Otaku: Japan's Database Animals*. Translated by Jonathan Abel and Shion Kono. Minneapolis: University of Minnesota Press, 2009.
Bakhtin, Mikhail Mikhailovich. "Forms of Time and Chronotope in the Novel." In *The Dialogic Imagination: Four Essays by M. M. Bakhtin*, edited by Michael Holquist, 84–225. Austin: University of Texas Press, 2006.

Barad, Karen. *Meeting the Universe Halfway*. Durham, NC: Duke University Press, 2007.
Barrett, Gregory. "An Interpretive Biography." In *Currents in Japanese Cinema: Essays*, edited by Satō Tadao, 263–73. Tokyo: Kodansha International, 1987.
Barthes, Roland. "Leaving the Movie Theater." In *The Rustle of Language*, 345–49. New York: Hill and Wang, 1986.
Bataille, Georges. *Eroticism*. London: Penguin, 2001.
Bazin, André. "The Western: Or the American Film Par Excellence." In *What Is Cinema?*, 147–48. Berkeley: University of California Press, 1997.
Beller, Jonathan. *The Cinematic Mode of Production: Attention Economy and the Society of Spectacle*. Hanover, NH: Dartmouth University Press, 2006.
Bernardi, Joanne. *Writing in Light: The Silent Scenario and the Japanese Pure Film Movement*. Detroit, MI: Wayne State University Press, 2001.
Berry, David. "The Postdigital Constellation." In *Postdigital Aesthetics: Art, Computation and Design*, edited by David Berry and Michael Dieter, 44–57. New York: Palgrave Macmillan, 2015.
Berry-Flint, Sarah. "Genre." In *A Companion to Film Theory*, edited by Toby Miller and Robert Stam, 22–44. Malden, U.K.: Blackwell, 1999.
Bordwell, David. *Ozu and the Poetics of Cinema*. London: BFI Publishing, 1988.
Bornhoff, Nicholas. *Pink Samurai*. London: HarperCollins, 1991.
Burch, Noel. *To the Distant Observer: Form and Meaning in the Japanese Cinema*. Berkeley: University of California Press, 1979.
Butler, Judith. *Bodies That Matter: On the Discursive Limits of Sex*. London: Routledge, 1993.
Caldwell, John. "Para-industry: Researching Hollywood's Blackwaters." *Cinema Journal* 52, no. 3 (spring 2013): 157–65.
Cambrosio, Alberto, and Peter Keating. *Biomedical Platforms*. Cambridge, MA: MIT Press, 2006.
Casetti, Francesco. *The Lumière Galaxy: Seven Keywords for the Cinema to Come*. New York: Columbia University Press, 2015.
Cathers, Kirsten. *The Art of Censorship in Postwar Japan*. Honolulu: University of Hawai'i Press, 2012.
Cazdyn, Eric. *The Flash of Capital: Film and Geopolitics in Japan*. Durham, NC: Duke University Press, 2002.
Clark, Bruce, and Mark N. B. Hansen, eds. *Emergence and Embodiment: New Essays on Second-Order Systems Theory*. Durham, NC: Duke University Press, 2009.
Condry, Ian. *The Soul of Anime: Collaborative Creativity and Japan's Media Success Story*. Durham NC: Duke University Press, 2013.
Corrigan, Timothy. "Glancing at the Past: From Vietnam to VCRS." In *A Cinema without Walls: Movies and Culture after Vietnam*, 11–50. New Brunswick, NJ: Rutgers University Press, 1991.
Crom, Louise. "Porno und Apokalypse: Der japanische Film heute." *Merian Japan* 11, no. 36 (1982): 112–13.
Curtin, Michael. *Playing to the World's Biggest Audience: The Globalization of Chinese Film and TV*. Berkeley: University of California Press, 2007.

Desser, David. "Global Noir: Genre Film in the Age of Transnationalism." In *Film Genre Reader III*, edited by Barry Grant, 516–36. Austin: University of Texas Press, 2003.

Doi, Takeo. *Amae no Kōsō* [Anatomy of dependence]. Tokyo: Kōbundō, 1971.

"Dokuritsu Puro mo Taisaku Shugi de Iku" [Independent productions heading for a blockbuster strategy as well]. *Seijin Eiga* 12 (October 1966): 12.

Domenig, Roland. "The Market of Flesh and the Rise of the Pink Film." In *The Pink Book: The Japanese Eroduction and Its Contexts*, edited by Markus Nornes, 17–48. Kinema Club, 2014.

———. "Women in the World of Pink Eiga." Unpublished paper presented at the conference "Female Japanese Filmmakers," University of Colorado, Boulder, October 5–7, 2000.

Eiga Gaidobukku 2001 [Film guidebook]. Tokyo: Chikuma Bunkō, 2001.

Eiga Nenkan [Film yearbook]. Annual publication. Tokyo: Jiji Tsūshin-sha / Jiji Eiga Tsūshin-sha, 1950–2006.

"Eiga Topikku Jānaru" [Film topic journal]. *Kinema Junpō* 1078 (March 1992): 166–67.

Ellis, Richard. "Disseminating Desire: Grove Press and 'The End[s] of Obscenity.'" In *Perspectives on Pornography: Sexuality in Film and Literature*, edited by Gary Day and Clive Bloom, 26–43. New York: St. Martin's, 1988.

"Ero Guro Kara no Dappi o Hakarau: Dokuritsu Pro Daihyō-sha Intabyū 4" [Planning to rid itself of ero-guro: Interviews with the representatives of independent production 4]. *Seijin Eiga* 26 (February 1968): 24–25.

Eto, Jun. *Seijuku to Sōshitsu: Haha no Hōkai* [Maturity and loss: The destruction of the mother]. Tokyo: Kawade Shibō Shin-sha, 1967.

Far Away from the Real: Nihon Eiga Nyū Wevu—"Riaru" no Kanate e. Tokyo: Esquire, 2000.

Foucault, Michel. *The History of Sexuality*, vol. 1: *An Introduction*. New York: Vintage, 1990.

Freeman, Elizabeth. *Time Binds: Queer Temporalities, Queer Histories*. Durham, NC: Duke University Press, 2010.

Friedberg, Anne. "A Denial of Difference: Theories of Cinematic Identification." In *Psychoanalysis and Cinema*, edited by E. Ann Kaplan, 36–45. London: Routledge, 1990.

Fujioka, Shinami. *Eigakan Bangaichi: Yoshiki e no Chōsen* [Outlaw theater: Challenging the common sense]. Tokyo: Noto Insatsu Shuppan Bu, 1998.

Furuhata, Yuriko. *Cinema of Actuality: Japanese Avant-Garde Filmmaking in the Season of Image Politics*. Durham, NC: Duke University Press, 2013.

Genette, Gerard. *Paratexts: Thresholds of Interpretation*. Cambridge: Cambridge University Press, 1997.

Gerow, Aaron. "From Independence to Detachment in Recent Japanese Film." In *Planet Eros: New Japanese Independent Cinema*, edited by Teresa Kwong, 9–12. Hong Kong: Hong Kong International Film Festival, 2002.

———. *Visions of Japanese Modernity: Articulations of Cinema, Nation, and Spectatorship, 1895–1925*. Berkeley: University of California Press, 2010.

Gillespie, Tarleton. "The Politics of 'Platforms.'" *New Media and Society* 12, no. 3 (2012): 347–64.

Gitelman, Lisa, and Geoffrey Pingree, eds. *New Media, 1740–1915*. Cambridge, MA: MIT Press, 2003.

Gledhill, Christine. "Rethinking Genre." In *Reinventing Film Studies*, edited by Christine Gledhill and Linda Williams, 221–43. London: Arnold, 2000.

"'Go-sha no Pinku Kōgeki' Kusokurae!" ["Five [major] company attack" eat shit!]. *Seijin Eiga* 33 (October 1968): 4–9.

Gotō, Bin. "Pinku Eiga Fūzoku-shi: Hito to Jiken" [Pink Film morals' history: People and incidents]. In *Pinku Eiga Hakusho*, edited by Shimaji Takamaro, 134–49. Tokyo: Kinema Junpō-sha, 1969.

———. "'76' Pinku Eiga Sōkatsu." In *Nihon Eiga 1977*, edited by Satō Tadao and Yamane Sadao, 121–23. Tokyo: Haga Shoten, 1977.

Gray, Jonathan. *Show Sold Separately: Promos, Spoilers, and Other Media Paratexts*. New York: New York University Press, 2010.

Hansen, Mark. "New Media." In *Critical Terms for Media Studies*, edited by Mark Hansen and W. J. T. Mitchell, 172–85. Chicago: University of Chicago Press, 2010.

Harootunian, Harry. "Ghostly Comparisons: Anderson's Telescope." *Diacritics* 29, no. 4 (1999): 135–49.

———. *History's Disquiet*. New York: Columbia University Press, 2002.

Haruhiko, Honchi. *Nihon Eiga Posutā-shū: Seijin Eiga-hen* [Japanese film poster collection: Adult film edition]. Tokyo: Wides Shuppan, 2001.

Haskell, Molly. *From Reverence to Rape*. New York: Penguin, 1974.

Hayashi, Sharon. "Traveling Film History: Language and Landscape in the Japanese Cinema, 1931–1945." PhD diss., University of Chicago, 2003.

High, Peter. *The Imperial Screen: Japanese Film Culture in the Fifteen Years' War, 1931–1945*. Madison: University of Wisconsin Press, 2003.

Higuchi, Naofumi. *Suna no Utsuwa to Nihon Chinbotsu: 70-Nendai Nihon no Chō Taisaku Eiga—Japanese Blockbuster Movies of the 70s*. Tokyo: Chikuma Shobō, 2004.

Hirano, Kyoko. *Mr. Smith Goes to Tokyo: Japanese Cinema under the American Occupation, 1945–52*. Washington, DC: Smithsonian Institution Press, 1992.

"Hitori heikin firumu 5 hon o torimakutta ga, gōkan toka rezu scene toka iroiro ate, daikōhyō." *Seijin Eiga* 84 (January 1973): 38–39.

Hunt, Lynn. "Introduction." In *The Invention of Pornography: Obscenity and the Origins of Modernity, 1500–1800*, edited by Lynn Hunt, 9–45. New York: Zone, 1993.

Igarashi, Yoshikuni. *Bodies of Memory: Narratives of War in Postwar Japanese Culture, 1945–1970*. Princeton, NJ: Princeton University Press, 2000.

Ishiro, Toshirō. "Memeshiki Eizō Ronsha-tachi" [Cowardly theorists of the image]. In *Gensō to Seiji no Aida: Gendai Nihon Eiga-ron Taikei 5* [Between illusion and politics: Modern Japanese film theory compendium 5], edited by Ogawa Tōru, 411–18. Tokyo: Tōju-sha, 1971. Originally printed in *Eiga Geijutsu* (November 1966).

Itō, Katsuo. *B-kyū Bideo Hakkutsu Kataroggu* [B-level video excavation catalog]. Tokyo: Seikyū-sha, 1988.

Iwao, S., et al. "Japanese and U.S. Media: Some Cross-Cultural Insights into TV Violence." *Journal of Communication* 31 (1981): 28–36.

Izbicki, Joanne. "The Shape of Freedom: The Female Body in Post-surrender Japanese Cinema." *U.S.-Japan Women's Journal* 12 (January 1997): 103–53.

Jameson, Fredric. "The Aesthetics of Singularity." *New Left Review* 92 (March/April 2015): 101–32.

———. "The End of Temporality." *Critical Inquiry* 29, no. 4 (summer 2003): 695–718.

Jordheim, Helge. "Against Periodization: Koselleck's Theory of Multiple Temporalities." *History and Theory* 51 (May 2012): 151–71.

Kadokawa, Haruki. "Kamui No Ken." In *Shisha Shitsu no Isu*, 266–75. Tokyo: Kadokawa Shoten, 1985.

———. "Satomi Hakken-den." In *Shisha Shitsu no Isu*, 202–9. Tokyo: Kadokawa Shoten, 1985.

———. *Waga Tōsō* [My struggle]. Tokyo: East Press, 2005.

Kadokawa, Tsuguhiko. *Gūguru, Appuru ni Makenai Chōsakuken-hō* [A copyright law that won't lose against Google and Apple]. Tokyo: Kadokawa, 2013.

———. *Kuraudo Jidai to "Kūru Kakumei"* [The age of the cloud and the "Cool Revolution"]. Tokyo: Kadokawa Wan Tēma 21, 2010.

"'Kadokawa Eiga' Stāto" ["Kadokawa Films" starts]. *Kinema Junpō* 690 (September 1976).

"'Kadokawa' Tataki, Soshite Yurimodoshi" ["Kadokawa" bashing and the backlash]. *Eiga Geijutsu* 370 (winter 1994): 5–26.

Kanehara, Ichi. "Orijinaru Bideo Mūbii: Meatarashii Ugoki mo Naku, Jūrai Rosen o Keishō" [Original video movie: No new activity, the usual lines are inherited]. In *Eiga Gaidobukku 2001*, 362–63. Tokyo: Chikuma Bunko, 2001.

Kawabata, Yasuo, and Kawachi Akira. "Nihon Eiga—Gaikoku Eiga Gyōkai Sōkessan: Keiei/Seisaku/Haikyū/Kōgyō no Subete" [Japanese film—foreign film business final accounts]. *Kinema Junpō* 1477 (February 2007): 186.

Kawasaki, Hiroshi. "Sukuriin Gyaru—Aidoru Eiga wa, Nihon Eiga no Saizenei o Shissō Suru Shigekiteki na Rosen na no de Aru" [Screen girl—idol films are the impulse-giving line of films rushing along at the very forefront of Japanese film]. *Image Forum* 57 (June 1985): 46–51.

Kawashima, Nobuko. "Desuku Nikki." *Seijin Eiga* 34 (November 1968): 29.

"Keisatsu Kenryoku e no Hangyaku no Merodi" [The melody of resistance against police power]. *Seijin Eiga* 84 (January 1973): 12–15.

Kinejun Eiga Bideo Iyābukku [Film and Video Yearbook]. Tokyo: Kinema Junpō-sha, 1990–99.

Kiridōshi, Risaku. "Poruno Eiga ga Sekai o Koroshitai Nara" [If porn films wanted to kill the world]. *Sei Media no 50-nen: Bessatsu Takarajima* 240 (1995): 111–22.

"Kitano Takeshi ga Kuruma kara Dete Kita Toki, Kono Hito wa Kantoku Dekiruna, to Omotte Shimatta" [When Kitano Takeshi got out of the car, I thought, this person can be a director]. In "Nihon Eiga no Shinjin Kantoku Chizu Shiriizu 5: 'Igyō-shū Kantoku' to wa Nani-ka?" [Japanese Film New Directors Map Series part 5: What is a nonbusiness director?]. *Kinema Junpō* 1075 (February 1992): 133–36.

Klopfenstein, Bruce C. "The Diffusion of the VCR in the United States." In *The VCR Age: Home Video and Mass Communication*, edited by Mark R. Levy, 21–39. London: Sage, 1989.

Kobayashi, Masaru. "Erotishizumu to Ero Rearu Eiga" [Eroticism and erotic-realism films]. In "Ai to Erotishizumu Joshoku Shinario Shū Kinema Junpō Bessatsu" [Love and eroticism: Female charm script collection], special issue, *Kinema Junpō* 2032 (July 1967): 98–101.

Koselleck, Reinhart. *Zeitschichten: Studien zur Historik* [Time layers: Studies on historiography]. Frankfurt: Suhrkamp, 2000.

Krämer, Sybille. "Das Medium als Spur und als Apparat" [The medium as trace and apparatus]. In *Medien, Computer, Realität. Wirklichkeitsvorstellungen und Neue Medien* [Media, computers, reality: New media and the imagining of reality], 73–94. Frankfurt: Suhrkamp, 1998.

Kubo, Masatoshi. "From Film to Video: How Japanese TV Found Its Niche in the Society of Visual Media." In *Japanese Civilization in the Modern World XIV: Information and Communication*, edited by Umesao Tadao, William W. Kelly, and Kubo Masatoshi, 77–103. Osaka: National Museum of Ethnology, 2000.

Kuwahara, Ietoshi. *Kirareta Waisetsu: Eirin Katto-shi* [Edited obscenity: A history of Eirin cuts]. Tokyo: Yomiuri Shinbun-sha, 1993.

Lamarre, Thomas. *The Anime Machine: A Media Theory of Animation*. Minneapolis: University of Minnesota Press, 2009.

Langford, Larry. *Fiction and the Social Contract*. New York: P. Lang, 1998.

Lazzarato, Maurizio. "Struggle, Event, Media." Republic Art, May 2003. http://www.republicart.net/disc/representations/lazzarato01_en.htm.

Lim, Bliss Cua. *Translating Time: Cinema, the Fantastic, and Temporal Critique*. Durham, NC: Duke University Press, 2009.

Manovich, Lev. *The Language of New Media*. Cambridge, MA: MIT Press, 2002.

———. "Postmedia Aesthetics." In *Transmedia Frictions: The Digital, the Arts, and the Humanities*, edited by Marsha Kinder and Tara McPherson, 34–44. Berkeley: University of California Press, 2014.

Marcuse, Herbert. *Eros and Civilization*. New York: Vintage, 1962.

Marlow, Eugene, and Eugene Secunda. *Shifting Time and Space: The Story of Videotape*. Westport, CT: Praeger, 1991.

Maruyama, Kazuaki. *Sekai ga Chūmoku Suru Nihon Eiga no Henyō* [The transformation of Japanese film that the world is taking note of]. Tokyo: Soshisha, 1998.

Maruyama, Masao. "Denken in Japan." In *Nihon no Shisō*, translated into German by Wolfgang Schamoni, 21–88. Frankfurt: Suhrkamp, 1988.

———. "Nikutai Bungaku kara Nikutai Seiji Made" [From literature of the flesh to politics of the flesh]. In *Maruyama Masao shū* [Maruyama Masao collection], vol. 4, 207–27. Tokyo: Iwanami Shoten, 1995.

Masubuchi, Takeshi. *B Kyū Eiga: Firumu no Ura Made* [B-level films: To the underside of film]. Tokyo: Heibon-sha, 1986.

Masumura, Yasuzō. "Supīdo ni Tsuite." *Shinario* 14, no. 2 (1958): 20–24.

Matsuda, Masao. "Media Kakumei no tame no Akushisu" [The axis for a media revolution]. In *"Hyōgen" kara "Media" e*, 51–60. Tokyo: Bijutsu Techō, 1973.

———. "Wakai Sedai no Eiga Shisō." *Shinario* 12 (1976): 44–49.

Matsushima, Toshiyuki. "Sengo no Dokuritsu Puro, Soshite Kadokawa Eiga" [The postwar independents, and then Kadokawa film]. In *Mainichi Gurafu Bessatsu "Nihon Eiga 40 Nen,"* March 1986, 144–46.

McDonald, Keiko. *From Book to Screen: Modern Japanese Literature in Film*. Armonk, NY: M. E. Sharpe, 2000.

McGray, Douglas. "Japan's Gross National Cool." *Foreign Policy* 130 (May 2002): 44–54.

Miyadai, Shinji. *Owari Naki Nichijō o Ikiro: Aumu Kanzen Kokofuku Manyuaru*. Tokyo: Chikuma Shoten, 1998.

Miyao, Daisuke. *Sessue Hayakawa: Silent Cinema and Transnational Stardom*. Durham, NC: Duke University Press, 2007.

Miyoshi, Masao. *Off Center: Power and Culture Relations between Japan and the United States*. Cambridge, MA: Harvard University Press, 1991.

Mizuno, Haruo. *Bideo de Miru Hyappon No Yōga* [100 foreign films to watch on video]. Tokyo: PHP Kenkyū-sho, 1992.

Morikawa, Kaichirō. *Shuto no Tanjō: Moeru Toshi Akihabara* [Learning from Akihabara: The birth of a personapolis]. Tokyo: Gentosha, 2003.

Mulvey, Laura. "Visual Pleasure and Narrative Cinema." *Screen* 16, no. 3 (autumn 1975): 6–18.

Muñoz, José Esteban. *Disidentifications: Queers of Color and the Performance of Politics*. Minneapolis: University of Minnesota Press, 1999.

Murai, Minoru. *Boku no Pinku Eiga-shi: Hadaka no Munendaiki* [My Pink Film history: A naked dream chronicle]. Tokyo: Yamato Shōbō, 1989.

———, ed. *Dokyumento Seijin Eiga: Shinetopia 10/15* [Document adult film: Cinetopia]. Tokyo: Million Shuppan, 1978.

———, "5-sha o Obiyakasu 300 Man Yen Eiga" [The 3-million-yen films that are threatening the 5 (major) companies]. In *Pinku Eiga Hakusho*, edited by Shimaji Takamaro, 93–95. Tokyo: Kinema Junpō-sha, 1969.

Nakamura, Hideyuki. *Eizō/Gensetsu no Bunkashakaigaku* [Cultural sociology of images and discourse: Film noir and modernity]. Tokyo: Iwanami Shoten, 2003.

Nakamura, Hogaru. *Nihon Bideo Sofuto-shi* [The history of video software in Japan]. Tokyo: Eizōshinbunsha, 1996.

"Nama no Hakuryoku! Pinku Jitsuen" [Raw impact! Pink jitsuen]. *Seijin Eiga* 38 (March 1969): 4–7.

Naoki, Sanjūgo. "Nihon Eiga Oyobi Eigakai" [Japanese film and film world]. In *Naoki Sanjūgo Zenshū* 21, 208–16. Tokyo: Jijinsha, 1991.

Neale, Steve. "Melo Talk: On the Meaning and Use of the Term 'Melodrama' in the American Trade Press." *The Velvet Light Trap* 32 (fall): 66–89.

Newman, Michael. *Video Revolutions: On the History of a Medium*. New York: Columbia University Press, 2014.

"1992 O-shōgatsu Mini Theater Eiga Tokushū" [1992 New Year's Day minitheater special]. *Kinema Junpō* 1071 (December 1991): 14–25.

"90-nen Eiga-kai 10 Dai-nyūsu Senshutsu" [Top ten news of the year 1990]. *Kinema Junpō* 1052 (February 1991): 108–9.

Noda, Masanori. "'Zen Media e Shinshutsu' o Gōgo Suru Kadokawa Haruki no Yabō" [The ambition of Kadokawa Haruki, who boasts of "advance into all media"]. *Tsukuru*, January 1983, 56–65.

Nomura, Masaaki. "Eiga-kai o Kassei-ka Saseta Oni-ko ni Jujitsu" [The changeling that revitalized the film world]. *Kinema Junpō* 1117 (October 1993): 58–63.

———. *Kaikan! Bideo Kyō Jidai* [Buying feeling! The age of video craze]. Tokyo: Rikurūto Shuppan, 1991.

Nornes, Markus. *Forest of Pressure: Ogawa Shinsuke and Postwar Japanese Documentary*. Minneapolis: University of Minnesota Press, 2007.

———, ed. *The Pink Book: The Japanese Eroduction and Its Contexts*. Kinema Club, 2014.

"Nugi Nugi Būmu de Kasegimakuru Tōei/Nikkatsu" [Tōei and Nikkatsu earn big money with the nudity boom]. *Seijin Eiga* 30 (July 1968): 5–11.

Ōbayashi, Nobuhiko. "Boku no Kadokawa Eiga-Dansō" [My Kadokawa Film fragments]. *Eiga Geijutsu* 370 (winter 1994): 34.

Oda, Katsuya. "Adabana wa Mankai da ga . . ." In *Nihon Eiga 1979*, edited by Satō Tadao and Yamane Sadao. Tokyo: Haga Shoten, 1979.

———. "Fukyō no Tanima ni Saku Pinku Eiga" [The Pink films that bloom in the valley of depression]. In *Nihon Eiga 1976*, edited by Satō Tadao and Yamane Sadao, 120–23. Tokyo: Haga Shoten, 1976.

———. "Pinku no Guerilla-sei no Genkai." In *Nihon Eiga 1980*, edited by Satō Tadao and Yamane Sadao. Tokyo: Haga Shoten, 1980.

"Okashitakunaru yō na 'sumashita joyū.'" [An actress so prim it makes you want to rape her]. *Seijin Eiga* 80 (September 1972): 30.

Ōkura, Mitsugi. "Ōkura, Mitsugi: Gendai Shakai no Chinseizai" [Contemporary society's tranquilizer]. In *Pinku Eiga Hakusho*, edited by Shimaji Takamaro, 26–28. Tokyo: Kinema Junpō-sha, 1969.

Ōtake, Hirō. *Nihon Eiga Gyakuten no Shinario* [Japanese film: A reverse scenario]. Tokyo: Wave Shuppan, 2000.

Ōtsuka, Eiji. *"Hoshi no Koe" o Kike* [Listen to the "voices from a distant star"]. Tokyo: Tokuma Shoten, 2002.

———. "Kigyō ni Kanri Sareru Kaiteki na Posutomodan no Tame no Essei" [An essay for the cozy postmodern(s) controlled by corporations]. *Saizensen*, May 2014.

———. *Kyarakutā Shōsetsu no Tsukurikata* [How to create a character novel]. Tokyo: Sekaisha Shinsho, 2013.

———. *Mediamikkusu-ka Suru Nihon* [A media-mix-izing Japan]. Tokyo: East Shinsho, 2014.

———. *Otaku no Seishin-shi: 1980-nendai Ron* [History of Otaku psychology: A theory of the 1980s]. Tokyo: Kodansha, 2004.

"Pinku Eiga-kai ni mo Oshiyoseta Gebaruto Kakumei no Namikaze!" [The storm of gebaruto revolution that has rolled over the Pink Film world!]. *Seijin Eiga* 42 (July 1969): 4–9.

"Pinku Eiga o Yokodori Shita Nikkatsu / Daiei no Kontan" [Nikkatsu that shoots Pink films on the side / Daiei's ulterior motives]. *Seijin Eiga* 32 (September 1968): 4.

"Pinku Eiga Tsūshin: Hadaka wa Honmono de Ikō yo!" [Pink Film report: In nudity, let's go with the real thing!]. *Seijin Eiga* 9 (September 1965): 18.

"Pinku Joyū no Butai Shinshutsu!!" [Pink actresses forge onto the stage!!]. *Seijin Eiga* 8 (April 1966): 38–39.

Pizer, John David. *The Historical Perspective in German Genre Theory: Its Development from Gottsched to Hegel*. Stuttgart: Hans-Dieter Heinz Akademischer Verlag Stuttgart, 1985.

Rancière, Jacques. "The Distribution of the Sensible: Politics and Aesthetics." In *The Politics of Aesthetics: The Distribution of the Sensible*, 7–46. London: Continuum, 2006.

Richie, Donald. *100 Years of Japanese Film*. Tokyo: Kodansha, 2002.

Rodowick, David. *The Virtual Life of Film*. Cambridge, MA: Harvard University Press, 2007.

Rohy, Valerie. "Ahistorical." GLQ 12, no. 1 (2006): 61–83.

Rosen, Philip. *Change Mummified: Cinema, Historicity, Theory*. Minneapolis: University of Minnesota Press, 2001.

"Ryūdō Suru Eigakai: 76 Nen o Kaiko Suru: Kawabata Kaichō no Jitsugen kara Kadokawa Shoten no Nagurikomi Sakusen made" [The film world in flux: Looking back at 1976: From the realization of chairman Kawabata to Kadokawa Shoten's assault strategy]. *Eiga Jihou* 249 (December 1976): 13.

Sano, Shinichi. *Nihon Eiga wa, Ima* [Japanese film, now]. Tokyo: TBS Buritanika, 1996.

Satō, Tadao. *Currents in Japanese Cinema*. Translated by Gregory Barrett. Tokyo: Kodansha International, 1987.

———. "Dokuritsu Puro no Eiga" [Films produced by independents]. In *Nihon Eiga Sengo Ōgon Jidai 7: Dokuritsu Puro* [The golden age of postwar Japanese film 7: Independent production], edited by Sengō Nihon Eiga Kenkyūkai, 186–99. Society for the Study of Postwar Japanese Film. Tokyo: Nihon Bukku Raiburarii, 1978.

———. "Nikkatsu Eiga Zenshi" [A complete history of Nikkatsu films]. *Kinema Junpō* 845 (October 1982): 27–32.

Schlegel, Friedrich. *434. Athenaeum Fragment*. Cited in *Genres in Discourse*, by Tzvetan Todorov. Cambridge: Cambridge University Press, 1990.

Scholz, Trebor, ed. *Digital Labor: The Internet as Playground and Factory*. New York: Routledge, 2013.

Sedgwick, Eve Kosofsky. *The Epistemology of the Closet*. Berkeley: University of California Press, 1990.

Sharp, Jasper. *Historical Dictionary of Japanese Film*. Plymouth, U.K.: Scarecrow, 2011.

Shigemasa, Takafumi. *Katte ni Eiga-shō/kō* [Writings and thoughts on film by my own convenience]. Tokyo: Matsumoto Kōbō, 1997.

Shimaji, Takamaro, ed. *Pinku Eiga Hakusho*. Tokyo: Kinema Junpō-sha, 1969.

Shindō, Kaneto. *Tsuinōsha-tachi: Eiga no Reddopāji* [The ones who had to pay additionally: Film's red purge]. Tokyo: Iwanami Shoten, 1996.

Shindō, Takae. "Ningen Fuzai o Hansei Shiyō" [Let's search our conscience on the absence of humans]. *Seijin Eiga* 3 (March 1966): 36–37.

Shinoda, Hiroyuki. "Media Mikkusu Kushi Shita Sofuto Bijinesu no Jittai" [The real circumstances of the soft business that made free use of media mix]. *Tsukuru*, February 1991, 98–111.

Shiozawa, Minobu. "Kadokawa Shoten to Yokomizo Seishi no 'Yattsu Haka Mura'" [Kadokawa Shoten and Yokomizo Seishi's "Village of Eight Gravestones"]. *Ryūdō*, November 1979, 260–72.

Shiozawa, Shigeru. "Ugokihajimeta Bideo Sangyō no Genjō Sōtenken" [A summary inspection of the emerging video business]. *Kinema Junpō* 527 (July 1970): 146.

Silverberg, Miriam. *Erotic Grotesque Nonsense: The Mass Culture of Modern Times*. Berkeley: University of California Press, 2009.

Simmel, Georg. *Philosophische Kultur* [Philosophical culture]. Leipzig: Alfred Kröhner, 1919.

Slaymaker, Douglas. *The Body in Postwar Japanese Fiction*. London: Routledge, 2004.

Steinberg, Marc. *Anime's Media Mix: Franchising Toys and Characters in Japan*. Minneapolis: University of Minnesota Press, 2012.

———. "Condensing the Media Mix: Tatami Galaxy's Multiple Possible Worlds." *Canadian Journal of Film Studies* 21, no. 2 (fall 2012): 71–92.

———. "Converging Contents and Platforms: Niconico Video and Japan's Media Mix Ecology." In *Asian Video Cultures: In the Penumbra of the Global*, edited by Joshua Neves and Bhaskar Sarkar. Durham, NC: Duke University Press, 2017.

———. *Naze Nihon wa "Media Mikkusu Suru Kuni" na no ka* [Why is Japan a "media-mixing nation"?]. Translated by Nakagawa Yusuru, supervised by Otsuka Eiji. Tokyo: Kadokawa E-Pub / Kadokawa Gakugei Shuppan, 2015.

———. "Platform Producer Meet Game Master: On the Conditions for the Media Mix." In *World Building: Transmedia, Fans, Industries*, edited by Marta Boni, Martin Lefebvre, and Marc Steinberg. Amsterdam: Amsterdam University Press, 2017.

Suga, Hidemi. "Imēji Tsuijūsha-tachi no Gukō" [The folly of the image imitators]. *Eiga Geijutsu* 370 (winter 1994): 27–29.

———. "Kaijū (Gojira) To Joyū: Kadokawa Eiga Ron" [Monsters/Godzilla and actresses: Kadokawa Film theory]. *Eiga Geijutsu* 349 (August–October 1984): 13–18.

Suzuki, Yoshiaki. *Pinku Eiga Suikoden: Sono Nijūnen-shi* [Pink Film outlaws of the marsh: The twenty-year history]. Osaka: Seishin-sha, 1983.

Tabb, William. *The Postwar Japanese System: Cultural Economy and Economic Transformation*. New York: Oxford University Press, 1995.

"Taidan Kadokawa Haruki to Yamane Sadao" [Talk between Kadokawa Haruki and Yamane Sadao]. *Kinema Junpō* 935 (May 1986): 76–83.

Takahashi, Eiichi. "Go-sha no Shijō o Doko Made Kutte Iru Ka" [To what degree are they eating the majors' market?]. In *Pinku Eiga Hakusho*, edited by Shimaji Takamaro, 189–95. Tokyo: Kinema Junpō-sha, 1969.

———. "Haikyū Men wa dō Natte Iru ka" [What about the distribution side?]. In *Pinku Eiga Hakusho*, edited by Shimaji Takamaro, 166–77. Tokyo: Kinema Junpō-sha, 1969.

Takamura, Eiji. "Japanese Film World Rises Again." *Kinema Junpō Tokyo Int'l Film Festival Edition Movie Marketing in Asia* 1, no. 4 (October 24, 2004): 1.

Tamaki, Katori. "Nihon Sekusupuroitēshon Eiga Kōbō-shi 1: Nihon de Saishō no Pinku Joyū ni Kiku, Shōwa Sanjūnendai Ero Eiga no Akebono" [The history of the rise of

Japanese exploitation film 1: Asking the first Pink Film actress, the dawn of the erotic film of the Shōwa 30s]. *Eiga Hihō* 90 (April 2007): 80–83.

Tanaka, Jun'ichirō. *Nihon Eiga Hattatsu-shi III* [The history of developments in Japanese film III]. Tokyo: Chūō Kōron-sha, 1976.

———. *Nihon Eiga Hattatsu-shi IV* [The history of developments in Japanese film IV]. Tokyo: Chūō Kōron-sha, 1976.

———. *Nihon Eiga Hattatsu-shi V* [The history of developments in Japanese film V]. Tokyo: Chūō Kōron-sha, 1976.

Tanaka, Stefan. *New Times in Modern Japan*. Princeton, NJ: Princeton University Press, 2009.

Tanioka, Masaki. *Kingu obu V-Shinema* [King of V-Cinema]. Tokyo: Ohta, 2002.

———. *V-Shinema Damashi: Ni-sen-bon no Doshaburi o Itsukushimi* [V-Cinema soul: Affection for a downpour of 2000 films]. Tokyo: Yotusya Round, 1999.

"Throw Away the Rope, Whip, and Knife!" *Seijin Eiga* 23 (November 1967): 4–6.

Todorov, Tzvetan. *Einführung in die fantastische Literatur*. Frankfurt: Ullstien, 1975.

Toyoshi, Ōguro, and Oshikawa Yoshiyuki. "Satō Junya Kantoku no 'Ningen no Shōmei'" [Director Satō Junya's "Proof of the Man"]. *Kinema Junpō* 721 (November 1977): 142–43.

Ueno, Kōshi. *Nikutai no Jidai* [The age of flesh]. Tokyo: Gendai Shokan, 1989.

Video Club Xanadeux: Bideo Chimanako Watching [Frenzied video watching]. Tokyo: Jitsugyōshi Nihon-sha, 1988.

Wakita, Yoshihiko. "Kadokawa Haruki Intabyū: Harada Tomyo wa Masashiku Tensai Shōjo Da." *Kinema Junpō* 890 (July 1984): 48.

———. "Kono Eiga Wa Zen-Enshuttsu-ka, Kankyaku ni Tai Suru Ore no Chōsenjō Da!!" [This film is my challenge to all directors and the audience!!]. *Kinema Junpō* 850 (December 1982): 90–94.

Wasser, Frederick. *Veni, Vidi, Video: The Hollywood Empire and the VCR*. Austin: University of Texas Press, 2001.

Williams, Alan. "Is a Radical Genre Criticism Possible?" *Quarterly Review of Film Studies* 9, no. 2 (spring 1984): 121–25.

Woolf, Virginia. *A Room of One's Own*. Guelph, ON: Broadview, 2001.

Wright, Will. *Sixguns and Society: A Structural Study of the Western*. Berkeley: University of California Press, 1975.

Yamada, Kazuo. *Nihon Eiga no 80 Nen* [80 years of Japanese film]. Tokyo: Isei-sha, 1976.

Yamada, Keizō. "Kōgyō Men wa dō Natte Iru no ka" [What about the exhibition side?]. In *Pinku Eiga Hakusho*, edited by Shimaji Takamaro, 178–88. Tokyo: Kinema Junpō-sha, 1969.

Yamakita, Shinji. *Kadokawa Haruki no Kōzai: Shuppankai—Eigakai o Yurugaseta Otoko* [Kadokawa Haruki's merits and demerits: The man who shook the publishing and film world]. Tokyo: Tokyo Keizai, 1993.

Yamamoto, Naoki. *Realities That Matter: The Development of Realist Film Theory and Practice in Japan, 1895–1945*. Ann Arbor: UMI, 2012.

Yamane, Sadao. "Kimyō na Ikimono ga Katsugeki o Yomigaeraseta" [A strange creature has resurrected the katsugeki]. In *Eiga no Katachi*, 154–68. Tokyo: Misuzu Shobo, 1996.

———. "Taishū no Yokubō to Eiga no Hihan" [The desire of the public and film criticism]. In *Gendai Nihon Eiga-ron Taikei: Tochaku to Kindai no Sōkoku* [Contemporary Japanese film discourse outline: The friction between nativity and modernity], edited by Ogawa Tōru, 548–62. Tokyo: Tōjusha, 1966.

———. "Tōei V-Shinema no Kanōsei" [Tōei V-Cinema's potential]. In *Nihon Eiga Jihyō '89–'92: Eiga wa Doko e Iku Ka* [Japanese film review '89–'92: Where is film going?], 58–68. Tokyo: Chikuma Shobo, 1993.

Yoda, Tomiko. "The Rise and Fall of Maternal Society: Gender, Labor, and Capital in Contemporary Japan." *South Atlantic Quarterly* 99, no. 4 (fall 2000): 865–902.

Yodogawa, Nagaharu. *Yōga Bideo De Mitai Besuto 150* [150 best foreign films you want to see on video]. Tokyo: Nihon Bungei-sha, 1992.

Yomota, Inuhiko. *Kawaii-ron* [Theory of Kawaii]. Tokyo: Chikuma Shinsho, 2006.

———. *Nihon no Joyū*. Tokyo: Iwanami Shoten, 2000.

Yoshiko, Minami. "Ōguro Toyoshi Sensei e" [To Ōguro Toyoshi Sensei]. *Kinema Junpō* 723 (December 1977): 58.

Yoshimoto, Mitsuhiro. *Kurosawa: Film Studies and Japanese Cinema*. Durham, NC: Duke University Press, 2000.

———. "Melodrama, Postmodernism and the Japanese Cinema." *East/West Film Journal* 5, no. 1 (January 1991): 28–55.

"Zadankai—Sutāto Shita Bideo Rentaru Jidai" [Roundtable discussion—the emerging age of video rental]. *Kinema Junpō* 889 (July 1984): 184–89.

Zielinski, Siegfried. *Zur Geschichte des Videorecorders* [The history of the video recorder]. Berlin: Wissenschaftsverlag Spiess, 1986.

INDEX

Abe Casio, 96–98, 123
Abe Shinzō, 213
Ace Pictures, 147
actors: Japanese, 44, 87; non-Japanese, 88; in Pink Film, 40, 57, 72; policies for, 59; scholarly focus on, 14
Adachi Masao, 56–57
Adachi Yumi, 136, 145
Adult Video Regulations Autonomous Round Table, 166–68. *See also* Biderin
advance tickets: financing, 115, 117; sales, 114; system, 117, 142–43, 145, 206
Adventure of Kōsuke Kindaichi, The (film), 119–20
Adventures of Miles and Otis, The (film), 143
Adventures of Sir Puss-in-the-Boots, The (film), 144
advertising: campaigns, 115, 117; culture, 21; Kadokawa, 103, 106–7
Affairs within Walls (film), 42, 44, 48–50, 57, 68
Afternoon When Flowers Fell (film), 139, 142
age, significance of, 129
Agency for Cultural Affairs, 214–15
Age of the Cloud and the "Cool Revolution," The (book), 210
Aikawa Shō, 180, 182, 188
AKA Serial Killer (film), 220
Akunin Senyō (film), 159
Akuryo Island (film), 114, 140

All under the Moon (film), 141
Althusser, Louis, 223
Altman, Rick, 8, 11
AMC, 206
Ampex, 167
Anchor Films, 196
Anderson, Benedict, 17
Anderson, Joseph, 21
Andō Mitsuru, 187
angura, 56–57
animation: animated film, 14, 137; Disney, 144; history, in Japan, 211; industry, 209, 211; Kadokawa, 147–48; trends in, 141, 178
anime, 2, 115–16, 130, 198; characters, 143; fans and, 198, 213; films, 166; impact of, 191; industry, 7; Kadokawa, 132, 139, 148; in media mix, 211–12; perception of, 213; in popular culture, 196, 216; popularity, 15; scholarship, 14, 209; screening practices, 139; spaces for, 76; trends in, 132; video and, 166, 169, 201
Anno Hideaki, 130, 147
Antarctica (film), 117, 143
Aoki Masuo, 35
Aoyama Misa, 82
Aoyama Shinji, 30, 161
Arai Haruhiko, 56, 120, 123
Arata Masao, 44
Argo Project, 141
Art Theatre Guild, 42, 55, 93, 101, 161

Asada Akira, 153–54
Asahi Shinbun (newspaper) 51, 104, 141, 147
Asian Pacific Film Festival, 144
Aso Tarō, 213–14, 216–21, 223
Astro Boy: character, 107; series, 116, 166, 216
At Some Point Somebody Will Be Killed (film), 114
audience, 4–5, 9, 12–16, 21; advance-ticket system and, 117; Euro-American, 123; formation of, 50; identification, 78–79; Kadokawa and, 106–8, 212; for Kadokawa Films, 122, 136; in media ecology, 197; numbers, 15, 26; perception of, 115; for Pink Film, 13, 29, 56, 61, 63–65, 74, 91; segmentation, 65, 111, 171; trends, 55, 66, 72, 96–97, 135, 139, 158–59, 172; youth, 65, 87–89, 132
Aum Shinrikyō, 181
auteurs, 44, 161; auteurism, 21, 125, 165; films, 55
AV (adult video): films, 173; genre, 169–70; market, 174, 196; section, 196; V-Cinema and, 192
Azabu (company), 200
Azuma Hiroki, 202

Baba Yasuo, 141
Back to the Future (film), 156
bakeneko film, 10
Bakhtin, Mikhail, 208
Balzac, Honoré de, 183
Bandai, 141, 163, 173, 191
Barad, Karen, 2
Barazoku, 65
Barcelona Olympics, 144
Barthes, Roland, 6
Battles without Honor and Humanity (series), 182–83
Bazin, André, 10–11
Beast to Die, The (film), 120, 131
Beautiful Mystery (film), 12
Beller, Jonathan, 218
Bender, Erich, 88
Benjamin, Walter, 170
Bergman, Ingmar, 48

Berlin International Film Festival, 42, 44, 48–49
Bernardi, Joanne, 217
Berry, David, 28
Bessatsu Naigai Jitsuwa (magazine), 25
Besson, Luc, 145
Betamax: recorders, 154, 167; tapes, 16
B-films: aesthetic, 196; American, 152; in Japan, 89, 158
Biderin, 167–69
Big Breast Hunter (film), 158
Billionaire, A (film), 53
Bizarre Experience: Wet Dream (film), 132
Black Princess—Angel from Hell (film), 158, 160
Black Rain (film), 105
Black Snow (film), 42, 44–50, 68, 75, 87
Blade of Kamui, The (film), 137
Blair, Tony, 215
Blind Spot of Peeping, The (film), 168
block-booking system, 55, 105, 115–17, 145, 163
blockbuster: advance-ticket system and, 117; budget, 104, 122; history, 116–17; Kadokawa and, 98, 111–13, 123, 126, 145; mentality, 115; perception of, 185; production, 134; realm, 104; screenings and, 141; strategy, 60, 83, 103, 118–20, 142–43
Blondie (serials), 217
Bloodbath Will Come (film series), 178
Blowback (film), 158
Blue Assault: Document of Abnormal Experience (film), 12
blue film, 33–34, 67
Blue Film Woman (film), 78
Blue Jeans Memory (film), 140
Blue Ribbon Award, 34
body: centrality of, 73; discourses of, 36–38; nation and, 77; politicization of, 38; as site, 37
Bordwell, David, 14
Boy (film), 35
broadcasters, 15; policies for, 59
Broccoli (company), 213
Brunetière, Ferdinand, 19

bubble: collapse, 185, 189; economy, 143, 145, 153, 172; era, 155–56, 174–75, 192, 202; video, 192
Bullet Train (film), 116
bunkobon (paperbacks), 100
Burch, Noel, 14
Burlesque in Japan—a Fairytale of the Night (film), 166
Burlesque in Japan—the Fantasy of Woman (film), 166
Butler, Judith, 28, 79
Butoh, 57

Cabaret (film), 130, 134
Caldwell, John, 9
Cannes International Film Festival, 1, 15, 144, 198
Capital City High Speed Trial 2 (film), 158
capitalism: commodity, 94; consumer society and, 41; desire and, 39; discourses of, 28; gender and, 76–78; history of, 8, 15, 17; in Japan, 29; Kadokawa and, 109; modes of, 14; presentation of, 37; temporality and, 18
Captain Tsubasa: character, 216; series, 216
Carlino, Lewis John, 145
Casetti, Francesco, 20–21
Castle of Sand (film), 116
Cathay, 144
CBS/Sony, 141
censorship, 68; debates on, 40; political, 47; strategies for, 74; wartime, 36, 52
Century Eiga, 43
chain drama, 73
characters, 2; in Kadokawa Film, 98, 120–21; in media mix, 102; in popular culture, 125–26, 132. See also *kyara*
Cherry Orchard, The (film), 141
chihō: discourses of, 60, 65–67; exhibitions in, 119, 139; movement to/from, 66, 72–73; *shinecon*, 206–7; theaters and, 61, 66, 92
chikan (groper): film, 9, 195; as subgenre, 30, 67, 92
Christian the Second Time Around (film), 140

CIC (distributor), 100
CIC Victor, 169, 192
cinema: American, 6; approaches to, 10, 16, 21, 23, 156; as art, 1–3; art house, 42, 44, 171; cinematic spaces, 98; cinematic traditions, 183; end of, 20–21, 222; eroticism, 40; hierarchies in, 107, 217; history of, 9; Hollywood, 7, 10; Japanese, 13–15, 20–21, 23, 77, 99, 143, 198; media ecology and, 3, 180; models, 179; perception of, 91; spectatorship, 218; temporality, 154; theater, 50, 139; video and, 165–66; world, 204
Cinema Japanesque, 198
Cinema Paradise, 200
Cine Qua Non, 141
Civil Information and Education System, 39
Civil Information Center, 44
class: discourses of, 42, 111; politics of, 27
Clifford, Graeme, 144
Code of Conduct (series), 159, 178–79
Code of Conduct Part 17—the Bastard That Kills Them All (film), 177
Coe, Fred, 100
Cold War: anxieties, 221; geopolitics, 19, 144; legacies, 21, 53, 221; representation of, 112; system, 3, 20, 127
colonialism, 17–18, 20, 75, 144
Columbia Pictures, 145, 172
Comic Market, 211–12
Committee on Film Production, 214
commodity culture, 26, 56, 59, 63
communism, and film industry, 53
Comptiq (magazine), 125, 212
Conde, David, 39
Condry, Ian, 209
consumerism, 18, 68, 174–75; culture of, 50, 55, 75–76, 80, 150, 171; discourses of, 68, 75; politics and, 111; society and, 41, 76, 103, 111
Content Promotion Law, 214
contents, 157, 210; business, 214; discourses on, 214–15, 217–18; economics of, 219; politics and, 214, 218
continuity, postwar, 17, 19, 27, 29, 52
Coo (film), 146

INDEX · 287

Cool Britannia, 215
Cool Japan, 15, 210, 215
copyright law, 52, 215
Copyright Law That Won't Lose against Google and Apple, A (book), 210
Corrigan, Timothy, 201
Crazed Instinct (film), 33
Creative Commons, 211
CR—*Ginpara Monster—the Surge's Final Attack* (film), 186
Crime Hunter—Bullet of Fury (film), 152–53, 156–58, 160, 164–65, 173–74, 176
Crime Hunter 2 (film), 158
Crom, Luise, 13
Cross the Funme Bridge (film), 116
Cruel Woodblock Print Story (film), 70
Cry of Passion, The (film), 32
cultural capital, 7, 21
Curtin, Michael, 215
Cute Devil, I'll Give You Something Good (film), 84–85

Daicon: at conventions, 211; Daicon Film, 211
Daiei, 144; adult films, 69; films, 40, 48; financial difficulties, 59, 70, 84–86, 101; Pink Film and, 27, 70; post-bankruptcy, 116, 141; subgenres, 65; trends, 41; wartime conditions, 52
Dai Nana Gurūpu, 62
Dainichi Eihai, 84–85
Dai San Productions, 45, 69
Dallos (film), 173
danchi: *danchi-tzuma* films, 9, 92; images of, 50–51; movement into, 65
Dark Water (film), 163
Davis, Sammy, Jr., 144
Daydream (film), 69
Day of the Jackal, The (film), 100
De Laurentiis, Dino, 145
Detective Story (film), 16, 127, 130, 138
Detestable Skin (film), 33
digital technology, 4
directors: *igyō* (non-[film] business), 161; in major studios, 42, 47, 56; in Pink Film, 13,

30, 43; as publicity, 161; scholarly focus on, 14. *See also* auteurs
Directors Guild of Japan, 46–47, 164
Directors' Production Association, 84
Dirty Hero (film), 120, 133–36
Discover Japan ad campaign, 67
disidentification, 79–80
Disney film, 144
dōjin mono ("amateur" media), 211; activity, 212
Dokuritsu Chēn, 43
dokuritsu puro, 51, 93
Don That Calmed Down, The (series), 179
double bill: Kadokawa and, 138, 140–41; screening, 119; system, 55, 60, 86
DreamWorks, 148
Dungeons and Dragons, 212
DVDs: categorization, 10; distribution, 198; distributors, 145; market, 197; marketing, 149, 199; numbers, 168, 200; rental, 185; shift to, 201; V-Cinema and, 185, 192; VHS and, 200
Dwango, 148, 213

Early Spring Story (film), 140
Ecstasy of the Angels (film), 42
Eel, The (film), 15
Eiga Geijutsu (magazine), 34, 55
Eiga Hihyō (magazine), 94
Eiga Hyōron (magazine), 41
Eiga Jihō (magazine), 106
Eiga Nenkan (magazine), 93, 104, 208
Eiren, 48–49, 59, 90, 206
Eirin, 59, 167; designation, 69; inspectors, 74; *Market of Flesh* and, 25, 44–46; perception of, 39; Pink Film and, 27, 53–54; standards, 74, 77, 87
eizō, discourse of, 14, 21–23
Emperor Hirohito, 153
Endōji Theater, 168–70
ENGEL (company), 196
Enomoto Toshirō, 83
Eon (company), 207
erodakushon, 32, 47
ero-guro (erotic-grotesque), 34, 65

ero-real, 40, 131, 184, 196, 202
erosu (eros): category, 178, 192
eroticism: criticism of, 39–40; in discourse, 34; and foreign film, 39–40
erotic realism, 13
Espo, 192
Eurospace (minitheater), 204
Evil Woman (film), 69
Excellent (company), 200
experience, discourses of, 19–20, 23, 80
experimental film, 56–58

Family Game (film), 82, 105, 123
Farewell to Space Battleship Yamato: In the Name of Love (film), 118
Federation of Credit Bureau of Japan, 190
Female Animal, Female Animal, Female Animal (film), 43
Female Convict: Scorpion (series), 193
Female Ninja Art Scrolls (series), 193
feminization, 50, 63, 68, 75–77
film: aesthetics, 8; discourses on (Japanese), 156–57; history and, 110; noir, 12; theatrical releases, 172, 174
film festivals: 15–16, 144; Euro-American, 13, 15, 21, 48–49; international circuit, 204
film history, 2, 14–15; as approach, 16; organization of, 13
film industry: budgets, 117; conditions of, 26, 51–52, 101–2, 133; decline of, 63, 139; distribution, 141; financing, 142–43; perception of, 133; practices, 3, 15, 103–4; production, 62; production costs, 106; production of stars, 124; production strategies, 145; traditions, 157; transformation, 84, 97–98, 140–42; unionization, 52, 85
film journalism, 13; on foreign films, 34–35, 101; in Japan, 14, 101; on Pink Film, 34–35, 42–44, 46–47
Film Noir (film), 161
film study: approaches to, 14–16, 21, 94, 99, 110, 157; director-centric, 56
Fireworks (film), 15
Five Star Story (film), 139
Flashdance (film), 137

flesh: discourses of, 37–38, 109; as trope, 40
Flick (film), 198
Flower and Snake (film), 199
Flower and Snake II (film), 199
Flower Petal Ninja—Momokage—the Big Ninja Technique Petal Turnaround (film), 196
Fordist production, 3, 21, 218; post-, 203, 222
foreign film: audiences, 108; distribution, 101; import of, 59; perception of, 34–35, 39–40; television and, 63; theater, 116, 170–72. See also *yōga*
For Real! (series), 179
Forsyth, Frederick, 100
Fossilized Wilderness (film), 114, 116
Foucault, Michel, 35
Fox (studio), 117, 192
Freeman, Elizabeth, 18, 28
Fuji Pony, 166, 190
Fuji Sankei, 118, 141
Fujita Takashi, 33
Fuji Television, 117–18, 141, 143, 166, 172
Fukasaku Kinji, 112–13, 122, 127, 182–83
Furuhata, Yuriko, 21

Gainax, 211
Gakken Publishing, 117, 141
gambling: category, 178; films, 185; group, 186. See also *kinyū*
Gang Wives (series), 194
Gates of Flesh, The (film), 37, 39, 69
gebaruto, 38; Pink Film, 58
Gekigan Seihai, 53
Genette, Gerard, 6
Genghis Khan / Blue Wolf: To the Ends of the Earth and Sea (film), 149
genre, 2–3, 6; cinema, 14; constructions of, 9–12; criticism, 10; as discourse, 12; discourses of, 162; problems of, 9–11; theory of, 6, 11
Gerow, Aaron, 55
Gillespie, Tarleton, 209
Girl Boss (series), 88
Girl School (series), 88
G.I. Samurai (film), 132, 143

Gitelman, Lisa, 31
Glacier Fox, The (film), 118
Glamorous Life of Sachiko Hanai, The (film), 12
Gledhill, Christine, 11
Glowing Autumn (film), 117
Godfather, The (film), 116
Godzilla, 127
Good Morning (film), 63
Gotō Bin, 91
Gotō Daisuke, 161, 193
Gōtō Kōichi, 58
Government Council on Intellectual Property, 214
Graduate, The (film), 100
Gray, Jonathan, 6
Great East Asian Co-Prosperity Sphere, 75
Great Shogunate Battle, The (film), 142
Greene, Graham, 33
Groper Diary: The Man Who Continued Caressing the Buttocks (series), 195
Grudge, The (film), 163
Guinea Pig (series), 163, 173

Haginiwa Sadaaki, 162, 177, 188
Haha no kai (Mother's Association), 29
½ of Eternity (film), 172
Hamano Sachiko, 68
Hankyū group, 85
Hansa Film, 48
Hansen, Mark, 219
Hanshin earthquake, 181
Happy 9 (company), 200
Hara Masato, 147
Harada Tomoyo, 16, 114, 123, 126–30, 138, 140–41
hardboiled (genre), 5, 100
Harmageddon: The Great Battle with Genma (film), 132
Harootunian, Harry, 17, 207
Hasebe Yasuharu, 114
Hasumi Shigehiko, 94, 110
Hata Masanori, 143
Hatano Tetsurō, 170
Hatsune Miku, 220

Hattori Mitsunori, 186–87
Hayakawa Hikari, 163
Heaven and Earth (film), 117, 134, 140, 142–45, 151
Heibon Punch (magazine), 64–65, 90
Helga (film), 88
Hello Kitty, 118, 125, 177
Herald (company), 207
Hero (company), 191
High School Teacher: Bondage, A (film), 81
Higurashi When They Cry (series), 211
Hirano Kyoko, 39
Hiroki Ryūichi, 30, 82
historical times, concept of, 18–20
history: discontinuity and, 38; discourses on, Japanese, 75, 132; of Japan, 17, 36, 156; Japanese films and, 113; Kadokawa and, 109–10, 112, 114, 128–33; time and, 18
H Man, The (film), 2
Hobbit, The (series), 125
hōga (national films), 207; discourses on, 101; exhibition, 206; releases, 145, 158
Hole in the Pants (series), 191
Hollywood, 6, 10–11, 14; remakes, 163
Honda Ishirō, 2, 124
Hoodlum Soldier, The (film), 48
Hori Kyūsaku, 44
Horiguchi Toshikazu, 118
Hori Productions, 124
horizon of expectation, 19
horror film, 10, 158, 162–63; boom, 173, 197; gender politics, 197; in rankings, 200
Hot Spring Massage Geisha (film), 70
House of Strange Loves, The (film), 70
Human Revolution, The (film), 116
Hussey, Olivia, 114

Ichikawa Kiichi, 103
Ichikawa Kon, 40, 53, 85, 103, 109
Ichikura Haruo, 158
Ida Motomu, 70
identification, 78–80
ideology: approaches to, 19, 79; impact of, 36; postwar, 79; switches in, 37

idol: craze, 115; films, 124–26; infrastructure, 128; in Japanese media culture, 124, 126, 143; in media mix, 125; trends, 129
Igarashi Yoshikuni, 35, 75, 129
Iijima Toshio, 31, 33
Ijūin Gō, 82. *See also* Hiroki Ryūichi
Ike Reiko, 88
Ikeda Hayato, 50, 55
Ikeda Takeshi, 146
Ikejima Yutaka, 57, 74
Image Forum (magazine), 57–58, 125
Imai Tadashi, 53, 69, 117
Imamura Shohei, 15, 69, 101
Imaoka Shinji, 83, 204, 208
Imazawa Tetsuo, 146
imēji-ka (becoming-image), 107–8, 114, 126
Impotent Man (film), 78
independent film, 7, 13; development of, 52–54, 80–81; discourses of, 52, 55–56; figures in, 103; major studios and, 54–55, 93, 139; politics of, 54; practices, 53; production and distribution, 27, 32, 48, 54–55, 80–81, 133, 139–41; terms for, 54; theater, 141; trading companies and, 142; trends in, 141
Index of Obscene Films, 31
industrial genre, 3, 5–10, 13, 18; agency of, 9; confusion and, 210; development of, 29, 63, 158; discourses of, 27, 98; history, 222; frameworks, 205; intertextuality, 129; as markers, 28; media mix and, 97; nation and, 112; qualities of, 98; study of, 15–17, 19–20, 23, 223
Inflatable Sex Doll of the Wasteland (film), 57
Inoue Yoshio, 85
Insect Woman (film), 69
International Monetary Fund, 59
In the Storehouse (film), 134, 140
Inugami Family, The (film), 102–7, 109, 112, 137
Invisible Man: Ero Doctor (film), 71
Ishida Tatsurō, 167
Ishido Toshirō, 47
Ishihara Shigeru, 182
Ishihara Yūjiro, 60, 65

Ishihara Production, 60
Ishii Sōgo, 119
Ishii Takashi, 199
Ishii Teruo, 70
Ishikawa Hitoshi, 82
Island Closest to Heaven, The (film), 114, 137
Itō Gō, 125
Itōchū, 172
Itoi Shigesato, 111
iTunes, 211
Izbicki, Joanne, 36
Izo (film), 198
Izumi Yuri, 32
Izutsu Kazuyuki, 123, 140

Jack—Pachinko Slot—the King of Darkness (film), 186
Jackson, Michael, 144
Jameson, Fredric, 10, 18–19, 170, 203, 215, 222
Japan Bicott, 166
Japanese Business Federation, 214
Japanese Imperial Army, 114
Japanese Red Army, 57
Japanese Self-Defense Forces, 112–13, 216–17; in film, 132
Japanese Thief Story (film), 48
Japan External Trade Organization, 214
Japan Foundation, 216
Japan Home Video, 158–59, 163; V-Movie, 159
Japan International Contents Festival, 214–15
Japan Satellite Communications (JSC), 175
Japan Sinks (film), 116
Japan Telecommunications Welfare Association, 84
Japan Video Software Association (JVA), 166–69, 173, 192
Japan Writers Guild, 164
Jarmusch, Jim, 145
Jaws (film), 116–17
J-bungaku (J-literature), 151
JCI, 141
J-Horror, 10, 14, 162–63
Jingi (series), 162, 179

INDEX · 291

jishu ("autonomous"): activity, 212; film, 7, 119, 220; term, 211
Jissōji Akio, 161
jitsuen (real performance), 72–73
Johnny's, 124, 140
Jokyōshi (female schoolteacher), subgenre, 195
Joy of Torture, The (film), 70
J-pop, 151
jukujo (ripe/older woman), subgenre, 30, 92
Julien, Sandra, 88
Jurassic Park (film), 137, 215
JVC, 167

Kadokawa: advertising, 103, 106–7, 138, 213; anime, 132, 139; audiences, 106–8, 111; audience segmentation, 147; blockbusters, 112, 115–16, 134; blockbuster strategy, 118–20, 123, 142–43, 145; books, 103; brand, 116–18, 140–41, 151; Broadway musicals, 99, 144; budgets, 103, 106, 113, 137; business strategies, 98–99, 118, 133, 136, 141–42; capitalism and, 109; catchphrases, 106; characters and, 98, 121, 148, 150–51, 175; company developments, 132; company history, 149–50; confusion and, 112, 115, 136–37; consumerism and, 111, 115; contradictions, 115, 120; criticism of, 107–8, 120; difficulties, 118, 123, 141–42, 144, 146; discourses of, 109, 115, 153; distribution practices, 120, 137, 140, 143, 148; fantastic spaces and, 136–37, 202; film history and, 110; film industry and, 96–97, 99, 108–9, 115, 139–40, 148; film releases, 155, 170; financing strategies, 142–43, 145; foreign markets and, 113–15, 144; games, 148, 151; geopolitics, 110–12, 114, 133, 135–36, 143, 151, 175; history and, 110, 112, 114–15, 128–29, 132, 149–50; Hollywood and, 144–45; identity politics, 134, 175; idol discourse, 127–28; idol films, 125; idols, 124–25, 128–29, 132, 148; idol strategy, 128–29, 142, 150; impact of, 96–98, 107–8, 118, 122–23, 150; impact of technology on, 119–20; independent production in, 134; industrial genre and, 150; Kadokawa Holdings, 149–50, 213; *kyara* strategy, 151; light novels, 147–48; literature and, 114, 119–20, 155; literature on, 117; magazines, 125, 139; major studios and, 104, 120, 140, 145–46; manga, 132, 139, 151; manga magazines, 147, 212; marketing, 213; media mix and, 123; media mix models, 102, 107, 111, 114, 118, 120, 132, 146, 175; media platforms and, 114, 119, 136; media texts, 150; *musume* (girls), 123, 126–28, 130; narratives, 137; nation and, 98, 151, 169, 223; New Kadokawa Films, 147, 149; opposition and, 102, 111, 115, 118, 139; perception of, 96–98, 103–4, 108, 116, 137–39; Pink Film and, 97–98, 107, 112, 115, 123; production, 134; production committee, 145; production strategies, 147; profits, 103, 140; public image strategies, 105, 132, 144; radio and, 106; realism and, 97; restructuring, 146; sales, 114; scholarship on, 96; self-referentiality, 107; shifts in business models, 148, 150; shifts in production, 120, 122–23, 139, 142; soundtrack, 104, 106, 120, 155; staff, 157, 162; star commodity, 122–23; styles, 137; television and, 104, 106, 155; temporality, 16, 128, 135–36, 144, 150–51, 155–57; theater, 140; tropes in, 136; use of narratives, 120
Kadokawa Gen'yoshi, 100–101, 109
Kadokawa Haruki, 1, 96–97, 106, 113, 140; on audiences, 128; as character, 112, 118, 129; criminal charges, 99, 146, 148, 174, 197; criticism of, 110, 120; as director, 117, 120, 127, 130, 133–34; film industry and, 102–4, 109, 116, 148; foreign markets and, 144; history and, 131–33, 149; Hollywood and, 137; idols and, 128–31; Kadokawa Haruki Corporation, 148; Kadokawa Haruki Mirai Fund, 149; Kadokawa Haruki Office, 96, 101, 103, 119, 123–24, 130, 137, 145–46, 148; major studios and, 102, 140; marketing of, 129; media-mix model, 146–48, 212, 221; opposition and, 99, 103–4, 109, 134–35; perception of, 148; personalization, 150; public figure of, 96,

98–99, 102, 108–9, 115, 117, 119, 133; realism and, 131; self-portrayal, 137, 150; strategies, 100–104, 115–16, 119, 143, 145, 146, 148

Kadokawa Tsuguhiko, 125, 139, 146, 150; business strategies, 147–48, 211, 213, 221; history and, 150; *kyara* strategy, 151; magazines, 147; media-mix model, 120, 139, 146–48, 212; on platform, 210–11, 220–21

Kadokawa Film: in comparison, 175–76, 194, 203, 215; confusion and, 112, 115, 210, 223; criticism of, 98, 103, 108, 142–43; developments in, 16, 19, 126–27, 151; difficulties, 140; directors, 123; discourse, 142; in film history, 96–99; history and, 111, 114, 150, 205; identity politics, 105, 129, 150, 175, 203; idol strategy and, 127, 130; impact of, 139, 165; as industrial genre, 4–5, 7–9, 23, 97, 147; major studios and, 140; marketing of, 129; opposition and, 109; personalization of, 133; Pink Film and, 137; practices, 149; realism and, 127; reception of, 104; releases, 145; scholarship on, 14; shifts, 134; strategies, 107, 117–18, 120, 191; temporality, 133, 137, 150, 205, 207

Kadokawa Publishing, 97–99, 109, 149; animation, 147; fairs, 101; film adaptations, 134; finances, 103, 106; history, 100–101, 133, 146, 148–49; magazines, 146; production, 139, 145; sales, 106–7

Kadokawa Records, 103
Kagemusha (film), 1, 96
Kaji Meiko, 88
Kamata Yoshitaka, 83
Kamen Rider (series), 199
Kanehara Ichi, 196
Kaneko Shūsuke, 172
Kanemori Yoshinori, 148
Kanō Kazuko, 57
Kansai Electric, 117
Kantō Movie, 43, 48, 90
Kara Jūrō, 56–57
Karatani Kōjin, 153–54
Kasahara Kazuo, 182
kasutori-zasshi (cheap magazines), 38–39
Kataoka Shūji, 158, 161

Katsu Shintarō, 65
kawaii, 126
Kawakita Kazuko, 172
Kawasaki Yoshisuke, 140
Kawase Naomi, 15, 198
Kawashima Nobuko, 34, 56
Kelly, Sharon, 88
Kenen, James, 100
Kennedy, George, 105, 114, 191
Kenya Boy (film), 115, 137
Key, The (film), 40
Kido Shiro, 52
Kim Dae Jung, 215
Kimba the White Lion (series), 166
Kinei, 207
Kinema Junpō (magazine), 38–39, 110; critics' poll, 103, 108; Kadokawa and, 103–4; Pink Film and, 57–58; on technology, 155; on video, 169, 174, 200
King Kong (film), 145
King of Debt, The (series), 188, 191
King of Minami, The (series), 162, 188–91
King of the Hitting Mark (film), 186
kinyū (finance): category, 178; characteristics, 185, 188; characters, 202; developments, 197; economy and, 190; films, 189, 190; history and, 190; subgenre, 187. *See also* gambling
Kishi Nobusuke, 45
Kitada Akihiro, 219–20
Kitano Takeshi, 15, 161
Kitasato Toshio, 58
Knapp, Gregory, 114
Kobayashi Akira, 65
Kobayashi Ichizō, 55, 70
Kobayashi Masahiro, 30, 161, 198
Kobayashi Masaki, 117
Kobayashi Masaru, 39–41, 131
Kobayashi Satoru, 25–26, 72, 78, 89, 93, 161
Kōdansha, 141, 147
Koei Net, 213
Koizumi Junichirō, 214
Kokuba Gumi, 207
Kokuei, 43, 66, 71, 73, 83–84, 177
kokusai-ka (internationalization), 132

Komatsu Sakyō, 116
Komatsu Takashi, 195
Komizu Kazuo/Gaira, 56, 193
Konuma Masaru, 161, 187
Koselleck, Reinhart, 18–20, 23, 222
Kowalski, Bernard, 100
Krämer, Sybille, 224
KSS: impact of, 178; Pink Pineapple, 195; production, 177, 196–97; series, 188; strategies, 191, 195, 198
Kudō Eiichi, 161
Kumai Kei, 60
Kurahara Koreyoshi, 117–18
Kurahashi Yumiko, 68
Kurosawa Akira, 1, 20, 36, 54, 59, 85, 96, 147
Kurosawa Kiyoshi, 30, 161
Kurosawa Mitsuru, 157, 193, 195
Kurosawa Productions, 54
Kusakabe Kyūshirō, 49
Kusakari Masao, 135
Kuwabara Masae, 90
kyara, 121, 125–26; strategy, 151

labor: casualized, 29–30, 80, 93, 104, 164; in film industry, 80, 84–86; gender divisions, 68, 75; in industrial genres, 8, 27–30; in postwar era, 36, 52; strikes, 52–53; unions, 53, 55, 85
La Comédie Humaine (novels), 183
Lara of the Wild (film), 58
Lazzarato, Maurizio, 210–12
leftist politics, 34, 38, 52; divisions in, 57; and filmmakers, 53; and independent films, 54
Legend, 196
Legend of the Eight Samurai (film), 122, 127, 137
Le Grand Meaulnes (film), 100
Lessig, Lawrence, 211
Let's Meet in a Dream (film), 126
Lévi-Strauss, Claude, 223
Lies (film), 40, 69
Lim, Bliss Cua, 156
Lindberg, Christina, 88
Lineage of the Tokugawa Women (film), 70
literary theory, 6

literature: criticism, 100; discourses on, 154; film and, 41, 99; of flesh, 20, 36–37, 69; publication of, 100
Little Girl Who Conquered Time, The (film): (1983), 16, 19, 127, 131–32, 138; (1997), 148
Lost Paradise: film, 147; publication, 147
Love Story: book, 100; film, 127, 134, 137
Lubitsch, Ernst, 39
Lucas, George, 117
Luhmann, Niklas, 219
Lunch Box (film), 204, 208

MacDowell, Andie, 144
MacKinnon, Catharine, 28
Mah-Jongg Demon (series), 187
Mah-Jongg Wolf Tale—Blow of Death! (series), 187
Mahjong Vagabond Chronicle (film), 137–39
Mainichi Hōsō, 141
Mainichi Shinbun (newspaper), 49, 147
Main Theme (film), 127, 130, 137
major studios, Japan: adult films and, 69–70; antiestablishment and, 88; companies, 27, 52; distinctions from amateurs, 47; elitism, 42; exhibition practices, 55, 60–62, 85, 141; financial difficulties, 59–60, 84–85, 174; hiring practices, 30, 42, 57; independent films and, 54–55, 139; Kadokawa and, 104, 120; Kadokawa Haruki and, 140; labor in, 164; perception of, 42, 54–55; Pink Film and, 58, 60–62, 69–71, 81, 83–84, 86–91, 93–94; production and distribution, 7, 9, 15, 21, 44, 55, 60–62, 69, 85–87; production breakdown, 160–61; profits, 101; stars, 125; strategies, 116, 133, 157; system, 3, 8, 56, 116, 119, 164; television and, 59, 94; theaters, 139; trading companies and, 142; video and, 166
Maki Kakuzo, 32
Makiguchi Yūji, 88
Mandarake, 213
manga, 15, 87, 116; characters, 178; criticism, 125; Kadokawa, 132, 139, 148; V-Cinema, 163
Manovich, Lev, 202

Mansion of the Lewd Snake (film), 73
Marcuse, Herbert, 80
Market of Flesh (film), 25–26, 30, 37, 73, 152
Maro Akaji, 57
Maruyama Masao, 34, 36–38, 109
Maruyama Shōichi, 108, 120
Marx, Karl, 109
Masao Miyoshi, 38
Master of Fraud Ippei (series), 188
Masuda Toshio, 142
Masumura Yasuzō, 40–41, 48, 69, 85, 156–57
Matano Seiji, 5
Maten, Guenther, 48
Matsubara Rumiko, 134
Matsuda Hitoshi, 193
Matsuda Masao, 219–20
Matsuda Yūsaku, 5, 105
Matsui Noboru, 162, 177, 186
Matsumoto Toshio, 56, 116
Matsushima Toshiyuki, 111
Matsushita, 145, 172
Mazinger Z (series), 116
MCA, 145, 172
McDonald, Keiko, 99
Me, Natalie (film), 100
Meat Mattress (film), 67
media discourse, 17
media ecology, 2, 5, 17, 21; capacities, 219; circulation, 201; demands, 204; discourses of, 220; film and, 23; history and, 197; industrial genres and, 3–4, 204; intensified, 154; in Japan, 99, 152, 197, 211, 213; Kadokawa, 123, 165; media mix, 199; organization, 218; principles, 221; shifts, 205, 215
media epistemology, 2, 23
media history, 20, 155; discourses of, 154
media mix: advertising campaign, 103; as approach, 14; discourse of, 215; ecology, 199; history of, 107; impact of, 178; intensification, 201; models, 102–3; series, 212; spread, 197; strategies, 1–2, 4, 16, 97–98, 100–104, 107, 115–16, 155; subgenre, 224; systems, 23, 142, 205–6, 222; talent agencies and, 125

media theory, as approach, 14, 31
mediation, 21
Meiji (company), 116
Meike Mitsuru, 12, 83
Melancholy of Suzumiya Haruhi, The (series), 148, 213, 215
melodrama, 10
Merian (magazine), 13
MGM/UA, 169, 172
Mifune Toshiro, 60, 65, 106
Mifune Production, 60
Miike Takashi, 161, 198
Million Films, 89, 93
Minami Saori, 129
Minami Yoshiko, 110
Ministry of Economy, Trade and Industry, 154, 185, 214
Ministry of Export and Trade, 214
Ministry of Foreign Affairs of Japan, 214
Ministry of Internal Affairs and Communication, 214
minitheater, 139, 170–72, 202, 204, 207; boom, 140–41, 172; film, 208
Mishima Yukio, 12, 57, 145
Misora Hibari, 124
Mistress (film), 61
Mitsui Bussan, 142
Mitsui financial group, 142
Mitsuishi Fujirō, 186
Mitsukoshi, 117
Miyadai Shinji, 156, 176
Miyazaki Hayao, 141, 216
Miyazaki Masumi, 193
Miyazaki Tsutomi, 162
Mizoguchi Kenji, 40, 85
Mizuno Ryo, 212
Moaning Teens (film), 32
Mochizuki Rokurō, 161
modern girl, 75
modernity, 10, 14, 17–18; cultures of, 35, 63; definitions of, 35, 60; discourses of, 40, 66–68; and gender, 75–78; interventions against, 18; and nation, 36, 50; and time, 17–18
Monday Girl (film), 69

Monna Katsuo, 186–87
Monroe, Marilyn, 126
monster films, 70, 124
moratorium generation, 129
Morikawa Kaichirō, 76
Morimura Seiichi, 104, 107, 112
Morita Akio, 154
Morita Yoshimitsu, 82, 123, 127–28, 147
Moritani Shirō, 116, 118
Mortensen, Viggo, 144, 192
Most Beautiful, The (film), 36
Mothra (film), 124
Motion Pictures Producers Association of Japan, 59
Motogi Sōjirō, 59
Mount Hakkodasan (film), 118
movie theaters, 3, 9, 16, 35, 42–43, 45, 51, 55; numbers, 20–21, 25–26
Mukai Kan, 56–57, 67, 78, 81, 89, 93, 161
Mukai Production, 56
mukokuseki eiga (anational films), 136, 157; action, 202
multiplex: boom, 141; business, 148
Muñoz, José Esteban, 79
Murai Minoru, 34
Murakami Akira, 44
Murakawa Tōru, 119–20, 131
Murata Shinobu, 188
Murder at Honjin Manor House (film), 101
Muroga Atsushi, 158
Musashino Kōgyō, 207
Museum: production, 184, 200; series, 194; strategies, 178, 198
Mushi Production, 166
music industry, Kadokawa and, 103
my-home-ism, 49–51, 55, 68
Mystery Train (film), 145

Nagai Go, 116
Nagai Tatsuo, 100
Nagata Masaichi, 52
Nagoya Video Library, 168
Naigai Times (newspaper), 34
Nakahara Shun, 141
Nakahira Kō, 69

Nakajō Kiyoshi, 180
Nakamura Genji, 12, 82
Nakamura Hideyuki, 12
Nakano Takao, 196
Nakasone Yasuhiro, 132
Nakata Hideo, 163
Naked Body (film), 69
Naked Embrace (film), 85
Naoki Sanjūgo, 216–18, 223
Narita Yusuke, 5
narrative: as approach, 6, 8, 10; changing role of, 97, 107, 120, 202; as commodity, 103; of decline, 14–16, 20–21; film, 73, 88; industrial genres and, 222–23; in Kadokawa, 109, 115; of transformation, 20, 23, 31
Narusawa Masashige, 69
Naruto (series), 2, 5
nation: as approach, 16, 21; construct of, 4, 17, 23, 27, 29, 35–36; of film industry, 96; gender and, 26, 29, 75, 80; identity and, 41, 64, 76–77, 79, 132; image of, 79–80; media ecology and, 223; media technology and, 155; postwar crisis of, 36; postwar discourse of, 38; sexuality and, 35; soft power and, 220; space of, 113
national cinema, as approach, 14
Natsuki Shizuko, 120
Navel of the Sun (film), 83
Neale, Steve, 6
Neeson, Liam, 144
Negishi Kichitaro, 16, 123, 127–28, 172
Neon Genesis Evangelion: film, 147; series, 130, 211
New: History of a Love Affair (film), 72
new wave directors, Japan, 54
Nichigeki Building, 167
Nichimen, 142
Nichols, Mike, 100
Nico Nico Douga, 21, 148, 213, 218
Night and Fog in Japan (film), 54
Nihon Herald, 145
nihonjinron (theories about the Japanese), 132
Nihon Keizai Shinbun (newspaper), 147
Nihon Shinema, 43, 71, 73

Nihon Terebi, 124, 141
Nihon Video Eiga, 159; V-Theater, 159
Niitaka Keiko, 57
Nikita (film), 145
Nikkatsu: actors, 65, 76, 86; adaptations, 193; adult films, 69; directors, 119; distribution, 60, 85; film genres, 5; financial difficulties, 59, 84, 86, 101, 174; history, 15, 55, 86; Kadokawa and, 104; nudity boom and, 74; obscenity charges, 44–45; Pink Film and, 9, 27, 37, 62, 70, 72, 88–89, 91, 93, 166; police and, 166; producers, 157; specialty, 152, 157, 166; strategies, 84–89; subcontracting, 54, 89; subgenres, 65, 72, 124; TBS, 200; theaters, 87, 89; V-Cinema, 158; V-Feature, 159; video production, 173, 200
Nikkatsu Roman Porno: actors, 87; characteristics of, 82, 86–87; in circulation, 170; directors, 123, 128, 161; discourses of, 94; film exhibition, 57, 89, 91; films, 15; history, 88, 174; impact of, 90; Pink Film and 9; producers, 193; as products, 168; as sources, 195; staff, 161; theaters, 167, 168
Nikkei Entertainment (trade paper), 172
ninkyō (chivalry) films, 65, 159, 178–79, 182, 197; V-Cinema and, 181
Nippon Herald, 147
Nippon Hōsō, 166
Nishimura Jukō, 116
Nishimura Kiyoshi, 161
Nishitomo, 141
Nomura Yoshitarō, 116
Norimichi Ichirō, 33
Nosaka Akiyuki, 100–101
nostalgia: media and, 4, 55–56; Shōwa-era, 156, 202; in subgenre, 179
NTV, 146
nudity: boom, 74; depoliticized, 94; portrayal of, 41, 44, 65, 69, 71–72, 88–89, 94; as provocation, 37; restrictions against, 46, 77
Number 2's of the Underworld (series), 194
Nye, Joseph, 215
nyū-hāfu, 134

Ōbayashi Nobuhiko, 16, 114–15, 119, 123, 127, 134
Obedient Belly Kingdom Japan: Intercourse, Birth (film), 71
obscenity: charges of, 25, 44–45, 87–88; conceptions of, 27, 38; trials, 44–48, 87, 89
Ochiai Masayuki, 147
OECD, 59
Official Development Assistance, 216
Ogawa Kinya, 61, 71
Ōguro Toyoshi, 109–10
Ōkawa Toshimichi, 152, 158
Ōkura: Eiga, 35, 43, 54, 71, 87, 93; in partnership, 166
Ōkura Mitsugi, 61, 66, 85–86, 89, 91
Ōkura Pictures (OP chain), 43, 61, 66, 83, 91–92
Ogawa Kinya, 43, 77, 89
Ogawa Shinsuke, 14, 67
Oguri Kōhei, 30
Okada Shigeru, 140
Okuyama Kazuyoshi, 198
Omen, The (film), 117
Ōmori Kazuki, 119, 139
Oniroku, Dan, 199
Original Net Animation, 21
Oshii Mamoru, 173
Oshima Nagisa, 21, 35, 42, 44–45, 54–55
otaku, 129
Ōtomo Katsuhiro, 161
Ōtsuka Eiji, 111, 129–30, 146–47, 209, 213
Our Seven Day War (film), 142
Outer Way, The (film), 161
OVA (original video animation) films, 173–74
Overseas Exchange Council, 214
Ōyabu Haruhiko, 120, 134
Ozawa Hitoshi, 180, 182–83
Ozu Yasujiro, 21, 63, 214

pachinko: films, 186–87, 190, 195; game, 185–86; in popular media, 185–86; profits, 185; subgenre, 159, 182, 185, 187, 196, 202
Pachinko Player Nami (film), 186
Pachinko Stories (series), 186
Palme d'Or, 1

Parasite Eve (film), 147
Parco, 111
Parent-Teacher Association, 9
Pass the Phone Please! (film), 70
Patriotism (film), 57
Peggy Sue Got Married (film), 137
Pervert Freak (film), 71
Pia Film Festival, 119
Pingree, Geoffrey, 31
Pink Cut (film), 82
Pink Film: actors, 40, 31, 57, 68, 70, 72, 83, 87, 94; advertising for, 66, 90, 177; aesthetics, 71–72, 77, 89, 131, 184; audiences, 13, 29, 56, 61, 63–66, 68, 74, 77–80, 83, 91–95; backlash, 70; body politics, 20, 26, 28–31, 73, 77; boom, 50, 55–56, 70, 83–84; business opportunities, 166; characteristics of, 13, 26–27, 29–31, 38, 40, 59, 63, 71, 92, 150; in circulation, 170; class and, 42, 65, 68, 71; in comparison, 164–65, 171, 175–76, 194, 203, 215, 223; compartmentalization, 87; confusion and, 26–29, 39, 63, 69, 71–74, 77, 80, 90, 95, 98, 194; contradictions in, 68, 71, 77, 79–81, 84; depoliticization, 92, 94–95; development as industry, 42–43, 46–47, 62–64, 69–71, 84, 94–95; directors, 13, 30, 40–41, 43, 50, 56, 68, 93–94, 128; discourse of, 19, 153, 194, 208; discourses on, 109, 135; distribution practices, 47, 83–84, 90, 93–94; exhibition practices, 61–62, 71–72, 94, 208; filmic textuality and, 177; foreign film and, 39–40, 88–89; gendered roles in, 39, 42, 67–68, 78; gender politics in, 68–69, 77–80, 135, 202; history and, 29, 68, 110, 155; identification in, 78–79; impact of, 7–9, 58, 69, 152, 158–59; as industrial genre, 3–4, 9, 152, 210; industrial practices, 12–13, 27, 56–57, 67, 80, 83–84; industrial trends and, 104; industry, 12; influence, 165; Kadokawa Film and, 97–98, 107, 112, 115, 123, 137; labor and, 80–81, 85–86, 93, 164, 190; mainstream coverage of, 34–35, 42–44, 46–47, 94; mainstream film and, 56, 63, 65, 91; market difficulties, 88–89; nation and, 64, 98, 169; negotiations of identity, 47–48, 50, 80; nomenclature, 31–35; as opposition, 27–29, 35, 39–41, 47–48, 50, 56–58, 65, 84, 93–94, 203; perception of, 9, 29, 47, 50, 91, 94–96; politics of, 52, 56–58, 63, 79, 83, 97; production practices, 29–30, 133, 158, 200; as products, 168; profitability, 42–43, 58, 61–62, 84, 91–92, 197; rural-urban tensions and, 65–68; scholarship on, 14–15, 56–57, 96; scriptwriters, 164; sexual politics, 26, 39, 41–42, 73–74; sexual violence, 3, 28, 30–31, 39, 42–43, 70–71, 73–74, 81–83; soundscape, 40; spatiality, 205; staff, 161; standardization, 157; strategies for increasing audiences, 71–72, 82–83; structural elements, 195; students and, 56–58, 65–66, 94; stylization of, 40–41, 92; television and, 59, 68, 73, 91, 94; in theaters, 168; time and, 23, 132, 156, 207; as training ground, 123, 161, 163; transformations, 204; underground culture and, 56–57; video and, 166, 196; violence, 74, 77, 82

Pink Film and major studios: competition, 86–91; distribution and exhibition practices, 42–44, 60–62; obscenity trials, 46–47; organization, 56; power balance, 54, 83–84; relationship, 58, 69–73, 80–81, 93–94

Pink Film budgets: average, 26–27, 29–32; changes in, 67, 83–84; in comparison, 47, 163, 86, 89–90, 103, 163; image of, 71; impact of, 40, 92; influence on, 59; trends, 11

Pink Film realism: aesthetics of, 54; appeals to, 68; aspirations of, 53; connotations of, 27, 38; discourses of, 67, 71; disparities, 29, 37; historicist, 128; modes of, 40; negotiations of, 39; oppositional themes, 27; response to, 39; role of, 13, 41

Pink Film theaters, 29, 43, 51, 64, 80, 95, 168, 177, 207; in comparison, 9; conditions of, 61–62, 92; gendered spaces of, 3–4, 68, 167, 169; numbers, 90–91; opening, 25; spread of, 35

Pink Ribbon (film), 74
Pink Ribbon Award, 34

Pinky Violence, 88–89, 193–95
platform: construction of, 224; discourses of, 205, 208, 210, 220, 222–23; models, 221; politics of, 211; space, 20; studies, 209
Pleasure of a Hussy, The (film), 72
police, Japanese, 25, 29, 33, 58, 122, 166
Pony, 166
Pony Canyon, 169, 214
Popeye (serials), 217
pop stars, Japanese, 103
Pornographers, The (film), 101
pornography, 13, 82; discourses on, 28, 35; Euro-American, 88
postwar period: conditions of, 10, 36; contradictions of, 28; critiques of, 49–50; discourses of, 13, 27–29, 31, 35, 41, 78; ideology, 79; image of Japan, 3, 48–49, 109; imagery in Japan, 36, 39; models of, 26–27, 111; post-postwar period, 29; reconstruction, 154; representation of, 110; subjectivity, 38; system, 19–20, 156, 179; trauma, 26
print media, 4, 17
program-picture: production systems, 160; strategy, 143, 159–60
Proof of the Man (film), 104–9, 112, 114
Proof of the Wild: book, 107; film, 112, 117–18, 124
publishing houses, 141
pure film movement, 14, 40

Quadruplex video system, 154, 167

radio, 141; advertisements, 103
Raiders of the Lost Ark (film), 137
Ran (film), 147
Rancière, Jacques, 3
RCA Columbia, 169, 192
realism: debates on, 41; discourses of, 39–41, 54, 67–68; independent film and, 53–54; in literature, 41; media and, 37; nation and, 41; opposition to, retreat of, 97
Record of Lodoss War (series), 212
Red Purge, 53
Red Tent, 56–57

Reems, Harry, 93
Resurrection of the Golden Wolf, The (film), 119
Rex: A Dinosaur's Story (film), 134, 136–37, 145–46
Richie, Donald, 14, 16, 21
Ring: film, 163; novel, 163; series, 197
Ring, The (film), 163
Rintarō, 132, 137, 148
Road to Becoming the Don, The (series), 178
Rocky (film), 135, 137
Rohy, Valerie, 194
Rosen, Philip, 18
Ruby Cairo (film), 144
rupture: and film, 19, 48; narratives of historical, 14, 17, 20, 26, 28, 31, 52, 74–75; technological, 4; as theme, 78
Ryoki (magazine), 39

Sacred Mother Kannon (film), 42
Sad Vessel (film), 83
Saeki Kōzō, 126
Sai Yōichi, 114, 123, 130, 141
Sailor Suit and Machine Gun (film), 120–22, 126–27, 140
Sailor Who Fell from Grace with the Sea, The (film), 145
Sakaguchi Ango, 36
Sakamiki Mayumi, 33
Sakamoto Rei, 83
Sakurai Shōichi, 187
S&M films, 72, 81–82
Sands of Kurobe, The (film), 60
Sano Kazuhiro, 82
Sano Shinichi, 117
Sanrio, 118
Santa Maria, 144
Sasaki Kōgyō, 207
Sasaki Yasushi, 39
Sasori in USA (film), 193
Satō Hisayasu, 82, 162
Satō Junya, 104, 112, 116, 142, 149
Satō Keiko, 66, 71
Satō Tadao, 15, 53, 56, 65–66
Satō Toshiki, 82, 162

Sawa Kensuke, 72
Sawai Shinichirō, 120, 123, 140, 149
Scan Doll (film), 195–96
School in the Crosshairs (film), 127, 140
Scorpion (series), 88
Second Tōei, 161
Sedgwick, Eve Kosofsky, 79
Segal, Erich, 100
Seibu culture, 111
seijin eiga (adult films), 25, 69, 89
Seijin Eiga (magazine): on Pink Film, 34–35, 56, 58, 68, 73–74, 82–83, 94–85; plot summaries, 32; on tours, 81; on video rentals, 165
seijin shitei (adult designation), 25
seisakuiinkai (production committee), 145, 147, 198
seishin shugi (spiritism), 36
sekai-kei (world type), 209, 224
Seki Kōji, 34, 71, 73, 168
Sekimoto Ikuo, 88
Sengen Seizō, 162
Sentō Takenori, 198
seppun eiga (kissing film), 39
Seven Samurai, The (film), 59
Seven Year Itch, The (film), 126
Sex Manual of Humanity (film), 89
sexploitation film, 9, 47, 91
sexual liberation, discourses of, 38–39, 41
sexual violence: attitudes to, 82; in Pink Film, 3, 28, 30–31, 39, 42–43, 70–71, 73–74, 81–83; in postwar literature, 37; as trope, 81–82
Shameless School (film), 87
Shaw Brothers, 144
Shichifukujin (Seven Lucky Gods of Pink Film), 83
Shichiji Yukihisa, 186
Shimizu Kentarō, 180, 182
Shimizu Kōjirō, 180
Shimizu Takashi, 163
Shindō Kaneto, 55
Shindō Takae, 12, 41
shinecon (multiplex), 205–8, 221
shingeki, 57

Shinkai Makoto, 209, 211
Shinoda Masahiro, 114
Shintōhō: audiences, 66; blockbusters, 116; distribution, 43, 92; financial difficulties, 59; history, 53, 58; Pink Film and, 93, 166; staff, 70, 89; subcontracting, 54
Shiota Akihiko, 161
Shirai Yoshio, 107–8
Shirakawa Kazuko, 87
Shishi Pro, 56
shitamachi (downtown), 180, 190, 203
shitennō (Four Devils of Pink Film), 82–83, 161–62, 177
Shōchiku: adult films, 69; budgets, 106; cinematic trends and, 39; films, 116, 161; financial difficulties, 59, 70, 85, 145; Kadokawa and, 102, 118, 145, 146; Multiplex Cinemas, 207; Nouvelle Vague, 69; Oshima Nagisa and, 54; Pink Film and, 27, 89; production, 133–34; Red Purge and, 53; Sister Picture, 157; strategies, 93; subgenres, 124; union, 86; wartime conditions, 52
Shōgun (musical), 144
Sholokhov, Mikhail, 179
shutaisei, discourses of, 38
Silk Road, The (film), 142
Simmel, Georg, 75
Singapore Sling (film), 146
Slayers (film), 147
Slaymaker, Douglas, 37
Sniper—The Shootist (film), 158
soft power, 214–15, 219–20
Sōmai Shinji, 120, 123, 126–27
Sony, 145, 154, 167, 172
soundtracks: in media mix, 104; sales, 103, 116
Sōzōsha, 54
Space Prince (film), 139
special-effects film, 2
Spielberg, Steven, 117
Stallone films, 156
Star Wars (films), 117, 137
Stein, Werner, 49
Steinberg, Marc, 210

Stiletto (film), 100
Stolen Heart (film), 163
Story from Echigo, A (film), 69
straight-to-video: films, 5, 152, 158; genre, 4; marketing, 199; numbers, 200; production, 173
Strategic Council on Intellectual Property, 214
Strawberry Statement, The: film, 100; novel, 100
Streisand, Barbra, 144
student movement, 38, 56–58, 94; perception of, 132; years following, 111
Studio Ghibli, 141
subgenre, 8, 92, 207; action, 89, 158, 193
subjectivity, 35, 37–38, 80; male, 68, 77–79, 83
Suga Hidemi, 127–28
Sugawara Hiroshi, 142
Sugimoto Miki, 88
Summer Vacation 1999 (film), 172
Sun over the Kurobe Gorge (film), 117
Sunscent Cinema Works, 198
Suntory, 172
Suō Masayuki, 30
Supernatural Tale Dismembered Ghost (film), 71, 77
Suponichi (newspaper), 34
surveillance, 14
Sutā tanjō! (TV show), 124, 126
Suwa Nobuhiro, 30
Suzaku (film), 15
Suzuki Kōji, 163
Suzuki Noribumi, 88
Suzuki Seijun, 37, 69
Suzuki Tomiko, 108–9

Taifun Club (film), 123
taiyōzoku (sun-tribe) films, 65
Tajiri Yūji, 83
Takabayashi Yōichi, 101, 134
Takada Kōji, 113–14
Takahara Kazuo, 161
Takahashi Akira, 82
Takahashi Banmei, 81, 161
Takahashi Hiroshi, 163
Takakura Ken, 65, 112–13, 124, 182
Takano Taira, 32
Takechi Tetsuji, 42, 44–47, 54, 69–70, 75
Take Me Out to the Snowland (film), 141
Takeuchi Riki, 176, 180, 188–89, 194
Takita Yōjirō, 30
Tamura Tajirō, 36–38, 69
Tanaka Hideo, 158
Tanaka Jun'ichirō, 53
Tanaka, Stefan, 17
Tanaka Yōzō, 123
Tani Naomi, 72–73, 76, 87
Taniguchi Yuri, 57
Tanioka Masaki, 165
Tanizaki Jun'ichiro, 72
Tanno Yūji, 87
Tanokin Trio, 140
TBS, 142, 172
technology: aesthetics and, 13, 73; costs of, 167; discourses of, 63, 167, 224; distribution and, 83; film, 21, 41; impact on lifestyle, 212; time and, 154
television: advertisements, 103, 106, 119, 189; animation, 178; cable, 172, 191; commercial imagery of, 135; as commodity, 55; film adaptations, 124; film industry and, 46, 58–60, 64, 91; film production and, 141, 143; format, 180, 189; idols and, 124; impact of, 63, 172; market, 191; in media ecology, 2; in media mix, 104; Pink Film and, 59, 68, 73, 91, 94; production model, 59; rise of, 59, 94; satellite, 119, 177, 191, 198–99, 201; series, 178, 198; scheduling, 65; scriptwriters, 164; set, 168; stations overseas, 216; video and, 154–55, 166
temporality, 16–20; geopolitics and, 111, 133, 217; of idols, 130; models of, 27, 28, 107; space and, 40, 207; star, 123
Terayama Shūji, 57, 161
Terranova, Tiziana, 212
Terrible Couple, The (film), 127
Teshigahara Hiroshi, 69, 116
Teshigahara Productions, 69

Tezuka Osamu, 116, 166

theater, 37, 44, 53, 56; building boom, 54–55; companies, 57, 72; contracting of, 55; decline of, 91–92, 101, 139; discourses of, 64; distribution of, 61, 66; film and, 73; foreign film and, 105; income, 42; major studios and, 57; numbers of, 21, 26, 45, 60–61, 139; second- and third-run, 60–62, 66, 90–91; specialty, 43, 64, 86, 90. *See also* minitheater

three sacred treasures, 55

time: approaches to, 19–20, 23, 28; discourses of, 154; geopolitics and, 157; Kadokawa and, 16–17; models of, 154–56; modernity and, 17–18, 40; technology and, 154

time-slip films, 131–32

TMC (company), 196

Tōei: action-film model, 174; adaptations, 103; advertising, 193; blockbusters, 116; budgets, 106; collaborations, 118; distribution practices, 88, 200; double-bill system, 55; financial difficulties, 59, 85; Goraku Ban, 157; international film festivals and, 48; Kadokawa and, 104, 120, 140; media mix, 193; *ninkyō* (chivalry) films, 178–79, 197; nudity boom and, 74; Pink Film and, 27, 69–70, 81, 89, 91, 93; police and, 166; presidents, 214; producers, 157; production companies and, 181; production practices, 88; resources, 175; sexually themed films, 170; specialty, 157; staff, 169; subgenres, 65, 170, 182, 194; Tōei Animation, 213; Tōei Central, 89, 93; video market and, 170, 173; video production, 173–74

Tōei Video: films, 158; history, 153, 166; multimedia strategy, 198–99; production, 173; shifts, 195, 199; subgenres, 184, 193; V-Cinema line, 157–60, 163, 179 196, 199

Tōhō: anime, 139; blockbusters, 116; films, 124, 140; financial difficulties, 59; independent productions and, 54–55, 69–70, 116–17; Kadokawa and, 103–4, 118, 140;

labor strikes, 52–53; New Action, 161; Pink Film and, 27, 89; strategies, 55, 65, 70, 117, 124; structure, 85; subgenres, 124; Tōhō Video Shop, 167–68; union, 86; video, 166; wartime conditions, 52

Tōhō Tōwa, 145

Tōhokushinsha, 158

Tōkatsu, 89, 93

Tokuma Shoten, 116, 141

Tokura Eiji, 49

Tokyo High Court, 87

Tokyo International Film Festival, 215

Tōkyō Kikaku, 32, 43

Tokyo Metropolitan Court, 42

Tokyo Metropolitan Police, 9, 27, 31, 44–45, 87–88

Tokyo Olympics, 49

Tokyū, 118

Tomb of Lead (film), 73

Tōmen (company), 142

Tomioka Tadafumi, 161, 195

Toneriko (film), 163

Tora-san (series), 89

Toshiba, 200

Toshiba Eizō, 141

Treaty of Mutual Cooperation and Security, 45

Truck King (magazine), 165

True Account: Hokkadio Yakuza War (series), 182

True Account: Okinawa Yakuza War (series), 182

True Account: Osaka Yakuza War (series), 182

True Account: Ryōzanpaku (film), 186

True Account: Ryōzanpaku—Pachislo Life—the Philosophy of Naniwa 2 (film), 186

True Scary Stories (series), 163

Tsuruoka Yoshiko, 57

Tsuruta Kōji, 65, 182

Tsuruta Norio, 163

Tsutaya, 192

Tusk of Evil, The (film), 5, 19

TV Asahi, 141

Twenty-Year-Old Youth (film), 39

2channel, 219
Two Female Dogs (film), 69

UCI, 206
Ueno Toshiya, 83
Ultraman (series), 161
Umezawa Kaoru, 32
Umezu Kazuo, 163
Underground Film Center, 57
Underworld Police P.O. Box 39—the Sex Video Woman File (film), 177
United States of America: approach centered on, 10, 18; film industry and, 144, 217; film production, 30, 85–86, 133; films, 12, 116, 152; hegemony, 221; history, 17, 20, 25, 210; image of, 80, 132–33; Japan and, 154, 216–17; in Japanese film, 105, 110, 135; media content, 172; media culture, 4, 59, 74; national politics, 221; navy, 167; occupation policies, 31, 39, 52–54, 85; opposition to, 45, 50; postwar Japan and, 41, 44, 50, 53–54, 75; promotion of, 75–76; restrictions on portrayal of, 45; television industry, 154

Valley of Deep Desire (film), 72
Valley of Desire, The (film), 34, 58, 71
V-America (series), 191
Variety (magazine), 125, 131, 138
V-Cinema: actors, 194, 200; adult entertainment, 166; aesthetics, 203; anime and, 166; audiences, 169, 173, 175, 180, 185, 199, 202; audience segmentation, 188, 190, 193; budgets, 163, 188, 193, 195, 199–200; business models, 197; characteristics of, 152–53, 155, 157, 161–62, 165; characters, 201–2; circulation, 164; companies, 162, 177, 198; in comparison, 165, 175, 194, 203, 215; confusion and, 155, 210, 223; cross-media relations, 177; developments in, 189, 205; difficulties, 191–92, 195, 197, 200; directors, 160–64, 200; discourses of, 189, 194, 200; discourses on, 163, 195, 200, 202; distribution practices, 191, 199–200, 202; economy and, 175, 184, 189–92, 202; in Euro-America, 161; exhibition practices, 191; filmic textuality, 177, 203, 207; film industry and, 200–201; financing, 158, 175; gender discourses in, 194; gender fantasies in, 165; gender politics, 193–95; genre and, 162, 165; history and, 155–57, 175, 178, 202–3; history of, 4–5, 152–53, 188, 202; idols, 194; image of, 164–65, 176, 181, 185, 193, 196, 199, 203; impact of, 7–9, 158–59; impossible rewind, 19–20, 160, 176, 179, 193, 201–2; as industrial genre, 5, 23, 151–53, 159, 161, 170, 181, 191, 199, 203; industrial practices, 163–64; industrial structure, 155, 164; in international festivals, 161; *jitsuroku* (true account) yakuza films, 182–84, 186, 190, 200–203; labor in, 161, 164, 200, 203; major studios and, 158; market, 181, 196; media channels and, 155, 163, 191; media ecology and, 165, 201; media history and, 153, 158, 182, 194–95; narratives, 197, 201–2; nation and, 169, 183, 203; as opposition, 203; output, 196; outsourcing, 199–200; perception of, 192; presentation of, 193; producers, 163, 190, 194; production, 161–64, 191, 196–97, 200; production practices, 160, 162, 164, 196, 202; production strategies, 174–75, 178, 193; profits, 174; program-picture and, 159–60; referentiality, 197; releases, 197; sales, 158, 175, 200; scholarship on, 14, 164–65; scripts, 164; scriptwriters, 164; sexual content, 194, 203; sexualization, 196; space and, 190, 203; spaces for, 176–77, 198, 205; staff, 162, 200; stars, 180, 188, 193, 202; star system, 161, 180; strategies for attracting audiences, 177; subgenres, 174, 176–78, 180–81, 186, 190, 194–95, 197–98, 202; talent, 163; technology and, 19–20, 153, 184–85, 196, 201; temporality, 185; temporal models, 201; temporal politics, 176, 203; texts, 175–76, 197; theaters and, 208; thematics, 179, 202; time and, 20, 153, 155–56, 170, 175, 194, 197, 202; as training ground, 162; video stores and, 185, 192, 196, 207

Venice Film Festival, 15
Verbinski, Gore, 163
V-Erotica (series), 192
VHS: medium, 185, 200; recorder, 167; tapes, 16, 201; technology, 20
Victor, 141, 145, 167
video: audiences, 168–69; business, 88; companies, 162; costs, 167–68; cross-media relations, 165–66, 171; discourses of, 169; distribution, 82; distribution outfits, 171; educational, 166, 173, 190; gender and, 169–70; genre and, 173; history, 173; home, 119, 165; home viewing, 170; impact of, 166–67; industry, 16; Kadokawa and, 136, 138, 141; marketing, 167, 169, 171; as medium, 17, 48, 156; minitheaters and, 172; original, 159; perception of, 154–55; Pink Film and, 31; platform, 148; production company and, 145; production costs, 172; profits, 168–69; releases, 172; rental, 83, 167–68; spatiality, 170; stores, 5, 152, 164, 173–74, 177; tape recorders, 154; technology, 4, 8, 19–20, 155, 166–67, 184; television and, 154–55, 166; temporality, 154–55; trends, 162–63
video market, 159; history, 165, 171–72; impact of, 171; major studios and, 170, 173; perception of, 166, 169; production for, 152–53, 158, 162–63; profits, 168–69; rental, 172
Videopia (magazine), 155, 166
Village of Eight Gravestones: film, 102–3, 116, 118; novel, 102–3
Violated Angels (film), 57
VIP, 159; V-Picture, 159
Virgin, 206
Virgin Diary of Violence (Female animal) (film), 78
Virus: book, 116; film, 112–14, 117–20, 126, 142–43
Visual Industry Promotion Organization, 214
Vocaloid, 220
Voices of a Distant Star (film), 209, 211, 224
V-Paradise (company), 201
V-World (series), 192

Waisetsuron (obscenity discourse), 38
Wakaba Natsuko, 76
Wakamatsu Kōji, 49; films, 38, 42, 44, 48, 57–58, 73, 83, 146, 191; Pink Film and, 56–57, 92; reputation abroad, 13; Shōchiku and, 70
Wakamatsu Productions, 48, 56–57, 89, 92, 120, 124
War Chronicles of Alexander (film), 148
Warner, 169, 192; Warner Brothers International Cinemas, 205
Warner-Mycal, 205–6
Watanabe Hiroshi, 147
Watanabe Hiroyuki, 180
Watanabe Hisashi, 158
Watanabe Mamoru, 42, 74
Watanabe Noriko, 114, 123, 130
Watanabe Tsutomu, 132
Watanabe Yūsuke, 69
Western (film genre), 11, 137
Wilder, Billy, 126
Wild Touch (film), 186
Williams, Allan, 10
Williams, Linda, 28
Woman from the Secret Club (film), 73
Woman in a Black Dress (film), 130
Woman in the Dunes (film), 69, 103, 116–17
Woolf, Virginia, 77–78
Wowow, 198
Wright, Will, 11
W's Tragedy (film), 120, 130, 139, 145

xx—*Beautiful Weapon* (series), 193

Yajima Midori, 68
Yakushimaru Hiroko, 112–13, 120–31, 138, 140
yakuza: ethics, 179; film industry and, 59, 104, 184; films, 65, 157–58, 170, 185, 190, 195, 202; films and confusion, 190–91; gender tropes, 179; history and, 183, 190; imagery, 176, 179; *jitsuroku* (true account) subgenre, 182, 186; nation and, 183; *ninkyō* (chivalry) subgenre, 181–82; portrayal of, 180, 183; production, 200; series, 194;

as subgenre, 178, 181, 196, 200; V-Cinema and, 192–93
Yamada Fūtarō, 193
Yamada Keizō, 90
Yamada Yōji, 161
Yamaguchi Momoe, 124
Yamamoto Satsuo, 48
Yamamoto Shinya, 56, 67, 92–93
Yamane Sadao, 64, 159–60, 165
Yamane Shigeyuki, 124
Yamashita Osamu, 72
Yamata no Orochi no Gyakushū (film), 211
Yamato (film), 149
Yamatoya Atsushi, 56–57
Yamazaki Kazuo, 139
Yana Tadashi, 44
Yoda, Tomiko, 75
yōga (foreign films), 101, 207; distribution and exhibition practices, 105, 119–20, 140, 144, 206; major studios and, 104, 117; releases, 118, 143; system, 118; theater, 111, 116, 118, 128, 136; video and, 169
Yokai Watch, 177
Yokomizu Seishi, 101–3, 119
Yomiuri Shinbun (newspaper), 147
Yomota Inuhiko, 57
Yoshida Genji, 139
Yoshida Kijū, 42
Yoshida Tatsu, 156–57, 169
Yoshimoto Mitsuhiro, 10, 21
youth: audience, 65, 87–89, 132; discourses of, 34, 129; films, 88, 124; idols and, 130–31
YouTube, 148, 209, 211, 213, 215
Yoyogi Tadashi, 89
Yuasa Namio, 83
Yuasa Noriaki, 85
Yū Pro, 161

Za Pīnattsu, 124, 126
Za Terebi (magazine), 125
Zatōichi (series), 65
Zemeckis, Robert, 156
Zero Woman (series), 193
Zeze Takahisa, 82, 162
Zielinski, Siegfried, 153

STUDIES OF THE WEATHERHEAD EAST ASIAN INSTITUTE, COLUMBIA UNIVERSITY

Selected Titles

Darwin, Dharma, and the Divine: Evolutionary Theory and Religion in Modern Japan, by G. Clinton Godart. University of Hawai'i Press, 2017

Dictators and Their Secret Police: Coercive Institutions and State Violence, by Sheena Chestnut Greitens. Cambridge University Press, 2016

Homecomings: The Belated Return of Japan's Lost Soldiers, by Yoshikuni Igarashi. Columbia University Press, 2016

Samurai to Soldier: Remaking Military Service in Nineteenth-Century Japan, by D. Colin Jaundrill. Cornell University Press, 2016

Accidental Activists: Victim Movements and Government Accountability in Japan and South Korea, by Celeste L. Arrington. Cornell University Press, 2016

The Red Guard Generation and Political Activism in China, by Guobin Yang. Columbia University Press, 2016

Imperial Genus: The Formation and Limits of the Human in Modern Korea and Japan, by Travis Workman. University of California Press, 2016

Ethnic Conflict and Protest in Tibet and Xinjiang: Unrest in China's West, edited by Ben Hillman and Gray Tuttle. Columbia University Press, 2016

Ming China and Vietnam: Negotiating Borders in Early Modern Asia, by Kathlene Baldanza. Cambridge University Press, 2016

One Hundred Million Philosophers: Science of Thought and the Culture of Democracy in Postwar Japan, by Adam Bronson. University of Hawai'i Press, 2016

Chinese Law in Imperial Eyes: Sovereignty, Justice, and Transcultural Politics, by Li Chen. Columbia University Press, 2016

The Life We Longed For: Danchi Housing and the Middle Class Dream in Postwar Japan, by Laura Neitzel. MerwinAsia, 2016

Conflict and Commerce in Maritime East Asia: The Zheng Family and the Shaping of the Modern World, c. 1620–1720, by Xing Hang. Cambridge University Press, 2015

The Nature of Knowledge and the Knowledge of Nature in Early Modern Japan, by Federico Marcon. University of Chicago Press, 2015

The Age of Irreverence: A New History of Laughter in China, by Christopher Rea. University of California Press, 2015

Yasukuni Shrine: History, Memory, and Japan's Unending Postwar, by Akiko Takenaka. University of Hawai'i Press, 2015

The Fascist Effect: Japan and Italy, 1915–1952, by Reto Hofmann. Cornell University Press, 2015

The International Minimum: Creativity and Contradiction in Japan's Global Engagement, 1933–1964, by Jessamyn R. Abel. University of Hawai'i Press, 2015

Empires of Coal: Fueling China's Entry into the Modern World Order, 1860–1920, by Shellen Xiao Wu. Stanford University Press, 2015

Casualties of History: Wounded Japanese Servicemen and the Second World War, by Lee K. Pennington. Cornell University Press, 2015

City of Virtues: Nanjing in an Age of Utopian Visions, by Chuck Wooldridge. University of Washington Press, 2015

The Proletarian Wave: Literature and Leftist Culture in Colonial Korea, 1910–1945, by Sunyoung Park. Harvard University Asia Center, 2015

Neither Donkey nor Horse: Medicine in the Struggle over China's Modernity, by Sean Hsiang-lin Lei. University of Chicago Press, 2014

When the Future Disappears: The Modernist Imagination in Late Colonial Korea, by Janet Poole. Columbia University Press, 2014

Bad Water: Nature, Pollution, and Politics in Japan, 1870–1950, by Robert Stolz. Duke University Press, 2014

Rise of a Japanese Chinatown: Yokohama, 1894–1972, by Eric C. Han. Harvard University Asia Center, 2014

Beyond the Metropolis: Second Cities and Modern Life in Interwar Japan, by Louise Young. University of California Press, 2013

Imperial Eclipse: Japan's Strategic Thinking about Continental Asia before August 1945, by Yukiko Koshiro. Cornell University Press, 2013

The Nature of the Beasts: Empire and Exhibition at the Tokyo Imperial Zoo, by Ian J. Miller. University of California Press, 2013

Public Properties: Museums in Imperial Japan, by Noriko Aso. Duke University Press, 2013

Reconstructing Bodies: Biomedicine, Health, and Nation-Building in South Korea since 1945, by John P. DiMoia. Stanford University Press, 2013

Taming Tibet: Landscape Transformation and the Gift of Chinese Development, by Emily T. Yeh. Cornell University Press, 2013

Tyranny of the Weak: North Korea and the World, 1950–1992, by Charles K. Armstrong. Cornell University Press, 2013

www.ingramcontent.com/pod-product-compliance
Lightning Source LLC
Chambersburg PA
CBHW070753230426
43665CB00017B/2338